FIFTY MAJOR THINKERS
ON EDUCATION

In this unique work some of today's greatest educators present concise, accessible summaries of the great educators of the past. Covering a time-span from 500 BC to the early twentieth century, the book includes profiles of:

- Augustine
- Dewey
- Erasmus
- Gandhi
- Kant

- Montessori
- Plato
- Rousseau
- Steiner
- Wollstonecraft

Each essay gives key biographical information, an outline of the individual's principal achievements and activities, an assessment of their impact and influence, a list of their major writings and suggested further reading. Together with *Fifty Modern Thinkers on Education*, this book provides a unique reference guide for all students of education.

Joy A. Palmer is Professor of Education and Pro-Vice-Chancellor at the University of Durham, England. She is Vice-President of the National Association for Environmental Education and a member of the IUCN Commission on Education and Communication.

Advisory Editors: **Liora Bresler** is Professor of Curriculum and Instruction at the University of Illinois, Urbana-Champaign. **David E. Cooper** is Professor of Philosophy at the University of Durham.

YOU MAY ALSO BE INTERESTED IN THE FOLLOWING ROUTLEDGE STUDENT REFERENCE TITLES:

Fifty Major Thinkers on Education
Edited by Joy A. Palmer

Fifty Modern Thinkers on Education
Edited by Joy A. Palmer

Key Concepts in the Philosophy of Education
John Gingell and
Christopher Winch

Key Concepts in Adult Education and Training 2nd edition
Malcolm Tight

Sport and Physical Education: the Key Concepts
Tim Chandler, Mike Cronin and
Wray Vamplew

FIFTY MAJOR THINKERS ON EDUCATION

From Confucius to Dewey

Edited by Joy A. Palmer

Advisory Editors: Liora Bresler and David E. Cooper

Routledge
Taylor & Francis Group

LONDON AND NEW YORK

First published 2001
by Routledge
2 Park Square, Milton Park, Oxon, OX14 4RN

Simultaneously published in the USA and Canada
by Routledge
270 Madison Ave, New York, NY 10016

Reprinted 2003, 2004 (twice), 2005, 2006

Routledge is an imprint of the Taylor & Francis Group, an informa business

Typeset in Times by Taylor & Francis Books Ltd
Printed and bound in Great Britain by TJ International Ltd, Padstow, Cornwall

British Library Cataloguing in Publication Data
A catalogue record for this book is available from the British Library.

Library of Congress Cataloging in Publication Data
Fifty major thinkers on education : from Confucius to Dewey / edited by Joy A.
Palmer ; advisory editors, Liora Bresler and David E. Cooper.
p. cm. – (Routledge Key Guides)
Includes bibliographical references.
1. Education–Philosophy–History. 2. Educators–Biography.
3. Education–History. I. Palmer, Joy. II. Bresler, Liora. III. Cooper, David
Edward. IV. Series.
LB17 .F56 2001
370′.92′2–dc21
[B]001019309

ISBN10: 0–415–23125–6 (hbk)
ISBN10: 0–415–23126–4 (pbk)

ISBN13: 978–0–415–23125–1 (hbk)
ISBN13: 978–0–415–23126–8 (pbk)

CHRONOLOGICAL LIST OF CONTENTS

CHRONOLOGICAL LIST OF CONTENTS

ALPHABETICAL LIST
OF CONTENTS

CONTRIBUTORS

Apple, Michael W. is John Bascom Professor of Curriculum and Instruction and Educational Policy Studies, University of Wisconsin-Madison, USA

Baker, Eva L. is Professor of Education at the University of California, Los Angeles, USA

Batho, G.R. is Emeritus Professor of Education at the University of Durham, England

Bergin, David A. is Professor of Educational Psychology at the University of Toledo, Ohio, USA

Bewley, William L. is Assistant Director at the National Center for Research on Evaluation, Standards and Student Testing, University of California, Los Angeles, USA

Chung, Shunah is Lecturer at Sookmyung University, Seoul, Korea

Cizek, Gregory J. is Associate Professor of Educational Measurement and Evaluation at the University of North Carolina, Chapel Hill, USA

Clarke, James A. is a Doctoral Student in the Department of Philosophy at the University of Durham, England

Cooper, David E. is Professor of Philosophy at the University of Durham, England

Dickerson, Adam B. is Research Affiliate of the Philosophy Program at the Research School of Social Sciences, Australian National University, Canberra, Australia

Dutta, Krishna is a freelance scholar based in London, England

Ellis, Nancy C. is Research Professor of Education at the University of Vermont, USA

FitzPatrick, P.J. is Reader Emeritus in the Department of Philosophy, University of Durham, England

Harris, Violet is Professor at the College of Education, University of Illinois at Urbana-Champaign, USA

Hart, Thomas E. is a Doctoral student in the Department of Philosophy, University of Durham, England

Hobson, Peter is Associate Professor in the School of Education Studies, University of New England, Armidale, NSW, Australia

Knight, David is Professor of Philosophy at the University of Durham, England

Laird, Susan is Associate Professor in the Department of Educational Leadership and Policy Studies, University of Oklahoma, USA

Martin, Jane Roland is Professor of Philosophy Emerita, the University of Massachusetts, Boston, USA

Monk, Ray is Professor of Philosophy at the University of Southampton, England

Noddings, Nel is Lee Jacks Professor of Education, Emerita, Stanford University, and Professor of Philosophy and Education, Teachers College, Columbia, USA

Oelkers, Jürgen is Professor in the Institute of Education at the University of Zurich, Switzerland

O'Hagan, Timothy teaches philosophy at the School of Economic and Social Studies, University of East Anglia, Norwich, Norfolk, England

O'Hear, Anthony is Professor of Philosophy at the University of Bradford, England

Palmer, Joy A. is Professor of Education and Pro-Vice Chancellor of the University of Durham, England

Peprnik, Jaroslav is Professor in the Department of English and American Studies, Palacky University, Olomouc, Czech Republic

Pickering, William is General Secretary of the British Centre for Durkheimian Studies, Institute of Social and Cultural Anthropology, Oxford, England

Prasad, Devi is educationist, artist and worker for international peace, based in New Delhi, India, Visiting Lecturer Bryn Mawr and Haverford Colleges, USA and Visiting Professor, Visva Bharati, India

Rack, Henry is formerly Senior Lecturer in Theology at the University of Manchester, England

Ridgway, Jim is Professor of Education at the University of Durham, England

Robinson, Andrew is Literary Editor of *The Times Higher Education Supplement*, England

Rowe, Christopher J. is Professor of Greek and Leverhulme Research Professor at the University of Durham, England

Russell, Joan is Assistant Professor and Director of Music Education at McGill University, Faculty of Education, Montréal, Canada

Seraphine, Connie Leean is Director, First Call Theological Education, Evangelical Lutheran Church in America, Chicago, Illinois, USA

Sevilla, Diego is Professor in the Department of Education, the University of Granada, Spain

Shen, Jianping is Assistant Professor in the Department of Teaching, Learning and Leadership, College of Education, Western Michigan University, Kalamazoo, MI, USA

Smith, Louis M. is Professor Emeritus in the Department of Education, Washington University, St Louis, USA.

Smith, Richard is Professor of Education at the University of Durham, England

Steitieh, Dalal Malhas is Professor in the Faculty of Educational Sciences at the University of Jordan, Amman, Jordan

Tawil, Hani A. is Professor in the Faculty of Educational Sciences at the University of Jordan, Amman, Jordan

Teitelbaum, Kenneth is Professor and Chairperson, Department of Teaching, Leadership and Curriculum Studies, Kent State University, Kent, Ohio, USA

Thompson, Christine is Associate Professor of Education at Pennsylvania State University, USA

Torre, Carlos Antonio is Professor of Education at Southern Connecticut State University, and Fellow, Yale University, USA

Tröhler, Daniel is Oberassistent at the Institute of Education of the University of Zurich, Switzerland

Tufekci, Aysel is a graduate student at the University of Illinois at Urbana-Champaign, USA

Villarini Jusino, Angel is Professor of Philosophy at the University of Puerto Rico

Walsh, Daniel J. is Associate Professor of Early Childhood Education at the College of Education, University of Illinois at Urbana-Champaign, USA

Willis, Arlette Ingram is Associate Professor at the College of Education, University of Illinois at Urbana-Champaign, USA

PREFACE

The twin volumes *Fifty Major Thinkers on Education: From Confucius to Dewey* and *Fifty Modern Thinkers on Education: From Piaget to the Present* are together intended to provide a valuable and fascinating resource for readers with an interest in 'influential lives' relating to critical thinking, action, and in more recent times research, which has influenced policy and practice in the field of education. As a pair, the two volumes consider influences upon educational thought and practice from the very earliest times through to the present day. In the first volume we examine the lives and influence of fifty individuals from the time of Confucius to the era of Dewey. The second volume continues where the first ceases, examining the contribution of a further fifty individuals from the time of Piaget to the present.

Each volume and each essay within it follows a common format. An opening quotation sets the scene at the start of each essay. Then, readers are provided with an overview of the subject's work and basic biographical information. Each author then engages in critical reflection which aims to illuminate the influence, importance and perhaps innovative character of the subject's thinking and, where appropriate, research and actions. In other words, authors have moved beyond the purely descriptive and have provided a discussion of the nature of the intellectual or practical impact that the life, thinking and works of each figure made or is making upon our understanding or practice of education.

At the end of each essay, we have provided information that will lead interested readers into further and more detailed study. Firstly, there are the references for the notes to which the numbers in the text refer; secondly there is a cross-referencing with other subjects in the two books whose thought or influence relates in some obvious way to that of the subject of the essay; thirdly there is a list of the subject's major writings (where applicable); and finally, there is a list of references for those who wish to pursue more in-depth reading on the subject.

By far the hardest task in assembling these volumes was deciding on the final list of 100 thinkers on education to be included. How can one begin, in a field so extensive as education, to select 100 individuals from over 2,000 years of thought? Inevitably, my advisory editors and I were inundated with suggestions and ideas for influential people who, for the obvious reason of lack of space, had to be left out. The 100 subjects finally decided upon include some very obvious 'great names' such as Plato, John Dewey and Jean-Jacques Rousseau, alongside some less well-known yet clearly influential people. In making our choice we also aimed to provide coverage of a range of fields within the vast and complex arena of teaching and learning – philosophy, psychology, thinking on the early years, on testing, evaluation and so on. Most importantly, we emphasise that this pair of volumes is certainly not exhaustive. As already mentioned our choice of subjects proved to be extremely difficult. Furthermore, the combined work certainly does not pretend to be an overview of the lives of the 100 greatest educational thinkers the world has ever known. We believe that it includes some people who would fall into the category of those who have had arguably the greatest global influence on educational thought and practice, but most importantly, *all* people in the books have made very substantial contributions to educational thinking in some form or another. It is hoped that some readers will derive great benefit and pleasure from the books because they introduce them to previously unknown lives. As a whole, I hope that the books will be of interest to all who would like to find out more about the lives of individuals past and present who have influenced thinking about knowledge and the education of the people of our world.

Joy A. Palmer

CONFUCIUS 551–479 BCE

> If one loves humaneness but does not love learning, the
> consequence of this is folly; if one loves understanding but does
> not love learning, the consequence of this is unorthodoxy; if one
> loves good faith but does not love learning, the consequence of
> this is damaging behaviour; if one loves straightforwardness but
> does not love learning, the consequence of this is rudeness; if one
> loves courage but does not love learning, the consequence of this
> is rebelliousness; if one loves strength but does not love learning,
> the consequence of this is violence.[1]

Confucius was the latinized name for Kong Qiu where Kong was the family
name and Qiu was the given. He is often revered as Kong Fuzi, with Fuzi
meaning 'master'. Confucius was born into an impoverished aristocratic
family. His father was a low-level military officer. It was said that Confucius
was only three when his father died and that Confucius did not even know
where his father was buried.

Confucius was married at the age of 19. He accepted public employment
as a storekeeper and later on as a superintendent of parks and herds. He
established his private school when he was about 30 years old (522 BCE) and
gradually gained his reputation for his expertise in 'rituals'. He then used his
prestige to gain access to the political arena, acting as an adviser to the
princes and nobility of the Kingdom of Lu as well as other neighbouring
states. His political agenda was to restore the 'Zhou rituals', which meant
the political and religious system established by the King of Zhou, founder
of the Western Zhou dynasty 500 year earlier.

At the age of 50 (502 BCE), Confucius became an official in the Kingdom
of Lu and about one year later became the Minister of Justice. He organized
a campaign to weaken the power of three aristocratic clans. The campaign
failed, and he lost his political future in the Kingdom of Lu. He was then a
political exile in the neighbouring kingdoms for fourteen years before one of
his former students, who was a high ranking official, helped him to resettle
in Lu. He was then 60 years old. The next five years before his death were
the most prosperous for his private school. During his lifetime, the private
school he established had enrolled 3,000 students. He died in 479 BCE were
he was 73.

There was no reliable evidence to point to the work written by Confucius
himself. However, it is generally agreed among historians that Confucius'
philosophic and educational ideas are recorded in, among others, the
following so called 'Four Books' – the *Analects of Confucius* (*Lunyu*), the
Book of Mencius (*Mengzi*), the *Great Learning* (*Daxue*), and the *Doctrine of
the Mean* (*Zhongyong*). In Chinese society, prior to the twentieth century,
these four classics were among the textbooks for those who planned to take
the imperial examination which selected officials for the imperial government. Among these books, the *Analects*, a book compiled by his disciples
after his death, is a collection of conversations with Confucius, containing
many of his most important sayings. Contemporary historians agree that the
Analects is among the most reliable for his remarks and activities. Therefore,
the following will draw heavily on the *Analects*.

The psychological foundation of Confucius' educational thought is that human nature is neutral at birth. He observed that 'By nature, people are close to one another; through practice, they drift far apart.'[2] Because of the neutrality of human nature at birth, the environment, including education, plays a very important role in raising the young. It was said that Mencius' mother moved three times in order to find a good environment for bringing up her son, who became one of the most important spokespersons for Confucius about one hundred years after his death.

Confucius' private school has been extolled as an institution which provided educational opportunity to the elite as well as the common people. He said: 'I instruct regardless of kind.'[3] He also said that 'To anyone who spontaneously came to me with a bundle of dried pork, I have never denied instruction.'[4] Although there have been debates as to the value of 'a bundle of dried pork' at that time and the extent to which his school was open to everyone, the students who had conversations with Confucius as reported in the *Analects* came from various social backgrounds.

However, the educational purposes for the elite and the common people appeared to be different. Confucius said that 'If the gentleman acquires the Way, he loves men; if the small man acquires the Way, he is easy to command.'[5] The 'gentleman' here represents children of the nobility, and 'the small man' those of the commoners. Therefore, there appeared to be differentiated educational purposes for those who came from various social backgrounds. Although his notion of educational opportunity was primarily to maintain the *status quo*, some of his outstanding students from poor family background did became important officials in the government. In Confucius' words, 'Those who excel in office should learn; those who excel in learning should take office.'[6] The notion of the scholar-official was the primary justification for the later imperial examination.

Confucius was heavily involved in teaching; and there are several texts about his ideas and practice related to teaching method and instructional content. Confucius paid attention to students' individual characteristics. In the *Analects* it was reported that Confucius commented on his students' individual differences and suggested that they were suited for various kinds of jobs. In his own words, 'To people above average, one can impart higher things; to people below average, one cannot impart higher things.'[7]

Confucius also expected his students to be motivated and active learners. In his words, 'No vexation, no enlightenment; no anxiety, no illumination. If I have brought up one corner and he does not return with the other three, I will not repeat.'[8] According to this quote, Confucius urged his students to take the initiative in learning. They should be eager in and dedicated to learning. When students were taught something, they were expected to draw relevant inferences from it.

In terms of instructional contents, Confucius tended to disregard practical knowledge. The following was recorded in the *Analects*: 'The Master said, "Inspire yourself with *Poetry*, establish yourself on *The Rituals*, perfect yourself with *Music*".'[9] Among others, Confucius used the so-called Five Classics – *The Book of Odes* (*Shijing*), *The Book of History* (*Shujing*), *The Book of Rites* (*Li*), *The Book of Changes* (*Yijing*), and *The Spring and Autumn Annals* (*Chunqiu*) – as the primary instructional materials. One of

Confucius' students, Fan Chi, requested to learn farming: Confucius responded 'I am not as good as an old farmer.' When Fan Chi requested to learn vegetable gardening, Confucius said: 'I am not as good as an old vegetable gardener.' After Fan Chi left, Confucius commented that Fan Chi did not have high aspirations.[10] His emphasis on studying classics rather than acquiring practical knowledge also has had significant influence on the history of Chinese education. During the imperial examinations, the test items were almost solely based on the classics.

In addition to intellectual education, moral education also played a very important role in Confucius' educational theory and practice. One of his students commented that 'The Master instructed in four aspects: culture, moral conduct, wholehearted sincerity, and truthfulness,'[11] with the last three aspects pertaining to moral education. According to Confucius' ethical theory, humanity is the supreme virtue and the total of all virtues, and it was manifested in many aspects of our lives. For example, Confucius said the following: 'To restrain oneself and return to the rituals constitutes humanity';[12] 'For a man of humanity is one who, wishing to establish himself, helps others to establish themselves, and who, wishing to gain perception, helps others to gain perception';[13] and 'A man of humanity places hard work before reward.'[14]

Confucius emphasized the importance of humanity in daily life in the way one treats parents and others. He said that 'What you do not wish for yourself, do not impose on others.'[15] Confucius also stressed the importance of humanity in governing. Confucius observed that 'If you yourself are correct, even without the issuing of orders, things will get done; if you yourself are incorrect, although orders are issued, they will not be obeyed.'[16] In another place in the *Analects*, he made a similar remark: 'If you can set yourself correct, what difficulty do you have in conducting state affairs? If you cannot set yourself correct, how can you correct others?'[17]

Confucius and his followers have had a tremendous impact on Chinese society in general and education in particular. The influence can also be felt in many other East and Southeast Asian nations. Although there have been ups and downs for the Confucian school in history, scholars from the school enjoyed high prestige in society and in the political arena. During some of the dynasties only scholars from the Confucian school could advise political leaders, a phenomenon called 'suppression of the hundred schools and the exclusive recognition of Confucian techniques'.

As to the influence of Confucianism on Chinese society, the following two aspects are the most obvious. First, many of the traditional values advocated by Confucius, such as filial piety, respect for the elderly, and moderation, still play a very important role in Chinese people's life. Second, Confucius and his followers emphasized education and learning, a tradition which can still be felt in China and many other neighbouring nations.

As to the influence of Confucianism on education, the following are the most important. First, the principle that 'Those who excel in office should learn; those who excel in learning should take office' has guided Chinese education.[18] This principle and the corollary notion of scholar-official became the justification for the imperial examination that selected officials based on individual merits, a system which was not abolished until 1905. In order to prepare the most able and virtuous rulers, Confucius held that education should be available to all, irrespective of social class. He was a pioneer in providing education to the common people.

Second, the Confucian school produced a large body of literature which formed the primary instructional materials for many centuries until the imperial examination system was abolished in 1905. There is no reliable evidence to indicate that the work was written by Confucius himself. Confucius was said to have edited *The Book of Odes*, one of the Five Classics. However, the orthodox works of Confucianism, such as the Four Books and the Five Classics, became the basic texts for preparing for the imperial examination. Because of Confucius' exclusive focus on classics to the extent of totally disregarding practical and scientific knowledge, Confucius and his followers are criticized for impeding China's progress in science and technology.

Finally, Confucius' purpose of education focused more on social rather than individual development. The moral values he advocated were ultimately related to governing and regulating social relationships. Confucius depicted a developmental path for his students – to achieve self-cultivation first, then family harmony, then good order in the state, and finally peace in the empire. Therefore, the real emphasis was on the social rather than private purpose of education. The emphasis on the social dimension is usually related to the instrumental purpose of education, i.e., to use education as a vehicle to achieve a purpose other than education per se. The training of talent loyal to the government was the fundamental principle of the official Confucian education. The instrumentality of educational purpose is still one of the most serious issues in current Chinese education.

Notes

1 Dawson, R. *Confucius: The Analects*, Oxford: Oxford University Press, 1993, p. 70.
2 Huang, C. *The Analects of Confucius (Lun Yu). A Literal Translation with an Introduction and Notes*, Oxford: Oxford University Press, p. 163, 1997.
3 Ibid., p. 158.
4 Ibid., p. 87.
5 Ibid., p. 166.
6 Ibid., p. 180.
7 Ibid., p. 83.
8 Ibid., p. 88.
9 Ibid., p. 97.
10 Ibid., p. 133.
11 Ibid., p. 91.
12 Ibid., p. 125.
13 Ibid., p. 85.
14 Ibid., p. 84.
15 Ibid., p. 125.
16 Ibid., p. 134.
17 Ibid., p. 135.
18 Ibid., p. 180.

Further reading

There is no reliable evidence to point to the work written by Confucius himself. Readers could consult the following to learn more about Confucius' thoughts in general and his educational idea and practice in particular.

Cheng, M., *A Study of the Philosophy of Education of Confucius and a Comparison of the Educational Philosophies of Confucius and John Dewey*, Laramie, Wyoming: University of Wyoming, 1952.

Huang, C., *The Analects of Confucius (Lun Yu). A Literal Translation with an Introduction and Notes*, Oxford: Oxford University Press, 1997.

Mayer, F., 'Confucius,' in *The Great Teachers*, New York: The Citadel Press, pp. 35–43, 1976.

Tong, K.M., *Educational Ideas of Confucius*, Taipei: Youth Book Store, 1970.

Zhu, W., 'Confucius and Traditional Chinese Education: An Assessment,' in R. Hayhoe (ed.), *Education and Modernization: The Chinese Experience*, Oxford: Pergamon Press, pp. 3–21, 1992.

JIANPING SHEN

SOCRATES 469–399 BCE

The unexamined life is not worth living for a human being.

These words are spoken by Socrates in Plato's *Apology*,[1] a largely fictional account of his speeches at the trial that led to his conviction and execution. We have no guarantee that Socrates actually uttered these words, or any others – or indeed that he thought anything in particular, since he wrote nothing himself, and we are forced to rely on numerous and often conflicting reports about him by those who did write: people like Plato, or Xenophon (to name what are probably our two most voluminous contemporary 'authorities'). But the eleven words quoted – six in Plato's original Greek – form an essential part of one highly plausible account of Socrates' thinking which we can put together, mainly from Plato's works.[2] Since this is an account that makes Socrates a particularly interesting figure from the point of view of educational theory – since, that is, it would give him a theory of outstanding interest for educationalists – there would be good reason for considering it in the context of the present volume even if it turned out that the real Socrates had no such theory at all (why prefer to discuss a duller person than a more brilliant theory)? In any case, since there is hardly any chance of a definitive solution to 'the problem of Socrates', as it is sometimes called, short of his returning from the dead, what will be presented here may as well represent what he stood for (and I believe that there are good, if less than conclusive, arguments for supposing that it was).[3]

Here are the main things we appear to know about the historical Socrates. Born in Athens, son of Sophroniscus – probably a stonemason – and Phaenaretê – a midwife – he served with great distinction as a heavy-armed infantryman on several campaigns, but never held any command; he generally avoided ordinary political involvement, but did serve on the executive committee of the democratic Council, a committee which also organized the business of the Assembly. On one occasion, in this role, he notoriously chose to stand out alone against the popular will. But he also – peacefully – resisted the bloody oligarchy of the Thirty Tyrants in 404, at the risk of his own life. Military service apart, he hardly left Athens, and spent most of his life talking, perhaps especially to the young. He was tried for impiety – or, more specifically, for not believing in the city's gods, but different ones, and for corrupting the young. He was sentenced to death, and executed. He left a wife and young children.

Socrates tends in modern discussions to be associated with a particular idea of teaching: one that is based on questions, and involves no direct transfer of information but rather allows the pupil to see the truth for himself or herself. In fact, Plato's Socrates typically denies that he is a teacher at all. He knows nothing, so that he actually has nothing to impart to anyone; if he is wiser than anyone else, it is because he is aware of his own ignorance, and so realizes that he needs to do something about it. So he goes about asking other people questions, in the hope (so he says) that he may find someone who possesses the knowledge that he himself is aware of lacking. But, in the event, none of the people he questions ever turns out to know anything worth knowing, unless it is some particular kind of expertise, like shoemaking or medicine; so all that he succeeds in doing is showing himself, and the other person too, if he's prepared to listen properly, that the other person doesn't know what he thought he knew. However, there is always an invitation, whether explicit or implicit, for the newly self-aware person to continue the inquiry along with Socrates; and this does at last begin to resemble our notion of Socratic method – the only difference being that we introduce it into a context which assumes that there are determinate truths to be learned, which we could mostly list if called upon to do so. Socrates, by contrast, not only says he knows nothing, but means it; he is not merely waiting for the other person to catch up with him, and gently prodding him or her in the right direction with supposedly neutral questions, but is himself actively involved in the search. (We do in fact find Plato's Socrates endorsing the idea of education as turning the soul towards – literally converting it to – the truth, but this is entirely compatible with the idea of learning as searching, and mainly serves to emphasize the idea that there are truths out there, as it were, waiting to be discovered: one idea that is surely Socratic.)

This is very far, however, from being the whole of Socrates' position; and it is the part that still needs to be supplied which is the more interesting. Socrates may not *know* anything much, but there are certainly plenty of things that he believes, and believes quite passionately. One such thing that he believes in is the importance of *reasoning things out*. This, of course, we might have derived immediately from the proposition about the unexamined life; but we might be inclined to object that that is to put it in a rather extreme way – why should life actually be *unliveable* if it is unexamined? Plenty of us do in fact live lives like that, and perfectly to our own satisfaction (we may say); what is more, surely most people would not be capable of examining anything rationally, let alone their lives? Socrates, it seems, would not be much bothered by the second point, since on the whole he seems prepared to talk to anyone (though if they are young, he evidently prefers them to be attractive). As for the first point, he would challenge it directly: if we all want to be happy, which he takes to be axiomatic,[4] then how are we going to know if what we are doing now is contributing to that, unless we think it through?

'We all want to be happy': for Socrates, it is the desire for the good – our own good – that drives us all. That is, he is a 'psychological egoist'; he believes that what in fact motivates us, always, is desire for our own happiness. But Socrates' brand of egoism is an unusual one. Whereas egoism immediately suggests selfishness, Socrates' notion of – his conviction about – what is good for the agent (any agent) actually turns out to include a central concern for others. So, for example, he gives *justice*, and indeed the other recognized virtues, pride of place in his conception of the good life. One should do nothing at all, he repeatedly insists (again, this is Plato's Socrates), unless it is just – though one should also, when circumstances demand it, act courageously, with restraint, with due respect to the gods, and so on. This already means an absolute commitment to safeguarding the rights of others (as we might put it), or being prepared to die for one's friends and fellow-citizens, if the circumstances demand it. His own behaviour also suggests an immediate and direct concern for others' welfare: his philosophizing is not merely for the sake of caring for his own soul – whatever the 'soul' may be, for him – but for the sake of others' souls too, i.e. those of the people he philosophizes with.[5]

'Caring for the soul' seems to mean, essentially, not being misled by the obvious attractions of so-called 'bodily', i.e. material, pleasures.[6] Here again justice enters the picture: a single-minded pursuit of such things – egoism of a more ordinary sort – would involve being prepared to trample over others if ever they get in our way. Socrates' response is that one should never treat anyone unjustly, even in return for injustice; one should never even *harm* anyone, under any circumstances. Thus, to take the extreme case, Socrates is prepared actually to die, rather than – as he puts it – harming the city and the laws by running away from prison and so avoiding the court's legal verdict. But the reason why he behaves like this is not out of any regard for 'moral values'. Rather, he thinks it simply a matter of what is good for him: what is best for him is to put up with the verdict, however unjust it may be, rather than to damage his city (to which he apparently has ties resembling, if not closer than, those that bind him to his parents).[7] Justice, that is, is a matter of knowing what is good and bad for oneself, in circumstances which might involve damage to others – just as courage is knowing what is good and bad for oneself in matters concerning one's safety and security, moderation or 'temperance' knowing what is good and bad in matters involving food, drink, sex, and so on.

Thus, in the terms of two of the Socratic paradoxes, 'all virtue is one',[8] and/because 'virtue is knowledge'. It is this second claim that takes us to what is probably the heart of the Socratic position. What the claim amounts to is that it is not only necessary, but *sufficient*, for 'virtuous' behaviour that we should know what is good and bad for us. If we know what is actually the best for us, then we *cannot* act otherwise. This is for one simple reason: that we all, and only, desire our own happiness. If we know what contributes to that end, then there is nothing – except for outside force – that can prevent us from doing it. Hence the extraordinary weight that Socrates lays on the importance of doing philosophy, of talking with anyone we can find to talk to about the crucial question, how we should live our lives (and how should we act *now*, in these circumstances).[9]

What is most peculiar about this position – and most interesting, from the point of view of theorising about education – is that it allows no room for the notion of an *irrational self*, of the sort with which most of us have grown up, and which we usually take for granted. That is, while there will be all sorts of impulses born in us (to get food and drink, have sex, form close relationships, and so on), there will be nothing in us – of the sort that Plato himself proposed – to counterbalance reason itself, and cause us to act contrary to what our reason has determined to be best for us (i.e. what reason has determined to be consistent with the universal desire for the good). Thus, in the words of the third Socratic paradox, 'no one does wrong/ goes wrong willingly/voluntarily'.[10] Plato gave us a bipartite soul, consisting of reason and unreason (the latter itself frequently divided into two), which allows, in the case of any action we may regret, cries of 'I don't know what came over me', 'I knew I shouldn't be doing it'; our more sober selves will have told us not to do it, but the beast within us rises up and overpowers reason. (Later philosophers then have to introduce the concept of the 'will', as adjudicator in the conflict between reason and unreason.) Socrates will treat such cries with scorn; if we do something, freely, that something will be what we decided was best for us. So, again, thinking things through, philosophy, Socratic 'dialectic' are all-important.

In fact, if we want to change behaviour, they will be the *only* things that matter. There will be no point in trying any other means, that is, any irrational means: beating people up, threatening them, offering them sweets; or 'educating the desires' in the way that Plato famously proposes (and puts into Socrates' mouth, perhaps thinking he is improving on the old man's ideas), by habituation – getting children to parrot improving verses, telling them the right stories, taking them to the best museums, and generally bringing them up in the right environment. If Socrates is right, there is absolutely no reason to believe that any of this will have anything but the most temporary effect; it may frighten people into conformity, or just stop them thinking about things, but if we want a *reliable* way of influencing the way people behave, then there is nothing for it but to talk to them, and go on talking to them.

This theory, a strict version of what is often labelled 'intellectualism', is virtually unique to Socrates – if it belonged to him at all (once again, it is essentially a reconstruction, based on someone else's writings; and what is more, the writings of someone who at some point – if the reconstruction is correct – must have come to find the theory unsatisfactory). Whether or not we think it plausible, it represents a thoroughgoing challenge to our ordinary notions, and to some of the usual assumptions of educational practice. According to Socrates, if it will do our children little good to be punished, neither will it do them much good even to be rewarded. There is just no substitute, except in the short term, for reasoning with them, and explaining why what we want them to do is good for them (if it is) – and, Socrates would want to know, have *we* thought that through?

Notes

1 Plato, *Apology* 38A.
2 Particularly from those usually (though perhaps not very securely) labelled as early: most people's lists will include *Charmides, Hippias Minor, Ion, Laches, Lysis, Crito*, and *Euthyphro*, along with the *Apology*. Other dialogues that contain clearly Socratic material are *Gorgias, Meno, Protagoras, Republic I*, and, I believe, *Symposium*.
3 For alternative views of Socrates, see e.g. Xenophon, *Memoirs of Socrates* (moral authority, guru?); Aristophanes, *Clouds* (scientist, expert public speaker); Vlastos (author of *Socrates: Ironist and Moral Philosopher*) and others listed under 'Further reading' – except for Penner, whose Socrates is a more philosophically complex and sophisticated version of the one described in the present essay.
4 See e.g. *Gorgias* 466A–468E, *Meno* 77A–78B.
5 This other-regarding aspect of Socrates' philosophy is perhaps most evident in the *Crito* and the *Symposium* – although it is perhaps permanently on display in the very practice of Socratic conversation.
6 See especially *Apology* 29D–30D.
7 The preceding four sentences are more or less a paraphrase of a major part of the argument of the *Crito*.
8 As Plato has Socrates argue at length in the last part of the *Protagoras*.
9 This is the kind of analysis generally hinted at, though never fully asserted (after all, Socrates knows nothing), in the 'dialogues of definition' like *Laches, Charmides*, or *Euthyphro*.
10 Clearly the pair of 'virtue is knowledge' (and vice ignorance), given the Socratic analysis: see e.g. *Meno* 87Bff., *Hippias Minor* 371E–373A with 376B, *Apology* 25D with 37A.

See also

In this book: Plato

Socrates' major writings

Socrates did not write anything. The dialogues of Plato in which his views are primarily represented, and which were cited in note 2, are widely available in translation, perhaps most conveniently in John M. Cooper (ed.), *Plato: Complete Works*, Hackett, Indianapolis, 1997. But for the *Symposium*, see also my translation and commentary (Aris & Phillips, Warminster, 1998) which gives what I believe is a proper emphasis to the Socratic elements in the character Socrates' contribution to the occasion.

Further reading

Irwin, Terence, *Plato's Ethics*, Oxford: OUP, 1995.
Kahn, Charles H., *Plato and the Socratic Dialogue: The Philosophical Use of a Literary Form*, Cambridge: CUP, 1996.
Kraut, Richard, *Socrates and the State*, Princeton, NJ: Princeton University Press, 1984.
Penner, Terry, 'Socrates and the Early Dialogues', in Richard Kraut (ed.), *The Cambridge Companion to Plato*, Cambridge: CUP, pp. 121–69, 1992.
—— 'Socrates', in Christopher Rowe and Malcolm Schofield (eds), *The Cambridge History of Greek and Roman Political Thought*, Cambridge: CUP, pp. 164–89, 2000.

Santas, G.X., *Socrates: Philosophy in Plato's Early Dialogues*, London: Routledge and Kegan Paul, 1979.

CHRISTOPHER J. ROWE

PLATO 427–347 BCE

[A] proper cultural education would enable a person, ... even when young ... and still incapable of rationally understanding why, ... rightly [to] condemn and loathe contemptible things. And then the rational mind would be greeted like an old friend when it did arrive.[1]

Plato belonged to an aristocratic Athenian family, members of which were among 'The Thirty Tyrants' who briefly ruled the city-state after its defeat by Sparta. As such, he may have been in personal danger after the re-establishment of a democracy during which, moreover, his teacher and friend, Socrates, was condemned to death in 399 BCE. Certainly Plato was to spend several years away from Athens, some of them as a royal tutor and political adviser in Sicily. On his return from his first visit to Sicily, he set up his famous Academy, a philosophical community that attracted young men from around the Greek world, including the Macedonian Aristotle. Plato continued to write and teach until he died at the age of 80.

Plato's preferred literary vehicle was the philosophical dialogue. More than twenty of these have survived, some of them – *Symposium*, for example, and *Phaedo* – as much masterpieces of dramatic art as of philosophical enquiry. In nearly all these dialogues, the main speaker is Socrates, although it is generally agreed that only in the early ones are the views expressed by this speaker those of the historical Socrates. By the time of such mature dialogues as *Republic*, probably composed during the 370s, 'Socrates' has become the mouthpiece for views original to Plato himself. The most important of those views, perhaps, is the theory of Forms (or Ideas, or Types) according to which what is most truly real are the immaterial, abstract entities, such as Beauty, of which empirically observable items in the physical world are but imperfect 'copies'.

From some of his teacher's convictions, however, Plato never seriously departed. Both men were convinced, above all, that the most important business of philosophy – and, indeed, of life – was morality. The morally good life alone ensures happiness and brings human fulfillment. And since a fully moral existence requires rational understanding of the virtues, of human nature and of truth, it follows, for both men, that an essential ingredient of the good life is philosophical reason. For neither Socrates nor Plato, moreover, is the understanding provided by moral reason of a piecemeal character: since 'virtue is one', the various virtues that are 'parts of it' must be grasped in their intimate unity (*Protagoras* 329).[2] This emphasis on unity culminates in Plato's claim that the enlightened philosopher attains knowledge of the supreme Form, that of the Good, which is the source of the intelligibility, nature and very being of everything else (*Republic* 509).

Plato's reflections on education, as on other subjects, remain among the most enduringly influential in the intellectual history of the West. Remarks on the purposes and nature of education are found in many of his dialogues. In *Protagoras*, for instance, we find Socrates challenging the credentials of the eponymous philosopher and other Sophists – paid teachers of well-heeled young Athenians destined for the professions – to teach people how to live properly, given their 'subjectivist' or 'relativist' attitude towards truth and morality. Again, in the famous 'slave-boy' section of *Meno* (82ff.), it is argued that some of our knowledge, at least – certainly mathematical knowledge – is not, strictly speaking, *learnt* at all. Rather the 'teacher' is 'reminding' the boy of – enabling him to 'recollect' – things he already and innately knows. (In *Phaedrus* (247), Plato picturesquely describes a pre-bodily life during which the soul is originally acquainted with the Forms, 'a reality without colour or shape ... but utterly real'. It is this acquaintance of which the pupil is 'reminded' by the 'teacher'.)

Educationists who emphasize children's innate cognitive endowment are often associated with a 'child-centred' approach to education, a 'hands off' policy of allowing the child's understanding naturally to 'blossom'. This was not at all the approach of Plato in *Republic*, at once his best-known dialogue and the one in which his thoughts on education were primarily elaborated. While education (*paideia*) may indeed 'clean and reignite a mental organ which everyone has', the strictest control of children's environment and upbringing is necessary if this 'organ' is not to be 'ruined and blinded' (*Republic* 527).

The apparent purpose of the seventy or so pages in *Republic* devoted to education is to prescribe a pedagogic programme for producing the Guardians or Philosopher-Kings who are to be the rulers of the imaginary state that Plato outlines in the dialogue. However, it is far from clear that Plato seriously intended the political system described, including its educational arrangements, as a blueprint for one to which people could sensibly aspire. As Plato explains, the point of the political discussion is to provide an *analogy*, 'on a large scale', for the individual person or 'soul'. Since a whole community is comparable, in certain respects, with an individual, reflection on the former may cast light both on what it is for a person to be just or moral and on why it is that only such a person can genuinely prosper and be happy. At the heart of the analogy is a comparison between the kinds or classes of people who make up the polity and the 'parts' of the individual soul or personality. Plato argues that, just as a flourishing state is one in which each class sticks to what it is most fitted for, so an individual flourishes only when each of his or her faculties does not trespass beyond its proper domain. In particular, just as the community should be ruled by those whose special talent and function is rational direction of public affairs, so the individual's life should be under the rule of the highest faculty – reason.[3]

The appropriate way, then, to regard the educational prescriptions in *Republic* is not as a programme for constructing a political utopia, but as recommendations for developing moral reason in the individual. The suggestion, for example, that the future Guardians should study mathematical subjects for ten years before moving on to 'dialectic' or philosophy is best seen as a light-hearted way of making the serious point that mathematics not only encourages the abstract, disciplined thinking essential to philosophical enquiry, but – since it deals with immaterial and timeless objects like numbers – 'attracts' the mind towards what is most 'utterly real', the realm of the Forms (*Republic* 523ff.). The aim of higher education, of which mathematics and dialectic are the main components, is not, for Plato, the amassing of information, knowledge 'for its own sake', or the acquisition of practical skills, but a 'reorientation of a mind from a kind of twilight to true daylight' (*Republic* 521). The 'reorientated' person will have risen above immersion in mundane empirical matters towards that articulate under-standing of the order of things without which his opinions, even if true, do not constitute the grounded knowledge that alone affords effective and stable guidance in life.

Plato is insistent, however, that it would be harmful to initiate the young into this rational moral understanding prior to an advanced stage in their education. Incapable of mastering such understanding, a premature attempt to get children to reason for themselves only serves to make them 'rebellious' and disrespectful of traditional wisdom. Hence, in the earlier sections of *Republic*, which discuss the 'cultural' (and physical) education of the young, Plato defends 'the notion that education is a training of character' above all else.[4] Close direction of the child's educational environment, especially in the very early years when it 'absorbs every impression that anyone wishes to stamp upon it' (*Republic* 377), is necessary, first, in order to counteract those pressures, including sensual appetites, that threaten to smother the innate, yet fragile, propensity for reason. It is also, and more positively, required if – as my opening citation indicates – the young are to acquire those affective dispositions, such as a love of 'grace and elegance', that are prerequisite to the eventual appreciation of 'the beauty of reason' (*Republic* 401). It does not matter that, for a considerable time, the young person has no conscious, rational grasp of why things are beautiful or good: the urgent task is to develop a character receptive to, indeed eager for, enlightenment and 'mental clarity'.

For Plato, culture at large, including music and architecture, forms an educational environment and, as such, has a power to shape impressionable young minds. Plato's particular focus is the effect upon character of literature, of the epics, odes and dramas that were not only the mainstay of Athenian education, but a primary medium for the dissemination, among the populace as a whole, of ideas and information. He criticizes most of this literature, including Homer, for failing to respect the gods, heroes and great men who, in modern jargon, were 'role-models' for the young. He is still more critical of the common practice of having young people 'represent ... mean-spirited or otherwise contemptible' people by acting parts or recitation, with the result that they take on the character of those they are 'imitating' (*Republic* 395). In Book X, Plato broadens his attack on literature: with few exceptions, the poets are to be 'banished from our community' for, by working on the emotions rather than by addressing reason, they are engaged in an 'ancient quarrel' with philosophy (*Republic* 607). Only art of the most ethically bracing kind is to be permitted.

Plato's paternalistic attitude towards cultural education has been a prime target for liberal critics of his programme. Much of this criticism, however, is guilty both of anachronism and of mistaking Plato's purpose. The arts whose effects Plato lamented were the *popular* ones of his day, not the effete pursuit of 'highbrows', and his concern should be compared with the one expressed by many people today over the effects, on impressionable children, of violence and vulgarity on TV, say, or of a relentless diet of brain-numbing pop music.[5] As for the purpose of Plato's programme of literary education, this was not to further the establishment of a totalitarian regime, but to emphasize in a dramatic way the massive impact of the cultural environment on the individual's eventual receptiveness to reason and morality. If, by contemporary lights, Plato displays scant respect for the 'autonomy' of the child, one may reasonably question whether he was mistaken in holding that genuine autonomy, as distinct from self-assertive *insouciance* towards tradition, is attained by young people encouraged to 'choose their own values', 'do their own thing', prior to any disciplined initiation into rational enquiry.

Anachronism and misunderstanding may also be responsible for the familiar charge of 'élitism' against Plato. Since it was only the sons of wealthy Athenians who were formally educated, in restricting higher education to the few Plato was being no more élitist than his contemporaries, or indeed than most educationists until very recent times. In one respect, moreover, Plato was radical for his day. Women, he argued, should receive the same higher education as men, the only relevant criterion being possession of 'the required natural abilities' (*Republic* 540). Plato would doubtless scorn modern calls for mass higher education, not because it should be the privilege of a future ruling élite, but because the 'natural abilities' people must have to benefit from demanding intellectual disciplines – and not some 'dumbed down' *ersatz* – are possessed by relatively few.

A more pertinent criticism is that, for reasons grounded in his questionable conception of knowledge, Plato's emphasis on the 'abstract' disciplines of mathematics and philosophy is unwarranted.[6] We should recall, however, that, for Plato, philosophy is not a hived-off, 'professional' pursuit, but the form of understanding that confers, first, 'the ability to take an overview' of other types of understanding and, second, the 'mental clarity' that enables a person to *explain*, to render articulate, the nature of and interconnections among the objects of knowledge (*Republic* 533–4).

Indifference to that kind of understanding and 'mental clarity' in an educational climate where the acquisition of information, practical 'skills', and 'autonomy' are more highly prized, helps to explain why Plato's theory of education – so deeply admired during past eras, such as the Renaissance – is nowadays more often attacked than applauded. That his views continue to attract comment, however, critical though it may generally be, only confirms the perception that the legacy of Plato's philosophy of education has been Western philosophy of education itself.[7]

Notes

1 *Republic* 401–2. References in the text cite the title of a dialogue and the page number of the Stephanus edition of Plato. All decent translations give the Stephanus numbering in the margins.

2 In this article, I do not dwell on the points shared by Plato and Socrates, since these are discussed in C.J. Rowe's article on Socrates in this volume.

3 The image of the person as a battleground for warring faculties, notably reason and

appetite, was ingrained in everyday Greek thinking as well as philosophy. See James Davidson, *Courtesans and Fishcakes: The Consuming Passions of Classical Athens*, London: Fontana, 1998.

4 Julia Annas, *An Introduction to Plato's Republic*, Oxford: Clarendon Press, p. 86, 1981.

5 See Iris Murdoch, *The Fire and the Sun: Why Plato Banished the Artists*, Oxford: Oxford University Press, 1977.

6 See R.S. Peters, 'Was Plato Nearly Right About Education?', in his *Education and the Education of Teachers*, London: Routledge and Kegan Paul, pp.119–32 1977.

7 Here I mimic Bernard Williams's remark that 'the legacy of Greece to Western philosophy is Western philosophy', 'Philosophy', in M. Finley (ed.), *The Legacy of Greece*, Oxford: Clarendon Press, p. 202, 1981. On one of Plato's major influences, see M.F. Burnyeat, 'The Past in the Present: Plato as Educator of 19th C. Britain', in A. Rorty (ed.), *Philosophers on Education: Historical Perspectives*. London: Routledge, pp. 353–73, 1998.

See also

In this book: Aristotle, Mill, Socrates

Plato's major writings

All of Plato's dialogues are translated in E. Hamilton & H. Cairns (eds.), *Plato: Collected Dialogues*, Princeton: Princeton University Press, 1961. The major ones are also available in Penguin translations. The translation of *Republic* I have used is by R. Waterfield, Oxford: Oxford University Press, 1993.

Further reading

Annas, J., *An Introduction to Plato's Republic*, Oxford: Clarendon Press, 1981.

Barrow, R, *Plato, Utilitarianism and Education*, London: Routledge & Kegan Paul, 1975.

Cross, R.C. and Woozley, A.D., *Plato's Republic: A Philosophical Commentary*, London: Macmillan, 1964.

Nettleship, R.L., *The Theory of Education in Plato's*, *Republic*, Oxford: Clarendon Press, 1935.

Peters, R.S., *Education and the Education of Teachers*, London: Routledge & Kegan Paul, 1977.

DAVID E. COOPER

ARISTOTLE 384–322 BCE

> [T]he best and most pleasant life is the life of the intellect since the intellect is in the fullest sense the man.[1]

Aristotle, one of the greatest and most influential educational philosophers of all time, was born in 384 BCE in the Northern Greek town of Stagira. He spent his early life in Macedonia and at about the age of 18 travelled to Athens to complete his education. He studied at Plato's Academy. Aristotle was certainly strongly influenced by Plato's teachings but later came to reject some of the most important of them. He is reported to have said: 'Plato is dear to me but dearer still is truth.'

After Plato died in 347 BCE, Aristotle left the Academy and travelled in Asia Minor and Greece, before he was invited in 343 BC by Philip King of Macedonia to act as tutor to his 13-year-old son, Alexander, the future conqueror of Persia and much of the then known world. Aristotle returned to Athens after Alexander became king in 336 BC and established a school of his own, known as the Lyceum, where he taught for twelve years. In 323 BC, due to growing Athenian hostility to Macedonians, Aristotle was forced to retire to Euboea where he died the following year.

Aristotle's work has had an enormous impact on Western thought, although it was not until the thirteenth century that the main body of his writing was rediscovered in Western Europe. After that time he was treated as an authority on most subjects and any new theories that disagreed with what Aristotle said were at first treated with suspicion. Unfortunately not all of Aristotle's writings have survived and what we do have are mainly copies of what are believed to be his lecture notes.

It is difficult to capture the full sweep of Aristotle's educational ideas in a brief essay such as this, but to help bring out the essential points they will be discussed according to the four components distinctive of any educational theory: theory of knowledge, of learning, of the person and the role of education in society. This will also serve to bring out the clear links between Aristotle's general philosophy and his educational views.

Knowledge

Unlike Plato, Aristotle did not believe that there are two separate orders of reality, but just one which we perceive through the senses. He did talk of ideal forms, not as transcendental entities but rather as a component of the actual material object. Whereas Plato's approach to knowledge was to reflect on an ideal world of unchanging perfect forms, Aristotle's was to examine more minutely the actual physical world in which we live. This has led to Plato being regarded as an idealist and Aristotle as a realist, in the sense of affirming the reality and objectivity of the physical world.

Aristotle also saw the world as a dynamic place where everything is continually evolving according to some inner purpose. All matter thus has a potential which it is striving to realize and in terms of education the aim is to help develop the child's potentialities into what he or she is best fitted to become.

Learning

How then is this knowledge built up in the human mind? Aristotle also rejected Plato's theory that knowledge is innate within us. For Aristotle, knowledge starts with sense perception – we observe objects or events and from these build up in our mind a general principle by which to understand and explain these. This is the process of inductive reasoning, which moves from particular observations to general conclusions. This is of course the prime method of reasoning used in science in contrast to the deductive method of mathematics. Once again the differences between Plato and Aristotle are apparent, with Plato primarily interested in mathematics and Aristotle in science.

Of course Aristotle realized that not all reasoning is inductive. Once we have established a general principle, we can deduce particular conclusions from it. For example, from the premises all men are mortal and Socrates is a man, we can deduce that Socrates is mortal. This is known as syllogistic reasoning, of which Aristotle wrote in some detail.

However for Aristotle the actual development of *new* knowledge generally comes about by induction and the process of learning is one of building up in the mind a picture of reality that corresponds with the real world outside. At birth our mind is like a blank slate but with capacities to act on impressions coming into it from the outside world. The role of the teacher is to help the child organize this vast range of empirical experiences, to help provide some structure for all these disparate elements. This has been a persistent model of the teacher's role ever since.

The person

Aristotle held that humans possess a soul, which gives form to the body, which is matter. Note that when Aristotle spoke of the soul he was not thinking of it in the way we do today, which is a thoroughly Christianized sense. It is unlikely he believed that the soul could exist apart from the body.

Given that everything in life has a purpose, Aristotle asks (in his *Nicomachean Ethics*) what is the purpose of humankind? His answer is to seek happiness. This is the sole self-sufficient good. But how do we achieve happiness? Basically, by being virtuous. If this sounds unconvincing to some, he develops his argument by making a distinction between intellectual and moral virtue. The former is equivalent to what we would call wisdom or intelligence and is mainly acquired by teaching and instruction, whereas moral virtue is concerned with our conduct towards other people and is mainly acquired by practice. When Aristotle says virtue is necessary for happiness, he is including both kinds.

We also need to remember that the classical Greek word we translate as virtue does not have exactly the same connotation as the English word 'virtue' (coming from the Latin *virtus*). The Greek word is *arete* which roughly translates as 'inner excellence' or 'fitness for purpose'. Bearing this in mind, it is easier to see why Aristotle regarded virtue so highly. If persons lack virtue, they are not functioning as they should, not fulfilling their purposes efficiently and therefore it is impossible for them to achieve happiness.

Of the two types of virtue Aristotle distinguishes in the *Ethics*, it is moral virtue in which he is most interested and he goes on to examine it in some detail. In trying to capture what is essential to it, he developed the idea that the virtuous action is generally a middle course between two extremes. For example, the virtue of generosity is a mean between meanness and prodigality. This doctrine has come to be known as the 'Golden Mean' and has appealed ever since to those moralists who believe in moderation in all things and not getting carried away by one's emotions.

Aristotle's argument that virtue is necessary for happiness may seem to take a merely expedient attitude to virtue, implying we should be good just because it is likely to bring us happiness. But here again there is a translation problem. *Eudaimonia*, the Greek word we translate as happiness, does not just mean a feeling of personal pleasure (as Aristotle himself points out),[2] it means living the good life. This includes being happy in the modern sense but it also means that the condition achieved is a stable long-term affair applying over one's whole life. As he says in a well-known passage that has passed into everyday usage: 'One swallow does not make a summer, neither does one day. Similarly neither can one day, or a brief space of time, make a man blessed or happy.[3] Aristotle also regarded *eudaimonia* as necessarily a public affair which involves playing one's proper role in society.

The next step in Aristotle's argument is to ask which of a person's activities best exhibits virtue in the fullest sense and is therefore most likely to bring us long-term happiness. His answer is *theoria*, or in English, contemplation or the pursuit of intellectual understanding. This is where the human being's distinctive function of reason is best exemplified. (This also brings to mind Aristotle's well-known definition of man as 'a rational animal'.) So in the end his conclusion is rather similar to Plato's, except that for Aristotle the contemplation will aim primarily at better understanding the physical, visible world around us rather than focusing on some mental world of abstract forms. It is also interesting to note the link between these two Greek thinkers and certain Eastern mystics and others who see meditation as our highest and most noble activity.

Education and society

The main source of Aristotle's ideas here is his *Politics* and like Plato he was influenced by his own aristocratic background and accepted that some people are slaves or manual labourers by nature while others are naturally endowed to be soldiers or rulers. He was however not as suspicious of democracy as Plato and favoured a form of government he called *polity* where the state is ruled by the best and wisest who are in a sense representative of all the people.

Like Plato, Aristotle believes the state should have complete control of education and use it to prepare the desired type of citizens needed by the state. Also like Plato, he was really only interested in the education of the free Greek citizen – workers and slaves only needed basic training for their future jobs.

Having now looked at Aristotle's basic assumptions in the areas of knowledge, learning, human nature and society, we can explore the implications of all this for his specific educational recommendations. He has the most to say about moral education and, as we have noted, held that moral virtue was mainly acquired by practice. As he says 'we become just by performing just acts, temperate by performing temperate ones, brave by performing brave ones'.[4] Hence the great importance of correct guidance by parents and teachers. If children are accustomed to the right moral habits from an early age, doing the right thing will become second nature to them. This has become a very influential model for moral education ever since.

Then he goes on to raise an objection to what he has just said. He says that if we become moral by doing moral acts, does this not imply we are already moral, for how otherwise could we do moral acts in the first place?[5] His answer to this question is a landmark in thinking about moral education and one that is still highly influential today. It involves once again making an important distinction, this time between acts in accordance with morality and moral acts proper. The actual behaviour may be exactly the same (e.g. helping someone in need), but the difference lies in the state of mind of the agent and his or her motives. For an act to be fully moral Aristotle says three conditions are necessary: (1) we must act with knowledge (2) we must deliberately choose the act for its own sake and (3) the act must spring from a fixed disposition of character.[6] These three features have become widely accepted as necessary features of fully fledged moral action.

Acts in accordance with morality, on the other hand, may be performed just out of habit, through fear of punishment, to gain approval and so forth. So Aristotle has resolved his own problem: it is quite possible to perform acts that correspond to morality before we are fully moral. This is in fact the only way to begin one's moral education and then as children mature intellectually the true reasons as to why they should act morally can be provided and children can then move towards principled moral action. Modern psychologists such as Piaget and Kohlberg have demonstrated empirically what Aristotle is saying here.

What about the rest of the curriculum apart from moral education? Here Aristotle does not have much to say explicitly but he would have had a graduated programme in some ways similar to Plato.[7] Up to about age 7 this would have been basically physical and character training. From 7 to puberty and then on to 21 is the period of public state-controlled education. The basic subjects would be gymnastics, reading, drawing and music. Of these, Aristotle wrote in most detail on the educational value of music.[8] Apart from their immediate value, these subjects are also designed to prepare the full Greek citizen for the final period of his education, which is understood to last for the rest of his life and extends beyond the confines of the school. The word 'his' is used advisedly here as Aristotle (unlike Plato) explicitly excluded women from higher stages of education.

This last stage is the period of liberal education, called liberal for two reasons. Remembering the derivation of the word 'liberal' (from Latin, *liber* = free), it is an education that frees the mind from ignorance and is also the education appropriate for free men. The subjects to be studied in this period are similar to those that we believe were taught at Aristotle's Lyceum, chiefly mathematics, logic, metaphysics, ethics, politics, aesthetics, music, poetry, rhetoric, physics and biology.

It is this final period that interested Aristotle the most and the one that he saw as being worthwhile in itself or of intrinsic value. This notion of the intrinsic value of education (as opposed to any vocational or practical advantages it may lead to) has been a constant theme in educational thought ever since, although many may feel today that there is a danger of losing sight of it in the present climate of economic rationalism. Aristotle was particularly derogatory about using education for any extrinsic or instrumental purposes and it is here that some of his aristocratic prejudices come out most clearly. Vocational education was fit only for the lower classes, for the Greek citizen it was the idea of education as making you a fuller and more cultured person that counted.

Overall many of the key themes emphasized by Aristotle remain with us in education to the present day, including his empiricist model of how we learn, the stress on early habit training in moral education followed by acquisition of a principled morality, the idea that happiness, virtue and contemplation are all interrelated and are key educational goals, and finally the ideal of liberal education with its stress on the intrinsic values of learning.

Notes

The following references to the *Nicomachean Ethics* include in brackets where appropriate the page and column numbers of Bekker's Greek text which are regularly indicated in English translations and enable location of the relevant passage in different versions.

1 *The Ethics of Aristotle* (The *Nicomachean Ethics*), trans. J.A.K. Thomson, London: Penguin Books, 1955, rev. 1976 by H. Tredennick, Book X, p. 331 (1177a–1178a).
2 Ibid., pp. 326–8 (1176a–1177a).
3 Ibid., p. 76 (1098a).
4 Ibid., pp. 91–2 (1103b).
5 Ibid., p. 97 (1105a).
6 Ibid.
7 See Books VII and VIII of the *Politics* for fuller details.
8 See Book VIII, *Politics*.

See also

In this book: Plato
In *Fifty Modern Thinkers on Education*: Piaget, Kohlberg

Aristotle's major writings

Collected editions

Barnes, J. (ed.), *The Complete Works of Aristotle – The Revised Oxford Translation*, Princeton: Princeton University Press, 1984.
McKeon, R. (ed.), *The Basic Works of Aristotle*, New York: Random House, 1941.
The Ethics of Aristotle, trans. J.A.K. Thomson, London: Penguin Books, 1955, revised 1976 by H. Tredennick.
The Politics of Aristotle, trans. T.A. Sinclair, Harmondsworth: Penguin Books, 1962.

Further reading

Books on Aristotle's ideas in general

Barnes, J. (ed.), *The Cambridge Companion to Aristotle*, Cambridge: Cambridge University Press, 1995.
Evans, J.D.G., *Aristotle*, Sussex: Harvester Press, 1987.

Books on Aristotle's educational ideas

Bauman, R.W., *Aristotle's Logic of Education* (New Perspectives In Philosophical Scholarship: Texts And Issues), Vol. 19, New York: Peter Lang, 1998.
Howie, G. (ed.), *Aristotle on Education*, London: Collier-Macmillan, 1968.
Lord, C., *Education and Culture in the Political Thought of Aristotle*, Ithaca and London: Cornell University Press, 1982.
Verbeke, G., *Moral Education in Aristotle*, Washington, DC: Catholic University of America Press, 1990.

Books with chapters on Aristotle's educational ideas

Frankena, W.K., *Three Historical Philosophies of Education*, Glenview, Illinois: Scott Foresman, 1965.
Rorty, A.O. (ed.), *Philosophers on Education*, London: Routledge, 1998.

PETER HOBSON

JESUS OF NAZARETH 4 BCE– AD 29

> While he [Jesus] was saying this, a woman in the crowd raised her voice and said to him, 'Blessed is the womb that bore you and the breasts that nursed you!' But he said, 'Blessed rather are those who hear the word of God and obey it!'[1]

Jesus of Nazareth as a teacher, preacher and reformer turned history inside out. Jesus taught as he lived. He lived in unconventional ways. His method and his message were the warp and woof of an unconventional mission – to challenge people to think in new ways.

Jesus was born in Palestine near the end of the reign of Herod the Great, probably around 4 BC. His parents were named Mary and Joseph and his family tree went back to King David who lived about 1000–961 BC. Jesus' home town of Nazareth was a town in southern Galilee, about a hundred miles north of Jerusalem and a few miles from Sepphoris, the largest city in Galilee. Palestine had been annexed to the Roman Empire since 63 BC and was ruled by kings appointed by Rome.

We know very little about his early years, but mainstream scholars think that Jesus learned to read and write in a local synagogue, with the Torah as his text. He had several brothers and sisters and his father was a woodworker who probably died before Jesus' public ministry began. As the oldest son, he presumably learned his father's trade making products such as yokes, ploughs, door frames, furniture and cabinets. Woodworkers were considered at the lower end of the peasant class since they didn't own land.[2]

One story told about Jesus at 12 years of age points to his interest in religion and portrays him as having a keen mind. Jesus and his family travel with others from Nazareth to the yearly celebration of Passover in Jerusalem. At the end of the festival, the family sets off to return to Nazareth and, after going a day, they realize that Jesus isn't with the caravan. Mary and Joseph return to Jerusalem, frantically searching for him.

Three days later, they finally discover him in the Temple, 'listening to the teachers and asking them questions'.

The Gospel According to Luke describes the impact the young boy had on these scholars: 'Everyone who heard him was surprised at how much he knew and at the answers he gave.' His distraught mother asks him, ' "Son, why have you done this to us? Your father and I have been very worried, and we have been searching for you!" Jesus answers, "Why did you have to look for me? Didn't you know that I would be in my Father's house?" But they did not understand what he meant.' Luke ends this story with a suggestion that Jesus was sensitive to his parents' wishes as he continued to mature into young adulthood. 'Jesus went back to Nazareth with his parents and obeyed them. His mother kept thinking about all that had happened. Jesus became wise, and he grew strong. God was pleased with him and so were the people.'[3]

About the age of 30, Jesus began his teaching and preaching ministry, but not in the conventional patterns of that day. He didn't fit the mould of a street preacher or a wandering prophet, roles that had been common throughout Jewish history. Nor did he resemble the élite of that day who had been educated in Greek philosophy.[4] These teachers were not only considered wise, but as having the authority that comes from being morally superior to the uneducated.

Jesus' teaching style was *egalitarian*. This, in itself, would have attracted attention within a highly structured and class-conscious society. As bees to honey, the lower classes of Jews couldn't get enough of this Rabbi from Galilee. His message of hope for a new day of mercy and justice attracted the poor and marginalized. Perhaps more influential than even these words was that Jesus treated everyone he encountered as having worth. His actions were congruent with his words. For instance, he took time to teach illiterate peasants, spent time with people who were despised (tax collectors), touched those considered unclean (lepers), and invited children to come and sit with him after his disciples tried to chase them away. Jesus repeatedly told his followers that they should look for truth and salvation – the Kingdom of God – within themselves. St Luke records:

> Once Jesus was asked by the Pharisees when the kingdom of God was coming, and he answered, 'The kingdom of God is not coming with things that can be observed; nor will they say, "Look, here it is!" or "There it is!" For, in fact, the kingdom of God is among [or within] you.'[5]

In contrast to the classically educated élite, Jesus claimed that his authority came not from himself as having a morally superior character, but from a spiritual source – his Father who had sent him into this ministry. In the early years of the Christian Church, the defenders of the faith, or apologists, attempted to present Jesus as the Divine Teacher with his authority from God. In the second century, Justin Martyr pointed out that Jesus brought to Roman and Jewish culture a morality that was higher than that of the philosopher élite because he was able to establish an intimate connection between himself (as divine teacher) and the uneducated and oppressed masses. He taught his followers that the divine could live in them.

The presence of divinity in the teacher engenders the powers of interpretation, understanding, communication and instruction that guide the students in the quest for the divine. Through a process of maturing, the students eventually become assimilated into the divine and attain divine status themselves.[6]

Origen, a third-century theologian, declared that through this process of maturation one could become a 'son of God'. Later in the early Church, this developmental process of maturation in the faith became the catechetical process, a learning process which usually took three years of training and apprenticeship in the Christian life.

However, Jesus was very reluctant to make divinity claims for himself. His relationship with his followers was that of master teacher to pupils. In Roman society there were two classes of teachers. One was a tutor hired by wealthy families to teach knowledge and moral character to the children in the household. The other role was that of master teacher who taught a group of students in the sciences and philosophy. A second-century Christian theologian, Clement, saw Jesus in both of these roles. First, Jesus tutored his disciples and other followers about the Kingdom of God and a new way of living in love. As a master teacher, he went deeper into God's plan for him and for the world with his twelve chosen disciples and a few others, including a non-Jewish woman from Samaria[7] and his friend, Martha, sister of Lazarus and Mary.[8]

Jesus was democratic in his teaching, but he taught with authority – an authority not based in academic degrees. In fact, the wisdom woven through his conversations with people and his many parables confounded the educated leaders of that day. They wondered how an itinerant preacher who came from a simple peasant family and a town like Nazareth could speak with such charisma and authority? How could a man who ignored strict Jewish laws – like healing on the Sabbath and eating with publicans – captivate hundreds and thousands of Jewish people from all walks of life?

Jesus' teaching authority was based on knowing that God had called him to a ministry of truth-telling. When he was being interrogated by Pontius Pilate before he was crucified, Jesus answered Pilate's question about whether he was a king by saying, 'You say that I am a king. For this I was born, and for this I came into the world, to testify to the truth.' Pilate's rejoinder, 'What is truth?' [9] has become the perennial question for seekers of knowledge.

Marcus Borg, a Jesus scholar, talks about Jesus having alternative wisdom in contrast to conventional wisdom.[10] Conventional wisdom is 'basically life within the socially constructed world'.[11] Jesus used the language of paradox and reversal to upset the conventional wisdom of his day which was based on traditions that he considered no longer adequate. Phrases like, 'Blessed are the poor,' 'The first will be last' and 'Leave the dead to bury the dead', convey unexpected messages which beg further thinking.

Jesus' chief teaching tool was the parable. Parables were good stories that invited people to consider a new way of thinking. Marcus Borg comments: 'The appeal is not to the will – not "Do this" – but rather, "Consider seeing it this way." As invitational forms of speech, the parables do not invoke external authority'.[12] Parables as a teaching pedagogy drew the listener into not only the story, but his/her own imagination as the images and the meaning of the story were pondered.

In the Gospels, Jesus tells his disciples why he speaks in parables.[13] He explains that parables contain mysteries about the Kingdom of Heaven, and people who are open to this will hear and understand. Jesus found that those who were uneducated and oppressed were likely to understand the meaning of his parables since they were ready to consider a new way of life.

Jesus lived what he taught. He embodied a challenge to the conventions of his day. The Jewish laws he broke, many of them bodily-oriented (eating, touching, gleaning grain), were not just private actions, but 'social miniatures that can support or challenge, affirm or negate a culture's behavioral rules or a society's customary codes'.[14] Jesus taught through his actions a way to challenge the political and social structures – the body politic. John Dominic Crossan points out that the body politic can also be the 'politic body'[15] when one's body interacts with society's norms in a way that challenges those norms.

Much of biblical scholarship in the second half of the twentieth century centred on study of the historical Jesus. Borg comments, 'It is remarkable, indeed extraordinary, that 2000 years after he lived, a Jewish peasant from Nazareth continues to be a figure of such towering significance.'[16] Several theologies in recent years have centred on the radical egalitarian life of Jesus. Liberation theology, which emerged in the late 1960s in Latin America with the writing of Gustavo Gutierrez,[17] proclaimed God's 'preferential option for the poor' based on Jesus' teachings and actions. Poor and often illiterate peasants were taught processes for studying the Bible that gave them insights into their plights and incentives to take action for the common good in their *barrios*. As a result, grassroots Christian groups called 'base communities' spread across Latin America and today continue to work for justice.

A Catholic educator in northeastern Brazil, Paulo Freire, championed the idea of 'praxis', the involvement of people in becoming aware of their oppression and learning how to leverage change in the social and political structures.[18]

In the US in the 1960s and 70s (and continuing today), religious institutions have joined civic groups and labour unions in forming broad-based community organizing campaigns on issues of justice identified at the grassroots. Housing and health care for the poor and working classes have been two major thrusts for these groups.

Another theology which is formed and energized by the story of Jesus is 'narrative theology'. It starts with the Bible as primarily a story. Stanley Hauerwas sees an ethical dimension in the biblical narrative which shows us how to live as people of God in the world.[19] Understanding Jesus as teaching a new way to live in the world that honours everyone's humanity and builds a just community is an ongoing legacy of Jesus as an egalitarian master teacher.

Notes

1 The Gospel According to Luke, 11: 27–28, *Holy Bible: New Revised Standard Version*, Nashville, TN: Thomas Nelson Publishers, 1989.

2 Marcus J. Borg, *Meeting Jesus Again for the First time*, San Francisco: HarperCollins Publishers, p. 26, 1994.
3 Luke 2: 49–52, *The Holy Bible: The Contemporary English Version*, Nashville, TN: Thomas Nelson Publishers, 1995.
4 Karen Jo Torjesen, 'You are the Christ: Five Portraits of Jesus From the Early Church,' *Jesus at 2000*, Boulder, CO: Westview Press, p. 80, 1998.
5 Luke 17: 20–21, *Holy Bible, New Revised Standard Version*, Thomas Nelson Publishers, 1989.
6 Torjesen (1998, p. 82).
7 John 4: 1–30, *Holy Bible, New Revised Standard Version*, Thomas Nelson Publishers, 1989.
8 John 11: 1–27.
9 John 18: 37–38.
10 Borg (1994, p. 75).
11 Ibid., p. 76.
12 Ibid., p. 74.
13 Matthew 13: 10–17; Mark 4: 10–11; Luke 10: 21–23.
14 John Dominic Crossan, *Jesus: A Revolutionary Biography*, HarperSanFrancisco: HarperCollins Publishers, p. 77, 1994.
15 Ibid., p. 76.
16 Marcus J. Borg, 'Introduction: Jesus at 2000,' *Jesus at 2000*, Boulder, CO: Westview Press, pp. 1–2, 1998.
17 Gustavo Gutierrez, *A Theology of Liberation*, rev. edn, trans. and ed. Sister Garidad Inda and John Eagleson, Maryknoll, NY: Orbis, 1988.
18 Paulo Freire, *Pedagogy of the Oppressed*, trans. Myra Bergman Ramos, New York: Continuum, 1982.
19 Stanley Hauerwas, *The Peaceable Kingdom*, Notre Dame, IN: University of Notre Dame Press, 1983.

See also

In *Fifty Modern Thinkers on Education*: Freire

Further reading

Borg, M.J., *Meeting Jesus Again for the First Time*, New York: HarperSanFrancisco, HarperCollins Publishers, 1994.
—— ed., *Jesus at 2000*, Boulder, CO: Westview Press, 1998.
Borg, M.J. and Wright, N.T., *The Meaning of Jesus: Two Visions*, New York: HarperSanFrancisco, HarperCollins Publishers, 1999.
Crossan, J.D., *Jesus: A Revolutionary Biography*, New York: HarperSanFrancisco, HarperCollins Publishers, 1994.
Ehrman, B.D., *Jesus: Apocalyptic Prophet of the New Millennium*, New York: Oxford University Press, 1999.
Johnson, L.T., *Living Jesus: Learning the Heart of the Gospel*, New York: HarperSanFrancisco, HarperCollins Publishers, 1999.
Powell, M.A. *Jesus as a Figure in History: How Modern Historians View the Man from Galilee*, Louisville: John Knox Press, 1998.
Neusner, J. *A Rabbi talks with Jesus: An Intermillennial Interfaith Exchange*, New York: Doubleday, 1993.

CONNIE LEEAN SERAPHINE

SAINT AUGUSTINE 354–430

> In your gift we find our rest. There are you our joy. Our rest is our
> peace. .... A body by its weight tends to move to its proper place.
> ... Things which are not in their intended position are restless.
> Once they are in their ordered position, they are at rest. My
> weight is my love.[1]

Aurelius Augustinus, whom we know as St Augustine, was born in 354 in the
small North African town of Thagaste. His mother Monica was a Christian;
his father Patricius was a pagan, who received baptism on his death-bed. At
the time of Augustine's birth, the Roman Empire in the West had less than a
hundred and twenty years to run before its final collapse: when he came to
die as Bishop of Hippo, that city was being besieged by the Vandals. The
writings he left were destined to be read in a world very different from his
own.

He was subjected to the disheartening procedures of education in those
days: learning by rote, a concentration upon single words to the neglect of
the whole, artificial composition, and instruction in Greek that nauseated
him – he never read Greek copiously and with ease. The whole process was
well seasoned with corporal punishment. He writes in the first book of the
Confessions about the pains and terror and boredom of his school-days, and
yet the education he received (at great cost to his parents) made him a
member of a caste that might find acceptance anywhere in the Roman world.

Augustine began to teach, first in Thagaste and then in Carthage. He
formed a stable liaison with a woman of a lower social class than himself,
and a son was born to them. His education had been literary, but he
encountered a philosophical writing by Cicero (now surviving only in
fragments) – the *Hortensius*, which placed the highest happiness in the quest
for Wisdom, and he was much moved by it. But a reading of the Bible
disappointed him, and he entered a subordinate rank among the Manichees
– a dualistic religion which made the Good principle be good indeed, but not
omnipotent. He eventually went to Rome and then to the Imperial City of
Milan, where he became Professor of Rhetoric. His faithful companion was
taken from him – she was an impediment to his advancement. His
Manichean beliefs petered out, and he veered to scepticism; but a reading of
books by 'Platonists' (Plotinus and Porphyry) led him nearer to Christianity.
His taking the final step in 386 is told in the eighth book of the *Confessions*
(written thirteen years after the event). His baptism took place at Milan.
Within three years, his mother and his son were both dead, and Augustine
returned to Africa and was ordained a priest. In 395, he was made a bishop
by force – such was a custom in those days – and bore for the rest of his life
the burden of administration which this entailed.

His voluminous writings include commentaries on Scripture, devotional
works, philosophical treatises against scepticism and on the freedom of the
will, educational works, the *Confessions* themselves, and writings against
theological opponents. The first, and obviously, of these was against the
Manichees. Then he wrote opposing the Donatists, an African sect that
wanted to limit the Church to those who were perfect. He also wrote in
opposition to the Pelagians, a sect of British origin that did not do justice to

the need for God's grace. Then, in the closing years of his life, he composed *The City of God*, directed at the paganism of an Empire now in dissolution. The effects of Augustine's thought on Latin theology have been incalculable. In the centuries that followed his death, when the Western Empire ended and the darkness came down, two things of Christian inheritance would have been found, along with fragments of pagan learning and literature, in the libraries of monasteries: one was the Latin Bible of St Jerome, and the other was writings by his contemporary, St Augustine. Whatever one thinks of his influence, it is there and it is undeniable.

The text of Augustine I put at the start of this essay was written by him in the setting of a meditation on the desire we have for God that runs through all our imaginings and wanderings. Just as bodies seek their 'natural place', according to the beliefs of those days, so do we seek him. He made us for himself, and our hearts will know no rest until they rest in him (*Confessions* I.i.1). But the text can also serve as a useful introduction to what Augustine has to say of education, for what stands out there is his contention that there must be a going-out from teacher to pupil, an encouragement that does not rest upon cruelty and punishment, a loving attempt to see the pupil's condition and to lead him on to what the teacher has to give.

He contrasts in the first book of the *Confessions* his experiences at school learning Greek with his acquisition of Latin, his native language. The punishments administered at school soured the language for him, and even the stories told by Homer were repellent, and had as it were gall sprinkled over them. Whereas the learning of Latin in his infancy took place without any pain or threat of punishment: his nurses caressed him, people made jokes, he played games with others: 'free curiosity has greater power to stimulate learning than rigorous coercion' (*Confessions* I.xiv.23). Even at school, the poetry of Virgil moved his heart, and he wept over the death of Dido (I.xiii.20). Later, the first step towards what was eventually his conversion came when (amid a largely literary education), he read the philosophical work by Cicero about the quest for wisdom. He writes in the *Confessions*: 'The book changed my feelings. It altered my prayers, Lord, towards yourself. It gave me different values and priorities' (III.iv.7). And the famous scene at Milan where he finally turns to God – even when we make allowance for the distance in time between the event and the narrative – is portrayed by Augustine as a change of heart, a relief from anxiety (VIII.xii.28–9).

The work *De catechizandis rudibus* shows the same preoccupations, but now in the practical setting of giving religious instruction. Deogratias (the catechist who had written for encouragement and advice) must not be despondent: it may well be that the pupils thought better of his discourse than he did. Any teacher at times will be painfully aware of the gap between what he has in mind and what he manages to express. He must strive to be cheerful – God loves a cheerful giver – and to let joy be felt in what he says (II.3 and 4). He must bear in mind that the love of God for us has been shown in the coming of Christ; and that this love we must make the foundation of all our teaching, so that the pupil 'hearing may believe, believing may hope, and hoping may love' (IV.8).

Difficulties may arise on the part of the pupil or of the teacher. The pupil's motives may be mixed when he seeks instruction. If so, we must not forget that the teaching itself can sometimes purify the intentions of the one who receives it. We should therefore not behave as if we were unmasking his insincerity, but enquire as best we can into his condition: we should endeavour to give instruction that will touch his heart and lead him on to better things (V.9).

Or the pupil may be already educated in other matters, and is probably familiar with passages from Scripture. Once more, we must go out to his condition. We should not talk as if he knew nothing, but rather speak as if we were reminding him of what he already knew. His difficulties and objections should not be peremptorily set aside, but discussed in a modest conversation (*modesta collatione*). And all matters should be brought back to 'the better way' (cf. I Corinthians xiii), the way of love (VIII.12). As for those pupils who have been trained in language and rhetoric (Augustine is thinking of people with his own educational background), they must be instructed in humility – not to be deterred by literary imperfections in the Scriptures, or by solecisms in what is said by ministers. They must be taught to see that what matters is the *content* of what is said. They need a change of priorities (as we saw Augustine put it in the *Confessions*): to prefer discourses that are true and friends that are wise (IX.13).

Or the difficulties may lie in the teacher himself. What he possesses inwardly has to be spelt out in detail that he finds tedious: he may be disheartened by what seems inertness in the pupil; his own private worries may impede his efficiency or – and this has a modern enough ring – he may be engaged in some fascinating work of his own, and have to leave it in order to teach (X.14).

Augustine does not claim to offer quick remedies for these difficulties. We need the charity of Christ towards our pupils, who himself used the analogy of the hen gathering the chickens under her (XI.15). We need in a sense to learn with our pupils when we teach – the old things can then become new to us (XI.17). Inertness should encourage us to get the pupil to express his feelings without fear; above all, we need patience (XI.18). Perhaps a change in posture will help – why not let him sit instead of stand? (XIII.19). As for our own preferred work, we should try to plan our work and our priorities, accepting with good grace the disturbance of our plan (XIV.20).

In both the *Confessions* and the *De catechizandis rudibus*, Augustine writes of the methods of teaching he prefers. In the *De Magistro*, he makes the apparently paradoxical suggestion that no one person can ever teach another – 'ye have one teacher, who is Christ', says the Gospel, and it is he, within us, who teaches. The *De Magistro* is a difficult dialogue: its style is circuitous and tentative, and one apparent conclusion is replaced by another (Burnyeat rightly comments on the resemblance to techniques in Wittgenstein's later writings). For an account of it, I cannot do better than refer the reader to Burnyeat's article (details below): it will be enough here to suggest that Augustine is not simply relying on a passage of Scripture. He is making a general philosophical point, although the route he takes to making it may perplex us. Words are signs of objects, and invite us to look; but we have to perform the looking for ourselves. Without the looking, the sign will not help (Augustine gives an example of an enigmatic word in the Book of Daniel). To attain intellectual knowledge, we need an interior light, and for this the teacher is but the outward occasion. The pupil is taught by the things themselves, as God reveals them inwardly to him.

'My weight is my love': we end where we began. The teacher needs to go out to the pupil's condition and to offer encouragement, but not simply so that information may be transferred from the mind of the one who teaches to the mind of the one who learns. Rather, the pupil must be aroused to use upon what is being said to him the powers that he has within. He must make his own what he is told; the teacher's language can go only so far.

Note

1   *Confessions* XIII.ix.10. I have consulted three writings of Augustine in composing this essay:

The *Confessions* (written in about 397) not only describes Augustine's own education, it tells of the academic world of his day, and the struggle in his life between Christianity and so much else. The three concluding books are in the form of a meditation in passages in the Book of Genesis. They have a philosophical interest (Augustine reflects there on the problem of time), but an educational interest too – they exhibit the ways in which a teacher then would 'draw out the sense' of a text. I cite the *Confessions* by book, chapter and paragraph number.

The *De catechizandis rudibus* ('On instructing the ignorant') was sent about 400 to a Christian catechist who was despondent over his achievements. It is a warm-hearted and eminently practical work, giving a good idea of how Augustine himself taught. I cite this by chapter and paragraph number.

The *De Magistro* ('On the Teacher'), written about 389, examines language, signs and significance, and puts forward the thesis that no one can teach another: enlightenment must come from within, where Christ is our teacher. I cite this by chapter and paragraph number.

See also

In this book: Jesus
In *Fifty Modern Thinkers on Education*: Wittgenstein

St Augustine's major writings

Augustine's works exist in confusingly many editions. A good proportion has been translated (in a variety of dates and settings) into English. Details of titles and translations are to be found in the five Chronological Tables in the indispensable biography, Brown (1967). But references to Augustine's works can be made, independently of the edition used, by book (if necessary) and by chapter. Paragraph numbers, which run continuously through the chapters, can usefully complement any reference.

To the three works mentioned in note 1, I add first the translation of the *Confessions* I have used:

Chadwick, H, *Augustine: Confessions, with introduction and notes*, Oxford: Oxford University Press, 1991.

I next give the titles of three other works that are linked with Augustine's views on education: *De doctrina christiana* (on Christian doctrine), *De musica* (on music), and *De civitate Dei* (on the City of God). I mention the last work because it shows the range of Augustine's acquaintance with the pagan culture that had shaped his own education. It is very long – most translations of it are also abridgments.

Further reading

Brown, P., *Augustine of Hippo: a Biography*, London: Faber and Faber, 1967.
Burnyeat, M., 'Wittgenstein and Augustine *De Magistro*', *Proceedings of the Aristotelian Society*, supplementary volume 61, pp. 1–24, 1987.
Harrison, S., 'Augustine on What we Owe to our Teachers', in A.O. Rorty (ed.), *Philosophers on Education: Historical Perspectives*, London and New York: Routledge, pp. 81–94, 1998.
Howie, G. (ed. and trans.), *St Augustine: On Education*, with introduction and notes, Chicago: Henry Regnery Company, 1969.
Marrou, H., *Saint Augustin et la fin de la culture antique*, Paris: E. de Boccard, 1938.
—— *History of Education in the Ancient World*, translated by George Lamb, London: Sheed and Ward, 1956.

P.J. FITZPATRICK

AL-GHAZZALI 1058–1111

> [T]here are two kinds of eye, an external and an internal; ... the former belongs to one world, the World of Sense, and ... internal vision belongs to another world altogether, the World of the Realm Celestial; ... each of these two eyes has a sun and a light whereby its seeing is perfected. ... He who never fares to that [latter] world, but allows the limitations of life in this lower world of sense to settle upon him, is still a brute beast, an excommunicate from that which constitutes us men. ... As the rind is to the fruit; ... as darkness in relation to light; as infernal to supernal; so is this World of Sense in relation to the World of the Realm Celestial. For this reason the latter is called the World Supernal or the World of Spirit, or the World of Light, in contrast with the World Beneath, the World of Matter and of Darkness.[1]

The Islamic ideology provided the world, especially in the early days of Islam, with a most powerful source of inspiration. The rich contributions which Islam has made in the various branches of science served as the bases for the development of modern science. Although many earlier Western writers tended to ignore this fact, recent investigators have stressed and recognized the importance of the Muslim contributions in all areas of human endeavour, especially in developing areas of scientific outlook.

Muhammed Ibn Muhammad Ibn Ahmed, Abu Hamid Al-Tusi Al-Ghazzali (or Al-Ghazzalli) Al-shafi was born in1058 at Tus in Khursan near the modern Meshed in Iran. He is also known as 'Hujjat Al-Islam' (The proof of Islam), 'Ornament of the faith', and 'Gatherer of multivarious sciences'. He was a major jurist, heresiographer and debater expert in the principles of doctrine and those of jurisprudence. Al-Ghazzali was an outstanding theologian, jurist, original thinker, mystic and religious reformer. His father died while he was still very young, and he and his brother Ahmed were left orphans at an early age. The members of his family were prominent in the study of Qanon Law. When Al-Ghazzali abandoned his teaching position at the Nizamyah school in Baghdad, he deputized his brother Ahmed, who was famous for his preaching, to replace him. There has been much discussion since ancient times whether his 'niba' (family name) should be Ghazzalli or Ghazzali. Al-Ghazzali died in Baghdad in 1111.

Al-Ghazzali received his education at Jurjan, adjacent to the Caspian Sea. Among his teachers was Abu Naser Al-Ismaili, then at Nayshabur, where he met many intellectual scholars such as Imam Al-Haramyn abu Al-Maali Al-Juwayni, who lectured in both Mecca and Medina, the two holy cities of Islam. Al-Juwayni was a theologian, a Mutakallim 'scholastic', who headed the famous Nizamyah school which Nizam Al-Mulk built and where Al-Ghazzali studied for eight years, 1077–1085. He studied theology, philosophy, logic and natural sciences. Al-Ghazzali then departed to Baghdad, where he joined the court of the Saljuks, in which he met the greatest scholars and poets patronized by the Persian wazir ('the minister of the court'), Nizam Al-mulk, the founder of Nizamyah school named after him, which was considered Baghdad's first great school of religious law, founded in 1067. Al-Ghazzali was appointed a professor there for four years, teaching theology and philosophy. Many scholars came to him for learning and consultation. Al-Ghazzali abandoned his post to become a wandering mystic. He went on pilgrimage to Mecca and then went to Damascus, where he lived in the mosque as was the custom of travellers at that time. There he wrote his masterpiece, *The Revival of Religious Sciences* (*Ihya Ulum Al-Din*). Al-Ghazzali wrote many deeply original religious books that synthesized the mystical and orthodox points of view.

Al-Ghazzali studied Christianity. He was especially familiar with the doctrines and faith of the Christian Greeks, and these had a fundamental impact upon his religious teaching. He also read the Greek philosophy of Plato, Aristotle and others. His several books were upon many different subjects. These books were closely related to the progress of his own spiritual and intellectual growth. Al-Ghazzali intended in his writings to expose ordinary men, as well as the scholarly élite, to his thoughts. He was interested in reaching everybody and to spread his ideas among all. Al-Ghazzali wrote at different levels for different audiences. At the higher levels he philosophized in a sophisticated way and enriched what he maintained at the lower levels. It is fair to say that Al-Ghazzali was, and still is, considered as one of the greatest writers and thinkers of Islam.

He made major contributions in religion, philosophy and sufism. As far as philosophy is concerned, to which he had been introduced by Al-Juwayni, he first wrote *Makasid Al-Falasifa* (*Objectives of the Philosophers*) which was greatly admired in the West, especially in the twelve and thirteenth centuries. This book is a presentation of the theories and thoughts of philosophers, as he understood them from original translation, and from studies of Al-Farabi (d. 950) and Ibn Sina (d. 1037). This he followed by a criticism of the doctrines of such philosophers, entitled *Tahafut Al-Falasifa* (*The Inconsistency (or Incoherence) of the Philosophers*). This was finished at the beginning of 1095. In this book, he concentrated on demonstrating the inconsistencies of other philosophers, especially those most influenced by the Greeks, and does not argue for any positive views of his own.

What impressed Al-Ghazzali most in philosophy was logic, and in particular the Aristotelian syllogism. However, in philosophy, Al-Ghazzali emphasized the inability of reason to comprehend the absolute and the infinite. He argued that religion and reason had, as their respective spheres, the infinite and the finite, respectively. In religion, particularly religious mysticism, Al-Ghazzali cleansed the approach of sufism of its excesses and re-established the authority of the Orthodox religion. Yet, he stressed the importance of genuine sufism which, he maintained, was the path to the attainment of absolute truth. His chief work in this area was *Al-Ikisad fi El Itikad* (*The Economy in Believing*). While this book makes full use of Aristotelian logic, including the syllogism, it also prepares for the wisdom or gnosis (Ma'rifa) of the Sufi.

Al-Ghazzali wrote, before his death, *Al-Munqith min Al-dalal* (*The Rescuer from Loss*), an account of the development of his religious opinions. Although many consider this book as an autobiographical sketch, it is not exactly an autobiography since it is arranged schematically not chronologically. In this book, he was much concerned with defending himself against the accusations and criticism that had been brought against his conduct and the views that he had expressed. This book is relevant to educationalists, since it emphasized the importance of the self-examining approach or method on which the truth-seeker must rely in order to continue his or her search for truth through a balance between religion and reason.

Certainly one of Al-Ghazzali's best known and most immortal books is *Ihya Ulum Al-Din* (*The Revival of Religious Sciences*), in which he presented his unified view of religion incorporating elements from three sources formerly considered contradictory – tradition, intellectualism and mysticism. This book provides a complete guide to a pious life, and is one of the very greatest works of religion written by a Moslem. The book is composed of four volumes. Volume I dealt with 'Ibadat' (cult practices), volume II dealt with 'Adat' (social customs), volume III dealt with 'Muhlikat' (vices or faults of character leading to perdition), and the last volume dealt with 'Munjiyat' (virtues or qualities leading to salvation). Each volume has ten books. The *Ihya* is thus a complete guide for the devout Muslim to every aspect of the religious life – worship and devotional practices, conduct in daily life, the purification of the heart, and advance along the Mystic way.

Al-Ghazzali's philosophical thoughts and ideas had a considerable effect on education, and his writings served to introduce logical thinking into Islamic educational thought. He undoubtedly performed a great service for devout Muslims at every level of education by presenting obedience to the prescriptions of the shari'a (Islamic law) as a meaningful way of life. In this way, he helped to develop the concept of self-control by both teachers and students in their pursuit of any educational activity. Al-Ghazzali's reflections on the nature of man's knowledge of the divine realm, and his conviction that the upright and devout man could attain to an intuition or direct experience of divine things, implied that in the realm of education a devout and hard-working learner should not be just a copier or follower. Rather, he could participate in developing and enriching the realm of knowledge, and the more sincere he was in his scholarly endeavours, the more opportunities he would have to add to authentic knowledge.

When considering Al-Ghazzali's thinking, one might jump to conclusion that he stood against rationalism. This conclusion is not really valid, since Al-Ghazzali forcefully argued that religion is the basis of rationality. Any form of rationality must, therefore, be delineated within the sphere of religion.

Al-Ghazzali's influence on educational thought was many-sided. To begin with, he emphasized the importance of raising a generation of faithful people who would be close to God and free from conflict among one another. Education should be in the service of society and bring up people with high moral standards. He also emphasized that education is a virtue, and that it should be congruent with the verses of the Holy Koran and the sayings of Mohammed, peace be upon him. Pedagogy, he argued, concerns what is in its essence a human process, and this meant that education cannot be properly practised except through humility, careful listening and the ability to respond on the basis of love and intimacy or collaboration among human beings.

Education, he insisted, is an essentially logical process, and should therefore start from the simplest aspects of life and proceed towards the most complicated. The job of the teacher is to explain even the most complex matters in the clearest terms. Pedagogy is, moreover, a moral process. Teachers should, therefore, have sympathy for their students, treat them kindly as if they were their sons, and guide and advise them. Teaching should not be a punitive process, but one of counselling. Teachers should, therefore, support their students and help them to fulfil their needs and achieve psychological and emotional stability. Teaching, Al-Ghazzali also explained, combines theory and practice. Hence teachers should serve as live models for students in their words and behaviour. As a cultural process, education vitally contributes to the future of a society in which individuals and groups grow and progress.

Al-Ghazzali's constant stress is upon teaching as a value-building process. Students should be encouraged to cultivate good behaviour based on a sound system of such values as telling the truth, faith, honesty, humility and the avoidance of arrogance. He emphasized that education is a total process that should take care of every aspect of human beings – intellectual, psychological, social, physical and spiritual. Teaching should be sensitively conducted, so that differences among students are recognized and they are helped to develop according to their own capacities and interests.

Al-Ghazzali died in December 1111. Under his bed a paper was found containing the following stanza:

> Do not believe that this corpse you see is myself, I am spirit and this is naught but flesh. I am a pearl which has left its shell deserted. It was my prison where I spent my time in grief. I am a bird and it was my cage when I had not flown forth and it is left as a token, praise be to God, who has now set me free.

Note

1 *Mishkat Al-Anwar*, Muhammad Ashraf, Kashmiri Bazar-Lahore, 1924.

See also

In this book: Aristotle, Ibn Tufayl, Plato

Al-Ghazzali's major writings

Ihya Ulum Al-Din, translated by K. Nakamura, The Islamic text Society: Cambridge, 1996.
Tahafut Al-Falasifah, translated by Sabih Ahmad Kamali, Pakistan Philosophical Congress: Lahore, 1963.
Miskat Al-Anwar, translated by W.H.T. Gairdner, Muhammad Ashraf, Kashmiri Bazar-Lahore, 1924.

Further reading

Carr, B. and Mahalingam, I. (eds), *Companion Encyclopedia of Asian Philosophy*, Part VI, London: Routledge, 1997.
Encyclopaedia of Islam, London: Luzak, 1965.
Qarbullah, Hasan, *The Influence of Al-Ghazzali Upon Islamic Jurisprudence and Philosophy*, Beirut: Dar el-Jil, 1993.
Smith, M., *Al-Ghazzali the Mystic*, London: Sheldon, 1944.
Watt, W. Montgomery, *The Faith and practice of Al-Ghazali*, London: Allen & Unwin, 1970.

HANI A. TAWIL

IBN TUFAYL *c.* 1106–85

> If there is a Being Whose perfection is infinite, ... then to lose hold of such a Being ... must mean infinite torture. Likewise, to preserve constant awareness of Him is to know joy without lapse, unending bliss, infinite rapture and delight.[1]

Abu Bakr Muhammad Ibn Abd Al-Malik Ibn Muhammad Ibn Tufayl al-Qaysi – ususally known simply as Ibn Tufayl (Abubacer, in Latin) – was a Spanish Muslim philosopher, physician, mathematician, poet and scientist. Born in Guadix during the first decade of the twelfth century, he practised medicine at Granada and was to become chief royal physician to the Muwahhid ruler, Abu Yaqub Yusuf, whom he served as a secretary for twenty years, eventually being appointed as a *wazir* (Minister) to his dynasty. In this office, he was to be succeeded in 1182, on his own recommendation, by his younger contemporary, Ibn Rushd (Averroes), one of the most illustrious philosophers of Islam and the one destined to have most impact on European thought in the centuries to come. Ibn Tufayl continued in public and diplomatic service until his death, in Marrakesh, in 1185. During this period of Muslim Spain, philosophy and learning flourished, and scholars such as Ibn Tufayl, Ibn Rushd and the great physician Ibn Zuhr (Avensoor) enjoyed patronage in the highest circles. Seville and Cordoba competed as great centres of learning and science.

Ibn Tufayl was an important critic of the writings of Al-Ghazzali, the greatest theologian of Islam, especially the latter's *Tahafut Al-falasifah* ('Incoherence of the philosophers'), which was also a critical target of Ibn Rushd. Ibn Tufayl is now, however, most famous for being the author of the celebrated philosophical fiction *Hayy Ibn Yaqzan* ('The living one, son of the vigilant'). This is one of the most remarkable books of the Middle Ages, and was to be translated into Hebrew in the fourteenth century, Latin in the seventeenth, and subsequently into most European languages. English versions were made by the Quaker, G. Keith, in 1674, and slightly later by C. Ashwell and S. Ockley. For the Arabic reader, the best critical edition is that of Léon Gauthier, with a French translation, first published in Algiers in 1900.

Hayy Ibn Yaqzan was admired by many distinguished figures during the Enlightenment period. The great German philosopher, Gottfried von Leibniz, knew it in its Latin translation and held it in high esteem. It has recently been suggested that the central idea of Daniel Defoe's famous novel, *Robinson Crusoe*, was borrowed from Ibn Tufayl's story, most probably from the Ockley translation of 1708. One may also see the story as a precursor of the European *Bildungsroman*, such as Goethe's *Wilhelm Meister*, popular at a rather later period, which tell of the education 'in the school of life' of young men and draw philosophical and moral lessons from this education. The book remains influential to this day. As one commentator has remarked, scholars still 'continue finding in it something fresh and meaningful' and it is 'still finding an appreciative audience not only among academics but also among students who have Islamic philosophy at heart'.[2]

The literal translation of the book's title is 'The living one, the son of the vigilant', or 'The alive son of the awake'. This title has great symbolic significance. 'The living one' stands for man or the human intellect, while 'the vigilant' stands for God or the divine intellect. It alludes to a verse of the holy Quran in which it is said of God that 'neither slumber nor sleep overtaketh Him'. Thus the book symbolically represents the theme that the human intellect partakes of the divine intellect, and hence has the capacity to know reality in its innermost truth, independently of prophetic revelations as recorded in the Scriptures. Ibn Tufayl uses the word 'intellect' in a very wide sense, so as to include something like mystical vision. This is in alignment with the philosophy of Neo-platonism, by which the doctrines presented in the book are considerably influenced.

Ibn Tufayl's aim in his masterpiece is to show, through the story of a boy's upbringing in 'a state of nature', that even without the help of tradition and revelation, man can attain to knowledge of the natural world and morality and, through this, to knowledge of God. In the story, Hayy is said to have been 'spontaneously generated' and to have been brought up, during his early years, by a deer. As a result of dissecting the deer, on its death, he comes to understand – through his own powers of observation and reflection – that death results from the dissolution of the union of spirit and body.

The novel offers interesting views on several problems of great philosophical importance. For example, is natural religion – religion, that is, without revelation – possible? The novel allows for this possibility in the most emphatic terms. Even if God had not revealed Himself through His prophets, He would have been discovered by scientists, mystics and

34

philosophers through their studies of nature, the human self and the universe. By the study of nature, it should even be possible to arrive at such attributes of God as His wisdom and love.

Ibn Tufayl's approach towards proving the existence of God and knowledge of His nature is a rational, empirical one *par excellence*. God is truly the unifying principle of the universe and the philosopher should have no trouble arriving at a proof of this truth. The mystic, by delving deep within himself, is able to obtain a vision of God in the aspiration of his own soul. For the mystic, this is not simply a 'vision', but living contact with ultimate reality, a union with God. It becomes evident to him that God and the human spirit are akin to one another. The human spirit genuinely partakes of the divine spirit: hence the title *Hayy Ibn Yaqzan*. This imposes a special obligation on each human being 'to endeavour, in whatever way possible, to attain His attributes, to imitate His ways, and remould his character to His ... [to] surrender all to Him'.[3]

In the novel, Ibn Tufayl also clearly brings out a distinction, of great importance in educational theory and practice, between two forms of knowledge – the logical or mediate form, and the intuitive or immediate one. It is only through the medium of the latter that we can have living experience of union with divine reality. The former, however, has the advantage of being expressible in words and hence of being communicable to others. Since there are no direct means of expressing intuitive knowledge, one must employ imagery and parables: hence Ibn Tufayl's use of the philosophical allegory.

Ibn Tufayl's importance to the philosophy of education resides in his insistence, unusual for his time, that human beings may, solely through the use of reason and the contribution of experience, come to understand and know a very great deal about their world and how should they act in it. As with later 'state of nature' theorists, such as John Locke and Jean-Jacques Rousseau, he tries to establish this by showing how human beings, considered in abstraction from all tradition and convention, might arrive at understanding and knowledge. However, his is a much wider conception of experience and reason than that of these later thinkers. His philosophy is a highly integrative one, in which a place is found for mystical experience as much as for ordinary sensory experience.

Notes

1 Ibn Tufayl, *Hayy Ibn Yaqzan*, trans. L.E. Goodman, Los Angeles: Gee Tee Bee, p. 137, 1984.
2 M. Schembri, 'Philosophy and Mystical Knowledge in Ibn Tufayl's *Hayy Ibn Yaqzan*', Ph.D. Dissertation: University of Malta, p. 4, 1997.
3 Ibn Tufayl, *Hayy Ibn Yaqzan*, p. 142.

See also

In this book: Al-Ghazzali, Locke, Rousseau

Ibn Tufayl's major writings

The History of Hayy Ibn Yaqzan, trans. S. Ockley, London: Darf, 1986.

Ibn Tufayl, *Hayy Ibn Yaqzan, a Philosophical Tale*, trans. L.E. Goodman, Los Angeles: Gee Tee Bee, 1984.

Further reading

Fakhry, M., *A History of Islamic Philosophy*, London: Longman, 1983.
Goodman, L.E., 'Ibn Tufayl', in S.H. Nasr and O. Leaman (eds), *History of Islamic Philosophy*, Part I, London: Routledge, pp. 313–29, 1996.
Lawrence, L.I. (ed.), *The World of Ibn Tufayl: Interdisciplinary Perspectives on Hayy Ibn Yaqzan*, Leiden: Brill, 1996.

DALAL MALHAS STEITIEH

DESIDERIUS ERASMUS (GERRIT GERRITSZOON) 1466–1536

> No man is born to himself, no man is born to idleness. Your children are begotten not to yourself alone, but to your country: not to your country alone, but to God ... it (is) a duty incumbent on Statesmen and Churchmen alike to provide that there be a due supply of men qualified to educate the youth of the nation. It is a public obligation in no way inferior, say, to the ordering of the army.[1]

Though never a schoolmaster, Erasmus was keenly interested in the aims and methods of education from an early age. The humanists, and he has been termed the 'Prince of Humanists', advocated a new curriculum and new methods of instruction in contradistinction to the 'Schoolmen'. They intended the New Learning not just for the clergy but for all Christian people, especially for princes and their tutors. They emphasized the formation of character and not the acquisition of knowledge *per se*. It has been written of Erasmus that 'he did more than anyone else to advance the Revival of Learning'.[2]

Erasmus was born in Rotterdam on 27 October 1466, the child of Gerard of Gouda, a priest, and Margaret, daughter of a physician of Zevenbergen. Named for St Erasmus, the martyred Bishop of Campania (died *c.* AD 303), his illegitimacy troubled him so much that as late as 1516 he sought papal dispensation for the circumstances of his birth.

He lost his parents due to the plague within a few months of each other in 1480. In retrospect, at any rate, he disliked all the schools which he attended. Sent first to the school at Gouda kept by Peter Winckel, later his guardian, he then went to the Catholic Choir School at Utrecht before going at the age of 9 to the school at Deventer, which was attached to the Church of St Lebuin where Alexander Hegius was headmaster and the famous scholar Sintheim was an assistant. He showed such promise at Deventer that one of his teachers told him: 'Well done Erasmus, the day will come when thou wilt reach the highest summit of erudition.'[3]

At 14 he was sent to the School of the Brethren of the Common Life at Bois-le-Duc which led to his lasting antipathy to monastic schools. He complained later of harsh discipline and poor teaching, writing:

> It is the mark of a good teacher to stand towards his charge
> somewhat in the relation of a parent. ... He will also in a sense
> become a boy again that he may draw his pupil to himself.[4]

Clearly a studious youth, he appears to have had a poor physique and no inclination to sport; he may even have been uncomfortable in the presence of boys.

Despite this, or perhaps because of this, he entered the Augustinian monastery of Emmaus at Stein near Gouda in 1483 and was ordained a priest in 1492. As a poor boy, the monastic life afforded him companionship and the leisure to study. His prolific production of literary works began when he was 18 with an Epitome of the *Elegantiae Linguae Latinae* of Laurentius Valla (*c.* 1405–1457), the widely used textbook of the great Italian scholar who made such a significant contribution to New Testament studies. In 1486 he wrote a formal epistle, *De Contemptu Mundi*, detailing the attractions of monastic life.

But Erasmus was ambitious and was evidently glad to leave the monastery in 1493 for the service of Henry, Bishop of Cambrai and Chancellor of the Order of the Golden Fleece. This gave him the opportunity of studying at the University of Paris in the Faculty of Theology. He devoted himself to the classics and made a start in learning Greek. After all, the humanists believed that the study of the classics led men to live righteous lives. In 1501 he declared:

> Latin erudition, however ample, is crippled and imperfect without
> Greek: we have in Latin at best some small streams and turbid
> pools, while they have the clearer springs and rivers flowing with
> gold.[5]

In 1499 he accompanied his pupil William Blount, Lord Mountjoy, to England and met John Colet and Sir Thomas More. He returned to Paris and dedicated his collection of *Adagia* to Mountjoy in 1500. These were more than 800 maxims in Latin and offered most contemporaries their first accessible overview of the classical past; there were twenty-six editions in his lifetime alone.

Driven from Paris by plague, he went to Orleans and then to Louvain where in 1502 he declined the Chair of Rhetoric. By 1505 he was back in Paris, editing Valla's annotations on the New Testament; by 1506 he was in Italy, working on the letters of St Jerome (*c.* AD 342–420), the learned Latin doctor whom Erasmus much admired.

In late 1507 Erasmus was writing to the great printer Aldus Manutius about a new edition of his translations from Euripides when he was offered and accepted the chance to go to Venice himself and prepare an expanded collection of Adages. A year or so later he moved to Padua and went on to reach Rome by the spring of 1509.

The only one of his books which is still read is probably *The Praise of Folly* (*Moriae Encomium*) which he appears to have composed in the space of seven days when he was staying in the house of Thomas More (who had four children) in England in 1509; the title was presumably a deliberate pun. In this book he attacks national pride, professional conceit, and especially ecclesiastical abuses and the monastic orders. The book ends with the contention that organized religion is a form of folly and that true faith comes from the heart, not the head. It was the forerunner to More's *Utopia* and became the best known secular work of the sixteenth century.

This second visit to England was probably the happiest period of Erasmus' life; as he wrote to Robert Fisher in 1499:

> When I hear my Colet I think I am listening to Plato himself; who will not admire an whole world of learning in Grocyn? What mind could be more penetrating than Linacre's? When did Nature ever create a disposition more friendly than More's? ... It is remarkable how thick springs up everywhere in this country the crop of classical studies.[6]

It was from Cambridge, where he was Lady Margaret Professor of Divinity, that Erasmus published *De Ratione Studii* (Paris 1511), apologizing for commenting on the art of instruction as Quintilian (*c.* AD 35–100) had already said it all. The concern was with the classics alone:

> There is ... no discipline, no field of study, – whether music, architecture, agriculture or war – which may not prove of use to the teacher in expounding the Poets and Orators of antiquity.[7]

He endorsed the classical conception of the orator, fusing the ideal of the orator with that of the grammaticus. The man of letters had to know how to deploy the spoken word especially as well as how to use language in writing. Arithmetic was summarily dismissed but mathematics generally had, although a part of the Quadrivium, become speculative rather than practical, a 'human' discipline related to philosophy:

> It is true, of course, that in reading an author for purposes of vocabulary and style the student cannot fail to gather something besides. But I have in my mind much more than this when I speak of studying 'contents'. For I affirm that in the slight qualification the whole of attainable knowledge lies enclosed within the literary monuments of ancient Greece.[8]

None the less, Erasmus' main contribution towards furthering the knowledge of ancient Greece was through his translations from Greek into Latin. He argued that there were three conditions which determine individual progress in learning:

> They are Nature, Training and Practice. By Nature, I mean, partly innate capacity for being trained, partly, native bent towards excellence. By Training, I mean the skilled application of instruction and guidance. By Practice, the free exercise on our own part of that activity which has been implanted by Nature and is furthered by Training.[9]

Colloquies were useful for the kind of teaching which Erasmus advocated. Also in 1611 he published *De Copia* (*De Duplici Copia Verborum ac Rerum*) ('Of Abundance') in Basle. It was a textbook written for St Paul's School, then being founded by Colet and was a storehouse of material for rhetorical uses; over 100 editions appeared during the century and it became the standard work in grammar schools all over Europe. The first part consisted of an extended vocabulary arranged to provide alternative words with which to elaborate a statement already made, the second different ways in which statements might be arranged. He set out the principle of gathering extracts under different headings, ranging over a great range of topics including contemporary themes such as children's manners, the misdemeanours of monks, the difficulties of marriage and the excesses of the nobility. Erasmus also revised Lily's textbook of Latin syntax which ultimately became the Eton Latin grammar.

Erasmus left England in 1514 for Basle, where the great printing-house of Johann Froben was prepared to publish at its own expense his Letters of St Jerome, which had been a cherished project for twenty years. The next years were to be restless. He worked on his Greek Testament, he became Counsellor to Charles I of Spain (later Charles V the Emperor) and wrote *Institutio principis Christiani* ('The Education of the Christian Prince') in 1516, the year More published his *Utopia*. Erasmus produced his Greek Bible that year with a fresh translation into Latin, writing in his Preface his desire to see the Gospel and Paul's Epistles translated into every language:

> The mysteries of kings it may be safer to conceal, but Christ wished his mysteries to be published as openly as possible. I wish that even the weakest woman should read the Gospel and the epistles of Paul.[10]

At first Erasmus supported the work of Martin Luther who challenged Church abuses as he also had done but later a bitter controversy occurred over Luther's violent threats to the social order.

In the 1520s as Erasmus continued to move around, from Louvain to Basle to Freiburg, and in the 1530s when he returned to Basle, he remained a figure with a great reputation and continued to publish prolifically. He was concerned with the Ciceronian controversy in the mid 1520s, advocating in a dialogue on Latinity which he called *Ciceronianus* (1528) that Latin should be the means of expression for modern living. In 1529 he published the most mature of his educational tracts *De Pueris instituendis*.

> A distinctive feature of it was the stress on the individuality of pupils: The Master will be wise to observe such natural inclination, such individuality, in the early stages of a child's life, since we learn most easily the things which conform to it.[11]

More, unable to accept Erasmus' advice to moderate his opposition to Henry VIII's religious settlement, died in 1535. Nonetheless, Bertrand Russell's judgment is probably fair that after Luther's revolt, for Erasmus and More: 'the world was too violent, on both sides, for men of their type. More suffered martyrdom and Erasmus sank into ineffectiveness.'[12]

They embodied the objection to everything systematic in theology or philosophy which characterized the reaction against scholasticism. Erasmus, working as Woodward remarked 'till death itself wrested the pen from his hand',[13] died at Basle on 12 July 1536. Ironically, this was the year when the best-known translator of the Bible into English, William Tyndale, was strangled and burnt at the stake at Vilvorde in Belgium as a heretic. In 1559, all of Erasmus' works were placed on the Papal Index of prohibited books but he was perhaps the earliest major European figure whose reputation was based on the printed word.

Notes

1 De Pueris Instituendis, 494A, 508D, in W.H. Woodward, Desiderius Erasmus Concerning the Aim and Method of Education, Cambridge: Cambridge University Press, pp. 187, 209–210, 1904.
2 D. Crystal, The Cambridge Encyclopedia, 2nd edition, Cambridge: Cambridge University Press, p. 392, 1994.
3 Letters, ed. F.M. Nichols, vol. 1, p. 26, 1901.
4 De Pueris Instituendis, 509B, in Woodward (1904, p. 211).
5 Erasmi Epistolae, ed. P.S. Allen, Oxford, no. 149, vol. I, p. 352, 1910.
6 Allen (1910, no. 118, vol. I, pp. 273–4).
7 De Ratione Studii, 523F, in Woodward (1904, p. 168).
8 De Ratione Studii, 522A, in Woodward (1904, p. 164).
9 De Ratione Studii, 497A, in Woodward (1904, p. 151).
10 Quoted in F. Seebohm, The Oxford Reformers, 3rd edition, p. 327, 1913.
11 De Pueris Instituendis, 500A, in Woodward (1904, p. 196).
12 B. Russell, History of Western Philosophy, 1946, p. 533.
13 Woodward (1904, p. 29).

See also

In this book: Russell

Erasmus' major writings

Erasmi Epistolae, Opus Epistolarum des Erasmi Roterodami, ed. P.S. Allen, 12 volumes, Oxford: Oxford University Press, 1910.
Epistles of Erasmus, trans. and ed. F.M. Nichols, 3 volumes, London: Longman, 1901–1918.
Erasmus and Cambridge, The Cambridge Letters of Erasmus, trans. D.F.S. Thomson, ed. H.C. Porter, Toronto and Oxford: Oxford University Press, 1964.
Adages, ed. M.M. Phillips, Cambridge: Cambridge University Press, 1964.
Colloquies, ed. and trans. C.R. Thompson, Chicago: Chicageo University Press, 1965.
The Education of a Christian Prince, ed. Lisa Jardine, Cambridge: Cambridge University Press, 1997.
Enchiridion Militis Christiani (The Manual of the Christian Knight), trans. F.L. Battles in Advocates of Reform, ed. M. Spinka, Philadelphia: SCM Press, 1953.
Praise of Folly, trans. John Wilson, 1668, Prometheus Books, 1994.
Desiderius Erasmus Concerning the Aim and Method of Education, W.H. Woodward, Cambridge: Cambridge University Press, 1904 including De Ratione Studii and De Pueris Instituendis, in translation.

Further reading

The place of publication is London unless otherwise stated.

Ackroyd, P., *The Life of Thomas More*, Chatto & Windus, 1998.
Adams, R.P., *The Better Part of Valor: More, Erasmus, Colet and Vives on Humanism, War and Peace, 1496–1535*, Seattle: University of Washington Press, 1962.
Bainton, R.H., *Erasmus*, Collins, 1969.
Bolgar, R.R., *The Classical Heritage and its Beneficiaries*, Cambridge University Press, 1954, 1964.
Caspari, F., *Humanism and the Social Order in Tudor England*, Chicago: University of Chicago Press and Cambridge University Press, 1954.
Charlton, K., *Education in Renaissance England*, Routledge & Kegan Paul, 1965.
Goodman, A. and Mackay, A. (eds), *The Impact of Humanism on Western Europe*, Longmans, 1990.
Hildebrand, H.J., *Erasmus and his Age*, 1970.
Huizinga, J., *Erasmus of Rotterdam*, Phaidon Press, 1952.
MacConica, J.K., *Humanists and Reformation Politics under Henry VIII and Edward VI*, Oxford: Oxford University Press, 1965.
Perkinson, H.J., *Since Socrates: Studies in the History of Western Education and Thought*, Longman, 1980.
Russell, B., *History of Western Philosophy*, Allen & Unwin, 1946.
Schoeck, R. J., *Erasmus of Europe: The Making of a Humanist, 1467–1500*, vol. 1, Edinburgh: Edinburgh University Press, 1990.
—— *The Prince of Humanists, 1501–1536*, vol. 2, Edinburgh: Edinburgh University Press, 1993.
Seebohm, F., *The Oxford Reformers*, 1867, 3rd edition, Longman, 1913.
Simon. J., *Education and Society in Tudor England*, Cambridge University Press, 1966.
Sowards, J.M., *Desiderius Erasmus*, Boston: Twayne Publishers, 1975.
Trapp, J.B., *Erasmus, Colet and More: The Early Tudor Humanists and their Books*, British Library, 1991.

G.R. BATHO

JAN AMOS COMENIUS 1592–1670

> Great Didactics is a general art of teaching everyone everything. And teach reliably so that the result must come. And teach gently so that neither the teacher nor the pupils feel any difficulties or dislike; on the contrary, both find it very pleasant. And teach thoroughly, not superficially, but bring everyone to a real education, noble manners and devout piety.[1]

Few 'great men' continue to live in the nation's memory and not in historians' books only. Comenius (Jan Amos Komenský in Czech) is one of them. Most of his countrymen remember his fate: a man who went into exile because of the situation in his country, a man who was ready to suffer for his beliefs. Persecution and exile are two topics that are very much alive in Czech collective memory.

In many poor households a framed print of 'Comenius taking leave of his country' could be seen in the early twentieth century. When independent Czechoslovakia came into existence, its first president, Thomas Masaryk, on his return from the USA, formulated his programme as developing the legacy of John Huss and Comenius. Comenius was respected by Slovaks too because he was born on the Moravian-Slovak border, actually the same region as Masaryk. One generation later, many Czechs were leaving their country to escape first from the Nazi persecution and ten years later to avoid the Communist dictatorship. Again, they had Comenius in their mind as a man who did not let adverse conditions break him and who wanted to do something positive for his nation, wherever he was.

But Comenius is much more than a model for exiled people. First, a word or two about his background. He lived in an interesting epoch when Europe split into two ideological spheres that came into conflict – the Mediterranean (Spanish-Austrian Catholicism) and the Northern civilization (the Protestantism of the Netherlands, Scandinavia, northern Germany). Comenius felt attracted to the latter both in religion and as a model of society and culture. The country from which he came was at that time not unimportant. Its borders enclosed large territories (lost since then, with Silesia and Lausitz) so that with its four million people it was nearly as big as England.

Comenius had his first foreign experience when he was a young man – he went to study theology at Heidelberg, a rare chance for Czechs even in the nineteenth and twentieth centuries. His career as a clergyman of the Unity of Brethren (the Moravians) was soon broken by the Habsburg Government decree banning his church and expelling from the country anyone who did not bow to the new order.

The young Comenius must have been an attractive personality because he found a family of the nobility (the Žerotíns) who were willing to keep him illegally on their estate, for some time at least. And when he really had to leave he always found new friends to protect him and encourage him (Leczynski and Radziwill in Poland, Geer in the Netherlands, Samuel Hartlib in England). Comenius was a pilgrim throughout most of his life. But until his death he remained a devotee of the 1620 uprising in Bohemia and supporter of the Winter King of Bohemia, Friedrich, and his wife Elisabeth Stuart (daughter of James I, King of Britain); when they visited Moravia in 1619 he undoubtedly came to meet them, and as late as 1668 he dedicated his writing 'Unum necessarium' to Friedrich's son Rupert, who was born in Prague in 1619, during the three-month reign of his father.

Although some of Comenius' travels had political objectives, for example, he travelled to Berlin to meet the Czech exiles, he brought a political message to The Hague, in Sweden he was received by Queen Kristina and by Chancellor Oxenstierna, and he met many influential people in England, he never thought of himself as a politician. Now we would call him simply an 'intellectual' (like Descartes, whom he met in 1642).

He was an educator whose local view matured to a global vision. As a theologian he could not help deliberating on why the 'fight for the good cause' was lost (with the Battle on the White Mountain in November 1620) and came to the conclusion that it was a punishment for previous Czech sins. His vision of the world was rather tragic because in addition to the fact that he never was allowed to see his native country again, there were several other misfortunes in his life, such as the death of his first wife and both of his children, the loss of his library at Fulnek in 1623, the destruction by fire of his lexicographical archives at Leszno in Poland, the death of his second wife, and last but not least the fact that just as he was being given a chance to reform education in England, with the support of some members of Parliament, a civil war broke out and he was obliged to leave. Nevertheless, the setting up of the British Royal Society is said to have grown from Comenius' inspiration.

In view of these peregrinations and various tribulations, the more admirable is his work. The tragic overtones colour solely his only work of fiction, *The Labyrinth of the World and the Paradise of the Heart*, in which the main character is a pilgrim, who encounters more folly than wisdom in the world. This religious allegory was similar to John Bunyan's later work, *Pilgrim's Progress*. However, the bulk of his writings are educational works, and in them he gradually developed his vision from the idea of improving the pupils in the classroom to the idea of improving mankind in general.

In 1630 he started work on a set of textbooks that were to contribute to national education. He favoured the learning of Latin to make the study of European culture easier. His very first textbook, *Janua linguarum reserata* (1631), was a success (it was translated into a dozen languages), and so was the *Gate of Tongues Unlocked* (1633) and *The School of Infancy* – a book for mothers. In these works he developed the principles that pupils should be taught what interests them and what will later be useful for them. Also he believed that 'all work and no play makes Johnny a dull boy' – the essentials of pedagogics that have never become out of date. Then he proceeded to the writing of the *Great Didactic* and elaborated his pansophic project, in which he defined the three sources of knowledge as senses, the reason and the Bible. The whole collection of his writings on education was brought out as *Opera Didactica Omnia* (1657). The universalization of knowledge was aimed at eliminating world tensions. *Orbis Sensualium Pictus* (1658, *The Visible World in Pictures*) was a work of lexicography.

Besides these fairly large works he occasionally wrote smaller tracts, such as *Via Lucis* (*The Way of Light*), in which he set out his programme and summed up his proposals for the reform of education; it was written for his English friends in 1642 but could be published only in 1668. *Faber Fortunae*, a tract on wisdom, was dedicated to the sons of his deceased political protector. *Panegyricus Carolo Gustavo* (1655) is a treatise describing a righteous monarch. Comenius' religious toleration, a sort of seventeenth-century ecumenism, manifests itself in several places (e.g. he admired the Jesuits and their interest in education, and expressed an understanding for the Jews).

Comenius continued watching the religious developments in the Thirty Years' War and when he realized that the Allies would not insist on reintroducing religious freedom in Central Europe, he took comfort in writing in Latin a history of his beloved church, under the telling name, *Historia persecutionum ecclesiae Bohemicae'* (originally meant as a chapter for the *Book of Martyrs* by John Foxe). Then, in Czech, he wrote another book, with a still more sorrowful title, *The Testament of the Dying Mother, the Unity of Brethren* (1650). His last years were marked by an increase in mysticism.

It is difficult to assess how much early modern education owes to Comenius – perhaps the new ideas would have arrived sooner or later anyway – but there can be no doubt that he was one of the pioneers. As a thinker he in some respects was before his age: he was one of the first modern advocates of education for women, and he felt both a patriot and an international citizen. As a brave and honest person who kept his faith in adverse conditions one cannot but feel admiration for him. The Communist regime could not suppress interest in him but tried to deprive his teaching of all religious orientation. Incidentally, even though the regime was proud of this intellectual, no-one was allowed to travel to Naarden in the Netherlands to pay homage to him at his grave (he died on 15 November 1670 in Amsterdam).

One quotation, the prophecy from his Testament, is familiar to millions in his native country: 'I believe that, after the tempest of God's wrath shall have passed, the rule of the country will again return unto thee, O Czech people.' These words became the theme of a protest song in the first days of the Soviet Russian invasion, which suppressed the Prague Spring of 1968. The song was banned and its singer could make a public appearance only twenty years later. But what an audience she had! Three-quarters of a million people at an open-air rally – a culmination of the Velvet Revolution in November 1989. Which of Comenius's contemporaries can rival that?

In Europe Comenius is not forgotten either: the 400th anniversary of his birth was commemorated by an exhibition, 'Comenius, European Reformer and Czech Patriot', in the Bodleian Library in Oxford, and by a colloquium in Amsterdam (besides international symposiums held in Prague). And at the university in Olomouc (Moravia), the thousands of students daily entering the Central Library, step across a metal inscription set in the floor of the entrance to this vast eighteenth-century building. It says: 'Let's make libraries from armouries. J.A. Komenský'. The quotation is reminiscent of the fact that after the Velvet Revolution in 1989, the Artillery Armoury was converted into the university library.

Note

1 Comenius, J.A. *The Great Didactic: of John Amos Comenius*, ed. M.H. Keatinge, 1910 (quote translated from the Czech by the author).

Comenius' major writings

Janua Linguarum reserata: The Gate of Languages Unlocked, trans. T. Horn; afterwards much corrected and amended by J. Robotham. sixth edition, London, Printed by James Young and sold by Thomas Slater, 1643.

Joh. Amos Commenii Orbis sensualium pictus: Joh. Amos Commenius's Visible World, trans. Charles Hoole, London, Printed for John Sprint, 1705.

The Great Didactic: of John Amos Comenius, trans. and with biographical, historical and critical introductions by M.W. Keatinge, 2nd edn, London, A. & C. Black, 1910.

The School of Infancy, with an introduction by Ernest M. Eller. Chapel Hill: University of North Carolina Press, 1956.

The Labyrinth of the World and the Paradise of the Heart, trans. and introduced by Howard Louthan and Andrew Sterk; preface by Jan Milic Lochman. New York: Paulist Press, 1998.

Further reading

Kyralova, M. and Privratska, J. (eds), *Symposium Comenianum 1982 – The Impact of J. A. Comenius on Educational Thinking and Practice*, Uhersky Brod: Jan Amos Komenský Museum, 1984.

Laurie, S.S., *John Amos Comenius, Bishop of the Moravians: his life and educational works*, 6th edn, Cambridge: Cambridge University Press, Pitt Press Series, 1904.

Murphy, D.J., *Comenius: A Critical Reassessment of his Life and Work*, Dublin: Irish Academic Press, 1995.

Needham, J. (ed.), *The Teacher of Nations: Addresses and Essays in commemoration of the visit to England of the great Czech educationalist Jan Amos Komenský, Comenius, 1641–1941*, Cambridge: Cambridge University Press, 1942.

Panek, J., *Comenius: Teacher of Nations*, Prague: Vychodoslovenske Vydavatelstvo, 1991.

Sadler, J.E., *J. A Comenius and the Concept of Universal Education*, London: Allen and Unwin, 1966.

Spinka, M., *John Amos Comenius: That Incomparable Moravian*, 1st edn 1943, Chicago, IL, The University of Chicago Press; 2nd edn 1967, New York: Russell and Russell, 1967.

Turnbull, G.H., *Hartlib, Dury and Comenius: Gleanings from Hartlib's Papers*, Liverpool: University Press of Liverpool, 1947.

van Vliet, P. and Vanderjagt, A.J. (eds), *Johannes Amos Comenius (1592–1670): Exponent of European Culture?*, Amsterdam, Oxford, North Holland, 1994.

Wright, C.J., *Comenius and the Church Universal*, London: Herbert Barber, 1941.

Young, R.F., *Comenius in England (1641–2)*, London: Oxford University Press, 1932.

JAROSLAV PEPRNIK

JOHN LOCKE 1632–1704

> A Sound Mind in a sound Body, is a short, but full Description of a Happy State in this World: He that has these Two, has little more to wish for ... of all the Men we meet with, Nine Parts of Ten are what they are, Good or Evil, useful or not, by their Education. 'Tis that which makes the great Difference in Mankind: The little, and almost insensible Impressions on our tender Infancies, have very important and lasting Consequences.[1]

John Locke was born near Bristol, England, to a father who was a lawyer and minor local government officer. The younger Locke studied medicine, 'natural philosophy' (i.e. science) and philosophy at Oxford. On graduation he held academic posts at different times in Greek, Rhetoric and Moral Philosophy. He became the personal physician of Lord Shaftesbury in 1667, and came to combine this with the role of tutor to his son, born in 1671. Shaftesbury removed himself to the Netherlands when he was accused of treason in 1683, and Locke accompanied the household into exile. After the accession to the throne of William of Orange, Locke returned to England and held posts sufficiently well paid, and so little onerous, that he was able to publish the bulk of the work on which his reputation rests from 1689 onwards.

That body of work includes four letters on toleration (the first published in 1689), and *An Essay Concerning Human Understanding* (1690, with further editions in 1694 and 1695). The *Essay* has come to be viewed as a classic Enlightenment text. Locke rejects the notion that human knowledge and moral capacity are innate, arguing that the individual should instead be regarded as a *tabula rasa* or blank sheet – literally an unmarked wax tablet – on which subsequent experience is imprinted. Thus he is generally regarded as an essentially empiricist philosopher, one who is disposed to be impressed by the extent to which our understanding is delivered to us through our own senses and experience of the world.

Elements of empiricism can easily be found in Locke's educational writings. As the quotation at the beginning of this essay shows, Locke strongly tended to think of children as 'white Paper, or Wax, to be moulded and fashioned as one pleases' (§ 217), yet the full context suggests a degree of caution. We should note that 'nine parts of ten' (above) are formed by upbringing or education, and give due weight to that last tenth. In *Some Thoughts Concerning Education*, his longest and best-known work on the subject, first published in 1693, Locke thinks of each child as having 'an original temper' or character:

> God has stampt certain Characters upon Mens Minds, which, like their Shapes, may perhaps be a little mended; but can hardly be totally alter'd, and transform'd into the contrary.
>
> (§ 66)

It follows from this that the educator should carefully observe the character of the individual child, to see where improvements can be made and where such efforts would rather be pointless or, worse, lead only to affectation, the very perversion of education – as Locke conceives it – where the child merely feigns understanding in order to please the grown-ups (ibid.).

Locke rejects training children through what we would now call extrinsic motivation, that is by appealing to their desires and aversions. Our knowledge may to a significant degree come via the senses, but to govern actions and to direct conduct by such motives as sensual pleasure and pain is 'to cherish that Principle in him [the child], which it is our Business to root out and destroy' (§ 48). That is why corporal punishment is to be avoided as far as possible. Locke's many warnings about the dangers of physical punishment, and its propensity to make a child cowed and low-spirited, no doubt proceed partly from his natural humanity and revulsion from what was the common practice of his age. But they derive also from the fact that such punishment works on the natural propensity to indulge pleasure, and to avoid pain, which is at all points to be opposed. Children are to be *educated*, and not merely *conditioned*, and this means their faculty of reason is to be strengthened, and their capacity to resist their desires steadily increased.

For Locke education is essentially what we would now call 'moral education': its aim is *virtue*. Due care is therefore to be taken 'to keep the Body in Strength and Vigour, so that it may be able to obey and execute the Orders of the *Mind*' (§ 31). The next business of the educator is 'to set the *Mind* right, that on all Occasions it may be disposed to consent to nothing, but what may be suitable to the Dignity and Excellency of a rational Creature' (ibid.). This twofold injunction makes sense of much that may seem odd to the modern reader. Locke advises us on a range of subjects, for example 'That Children be not too *warmly clad or Covered*, Winter or Summer' (§ 5), or that, as soon as a child has a sufficient head of hair, he should go without a cap day and night: 'there being nothing that more exposes to Head-ach, Colds, Catarrhs, Coughs, and several other Diseases, than keeping the *Head warm*' (ibid.). The reader is instructed on, among other topics, children's diet,[2] sleep and footwear,[3] the consequences of sitting on the cold ground when hot with exercise (§ 10: often fatal, it seems) and, at considerable length, the importance of regular movements of the bowels (§ 23f.).

This is not the sort of thing we would expect to find in a modern book on education. For Locke, however, 'education' has more the sense of 'upbringing' (the German *Erziehung*) than of school-based education in the modern sense. And he is writing for the class of people whose sons (their daughters are barely mentioned here) are to grow up into gentlemen under the individual guidance of tutors: these people are interested in the wider question of how their offspring are to grow into satisfactory manhood, and not simply in their intellectual attainments.

So it is a mistake to focus exclusively on what Locke has to say about intellectual and moral development, as most introductions to his theory of education do,[4] and ignore the rest of *Some Thoughts* as merely quaint. It is significant that Locke was an active medical practitioner. For example, he conducted what we would now call field-trials of *cinchona*, a predecessor of quinine, and recorded its effects on his patients.[5] To someone who believes that the impressions of the bodily senses are significant sources of knowledge, it is of the first importance that those senses should be in good repair. To this end many of Locke's scientific contemporaries enthusiastically experimented with a range of diets, drugs and regimes, partly in order to discover which made the senses most alert and receptive. [6] Our modern tendency to divide professional responsibility for the growing child between the doctor and the teacher ('Personal, Social and Health Education' notwithstanding) would probably have puzzled Locke.

Some Thoughts presents us with a thoroughly secular picture. The child is not born with the idea of God or of moral truths; he does not possess innate moral goodness just waiting to be liberated and activated. It is *education* that turns the self-centred, demanding – Locke has no romantic view of childhood – infant into the rounded young man. The picture is at the same time in many respects a traditional one. Children are like travellers newly arrived in a strange country (§ 120), and have to learn its customs and ways. They are to learn these, like all else, not by being taught rules, but through practice. If the occasion for practice does not occur naturally then it must be manufactured. Practice 'will beget Habits in them, which, being once established, operate of themselves easily and naturally' (§ 66).

The skill of the tutor, then, lies in finding such occasions, and marrying the process of habituation to the active development of the child's power of reason. The key is that the child should be brought to *want* to learn. There is no question of simply waiting for this to happen: it is to be engineered. The teaching of reading supplies an instructive case. Locke describes how he helped set up a conversation for a child to over-hear, along the lines that reading makes heirs and elder brothers into gentlemen 'beloved by everybody' (§ 148); it is a favour for younger brothers to be taught to read at all – they can be illiterate ignoramuses, if that is what they choose. The effect, apparently, was to make the object of this benign manipulation passionate to learn to read. More generally, Locke tells us, the acquisition of literacy should be turned into a kind of sport, through the use of 'Dice and Play-things, with the Letters on them, to teach Children the *Alphabet* by playing' (ibid.).

It was this refusal to trust children to want to learn *naturally* that so enraged Rousseau:

> People make a great fuss about discovering the best way to teach children to read. They invent 'bureaux' and cards, they turn the nursery into a printer's shop. Locke would have them taught to read by means of dice. What a fine idea! And the pity of it! There is a better way than any of those, and one which is generally overlooked – it consists in the desire to learn.[7]

Here we see the difference between what may be called the child-centred, permissive philosophy of education on the one hand and, on the other, a philosophy which is liberal and humane but doubts that children will be particularly inclined to learn unless they are properly taught. Locke is far from inhumane. He understands that childhood has its own needs and, as we might now put it, its own developmental psychology: for example, he does not doubt that children need play and toys (§ 39). But this is not child-centredness: the education he proposes has in view less the happy and fulfilled child than the civilized and accomplished adult the child will become.

That adult will above all possess good habits, moral and otherwise. He will have acquired the virtue which is harder to come by, and more important, than all the knowledge of the world (§ 70); yet he will also love and value knowledge and – a true lifelong learner – will understand how and where to find knowledge when he wants to (§ 195). Even though he is well born he will not despise manual trades, learning carpentry or gardening (§ 204), or how to grind and polish optical glasses (§ 209); these activities are properly recreational and fulfilling, and guard against the 'lazy, listless Humour, that idly dreams away the days' (§ 208).

Although Locke's advice on the upbringing of the seventeenth-century young gentleman does not translate easily into the conditions of modern mass education there is still much in his account to inspire and instruct the educator and parent now. For example, the teacher's role in constructing opportunities for the pupil to learn, even if in *Some Thoughts* it sometimes seems manipulative, has not grown less important in a world where commercial pressures and the reconstruction of the child as infant consumer make the 'natural' education of Rousseau's Émile, based on his innate and healthy curiosity, increasingly implausible. It is attractive too, at a time when we are subjected to comprehensive (and often conflicting) theories of learning and guidelines setting out, often in minute detail, the authoritative way of teaching every subject on the curriculum, that Locke presumes only to offer 'some thoughts'. His modesty, and sympathy with the world of the child, are apparent throughout his text. But one would still want to put in a good word for peaches and plums.

Notes

1 *Some Thoughts Concerning Education*, § 1. All references are to *Some Thoughts Concerning Education*, unless otherwise indicated. I have followed the orthography and spelling of Yolton and Yolton's 1989 edition.
2 '*Melons, Peaches*, most sorts of *Plumbs*, and all sorts of *Grapes* in *England*, I think Children should be *wholly kept from*, as having a very tempting Taste, in a very unwholesome Juice' (§ 20). Strawberries, gooseberries and cherries are however apparently safe.
3 'I would also advise his *Feet to be washed* every Day in cold Water; and to have his *Shooes* so thin, that they might leak and *let in Water* ... he that considers how Mischievous and Mortal a thing, taking *Wet in the Feet* is to those, who have been bred nicely, will wish he had, with the poor People's Children, gone *Bare-foot*; who, by that means, come to be so reconciled, by Custom, to Wet in their Feet, that they take no more Cold or Harm by it, than if they were wet in their Hands' (§ 7).
4 E.g. Yolton and Yolton (1989): 'The feature of *Some Thoughts* not discussed in this introduction, that portion dealing with the care of the child's body and bodily health' (p. 35).
5 Lisa Jardine, *Ingenious Pursuits*, Little, Brown, pp. 282–3, 1999.
6 See *ibid.* Locke was more conscious than many of his peers that the medicine of his time, which he calls 'physic', was as prone to cause illness as to cure it. He writes, 'Nor upon every little Indisposition is *Physick* to be given, or the Physician to be called to Children – no body can have a pretence to doubt the Advice of one, who has spent some time in the Study of Physick, when he counsels you, not to be too forward in making use of *Physick* and *Physicians*' (§ 29).
7 Rousseau, *Émile*, Book 2.

See also

In this book: Rousseau

Locke's major writings

A Letter Concerning Toleration, 1689.
An Essay Concerning Human Understanding, 1690.
Two Treatises of Government, 1690.
Some Thoughts Concerning Education, 1693.
(All available in the Clarendon edition of the works of John Locke, published by Oxford University Press.)

Further reading

Axtell, J., *The Educational Writings of John Locke*, Cambridge: Cambridge University Press, 1968.
Stephens, R.C., *John Locke and the Education of the Gentleman*, University of Leeds: Institute of Education Research Studies, 14, 1956.
Yolton, J.W. and Yolton, J.S., Introduction: John Locke, *Some Thoughts Concerning Education*, Oxford: Clarendon Press, 1989.

RICHARD SMITH

JOHN WESLEY 1703-91

> The bias of nature is set the wrong way. Education is designed to
> set it right.[1]

John Wesley was born at Epworth, Lincolnshire, on 17 June 1703, the
second surviving son of Reverend Samuel Wesley, Rector of Epworth, and
his wife Susanna. Educated at Charterhouse and Christ Church, Oxford,
Wesley was elected fellow of Lincoln College in 1726 and ordained. From
1725 he determined to live a holy life by vigorous self-discipline and from
1729 led a like-minded group nicknamed 'the Holy Club' and 'Methodists'.
As a missionary in Georgia in 1735-7 Wesley was influenced by Moravian
immigrants and on his return to England they convinced him that salvation
could only come by faith in Christ rather than in his own efforts and
on 24 May 1738 he experienced an evangelical conversion. Thereafter as a
travelling evangelist he organized religious societies which became a
nationwide network serviced by lay preachers. From 1744 an annual
conference of preachers laid down rules for the organization. Though
claiming that he had not separated from the Church of England, in 1784
Wesley registered his Conference as a legal entity and began to conduct his
own ordinations, initially for America. After his death on 2 March 1791
Methodism developed into a new family of churches, dividing into several
branches during the nineteenth century. Though part of an international
evangelical revival movement, Wesley's Methodism was distinctive for its
centralized organization, rejection of Calvinistic predestination and
controversial advocacy of Christian perfection.

Wesley was a prolific writer, though much of his output consisted of
abridgements of other authors, tailored to his own views. Despite his wide
intellectual and cultural interests, Wesley's overriding concern was to use
culture to promote religion, and he had a strong interest in the supernatural.
His educational work has to be viewed in the light of his overriding religious
concerns and beliefs after his conversion.

The evidence for the influence of published and other sources on Wesley's
educational ideals and practice is mostly indirect and deduced from
apparent echoes and parallels. He cites Milton and the Pietist system at
Jena but only for the principles of continuous education in one place and the
constant presence of masters with the children, respectively. Wesley's
Instructions for Children (1743) were avowedly adapted from Pierre Poiret
and Claude Fleury; his *A Token for Children* (1749) from the Puritan James
Janeway; and reading lists for his preachers and Kingswood school reflect
the advice of Philip Doddridge, head of a Dissenting Academy. Though not
directly acknowledged by Wesley, echoes and close parallels have been
claimed between his prescriptions and Locke's *Some Thoughts on Education*,
the Jansenist Port Royal schools and possibly Comenius.

Wesley's most obvious inspiration can be found in his mother's system of
child-rearing and education at Epworth, together with his observations on
the Pietist and Moravian schools in Germany he visited in 1738 and
published in his *Journal*. Susanna Wesley was concerned to educate children
in obedience and godliness from the earliest possible age before worldly
corruption set in. This contrasts with contemporaries who thought religious

education should be left to later years and Susanna allowed little to individual variations or a child's powers of discovery. To enforce godliness and good learning it is necessary to 'break the will' and conform the child's behaviour to that of its parents until it can make its own (well-conditioned) decisions. Rewards and punishments may be used, with physical chastisement if necessary.[2] John Wesley applied these principles to obedience to masters in school.

His view of the purpose of education was based on his reading of human nature and God's dealings with humanity. He explicitly rejected the view of Rousseau and others that human nature is naturally good. Rousseau's *Émile* was 'the most empty, silly, injudicious thing that ever a self-conceited infidel wrote'.[3] Wesley believed that since the Fall we have inherited Adam's sinful nature. As we can only be saved by God's grace it might be thought that Wesley would not share contemporary optimism about the saving power of education. Certainly he wrote that 'All our wisdom will not even make them [children] *understand*, much less *feel*, the things of God.'[4] Nevertheless, Wesley liked to appeal to reason as well as religion. He rejected predestination and believed that human beings are given freedom by God to accept or reject salvation and can make progress in religious and moral achievement by preparing for and cultivating the gifts of grace. Like Locke he rejected innate ideas and stressed the power of sense-impressions. Hence education has an important role in cultivating mental as well as moral and religious achievement. This explains the 'bias of nature' remark (which echoes Milton) and Wesley's belief that 'the only end of education is to restore our rational nature to its proper state. Education, therefore, is to be considered as reason learned at second-hand, which is, *as far as it can* [my italics], to supply the loss of original perfection.'[5] Although his ultimate concern was for conversion and a holy life, even for very young children, Wesley gave much attention to education by his publications and advice tailored to the capacities of his followers.

Pietist and Moravian influence is evident in Wesley's Kingswood school, whose regime closely resembled that of Halle, Herrnhut and Jena. Whether or not he had direct knowledge of Comenius' educational ideals, he certainly learnt much from Comenius' Moravian disciples and, like Locke and Comenius, emphasized the necessity of thoroughly mastering a subject before moving on to a new one.

Wesley's contribution to social reforms has often been exaggerated. Given his busy life and the relatively low status of his followers, it is not surprising that he failed to lead large-scale campaigns in the manner of Wilberforce and his associates. While he condemned the slave-trade and praised Sunday schools, his followers were more directly involved in these causes. This was largely also the case with education more generally. For girls he recommended schools run by female friends while criticizing female academies for frivolity and condemning the bringing up of girls 'as if they were only designed for agreeable playthings'.[6] Wesley nevertheless took more direct action in education than in any other of his social concerns. He founded a few charity schools himself and published a number of books for general and religious education including prayers, hymns and Bible extracts for children and a number of textbooks and selected texts for his Kingswood school. In addition, he contributed to adult self-education by publications, book-lists for preachers and individual correspondence. His *Christian Library* (1749–55) offered a wide-ranging collection of devotional works. He abridged works on science (*A Survey of the Wisdom of God in Creation, 1775*) and history though frankly acknowledging that 'My aim in writing history (as in natural philosophy) is to bring God into it.'[7] Here he was acting as a kind of semi-popular educator or middleman between the cultured élite and the less educated.

However, Wesley's most substantial and lasting contribution to education was his Kingswood school, opened in 1748. This was designed as a kind of junior grammar school with a strong emphasis on religious nurture. Though aimed at the general Christian public it was later used increasingly to educate the sons (and occasionally daughters) of his travelling preachers. Like many evangelicals and other serious people, Wesley distrusted the old public schools for their dubious educational methods as well as their moral and religious failings. He claimed that they were mostly situated near large towns and so open to corruption; children were admitted regardless of character; most of the masters had no more religion than their pupils. Instruction was poorly planned, with elementary work neglected in favour of Latin and Greek and the work was not properly graded in order of difficulty. But Kingswood combined seclusion with access to Bristol; only selected boarders were taken and would remain in the school without a break to avoid parental interference. The aim was a Christian education by 'forming their minds, through the help of God, to wisdom and holiness, by instilling the principles of true religion, speculative and practical, and training them up in the ancient way, that they might be rational, scriptural Christians'.[8]

Rising at 4.00 a.m., academic work was supplemented with religious exercises. No play was permitted, for 'he that plays as a boy will play as a man'.[9] As with Pietists, recreation consisted of walking, gardening and other physical labour; and children were always to be accompanied by a master. A plain diet was provided and mattresses instead of feather beds (there is a parallel with Locke here). The boys were to be educated between 6 and 12 years of age in 'reading, writing, arithmetic, English, French, Latin, Greek, Hebrew, history, geography, chronology, rhetoric, logic, ethics, geometry, algebra, physics, music'.[10] However, some of these subjects were not covered in Wesley's book-lists and references to science may suggest that this was a form of recreation as at Halle. The core curriculum was predominantly classical, once past basic English instruction, and apparently pursued in the traditional way through verses, 'themes' and 'declamations'. On the other hand, Wesley laid emphasis on graded instruction; the classical authors were selected from what he saw as the earliest and purest authors; and, like the Pietists, he omitted 'indecent' authors. More distinctive was the inclusion of one of Wesley's favourite religious authors at the head of each year's list for reading and translation.

Wesley also projected a four-year 'academical' course, adding modern works in science, history and literature to the classics. With characteristic self-confidence he claimed that 'whoever goes through this course will be a better scholar than nine in ten of the graduates at Oxford and Cambridge'.[11] This design was suspended until the late 1760s when Methodists were being prevented from graduating at Oxford. In 1775 suggestions were made to educate preachers at Kingswood but it is unlikely that any completed the 'academical' course. Occasionally a preacher had a short stay there and Wesley sometimes gave Oxford-style tutorials to preachers. He frequently lamented Kingswood's lack of conformity to his ideal for, apart from intractable boy nature, the masters rarely possessed all the necessary qualities of piety and teaching and management skills. Yet the school survived many vicissitudes, eventually becoming a modern public school.

Wesley's significance and influence as an educationalist is not easy to establish. While many evangelicals and Methodists shared his views on original sin, child nurture and the role of education, some allowed for 'innocent' play and the educative use of children's curiosity. In the perspective of seventeenth-century and eighteenth-century suggestions for educational reform, Methodist and evangelical attitudes appear largely conservative, though with some modifications in terms of graded instruction and close supervision. What stands out is their analysis of human nature as fallen and the concern for education as a necessary, if imperfect, instrument to prepare children for salvation. Traditional education must therefore be pursued in a religious context. This was clearly in opposition to the contemporary rise in optimism about human nature and what can be achieved by education alone. At Kingswood until late in the nineteenth century the office of Governor was held by elderly ministers who controlled management as well as religion and hampered the ability of headmasters to modernize the curriculum.

Like the Church of England and Nonconformists in the nineteenth century, Wesleyans aspired to educate their own people in elementary and secondary church schools and teacher training colleges. By the end of the century most Nonconformists had abandoned hope of denominational schools in favour of secular school board schools which would at least save their children from Anglican indoctrination. The Wesleyans, though divided on this issue, persisted longer with their own schools. Wesley had praised Sunday schools, evidently hoping they would promote religion as well as education, and Wesleyans were prominent in founding them.[12] However, Wesleyan ministerial attempts to control them and limit them to reading and catechetical instruction often led to secessions and loss of denominational control. Despite continuing attempts to combine education with a Wesleyan religious ethos, developments in Wesleyan educational institutions during the nineteenth century often seem to reflect the pressure of social aspirations as much as the religious aims inherited from Wesley. Nevertheless, their persistence testified to a desire to insulate Methodists from worldly snares while fulfilling some of their social and educational ambitions, a significant aspect of nineteenth century church-based education. In America Methodism developed an extensive denominational college and university system impossible in Britain, though only the shortlived Cokesbury College seems to have followed the Kingswood pattern closely.

As to Wesley's wider cultural and educational concerns expressed in his publications, his legacy seems to have been reprints, mainly for Wesleyans, into the early nineteenth century; and his *Wisdom of God in Creation* and best-selling folk remedies in *Primitive Physick* were reprinted even longer. Yet as an adapter of 'high' to 'popular' culture with a religious basis, it is arguable that Isaac Watts' works of a similar nature had a longer life and wider influence. At the most 'popular' level of the tract, it is surprising that

Wesley only founded a tract society in 1782 to distribute his brief *Words* to various sinners and they lacked the chapbook style and efficient distribution system achieved by Hannah More.[13]

Notes

1. 'A Thought on the Manner of Educating Children', in *Works*, XIII, p. 476, 1872.
2. John Wesley, *Journal*, ed. W.R. Ward, in *Works*, bicentennial edition, XIX, pp. 286–91, 1990; *Sermons*, ed. A. Outler in *Works*, bicentennial edition, III, pp. 367–8, 1986.
3. 'A Thought on the Manner of Educating Children', in *Works*, p. 474, 1872; similarly in *Journal* in *Works*, bicentennial edition, XXII, p. 284, 1993.
4. John Wesley, *Letters*, ed. J. Telford, VI, p. 39, 1931.
5. John Wesley, *Sermons*, in *Works*, bicentennial edition, III, p. 348, 1986, quoting William Law, *Serious Call*.
6. John Wesley, *Sermons* in *Works*, bicentennial edition, III, 396, 1986.
7. John Wesley, *Letters*, VI, p. 67.
8. 'Plain Account of Kingswood School', 1781, in *Works*, XIII, p. 293, 1872.
9. A German proverb quoted in 'A Short Account of the School in Kingswood', 1768, in *Works*, XIII, p. 283, 1872; and 'Plain Account', 1781, in *Works*, XIII, p. 294.
10. 'Short Account' in *Works*, XIII, p. 283. In the 'Plain Account' in *Works*, XIII, p. 295 the last two subjects are given as 'natural philosophy' and 'metaphysics'.
11. 'Short Account', last sentence, in *Works*, XIII, p. 289; cf. 'Plain Account' in *Works*, XIII, pp. 296–301 listing his criticisms of Oxford and Cambridge.
12. John Wesley, *Journal*, ed. N. Curnock, 1916 reprinted 1938, VII, pp. 3, 306, 377.
13. V.E. Neuburg, *Popular Education. A History and Guide*, Harmondsworth: Penguin, pp. 131–7, 1977.

See also

In this book: Comenius, Locke

Wesley's major writings

The Bicentennial Edition of Wesley's *Works*, 34 vols, ed. F. Baker and R.P. Heitzenrater, Oxford: Oxford University Press, continued by Abingdon Press, Nashville, 1975–) is in progress. For some writings the older edition of the *Works*, 14 vols, Wesley Conference Office, 1872, reprinted Grand Rapids: Zondervan, n.d. is still necessary; also the *Journal*, ed. N Curnock, London: Epworth Press, 1916 reprinted 1938, vols. VII and VIII for 1787–91; *Letters*, ed. J. Telford, London: Epworth Press, 1931, vols. III–VIII for 1756–91.

The following items deal directly with education:

Journal, ed. W.R. Ward in *Works*, bicentennial edition, XIX, pp. 286–91,1990 (Susanna Wesley's child-rearing).
Sermons, ed. A. Outler on 'Family Religion', 'The Education of Children', 'Obedience to Parents' in *Works*, bicentennial edition, III, pp. 333–72, 1986.
'A Thought on the Manner of Educating Children', in *Works*, XIII, pp. 474–7, 1872.
Instructions for Children, London, M. Cooper, 1743 (emphasizes doing all to the glory of God and repression of the passions).
'A Short Account of the School in Kingswood', Bristol, F. Farley, 1749; reprinted in Ives, *Kingswood School*, pp. 11–18; 1768 edition in *Works*, XIII, pp. 283–9, 1872.
'A Plain Account of Kingswood School', in *Works*, XIII, pp. 289–301, 1781.

Further reading

Body, A.H., *John Wesley and Education*, London: Epworth Press, 1936.

Ives, A.G., *Kingswood School in Wesley's Day and Ours*, London: Epworth Press, 1970.

Matthews, H.F., *Methodism and the Education of the People 1791–1851*, London: Epworth Press, 1949.

Naglee, D.I., *From Font to Faith. John Wesley on Infant Baptism and the Nurture of Children*, New York: American University Studies, Series VII, Vol. 24, P. Lang, 1987.

Prince, J.W., *John Wesley on Religious Education*, New York and Cincinnatti: Methodist Book Concern, 1926.

Sangster, P., *Pity My Simplicity. The Evangelical Revival and the Religious Education of Children*, London: Epworth Press, 1963.

HENRY D. RACK

JEAN-JACQUES ROUSSEAU 1712–78

> Everything is good as it leaves the hands of the Author of things; everything degenerates in the hands of man.[1]

Jean-Jacques Rousseau, self-taught genius of the Age of Enlightenment, was born in 1712 in Calvinist Geneva to parents of the bourgeois class. His father was a feckless watchmaker. His mother died a few days after his birth. Proud to be a citizen of his native city, he none the less left it as a young man, and later quarrelled, bitterly and publicly, with its rulers. He lived most of his adult life as an outsider in France, where he became an ornament, as well as a thorn in the flesh, of its glittering cultural world.

Rousseau's personal qualifications as an educational theorist were minimal. He had received little formal schooling and he abandoned his five children, born to his common-law wife Thérèse Levasseur, to the orphanage. In 1740–1 he was private tutor to the two sons of a minor nobleman of Lyons, but acknowledged that he had little aptitude for the job.[2]

None the less, Rousseau wrote one of the greatest works on developmental psychology, *Émile, or on Education*, published in 1762, the same year as the *Social Contract*.

Émile consolidated Rousseau's fame, but led to his banishment and exile after it was condemned by the Paris Theology Faculty and then by the Paris *Parlement*, which ordered his arrest. The Genevan authorities followed suit, ordering that both the *Émile* and the *Social Contract* be burnt, as 'foolhardy, scandalous, impious, tending to destroy the Christian religion and all governments'. Finally, the Archbishop of Paris issued a 'condemnation of a book entitled *Émile, or on Education* by J.-J. Rousseau, citizen of Geneva'. The most important charge was that the author denied original sin. In his detailed reply, published a year later, Rousseau re-emphasized that denial: 'The fundamental principle of all morality ... is that man is a naturally good creature, who loves justice and order; that there is no original perversity in the human heart, and that the first movements of nature are always right.'

After exile in Switzerland and England, Rousseau returned to Paris in 1770. His output continued unabated. He produced a reasoned constitutional proposal for Poland, but devoted most of his energy to works of self-justification, which were published only posthumously. Rousseau's behaviour in his last years is often described as paranoid. But his sense that he was surrounded by people plotting to blacken his name had some foundation. His works had gained him many enemies among the authorities of Church and state, but also among his former friends in the intellectual élite whom he had systematically alienated. He died at Ermenonville, his last place of retreat, in 1778.

The *Émile* constitutes an imaginary educational experiment. Rousseau's goal was to show how it is possible to raise an individual who could function as an autonomous agent even in the illegitimate political order of his time. There, since the public institutions of schools and colleges were irredeemably corrupted, the only solution was to withdraw both pupil and teacher from society, and conduct the experiment in isolation from it.

Rousseau took a consistently naturalistic approach to education in the *Émile*, maintaining that the child is naturally good and made wicked only by its environment. He held that knowledge comes from the senses, and that children should engage actively with a well-ordered environment, and learn by interacting with it. Since movement is crucial to this learning process, it should be encouraged from birth. Thus Rousseau was hostile to swaddling infants and to controlling toddlers with leading reins. The growing boy was to be introduced to the natural sciences by practical lessons, 'learning by doing', preferably in the open air, far from the dry pedantry of textbooks and laboratories. In the imaginary micro-environment, the pupil's natural drives, those that are healthy, self-sustaining and non-exploitative, could be fostered, and the distorting effects of the larger society could be kept at bay. Paradoxically, the greatest artifice is needed to guarantee the survival of the natural within a corrupt modern society: 'In the present state of things a man abandoned to himself in the midst of other men from birth would be the most disfigured of all. ... All the social institutions in which we find ourselves submerged would stifle nature in him and put nothing in its place' (37).

If the educational experiment of the *Émile* succeeds, the tutor will have produced 'a savage made to inhabit cities' (205), a street-wise adult who is happy and autonomous. In order to bring about the desired state, it is important to instil a degree of stoical realism about oneself and one's environment: 'The truly free man wants only what he can do and does what he pleases. That is my fundamental maxim. It need only be applied to childhood for all the rules of education to flow from it' (84). Freedom must not degenerate into caprice. To be an autonomous agent is to be master of oneself, above all master of one's own imagination. To be capricious and spoiled is to be mastered by impulse, by false dreams and unsatisfiable ambitions. Enduring happiness can be guaranteed to no one, but the truly free person has at least the inner resources to attain it.

That pupils should be introduced to different topics in a particular order, corresponding to the development of their capacities, was not a novel insight of Rousseau. But he went far beyond his predecessors in valuing the experience of the child and in theorizing its qualitative difference from the adult's: 'Love childhood; promote its games, its pleasures, its amiable instinct' (79); 'Childhood has its ways of seeing, thinking and feeling which are proper to it. Nothing is less sensible than to want to substitute ours for theirs' (90). Later developmental psychology owes much to Rousseau's pioneering work in the *Émile*. In a draft of the book, Rousseau distinguished four 'ages of man': the age of nature (0–12 years); the age of reason or intelligence (12–15); the age of force (15–20); the age of wisdom (20–25). These are followed (whimsically) by 'the age of happiness – for the rest of life'. These headings disappeared from the final version, but serve as a guide to its structure. There Rousseau added a three-stage schema of ethical development: (a) in infancy and childhood the pupil should be ruled by *necessity*; (b) between childhood and puberty by *utility*; (c) from the advent of sexuality by *morality* (167).

Progress through the early stages of ethical training is governed by the principle of 'negative education'. At least until the age of 12, 'the first education should be purely negative. It consists not at all in teaching virtue or truth but in securing the heart from vice and the mind from error' (93). Rousseau was particularly anxious to postpone the acquisition of an inappropriate moral vocabulary, since 'before the age of reason one cannot have any idea of moral beings or of social relations. Hence so far as possible words which express them must be avoided' (89). During the period of negative education, the child is to be surrounded by an environment of artificial necessity, encountering obstacles which appear to be the inevitable outcome of his own behaviour, rather than willed by others. As a result he should become 'patient, steady, resigned, calm, even when he has not got what he wanted, for it is the nature of man to endure patiently the necessity of things but not the ill will of others' (91).

According to Rousseau's schema, negative education begins to give way to positive at the age of reason, but is only fully superseded at adolescence (the age of energy). Then Émile enters the moral world, as the tutor 'discloses to him ... all his moral relations' (318). The key to the new world is amour-propre, 'the first and most natural of all the passions' (208). Amour-propre involves reflexion. One constructs one's own self through interaction with other selves, exchanging recognition and approval, contempt and rebuffal. The tutor must ensure that his pupil, now entering society, interacts with others who are worthy of his interaction, who recognize in him what is worthy of recognition, and provide him with a true mirror of himself. But amour-propre is a 'useful but dangerous instrument' (244), since this new interactive world is no longer fully within the tutor's control.

Negative education made a virtue of delay. Rousseau held that children are incapable of moral (as opposed to instrumental) behaviour until puberty. Before that, since they are not naturally cruel, but are driven by an 'innate repugnance at seeing another creature suffer', they can treat their fellow human beings (along with other animals) compassionately. But only later, through imagination and amour-propre, do they come to recognize them as bearers of rights, entitled to justice. And only then, according to Rousseau, can they understand the idea of God. So, counter to accepted practice, Émile receives no religious instruction until adolescence. Still more surprising is Rousseau's attempt to delay the pupil's first sexual encounter until the age of 20. Even then, consummation is postponed for another five years, while Émile is educated in, though not corrupted by, the ways of the world, travelling abroad and studying politics and society. Until the moment of his marriage, the tutor orchestrates Émile's sex life, finding him an ideal spouse, Sophie, and organizing an appropriate education for her. Rousseau stressed, against received Enlightenment wisdom, that there are fundamental physiological differences between men and women, which should be recognized by the allocation of complementary, rather than identical, roles to the two sexes, and reinforced by radically different kinds of education. Thus Émile was spared religious instruction until adolescence, Sophie is subjected to it from infancy. Above all, Émile was raised to be autonomous, Sophie to be personally dependent.

Rousseau justified his unfashionable sexual inegalitarianism by claiming that here, as before, he was reconstructing a 'natural' order of things within a social environment, allowing men and women once again to complement each other rather than compete.

The impact of the *Émile* on both parents and educationalists was immediate. By the end of the century, its influence was felt throughout the Western world, though resistance to it was stronger in Catholic than in Protestant countries.[3] Parents, aristocrats and bourgeois alike, were the most receptive group. Upper-class mothers were persuaded to breast-feed their children, instead of sending them to wet nurses. Some parents 'returned to nature' in rejecting swaddling clothes and allowing their children to run barefoot indoors and out. Others encouraged them, however fancifully, to acquire the skills of artisans. Among theorists, responses were mixed. Some held that Rousseau was unoriginal and derivative, others that he was absurdly utopian and extreme. But historians agree that his work had a powerful and lasting influence on theoretical debate throughout Europe. 'Progressive' educational thinkers from Pestalozzi and Froebel in the eighteenth and nineteenth centuries to Montessori and Piaget in the twentieth were all indebted to the *Émile*.

From the moment of its publication, the *Émile* aroused fierce criticisms, which have continued to this day. The accusations of utopianism, élitism, totalitarianism and sexism have constantly recurred. To the charge that the precepts of the *Émile* are mere utopian fantasy, inapplicable to reality, it could be responded that the book is best understood as an exercise in model building, the construction of an ideal type, to which empirical examples could correspond more or less closely: it is not intended as a first-order description of those examples. The second charge, that, if it were applied in reality, then it could be by only a tiny élite in an inegalitarian society, would have been accepted by Rousseau. He would have argued that the educational system of the *Émile*, and it alone, was applicable in the corrupt society of his time, whereas a different, democratic system would be appropriate to an ideal democratic political order. According to the third charge, of totalitarianism, the tutor subjects the pupil to undignified deception and manipulation which must frustrate the ultimate aim of producing an autonomous adult. It could be responded that, without elaborate stage setting in childhood, the pupil will become the slave of whims, caprices and fashions before he has had a chance to develop his own personality and become truly master of himself. Though this response is true to Rousseau's deepest thought, he himself was never fully convinced that his method of 'preparing from afar the reign of freedom' (63) would succeed. He showed his own reservations about it in *Émile et Sophie, ou les solitaires,* an unfinished, unpublished sequel to the *Émile.* In this, the young lovers, once exposed to the corrupt world of Paris, did not reach a happy ending, but marital breakdown, adultery and separation. The fourth charge is that the different forms of education which Rousseau advocated for men and women would result in inequality, not 'complementarity', as he claimed. As a result, women would never reach moral or intellectual maturity, let alone political or economic independence. Mary Wollstonecraft was the first of many critics to point to Rousseau's duplicity on this vital question. Though there is still resonance in Rousseau's reflexions on sexual difference and identity, the prescriptions he derived from them have not withstood the test of time.

Notes

1 Jean-Jacques Rousseau, *Émile,* Book I, trans. A. Bloom New York: Basic Books, p. 37, 1979. All further page references are to this translation.
2 Despite that, Rousseau used his experience to write two brief treatises on education, the *Mémoire* and the *Projet,* which he presented to his employer. They contain several original theses which he would develop later in the *Émile.*
3 See Leith (1977, p. 19).

See also

In this book: Pestalozzi, Froebel, Montessori, Wollstonecraft
In *Fifty Modern Thinkers on Education*: Piaget

Rousseau's major writings

The standard edition of Rousseau's works in French is Jean-Jacques Rousseau, *Œuvres complètes,* ed. B. Gagnebin, M. Raymond, Paris, Gallimard: Bibliothèque de la Pléiade, 5 volumes, 1959, 1964, 1969, 1995.

The standard English translation (not yet completed) is Jean-Jacques Rousseau, *Collected Writings,* series editors, R. Masters, C. Kelly, Hanover, NH: University Press of New England, 1990 ff.

Not yet available in the *Collected Writings*:

Émile, or on Education, trans. A. Bloom, New York: Basic Books, 1979.

Further reading

Cranston, M., *Jean-Jacques: The Early Life and Work of Jean-Jacques Rousseau, 1712–1754,* London: Allen Lane, 1983.
—— *The Noble Savage: Jean-Jacques Rousseau, 1754–1762,* London: Allen Lane, 1991.
—— *The Solitary Self: Jean-Jacques Rousseau in Exile and Adversity,* Chicago: University of Chicago Press, 1997.
Dent, N.J.H., *Rousseau: An Introduction to his Psychological, Social and Political Theory,* Oxford: Blackwell, 1988.
Jimack, P., *Rousseau, 'Émile',* London: Grant and Cutler, 1983.

Leith, J.A. (ed.), *Facets of Education in the Eighteenth Century*, in *Studies on Voltaire and the Eighteenth Century*, vol. 167, Oxford: Voltaire Foundation and Taylor Institution, 1977.

O'Hagan, T., *Rousseau*, London: Routledge, 1999.

Rorty, A.E.O., 'Rousseau's Educational Experiments', in A.E.O. Rorty (ed.), *Philosophers on Education*, London: Routledge, 1998.

Wokler, R., *Rousseau*, Oxford: Oxford University Press,1995.

Wollstonecraft, M., *A Vindication of the Rights of Woman*, Harmondsworth: Penguin, 1992.

TIMOTHY O'HAGAN

IMMANUEL KANT 1724–1804

> How then is perfection to be sought? Wherein lies our hope? In education, and in nothing else.[1]

Kant is a central figure in Western intellectual history, and has had a significant impact on educational thinking through his enormously influential work in philosophy. An academic philosopher at a provincial German university, he led an uneventful and orderly life but his writings transformed modern thought. The son of a harness-maker, Kant was born on 22 April 1724 in Königsberg, the capital of East Prussia (now Kaliningrad, Russia). From 1740 to 1746 he studied mathematics, natural science, theology, philosophy and classical literature at the University of Königsberg. He then spent eight years as a private tutor to the children of various wealthy families in the local area before returning to the university as a lecturer. In 1770, at the age of 46, Kant was appointed to the university's chair of logic and metaphysics. By this time he had published a number of treatises on various scientific and philosophical matters, but his fundamental contributions to philosophy began only in 1781 with the publication of the epoch-making *Critique of Pure Reason*, which dealt with the main problems of metaphysics and epistemology. Other major works soon followed, including the *Groundwork of the Metaphysics of Morals* (1785) and the *Critique of Practical Reason* (1788), on moral philosophy, and the *Critique of the Power of Judgment* (1790), on aesthetics. Kant died on 12 February 1804. Almost all philosophical developments since then have been in some way influenced by his work. Kant's influence on educational thought, including both educational psychology and the philosophy of education, can be seen particularly in such thinkers as Pestalozzi and Herbart, who were influenced by and reacted to central themes in his epistemology and moral philosophy.

Despite a deep and abiding interest in the subject, Kant never wrote a systematic treatise on education. However, a work entitled *Immanuel Kant über Pädagogik* (1803) was published shortly before Kant's death by F.T. Rink, a former student.[2] This work, an English translation of which was published in 1960 as *Education*,[3] purports to be based upon Kant's notes for a series of lectures on pedagogy which he delivered on four occasions during the 1770s and 1780s. It is now known that this work in fact consists largely of paraphrases and misquotations of passages in Kant's other writings, which Rink has placed in some semblance of order.[4] It is therefore not an authoritative expression of Kant's views on education. In order to discover those views it is necessary to turn to Kant's main philosophical writings and the many remarks on education scattered through his discussions of ethics, history and politics.

The details of Kant's 'critical philosophy' are very complex, but the notion of autonomy provides one important unifying theme. Deeply influenced by the thought of Jean-Jacques Rousseau, Kant's epistemology and moral philosophy can both be seen as profound treatments of Rousseau's claim that 'obedience to a law which we prescribe to ourselves is liberty'.[5] In the *Critique of Pure Reason* Kant begins with the problem of how it is possible for us to have *a priori* knowledge of the world, such as that provided by mathematics and geometry. He argues that this could only be possible if the basic features of the world (such as space, time and causality) are dependent upon the essential nature of the mind. Human cognition is thus not simply the passive reception of data but also involves a structuring activity of the mind, in which certain innate 'categories' are imposed upon the 'manifold' given by the senses. Hence, our reason is autonomous in that its fundamental theoretical principles are not attempts to 'match up' to an external reality, but are rather laws that reason prescribes to itself and thereby to the experienced world. However, the deterministic, spatio-temporal world of our experience does not exhaust reality. Underlying the 'phenomena' that we experience there is a realm of 'noumena' of which we can have no determinate knowledge. Human beings exist both in the phenomenal realm, as causally determined parts of the natural order, and in the noumenal realm, as potentially autonomous moral agents. As moral agents we can be autonomous, Kant argues, because acting morally is not a question of obedience to something external to ourselves, such as God's commands or the norms of our culture. Instead, the moral law is again a law that reason prescribes to itself. An act is morally worthy only if it is done purely for its own sake, and not if it is done, for example, out of habit, out of deference to religious or political authority, or as a means to satisfy some further end, such as a desire for happiness. That is, according to Kant, the central fact about the moral law is that it is unconditionally obligatory. It must therefore constrain us simply in virtue of our rationality, and not because of any particular desires or preferences we might have. Hence in following the moral law we are moved to act solely by that which is essential to us, namely our reason, and are thereby autonomous. Kant further argues that for the moral law to be unconditional in this way it must be able to be consistently universalized, or in other words recognizable as binding by all rational beings, and must constrain us to respect the intrinsic value of all rational beings.

Kant thus sharply separates the sphere of nature from the sphere of morality, but he conceives of education as the process that links the two – that is, that leads the child from a state of compulsion by natural desire to a state of being able to perform the right act simply through an understanding that it is the right act. Hence, according to Kant, the ultimate aim of education should be the formation of moral character. In this he again shows the influence of Rousseau, but Kant has a very different conception of

61

the origin and basis of morality from Rousseau, and thus has a correspondingly different account of what is involved in the development of moral character. Moral character for Kant means the capacity to be motivated to act purely on the basis of a rational grasp of the moral law and not on the basis of some natural desire. Because he thus sees rationality as a necessary condition of morality, he holds that the child is neither naturally good nor naturally evil, but rather is naturally non-rational and thereby non-moral. The child does not begin life with a capacity for rational autonomy, but must be led to develop such a capacity through the process of education. This means that education cannot consist simply of the formation of certain habits (for example, through rote learning), for acting from habit is not acting morally. All education must be aimed at eventually leading children to think for themselves and become autonomous individuals capable of genuine moral action. Kant did not claim to know the best way to achieve this end, although he suggested that Rousseau's *Émile* contains many valuable suggestions. Kant did argue that most contemporary educational practices were useless, if not harmful, because they encouraged conformity and deference to authority rather than autonomy. He thus recommended the establishment of experimental schools in order to find the best methods for developing moral character in children, and was an enthusiastic supporter of the educational reformer J.B. Basedow, who ran the 'Philanthropinum' in Dessau, an experimental school based on Rousseau's principles.

Although Kant does not attempt to offer much in the way of concrete proposals for educational reform, he does provide a general outline of the process of education, as involving the three components of nurture, discipline, and instruction or cultivation. At the earliest ages children require only nurture. That is, they must have their natural needs for such things as food, warmth and affection met. As they grow older, they begin to require discipline. If children were left to themselves they would remain animals, acting on whatever immediate impulse they felt, and would never become teachable. They must therefore be forced to restrain their desires as a necessary precondition for the development of their rationality, but such compulsion must be kept to the minimum. Kant thus writes that 'Man must be disciplined, because he is by nature raw and wild. ... Discipline implies compulsion; but as compulsion is opposed to freedom and freedom constitutes man's worth, the compulsion of discipline must be so applied to the young that their freedom is maintained.'[6] This means that children should be allowed the maximum amount of freedom compatible with their own safety and the freedom of others. Kant thus argues, unlike Rousseau, that public education in schools is better than private education at home, for in school children will have more opportunity to interact with, and learn to respect the autonomy of others. The remaining component of education is instruction or cultivation. Children must develop their capacities for thought and understanding, and learn the skills and knowledge they will require as adults. Throughout such instruction children must not be taught just to do things mechanically, but must always be led to understand the point of what they are doing. For this purpose Kant tentatively recommends the use of the Socratic method of question and answer, and also suggests that the teaching of theory be united with practice. Most importantly, this component of education will also include moral instruction, or the inculcation of habits of performing outwardly right actions. Of course acting from such habits does not constitute genuine moral behaviour, but it is an important first step towards it. In the final part of moral instruction children must be led to understand the unconditional value of morality, and thus as it were re-establish their habits of right action on the correct foundation. This is the ultimate aim of education, and all prior discipline and instruction should be directed at leading children to take for themselves this final step into autonomy and genuine adulthood.

In aiming to develop moral character in the individual, the process of education thereby also aims at the development of an ideal political community. For someone who acts from an understanding of the moral law thereby wills a state of affairs in which the autonomy of all rational beings is respected and fulfilled. Such a state of affairs would be a political community with laws that corresponded to moral demands and this, Kant argues, would involve the organization of the polity on liberal and republican principles. He thus writes: 'Let education be conceived on right lines, let natural gifts be developed as they should, let character be formed on moral principles, and in time the effects of this will reach even to the seat of government.'[7] In fact Kant sees the development of the human being, from the natural state of infancy to the autonomy of adulthood, as parallel to the development of the human race as a whole. With the typical optimism of the Enlightenment, he sees history as the story of the human race struggling to perfect itself through its own efforts – passing from a state of barbarism to a state of civilization and finally, at some distant point in the future, achieving a state of genuine moral community and perfect political organization. Education thus has the momentous task not only of developing the moral character of the individual but also, in virtue of that, of working towards the perfecting of the human race.

Notes

1 I. Kant, *Lectures on ethics*, trans. L. Infield: New York, Harper and Row, p. 252, 1963.
2 *Immanuel Kant über Pädagogik* in *Kants gesammelte Schriften*, vol. 9, Berlin, de Gruyter, pp. 437–99, 1923.
3 Kant, *Education*, trans. A. Churton, Ann Arbor: University of Michigan Press, 1960.
4 See T. Weisskopf, *Immanuel Kant und die Pädagogik*, Zurich, EVZ-Verlag, 1970. For a brief summary of Weisskopf's claims, see L.W. Beck, 'Kant on Education' in his *Essays on Kant and Hume*, New Haven: Yale University Press, pp. 194–7, 1978.
5 J.-J. Rousseau, *The Social Contract*, trans. G. Cole, London: Everyman, Book 1, chapter 8, 1993.
6 Kant, *Lectures on ethics*, p. 249.
7 Ibid., p. 253.

See also

In this book: Herbart, Pestalozzi, Rousseau

Kant's major writings

The standard critical edition of Kant's works is *Kants gesammelte Schriften*, ed. Deutsche Akademie der Wissenschaften, 29 vols, Berlin, de Gruyter, 1902–83. Recommended English translations of his major works are as follows.

Critique of Pure Reason, trans. P. Guyer and A.W. Wood, Cambridge: Cambridge University Press, 1998.
Practical Philosophy, trans. M.J. Gregor, Cambridge: Cambridge University Press, 1996.
Critique of the Power of Judgment, trans. P. Guyer, Cambridge: Cambridge University Press, 2000.
Lectures on Ethics, trans. J.B. Schneewind and P. Heath, Cambridge: Cambridge University Press, 1998.
Political Writings, ed. H. Reiss, trans. H.B. Nisbet, Cambridge: Cambridge University Press, 2nd edn, 1991.

Further reading

Beck, L.W. 'Kant on Education' in his *Essays on Kant and Hume*, New Haven and London: Yale University Press, pp. 188–204, 1978.
Crittenden, P. *Learning to be Moral: Philosophical Thoughts About Moral Development*, Atlantic Highlands and London: Humanities Press International, chapter 7, 1990.
Frankena, W.K. *Three Historical Philosophies of Education: Aristotle, Kant, Dewey*, Scott, Foreman and Co., Glenview, chapter 3, 1965.
Herman, B. 'Training to Autonomy: Kant and the Question of Moral Education', in A.O. Rorty (ed.), *Philosophers on Education: New Historical Perspectives*, London and New York: Routledge, pp. 255–72, 1998.

ADAM B. DICKERSON

JOHANN HEINRICH PESTALOZZI 1746–1827

It is Life that forms and educates. (*Das Leben bildet.*)[1]

Pestalozzi's educational thinking arose from the republican ideology discussed intensively in the second half of the eighteenth century in Switzerland. Influenced by the historian and literary critic Johann Jacob Bodmer, the republican discussion in Pestalozzi's home town of Zurich became radical and emerged as a reform movement in which he was politically socialized during the 1760s. The ideal the young republicans stood for was a paternalistic, virtuous and aristocratic republic, where education would be integral to political understanding. Pestalozzi's political involvement, and the fact that his family did not belong to the upper class (his father died when he was 5), made it impossible for him to pursue a career either as a clergyman or a politician. In keeping with the anti-commercial republican ideology and the shining example of Rousseau's *Émile* (1762), he decided to become a farmer – dreaming of a virtuous life far away from the perceived vices and corruption of a trading city like Zurich.

In 1767 he went to Berne to begin an apprenticeship in modern farming.

Berne was an agricultural republic and the Bernese believed themselves to be the true heirs of the Roman Republic. The Bernese reformers were politically not as radical as those in Zurich and focused mainly on the improvement of agricultural production. It is in this context of the so-called 'economic patriots' that Pestalozzi first learned that a flourishing economy can be advantageous for country people as well. After buying land for a farm of his own, he fell victim to the disastrous European crop failure of 1771–2. That is the reason he installed looms in the cellar of his farmhouse, employing the poor of the neighbouring villages to weave cotton at low wages. Faced with the growing poverty around him, he decided to establish an institution for poor children in 1774. The idea was that children would support their own cost of living while working in cotton production, and Pestalozzi promised to teach the children the basic knowledge needed by poor people. However, the failure of the children to be able to support themselves led to the collapse of the institution in 1780.

His plea for a commercial basis to solve the problem of poverty prompted Pestalozzi to contact the most important Swiss journalist and editor of the eighteenth century, the philosopher and philanthropist Isaak Iselin. Iselin supported Pestalozzi's writings and helped him with his first novel *Lienhard und Gertrud* (1781), describing the reform of a corrupted village by a virtuous prince. Influenced by the German natural rights theories and the French physiocrats, Iselin, a prominent critic of Rousseau, had a deep impact on Pestalozzi's theoretical thinking, which became more cosmopolitan, Christian and natural-rights orientated. For more than a decade the relationship between our natural and our social state became the dominant topic of his thinking. He dropped the idea of people being an organic community by claiming a fundamental distinction between the political sphere of the state and the personal religious sphere. After Iselin's death in 1782, Pestalozzi started to write about social and political problems, such as crime and infanticide. His scepticism towards human nature grew and he dropped the optimistic, religiously tempered natural-rights republicanism of his deceased mentor. Man was regarded as a wild animal, selfish, pre- and basically anti-social, and education therefore was mainly identified with socializing by apprenticeship and with the function of preparing people for work. The social function of religion was limited to fostering harmony between the different social classes.

After the French Revolution of 1789, Pestalozzi focused on the meaning and role of freedom. Mainly influenced by German critics of the Enlightenment, like Jacobi, he developed a concept of personal freedom, identified by many scholars with Kant's ethics. In 1797 he published his most important philosophical work, the *Nachforschungen*, where he draws a parallel between individual development and that of the human species. On this basis, he tried to solve the fundamental social problems by proposing a third, inward state as the true solution of the conflict between the state of nature and the state of society. This state of inner morality is indebted to his view of true Christian religion and is advocated particularly for political leaders, since the temptation to abuse power seemed to Pestalozzi to be the major problem of social life. He rejected the idea of egalitarian democracy on the grounds that people were insufficiently educated and hence excessively selfish. Attainment of the state of morality would require, therefore, an early and complete socialization into the state of society in order to counteract this selfishness and promote strength of will. For this destruction of egoism, education in the family is crucial, for love is the central emotion within the familial context, and it is this which enables the child to foster its original good will. Strength of will is necessary for making judgments where there are conflicts between a feeling of injustice and love or altruism. The state of inner morality is necessary, therefore, if men are to decide and act in a moral way.

The Helvetic Revolution of 1798 changed Pestalozzi's life dramatically. Confident that this revolution would re-establish the old virtuous republic, and convinced of the moral integrity of the new leaders, he soon outlined a plan for an industrial institute for the children of the poor. Sent by the new government to Stans, Pestalozzi spent seven months in a convent trying to establish and organize an institute until the building was requisitioned by French troops in June 1799. These seven months were decisive in Pestalozzi's life and many scholars claim that Stans ought to be regarded as the birthplace of modern pedagogics. The basis of this assessment is a letter, published in 1807, in which Pestalozzi advocated, on the basis of his experience with the children, a new three-stage educational system. The first and basic stage is family life, where the main goal is to open the hearts of children by satisfying their basic needs. The second stage aims to encourage the practice, in everyday life, of the altruistic impulses inspired at the first stage. The third step introduces reflection on this everyday life, enabling children to understand what moral judgment is. Therefore, schools have to be guided by an overall educational concept of *Menschenbildung*, one of the 'formation of man', in which knowledge is always tied to moral standards.[2]

It is crucial to understand how, by 1807, this ideology of *Menschenbildung* had become so important. There are at least two central and, perhaps, somewhat opposed elements to be considered. The first is Pestalozzi's disappointment at the new political system. Parliamentary debates on the tax system convinced him that the selfishness of the élite is not to be abolished by the change of a governmental system. Politics, indeed, cannot be fundamental, since good politics is impossible unless people are first morally educated. This conclusion indicates a total inversion of the old republican doctrine. It is not in the political or public sphere that people must first be educated, but in the 'living-room' (*Wohnstube*). According to this inversion, it is not the Prince, but the mother, who is a moral leader. She becomes the pivotal point between God, children and the world outside the *Wohnstube*. The focus is not, in terms of Rousseau's dichotomy, the *citoyen*, but the human being: 'I'm not a Zuricher, I'm not a Swiss anymore. We don't have a fatherland anymore. Let us stay human beings and not forget the concerns of mankind until our death.'[3] Therefore the whole social and political destiny of a nation depended on true education, and the realization of this education depended on wise leaders.

The second element, though one reason for Pestalozzi's tremendous success after 1800, is rather at odds with the first. At the very moment when he was replacing the old paternalistic, republican ideology by the depoliticized, maternalistic idea of the *Wohnstube*, the Helvetic Government, especially the Kantian Minister of Science and Education, Philipp Albert Stapfer, believed Pestalozzi would be the ideal person to oversee the new school system. Pestalozzi's 'method' was deemed capable of solving all the educational ambitions of the young nation. The training of teachers would be based on Pestalozzi's notion of knowledge that was morally ennobling. In 1800 Pestalozzi became the first national trainer of teachers and saw his didactic schoolbooks printed.

The central thought behind this method was that all men are subject to basic forces, prestructured by eternal laws of nature. Hence the aim of education is to develop those forces naturally or psychologically. All three major dimensions of human nature – the head, the body and the heart – are to be understood as 'germs' awaiting this educational development, as Pestalozzi stresses in his crucial book *How Gertrude Teaches Her Children* (1801). Once developed naturally, they form together an overall harmony allowing morality to reign. Despite the apparent paradox of a *natural* transition from a state of nature to a state of morality – and despite the mechanistic character of the exercises in his didactic books – both Pestalozzi's method and his Institute in Burgdof were becoming famous throughout Europe. It was less the idea of founding the educational system of the modern state on familial or motherly love than the holistic ideology of *Menschenbildung* that fitted well into contemporary currents of thought, such as German romanticism and Humboldt's humanism. What was found appealing was less the mechanical method than the 'spirit' of that method, the view of education not as the teaching of knowledge, but as the strengthening and harmonizing of intellectual and other psychological forces. Testimonies to Pestalozzi's influence were the founding of Institutes based on his method in various countries, including Germany, France, England and the United States and the appearance, within the first four years after the publication of *Gertrud*, of almost 200 titles discussing Pestalozzi's method.

The first decade of the nineteenth century was a tremendous success and a tribute to Pestalozzi's skill in bringing educational concerns into the broader public discussion. After leaving Burgdorf for political reasons, Pestalozzi was offered several locations to accommodate his Institute. After a short collaboration with Philipp Emanuel Fellenberg in Münchenbuchsee, Pestalozzi moved his Institute 1805 to Yverdon in the French part of Switzerland, where he stayed until 1825. His success was, however, mixed: for his decontextualized method, based upon supposedly eternal and natural laws, could be applied in any political system. Prussia, for example, exploited his ideas in order to construct a national, military-orientated school system. Convinced that his method could be the basis of a national renaissance, Pestalozzi urged the Swiss Diet to make his method the foundation of school education in Switzerland. The official report published in 1810, however, showed that neither the mechanical method of teaching nor the familial structure of the Institute could be adapted to a public school system.

The second decade of the nineteenth century was one of confusion. Quarrels among Pestalozzi's collaborators and his own inability both to manage a large institution and to arrange for his succession led to the decline of the Institute. In this situation, Pestalozzi began not only to dissociate himself from his method, but to regret his attempt to reduce the theory of education to one of eternal natural laws. Increasingly turning to a Christian point of view, he worried, too, that his Institute, originally intended for poor children, mostly accommodated children of rich parents. In 1818, therefore, he opened a parallel institute for poor children, focusing on a broad apprenticeship that would enable the young to find a decent way of life. The experiment, however, failed only a year later for financial reasons. The integration of these poor children into the main Institute caused new problems, for differential treatment of wealthy and poor children was not accepted.

In 1813, Pestalozzi had started a book about his educational theory which appeared only in 1826 as the *Schwanengesang*, which may be regarded as his educational testimony. In this book, we find surprisingly many parallels to the *Nachforschungen* of 1797, though without the praise of political leaders and with a new emphasis on an optimistic Christian anthropology. While human forces are still understood teleologically, it is only in connection with children's initial development that eternal natural laws are deemed relevant. The emphasis is now on the practical relevance of different social and familial contexts: it is these which are decisive. Moreover, each individual is now held to possess a unique character, resistant to theoretical or systematic generalization. This signified the end of the dream that there could be a general, decontextualized and eternally valid theory of education. Real life within a specific context is the basis of education, and the better family life is, the better the education will be.

The *Schwanengesang* was published after Pestalozzi's return to his old farm. He died one year later in 1827. By this time, neither radical reform of the school system nor the idea of *Menschenbildung* was a fashionable topic. In Switzerland, however, the climate changed when the liberal movement won a majority in the 1840s. This movement needed its heroes and nobody was a more ideal representative of peacefulness, unselfishness, faithfulness and educational ambitions than Pestalozzi. Although, as is often the fate of such heroes, his texts were little read, Pestalozzi had become, by the end of the nineteenth century, a decisive symbol of national integration. His 150th anniversary in 1896 was the first national holiday. Beyond this political canonization – which in its own way was of educational import – educational researchers have continued to discuss the main problem that Pestalozzi had raised and addressed: the relation between school education and the public virtue of the men and women it has helped to 'form'.

Notes

1 *Schwanengesang*, in *Pestalozzis Sämtliche Werke* (*PSW*), XXVIII, p. 83.
2 *Stanser Brief*, in *PSW*, XIII, pp. 14f.
3 *Letter to David Vogel*, in *Pestalozzis Sämtliche Briefe*, vol. 5, Zurich, pp. 35f., 1961.

See also

In this book: Humboldt, Kant, Rousseau

Pestalozzi's major writings

Pestalozzis Sämtliche Werke (*PSW*), vols I–XXIX, Leipzig/Zurich, 1927–96.
Von der Freiheit meiner Vaterstatt, 1779, in *PSW*, I.

Über Gesetzgebung und Kindermord, 1783, in *PSW,* IX.
Meine Nachforschungen über den Gang in der Natur in der Entwicklung des Menschengeschlechts, 1797, in *PSW,* XII.
Wie Gertrud ihre Kinder lehrt, 1801, in *PSW,* XIII.
An die Unschuld, den Ernst und den Edelmuth meines Zeitalters und meines Vaterlandes, 1815, in *PSW,* XXIV.
Schwanengesang, 1826, in *PSW,* XXVIII.
Pestalozzi's Educational Writings, ed. J.A. Green, London, 1912.

Further reading

Hager, Fritz-Peter and Tröhler, Daniel (eds), *Pestalozzi – wirkungsgeschichtliche Aspekte. Dokumentationsband zum Pestalozzi-Symposium 1996*, Neue Pestalozzi-Studien, vol. 4, Berne: Haupt, 1996.
Oelkers, Jürgen and Osterwalder, Fritz (eds), *Pestalozzi – Umfeld und Rezeption. Studien zur Historisierung einer Legende*, Weinheim: Beltz, 1996.
Oelkers, Jürgen, Tröhler, Daniel and Zurbuchen, Simone (eds), *'Methode' um 1800: Ein Zauberwort? Der Erfolg Pestalozzis im historischen Kontext*, Neue Pestalozzi-Studien, vol. 7], Berne: Haupt, 2001, work in progress.
Stadler, Peter, *Pestalozzi. Geschichtliche Biographie*, vols 1 and 2, Surich, NZZ, 1988/93.
Tröhler, Daniel (ed.), *Pestalozzis 'Nachforschungen' I: textimmanente Studien / 18 neuendteckte Briefe Pestalozzis*, Neue Pestalozzi-Studien, vol. 5, Berne: Haupt, 1998.
—— (ed.), *Pestalozzis 'Nachforschungen' II: kontextuelle Studien. Tagungsakten des interdisziplinären Kolloquiums am Pestalozzianum im April 1998*, Neue Pestalozzi-Studien, vol. 6, Berne: Haupt, 1999.

DANIEL TRÖHLER

MARY WOLLSTONECRAFT 1759–97

> The most perfect education, in my opinion, is such an exercise of the understanding as is best calculated to strengthen the body and form the heart. Or, in other words, to enable the individual to attain such habits of virtue as well render it independent. In fact, it is a farce to call any being virtuous whose virtues do not result from the exercise of its own reason. This was Rousseau's opinion respecting men: I extend it to women.[1]

Mary Wollstonecraft was born in London into a family whose high-living, frequently abusive father repeatedly uprooted his wife and five children, squandered their money, and generally reduced their prospects. At the age of 18, after receiving a haphazard education in what by all accounts were miserable, unloving circumstances, she left home. Wollstonecraft spent the next nine years in the service of the three occupations that were then open to unmarried women. First she was a companion to a widow living in Bath. Next, with the help of a sister and a close friend, she established and ran a school for girls. When that venture failed, she became a governess.

One wonders what would have happened had not Joseph Johnson come to Wollstonecraft's rescue. When she was dismissed from her last position, the man who had published her 1786 tract *Thoughts on the Education of Daughters* gave her housing, hired her to write for his new *Analytic Review*, and admitted her to an intimate circle of literary friends whose number included William Blake, William Godwin and Tom Paine. In this heady environment Wollstonecraft came into her own. After calling Wollstonecraft's ideas in *Thoughts on the Education of Daughters* 'fragmentary, limited, and largely subjective', one biographer wrote, 'The great leap ahead in her thinking was still several years away.'[2] In 1790 Wollstonecraft published *A Vindication of the Rights of Man*, a reply to Edmund Burke's *Reflections on the Revolution in France*, that made her name known. But it was *A Vindication of the Rights of Woman*, published in 1792, that represented her great leap forward.

Praised by radical thinkers of the time and damned by the conservatives, Wollstonecraft's treatise brought her fame both in England and abroad. Indeed, arriving in revolutionary Paris in late 1792, the author of what is now universally acknowledged to be a feminist classic discovered that a French translation of that work had preceded her. Tragically, Wollstonecraft would not have the opportunity to repeat this achievement. In August 1797, shortly after her marriage to Godwin, the author of the acclaimed radical treatise *Enquiry Concerning Political Justice*, and just five years after the publication of *A Vindication of the Rights of Woman*, Wollstonecraft died after complications in childbirth. The child lived, however, and her portrait, like that of her mother, now hangs in London's National Portrait Gallery, for at age 19, Mary Wollstonecraft Godwin Shelley wrote the great gothic novel *Frankenstein*.

Susan B. Anthony, Elizabeth Cady Stanton, Emma Goldman, Virginia Woolf, Simone de Beauvoir are among the many feminists who have paid tribute in their own writings to Wollstonecraft. More often than not, however, *A Vindication of the Rights of Woman* has been read as a purely political text. Rousseau said in *Émile*, a book that Wollstonecraft discussed at length in her second *Vindication*, 'Read Plato's *Republic*. It is not at all a political work, as think those who judge books only by their titles. It is the most beautiful educational treatise ever written.'[3] In fact, the *Republic* is both a political and an educational treatise. So is Rousseau's *Émile* and so is *A Vindication of the Rights of Woman*.

A celebration of the rationality of women, *A Vindication* constitutes an attack on a view of female education espoused by Rousseau and countless others that would render women artificial and weak by subordinating cultivation of understanding to the acquisition of some 'corporeal accomplishment.'[4] To be a moral individual, Wollstonecraft said, one must exercise one's reason: 'The being cannot be termed rational, or virtuous, who obeys any authority but that of reason.'[5] The exercise of reason requires, in turn, that knowledge and understanding be cultivated. In other words, an education of the mind is essential for the rationality that is the mark of the truly virtuous person.

If the requirements of morality and also of immortality demand that woman's education develop her reason as fully as possible, so, according to Wollstonecraft, do the requirements of the wife–mother role. In vindicating women's rights, she did not abolish this position for women, or even invite men to share with women the tasks and responsibilities associated with life in the private home. Rather, she rejected the education in dependency that Rousseau prescribed. A woman must be intelligent in her own right, she argued, because she cannot assume that her husband will be intelligent. Moreover, 'Meek wives are, in general, foolish mothers.'[6]

Wollstonecraft was a true daughter of the Enlightenment. Reason served as the starting point for her political philosophy, as it did for John Locke's. She believed that there are rights that human beings inherit because they are rational creatures; that rationality forms the basis of these rights because reason, itself God-given, enables them to grasp truth and thus acquire knowledge of right and wrong; that the possession of reason raises humans above brute creation; and that through its exercise they become moral, and ultimately political agents. If, however, Wollstonecraft embraced a world-view shared by others, she was the one who argued systematically for bringing women into its domain. The originality and profundity of her ideas are to be found not in her Enlightenment philosophy *per se* but in the way she extended the fundamental tenets of that philosophy to women.

In *A Vindication of the Rights of Woman* Wollstonecraft set herself a threefold task: to rebut the presumption that women are not rational but are slaves to their passions; to show that if the rights of man are extended to females, women's domestic duties will not suffer; and to propose an education and upbringing for females that will sufficiently develop their ability to reason independently so that they will clearly deserve the same political rights as men. She carried out her first task brilliantly. Documenting the details of what has since been called female socialization, she displayed a sensitivity to the educative powers of the community perhaps matched only by Plato. She also proposed an experiment in living. Since women have been denied the very education necessary for the development of reason, it is impossible, she said, to know if they are rational by nature. Cultivate their understanding and then see if women are not rational creatures. By shifting the burden of proof onto those who would deny female rationality, she thus turned a question about political rights into one about education.

Wollstonecraft's approach to her second task was equally inspired. Incorporating the characteristics of rationality and personal autonomy that the Enlightenment associated with the good citizen into her redefinition of the wife–mother role, she made the performance of women's domestic duties dependent on the extension of the rights of man to woman.

To accomplish her third task Wollstonecraft made another remarkable move. It must be understood that although the idea of female education she put forward in *A Vindication* constituted a wholesale rejection of Rousseau's recommendations for the education of girls, it incorporated the education Rousseau designed for males. In other words, even as she appropriated the Enlightenment's philosophy of men's rights for women, she claimed Rousseau's philosophy of the education of boys and men for her own sex. Needless to say, Rousseau would have been horrified. And he would have been all the more distressed to learn that she wanted men and women not only to receive identical educations but to be educated together.

In the nineteenth and twentieth centuries reformers began translating Wollstonecraft's coeducational dream into practice. By the end of that period coeducation had become a fact of life for millions and millions of people around the world. The trouble is that this great historical development turned out to be a carrier of old inequities and the creator of new problems for women. Wollstonecraft could not have anticipated that when the official tracking system of separate schools with distinctive curricula for males and females became all but extinct, a *de facto* gender tracking system within coeducation would develop to take its place. But one has.[7] She could not have foreseen that the coeducational classroom climate would be a chilly one for women. But it is.[8]

In 1932 Virginia Woolf wrote that the originality of *A Vindication* 'has become our commonplace'.[9] So far as Wollstonecraft's educational vision is concerned, this judgment was premature. Now that history has caught up with Woolf's verdict, one task facing those who share Wollstonecraft's abiding interest in women's education is to ensure that coeducation is 'girl and woman friendly'. Another equally important task is to design an education for both sexes that incorporates the virtues of rationality and self-governance that Rousseau attributed to men and also the virtues of patience and gentleness, zeal and affection, tenderness and care that he attributed to women.[10]

Notes

1 Mary Wollstonecraft, *A Vindication of the Rights of Woman*, ed. Carol H. Poston, New York: Norton, p. 21, 1975.
2 Eleanor Flexner, *Mary Wollstonecraft*, New York: Coward, McCann, and Geoghegan, p. 61, 1972.
3 Jean-Jacques Rousseau, *Émile*, trans. Allan Bloom, New York: Basic Books, p. 40, 1979.
4 Wollstonecraft, *A Vindication of the Rights of Woman*, p. 23.
5 Ibid., p. 191.
6 Ibid., p. 152.
7 Jane Roland Martin, *Coming of Age in Academe*, New York: Routledge, pp. 77–84. 2000.
8 Ibid., pp. 85–90.
9 Virginia Woolf. 'Mary Wollstonecraft.' in Wollstonecraft, *A Vindication of the Rights of Woman*, p. 221.
10 Jane Roland Martin, *Reclaiming a Conversation*, New Haven: Yale University Press, chapter 5, 1985.

See also

In this book: Plato, Rousseau, Locke

Wollstonecraft's major writings

Maria, A Fiction, in *A Mary Wollstonecraft Reader*, ed. Barbara H. Solomon and Paula S. Berggren, New York: New American Library, 1983.
Thoughts on the Education of Daughters, in *A Mary Wollstonecraft Reader*, ed. Barbara H. Solomon and Paula S. Berggren, New York: New American Library, 1983.
A Vindication of the Rights of Men, in *A Mary Wollstonecraft Reader*, ed. Barbara H. Solomon and Paula S.Berggren, New York: New American Library, 1983.
A Vindication of the Rights of Woman, ed. Carol H. Poston, New York: Norton, 1975.

JOHANN GOTTLIEB FICHTE

Further reading

Eisenstein, Zillah, *The Radical Future of Liberal Feminism*, New York: Longman, 1981.
Flexner, Eleanor, *Mary Wollstonecraft*, New York: Coward, McCann, and Geoghegan, 1972.
Ferguson, Moira and Janet Todd, *Mary Wollstonecraft*, Boston: Twayne Publishers, 1984.
Krammick, Miriam Brody, 'Introduction', Mary Wollstonecraft, *A Vindication of the Rights of Woman*, Harmondsworth: Penguin Books, pp. 7–72, 1982.
Martin, Jane Roland, *Reclaiming a Conversation*, New Haven: Yale University Press, 1985.

JANE ROLAND MARTIN

JOHANN GOTTLIEB FICHTE 1762–1814

The summons to free self-activity is what one calls education.[1]

J.G. Fichte was born in Rammenau, in Western Saxony on 19 May 1762. After attending school at Pforta, he entered the theology faculty of Jena University. Fichte soon undertook an exhaustive study of Kant's critical philosophy and 1792 saw the anonymous publication of *Attempt at a Critique of All Revelation*, which was initially thought to be penned by Kant himself. The subsequent realization that the author was a young, relatively unknown philosopher caused a sensation within academic society, and Fichte was offered the prestigious chair of philosophy at Jena University. On his arrival in 1794, he rapidly composed the first presentation of his *Wissenschaftslehre*[2] ('Doctrine of Science'), the 1794–95 *Foundations of the entire Wissenschaftslehre*. Fichte conceived of his *Wissenschaftslehre* as the completion of Kant's transcendental idealism. Drawing upon Kant's conception of transcendental subjectivity, Fichte sought to ground all 'science' or systematic knowledge in the spontaneous activity of the 'Absolute I'. The entire *Wissenschaftslehre* was initially intended to derive transcendental theories of aesthetics, nature, religion, natural right and morality from the spontaneity of the I.[3] Only the latter two received systematic exposition, the *Foundations of Natural Right* appearing in 1796–7 and the *System of Ethical Theory* in 1798.

Despite his initial success at Jena, Fichte became unpopular with his colleagues and superiors. Whilst this was partly due to his reputation as a dangerous, revolutionary thinker,[4] it was also due to his volatile personality, Fichte habitually responding to his critics in an arrogant and abusive manner.[5] The apparently atheistic sentiments expressed in a 1798 article[6] therefore provided an ideal opportunity for revenge. The ensuing 'Atheism Controversy' resulted in Fichte's dismissal in 1799. Fichte moved to Berlin where he continued to develop and teach his *Wissenschaftslehre*. In 1805 he accepted an appointment at the University of Erlangen. This appointment was terminated by the Napoleonic invasion of Prussia in 1806, Fichte fleeing to the safety of Königsberg. With the declaration of peace of 1807, Fichte

73

returned to occupied Berlin and, after developing a plan for the foundation of a new university, delivered his infamous *Addresses to the German Nation*, a series of speeches promoting the unity and autonomy of the German nation. In 1810, Fichte was appointed as the first Rector of the new University of Berlin. Whilst supervising the development of the university, Fichte also continued to revise and develop his *Wissenschaftslehre*. He died on 29 January 1814, at the age of 52.

The following seeks to provide an account of Fichte's early conception of education. This conception is intimately related to, and even presupposes, Fichte's first presentation of his transcendental idealism. I shall therefore preface this account with a brief discussion of the fundamental features of the latter.

The 1794–5 *Wissenschaftslehre* constitutes an attempt to found theoretical and practical knowledge upon the spontaneous activity of the absolute I, to discover the 'necessary' 'acts of the mind' that facilitate human cognition and action.[7] The activity of this I is threefold: it posits itself, it posits the not-I, and it posits the relation of mutual limitation between I and not-I. From this threefold positing, the foundations of theoretical and practical knowledge are to be derived. In his treatment of theoretical knowledge, Fichte presents this activity as constituting the fundamental structures of reality, determining the basic aspects of the world. For Fichte, all being is essentially *for* the I, is posited by the I. Now to say that the activity of the I *constitutes* reality is not to say that it materially produces reality in its entirety. Fichte is *not – pace* Schelling and Hegel – advocating a doctrine of 'subjective idealism', according to which the world simply *is* the I.[8] Indeed, he describes his particular variety of critical idealism as 'real-idealism or ideal-realism'.[9] The 'realistic' aspect of Fichte's idealism is to be found in the doctrine of the *Anstoss*.[10] Admittedly, this is a highly attenuated form of realism – the *Anstoss* being neither an external object, nor a thing in itself, but *'an original fact occurring in our mind'*.[11] Yet whilst it is necessarily *for* the I, the *Anstoss* designates an element of brute contingency that cannot be attributed to, nor explained by, the I's activity. This contingency is both a hindrance (*Anstoss*) to the I's infinite activity *and* a stimulus (*Anstoss*) to further activity. It is by virtue of the necessity encountered in the *Anstoss* that the I is led to determine itself (limit itself) and the not-I.[12]

In the practical part of the 1794–5 *Wissenschaftslehre*, the *Anstoss* is presented as the 'feeling' (*Gefühl*) encountered by the finite, empirical I. This feeling limits its activity, determining the finite I sensuously. Yet it also provokes it to further activity. For insofar as the finite I is determined heteronomously, it cannot act in accordance with its nature as infinite, spontaneous I. It must therefore overcome this hindrance to its activity, and attempt to realize its absolute autonomy. Yet this can never be achieved, the absolute I being presented as a regulative Idea, an unachievable goal for rational thought and action. We *should*, however, endlessly *strive* to attain this Idea, overcoming all that is not-I in an attempt to achieve absolute autonomy. This, according to Fichte, is the 'vocation of man in itself'.

But how is the ordinary, non-philosophical person to become aware of this ethical vocation and of the autonomy and freedom which she should strive to achieve? Given Fichte's conviction that 'The majority of men could sooner be brought to believe themselves a piece of lava in the moon than to take themselves for an I',[13] the attainment of such awareness would seem unlikely. Is this awareness merely granted to those philosophers who have grasped the truth of Fichte's transcendental idealism? The answer to these questions is to be found in Fichte's conception of education.

In his 1794 essay *Concerning the Concept of the Wissenschaftslehre* Fichte tells us that philosophers must not give laws to the human mind but must rather attempt to describe it, assuming the role of 'writers of pragmatic history'.[14] This declaration of the philosopher's task is of crucial importance. For Kant, the goal of a 'pragmatic history' is the promotion of the happiness and welfare of the human race. It achieves this goal by teaching humanity to avoid misfortune through 'prudence'.[15] For Fichte, the task of the *Wissenschaftslehre* is 'pragmatic' insofar as it serves an educative function, awakening humanity to its autonomy and spontaneity. He differs from Kant, however, insofar as the ultimate goal of this 'history' is not happiness, but morality – the activity of the agent in accordance with a rational, self-given moral law.

The notion of 'pragmatic history' plays a central role in the 1794–5 *Wissenschaftslehre*, Fichte telling us that the *Wissenschaftslehre* is to be 'a pragmatic history of the human mind'.[16] This history is provided in the brief – yet crucial – 'Deduction of Representation' which completes the theoretical portion of the *Wissenschaftslehre*.

Having derived the productive imagination and the *Anstoss* from an exploration of the proposition 'The I posits itself as limited by the not-I',[17] Fichte turns in this section to consider the way in which this account might be transmitted to the non-philosophical consciousness. Fichte argues that the non-philosophical consciousness is, under the supervision of the philosopher, to traverse the series in reverse, proceeding from sensation to reason. Through repeated reflection upon its initial encounter with the *Anstoss* it is to construct its world and, having done so, grasp its own autonomy and spontaneity – realizing that its activity underlies the representation of an apparently mind-independent world. The transcendental philosopher does not direct this process, nor coerce the non-philosophical consciousness into accepting the truths of transcendental idealism. She is merely a silent guide, pointing out the activity that occurs.

This process is significant in several respects. It is the means whereby the non-philosophical consciousness gains access to the standpoint of transcendental philosophy. For having attained reason, it can now begin to study the *Wissenschaftslehre*, grasping the abstract foundational principles with which it begins and its complex discussion of theoretical knowledge. It can therefore explore the foundations and limits of theoretical reason. Yet it can also, crucially, proceed to the practical part of the work – the exploration of the foundations of practical knowledge. It can, in other words, grasp the necessity of acting in accordance with a self-given rational law. The *Deduction of Representation* is therefore the *means* whereby the natural consciousness realizes its moral vocation. This is its truly 'pragmatic' aspect.

But what of the relation between the non-philosophical consciousness and the transcendental philosopher who 'calmly follow[s] the course of events'?[18] The role of the philosopher calls to mind Rousseau's *Émile*, the transcendental philosopher's unobtrusive supervision constituting a type of 'negative education'. The philosopher has initiated the process (by pointing out the *Anstoss*), and observes this process. Yet the non-philosophical consciousness is unaware of any education taking place.

An interesting implication of this process is that the non-philosophical consciousness may, having reached the standpoint of transcendental philosophy, communicate this knowledge to another non-philosophical consciousness. The tutee can become the tutor, training another tutee, who in turn trains another, and so on. The 'Deduction of Representation' therefore suggests a circular educative process without end. This, of course, implies that the tutee must become aware that she has been educated. She must, in other words, be able to recognize that another free being has educated her.[19]

This leads us to an aspect of Fichte's philosophy that is central to his conception of education, his concern with intersubjectivity, with the nature, and philosophical significance of, the relations *between* subjects. This concern is first introduced in *Some Lectures Concerning the Scholar's Vocation* (1794). The question of the vocation of the scholar poses, Fichte claims, several other questions, including that of the 'vocation of man in itself' (*an sich*), the vocation of man considered in isolation from 'any relation to rational beings like himself'.[20] We have already discussed this vocation: it is the finite subject's striving to realize the autonomy and rationality of the absolute I. Now insofar as the finite agent is dependent upon the not-I (ultimately, the *Anstoss*), she must – in order to achieve autonomy – transform the not-I (or 'nature') in accordance with her necessary practical concepts of how things *ought* to be.

In the second lecture, Fichte points out that man does not live alone but with other beings like himself, in society (*Gesellschaft*), which Fichte defines as 'the relationship in which rational beings stand to each other'.[21] Now, according to Fichte, it is only through this relationship that the agent becomes aware of, and realizes, the vocation of man as such. This relationship is a specific relationship that *should* obtain between human agents insofar as they are *rational beings*. It is a relationship in which the participants acquire a sense of freedom and moral obligation, *learning* to be ethical. It is therefore an *educative* relationship. Yet it is also – and this is of fundamental importance – a non-coercive, *reciprocal* relationship. For it is entirely wrong, Fichte claims, to coerce another to realize his freedom.[22] The other must be invited to realize her freedom through open and free interaction. In short, each member of this relationship must be both teacher and tutee, generously offering knowledge, but equally ready to receive it. Fichte describes this as the 'loveliest bond of all – the bond of free, mutual give and take' and suggests that people of all races and creeds may enter into it.[23]

Now through such an educative relation, each member of humanity can realize her vocation, everyone striving together to achieve absolute autonomy and rationality. If this unrealizable goal could be attained each member of society would be a completely rational, ethically perfect being. They would be entirely identical and unified, the autonomous legislation of each subject according with the universally valid moral law. Such a society would be Kant's 'kingdom of ends', a society in which each member is both author and subject of the law. We must strive to achieve this goal, the vocation of man in society consisting in an endless process of 'unification' or 'communal perfection', a process sustained by a specific mode of intersubjectivity – education.[24] The vocation of the scholar is to guide and supervise this process, to place her knowledge in the service of the human species.[25] Following Lessing, Fichte claims that the 'scholar is the *educator* of mankind'.[26] And insofar as the transcendental philosopher is a scholar, her true vocation lies in the application of her philosophy – the transformation of theory into practice.

Fichte's conception of education is further developed in his 1796–7 *Foundations of Natural Right*. In section 1 of this work Fichte attempts to demonstrate that intersubjectivity is a condition for the possibility of self-consciousness, claiming that the infinite activity of a rational being must be limited if it is to attain self-consciousness. This limitation is no longer to be explained by the abstract device of the *Anstoss*, but by a primordial encounter with an other rational being in which the subject is 'summoned' by the other rational being to exercise its free activity.

Fichte claims that this relationship of 'recognition' (*Anerkennung*) is an *educative* relationship, in which each educates the other to an awareness of her autonomy – 'The summons to free self-activity is what one calls education.' Fichte thereby places education and intersubjectivity at the heart of his transcendental idealism, claiming that the rational being only achieves self-consciousness and autonomy through an educative relationship to another finite rational being – that subjectivity and intersubjectivity are interdependent. 'All individuals must be educated to be men; otherwise they would not be men.'[27] Education is therefore not merely something which takes place within the confines of the classroom, nor simply a social phenomenon – but the very means whereby we *become* human, that is, grasp our autonomy and rationality.

The issue of the influence of Fichte's early conception of education is hard to assess. Whilst Fichte's later work influenced German educational practices, his early work has had little direct impact. This is undoubtedly due to the fact that Fichte's philosophy has, until recently, been eclipsed by the idealism of Schelling and Hegel. Fichte's 'subjective idealism', it has been claimed, is riddled with contradictions and inconsistency, his emphasis on intersubjectivity conflicting with his notion that the world is 'created' by an Absolute I. Whilst such an interpretation of Fichte's project is entirely mistaken, it owes its popularity to the fact that it was first advanced by Schelling and Hegel. Indeed, in Hegel's case, this misleading interpretation served to obscure his enormous debt to Fichte – a debt that is clearly visible in his concept of education. For it is Fichte's 'Deduction of Representation' that provided the inspiration for Hegel's acclaimed *Phenomenology of Spirit*, in which natural consciousness is cultivated to the standpoint of science. Insofar as Hegel's philosophy has greatly influenced educational thought, it is perhaps fair to say that Fichte has exerted a hidden and indirect influence upon our thinking about education.

Notes

1 Fichte, *Foundations of Natural Right*, ed. F. Neuhouser, trans. M. Baur, Cambridge: Cambridge University Press, p. 38, 2000. Translation modified.
2 Following the practice established by D. Breazeale, I leave Fichte's neologism *Wissenschaftslehre* untranslated.

3 *Fichte – Early Philosophical Writings*, trans. D. Breazeale, Ithaca and London: Cornell University Press, p. 135, 1988.
4 This reputation was largely due to Fichte's 1793 treatise on the French Revolution.
5 On this point, see *Fichte – Early Philosophical Writings*, pp. 341–54.
6 *On the Belief in the Divine Governance of the World.*
7 *Concerning the Concept of the Wissenschaftslehre* in ibid., p. 126.
8 Fichte is making the far less extravagant claim that a fundamental subjective activity underlies, and facilitates, all human knowledge. To say that all being is 'for' the I, is simply to say that it is impossible to somehow 'remove' this activity and examine a mind-independent 'reality'.
9 Fichte, *The Science of Knowledge*, trans. P. Heath and J. Lachs, Cambridge: Cambridge University Press, p. 247, 1982.
10 Ibid. p. 189
11 Ibid. p.196. Translation modified.
12 An excellent explanation of the *Anstoss* is to be found in D. Breazeale's essay 'Check or Checkmate? On the Finitude of the Fichtean Self', in *The Modern Subject: Conceptions of the Self in Classical German Philosophy*, Albany: SUNY Press, pp. 87–114, 1995.
13 *Fichte – Early Philosophical Writings*, p.162, fn. 2.
14 Ibid. p. 131.
15 See Kant, *Grounding for the Metaphysics of Morals*, trans. J.W. Ellington, Indianapolis and Cambridge: Hackett Publishing Co. Inc., p. 26, fn. 5, 1993.
16 Fichte, *The Science of Knowledge*, pp. 198–9.
17 Ibid. p. 122. Translation modified.
18 Ibid. p. 199.
19 I owe these points to Alexis Philonenko's excellent discussion of the 'Deduction of Representation', in Philonenko, *La liberté humaine dans la philosophie de Fichte*, Paris: Librairie Philosophique J. Vrin, pp. 303–16, 317–32, 1980.
20 *Fichte – Early Philosophical Writings*, p. 152.
21 Ibid., pp. 153–4.
22 Ibid., p. 159.
23 Ibid. p. 161.
24 Ibid., p. 160.
25 Ibid. p. 172.
26 Ibid., p. 175.
27 Fichte, *Foundations of Natural Right*, p. 38. Translation modified.

See also

In this book: Hegel, Kant, Rousseau

Fichte's major writings

Sämmtliche Werke, 8 vols, ed. I.H. Fichte, Berlin: Berlin, 1845.
Gesamtausgabe der Bayerischen Akademie der Wissenschaften, ed. R. Lauth, H. Jacob and H. Gliwitsky, Stuttgart-Bad Cannstatt, Frommann-Holzboog, 1964–.
Early Philosophical Writings, trans. D. Breazeale, Ithaca and London: Cornell University Press, 1988.
Foundations of Natural Right, ed. F. Neuhouser, trans. M. Baur, Cambridge: Cambridge University Press, 2000.
Foundations of Transcendental Philosophy (Wissenschaftslehre) nova methodo (1796/99), trans. D. Breazeale, Ithaca and London: Cornell University Press, 1992.
Introductions to the Wissenschaftslehre and Other Writings (1797–1800), trans. D. Breazeale, Indianapolis: Hackett Publishing Company, Inc., 1994.

The Science of Knowledge, trans. P. Heath and J. Lachs, Cambridge: Cambridge University Press, 1982.

Further reading

Breazeale, D., 'Check or Checkmate? On the Finitude of the Fichtean Self', in *The Modern Subject: Conceptions of the Self in Classical German Philosophy*, Albany: SUNY Press, 1995.
Hohler, T.P., *Imagination and Reflection: Intersubjectivity in Fichte's Grundlage of 1794*, The Hague: Nijhoff, 1982.
Neuhouser, F., *Fichte's Theory of Subjectivity*, Cambridge: Cambridge University Press, 1990.
Zöller, G., *Fichte's Transcendental Philosophy: The Original Duplicity of Intelligence and Will*, Cambridge: Cambridge University Press, 1998.

JAMES A. CLARKE

WILHELM VON HUMBOLDT 1767–1835

> The grand, leading principle, towards which every argument unfolded in these pages directly converges, is the absolute and essential importance of human development in its richest diversity.[1]

John Stuart Mill used this quotation of Humboldt as the motto for his famous Essay *On Liberty* that was published in 1859. While writing the essay Mill read Humboldt's *The Sphere and Duties of Government*, translated into English and published in 1854 when Mill started writing *On Liberty*. Originally written in 1792 Humboldt's book was published only in fragments during his lifetime. The German *Ideen zu einem Versuch, die Gränzen der Wirksamkeit des Staats zu bestimmen*[2] was part of the complete edition of Humboldt's work. [3] It was widely ignored in Germany but became a main source for liberalism in the English language in the nineteenth century.

Humboldt's *The Sphere and Duties of Government* was a work of youth. Wilhelm von Humboldt and his younger brother Alexander (1769–1869), the famous explorer and natural scientist, were educated privately; neither attended school. Wilhelm von Humboldt started his university studies in 1787 at the University of Francfort/Oder near Berlin. He left Francfort after a year in order to go to the Reform University of Göttingen to study law and classical philology. He visited revolutionary Paris in 1789 and finished his studies in 1790. Two events influenced the early work on government: the revolution in France and Humboldt's experiences of Prussia's civil service. He was in the service for only one year and resigned in 1791. After marrying Karoline von Dacheröden in the same year Humboldt lived for ten years without any office in private seclusion as an independent scholar.

His extensive studies were influenced by an enduring discussion of Kant's philosophy, his readings of classical antiquity, and Friedrich August Wolf's ideas on philology and education. Humboldt became part of the Weimar circle, a close friend to both Goethe and Schiller, without publishing anything apart from small fragments. Not by chance his first book was devoted to a topic of the Weimar circle, namely Goethe's epic poem *Hermann and Dorothea* that was published in 1798 and became an immediate success among the educated public. Humboldt shared the view of his contemporaries and wrote a very favourable review that appeared in 1799.[4]

In 1802 Humboldt accepted a civil office. He became Prussian counsellor[5] at the Holy See in Rome where he lived with his family for more than six years. Prussia was defeated by Napoleon's troops in 1807. After that the Prussian state was completely reorganized, especially the system of higher education. Humboldt entered the section of culture and public education within the Prussian Ministry of the Interior.[6] For two years (1809/1810) he was one of the main forces behind educational reforms and the founding of the University of Berlin that very soon became one of centres of European intellectual life. Matthew Arnold mentioned Humboldt's leading role in his *Schools and Universities on the Continent* (1868) at a time when Humboldt was widely forgotten in his own country.

The University of Berlin opened in 1810. After that Humboldt changed office and became legation counsellor of the Prussian court in Vienna where he took part in the Vienna Congress (1814/1815) that re-established Prussia's role as a superior force in Europe. Humboldt was counsellor at the Prussian legation in London for two years (1817/1818) but left the civil service at the end of 1819 after serious conflicts with the Prussian Chancellor Hardenberg. After that Humboldt lived again for ten years in privacy. In 1830 he returned to office and became minister in Prussia's state council (for biographical details see Menze 1975, Scurla 1976).

His work was wide ranging, constructed around central themes and subjects of what were later called philosophical anthropology, but it was never finished. Only small parts were published during Humboldt's lifetime, and his influence did not grow until the end of nineteenth century when he was discussed by such scholars as Wilhem Dilthey and, in education, Eduard Spranger. Humboldt's interest in education was led by his studies of classical antiquity. The spirit of especially Greek antiquity is considered to be the measure of modern individuality. The Greek's 'character' for Humboldt was the role model for the ideal individuality (*Werke* Vol. II, p. 26).[7] Life was raised by the Greeks to ideal forms and the ideal forms were transformed into life again (ibid., p. 29). This was done by the five media of culture, namely art, poetry, religion, morals and history (ibid., p. 32). These are Humboldt's fields of interest, later supplemented by studies in the history of language that influenced no less an author than Noam Chomsky.

Humboldt's theory of education is not of a piece. It is fragmented as is the whole of his work, but clearly recognizable. The basic idea is the relation between man and world. Education is interchange and development, not scholarship in the sense of organized knowledge. Humboldt called it the 'interaction' between the susceptibility and self-acting of man (*Werke* Vol. I, p. 237). Knowing and acting have to be organized within a man's circle of experience, providing what is called 'accurate development of the powers of man' (ibid., p. 51). The notion of 'development', quoted by Mill, is twofold. On the one hand Humboldt refers to the evolution of mankind within the succession of generations (ibid., pp. 51–2); on the other hand 'development' is considered to be the way for human individuals to reach the general ideas of mankind (ibid., p. 54). Thus 'individualism' is not subjectivism. Humboldt's thoughts are Platonic; the aim of education is to transform the 'individuals of real life' into *general ideas* (ibid., p. 54) that will guide the life of individuals without forcing them to go in a specific direction (ibid., p. 55).

In a work of 1797,[8] Humboldt mentioned Shaftesbury's concept of the 'inward form'[9] that is of crucial importance for the whole German classical philosophy of education (Oelkers 1999). In Humboldt's terms, experience means continuously transforming man's observations of world and life into the mind's inner form which is the centre of learning (*Werke* Vol. I, p. 347). Learning is nothing else than the 'continuous correspondence between our mode of *being* and our mode of *judging*', i.e. our existence in praxis and theory (ibid.; my italics). Both modes work together. Humboldt thus overcomes the Kantian dualism of theoretical and practical reason and thereby the theory of the two worlds. Reasoning means observing and concluding *in one single* 'character' that cannot be divided into one part that is 'practical' and another part that is 'theoretical' (ibid., p. 348). What Humboldt called 'character' should be considered as a unique form of individuality that cannot be the object of education but *is* education's subject.

Here Humboldt followed the late Kant, especially the theory of aesthetic judgement in the *Critique of Judgement*. Education should strive for the 'beautiful individuality' that is able to build its inner form through *all* experience and not just through scholarship. What is later called the 'wholeness' of education has Humboldt as one of its main sources. Education is not something imposed upon a *tabula rasa*, but also not the mere development of an innate nature. Humboldt contradicts both Locke and Rousseau. His notion of 'character' refers to the *singularity* of the individual that will learn by himself only what is homogeneous to his inner form. As soon as the character is awoken, it adopts, out of all the things that influence it, only those that are fitted to it (ibid., p. 348).

This does not exclude general standards[10] but they have to be made concrete by individuals. '*Bildung*',[11] in the final analysis, is that experience of finding out what are the 'imprints of humanity and humanism' in the experience of life, while excluding everything that is 'mechanical' (ibid., pp. 508–9). The best ideas of mankind are to be found in authentic poetry, philosophy and literature, and true 'inner education'[12] is to be gained through cultivation and not by instruction. It is, in the eyes of Humboldt, the central error of educational theory to seek specific 'laws' of human action from which the working principles of education can be derived. On the contrary, what really influences the continuous building of one's character is 'true art' and 'true philosophy'. And there is no limit to the improvement of man (ibid., p. 512).

In all these aspects Humboldt is a Platonist, following the strong influence of Neoplatonism in the English and continental development of art, literature and, to some extent, also philosophy in the eighteenth century (see Baldwin and Hutton 1994; for Neoplatonism also Hankins 1994). This was relevant, too, for Humboldt's late theory of historiography,[13] which considered history to be guided by ideas, so that all historians should endeavour to describe the working of ideas behind the events of history. History is not contingent but guided by ideas, just as all individuals are. In this sense history too is education. 'The business of the historian is to portray the striving of an idea to gain reality' (Humboldt 1971, p. 303). This is because history is composed out of individuals, and 'every human individuality is nothing else than an idea come into appearance' (ibid., p. 302).

In one of Humboldt's fragments written before the *Sphere and Duties of Government*,[14] a short (and the only) definition is given of what should count as 'education' and what should not. 'All education originates from the inner soul of man, all external arrangements or events can only initiate but not cause education' (ibid., p. 87). This idea, the self-causation of education, became Humboldt's strongest single influence on what was later called neo-humanism. Even though Humboldt did not found anything like a school of thought, his theory of education, fragmented as it is, was used to react against formal schooling in the nineteenth century and to promote progressive humanism. Today's link with the psychology of 'wholeness' is actually *not* what Humboldt had in mind. He is Platonist enough to expect morality[15] to develop as the result of an education that it is guided by ideas and not, or not exclusively, by schools.

John Stuart Mill learned exactly this from Humboldt: The 'Greek ideal of self-development' (Mill 1974, p. 127) points to the 'cultivation of individuality', not just to individuality as such (ibid., p. 128). 'Individuality' *is* 'development' (ibid.). Any attempt by the state 'for moulding people to be exactly like one another' (ibid., p. 177), that is, to equalize their morality and thus the inner world of individuals, contradicts this premise of the *cultured individual*. Humboldt did not find many readers in the English-speaking world even though he formulated a theory, though very fragmented, that looked for a third way besides sensualism and naturalism, which were the two main forces in the eighteenth-century theory of education and are still influential. In Germany, Humboldt was mostly regarded as one of the founding fathers of the theory of *Bildung*, although he did not create this theory, despite the claim made by the editor of his *Gesammelten Schriften*.

But Humboldt is to be read not simply as a philosopher who shaped categories like *Bildung*. He was at the same an active diplomat, a politician with high influence in the state of Prussia and throughout Europe, and a scholar working in very diverse fields of knowledge. What he called education or *Bildung* is not a specifically German concept of apolitical 'inwardedness', but an experience of culture that has, in one way or another, consequences for the formation of mind and character without the intervention of the state. The *cultivation* of the inner world is what should be the result of education that is nothing less than a lifelong process of observation, learning and thinking. Humboldt thus had in mind not a narrow, but a broad concept that considered education to be the flexible sum of all intellectual and especially aesthetic experiences a man or a woman can have.

Notes

1 *The Sphere and Duties of Government* (Humboldt 1854).
2 *Ideas for an attempt to define the limits of effectiveness of the state.*

3   *Gesammelte Werke*, ed. by Carl Brandes, Vols 1–7, Berlin 1841–52. Humboldt's *Gesammelte Schriften* were published later by the Prussian Royal Academy of Sciences, 17 Vols, Berlin 1903–36.
4   *Aesthetische Versuche. Erster Teil. Ueber Goethes 'Hermann and Dorothea'*, Braunschweig, 1799.
5   *'Ministerialresident'*.
6   Home Office.
7   *Latium und Hellas oder Betrachtungen über das classische Alterthum* in *Werke*, Vol. II, pp. 25–64, 1806.
8   *Plan einer vergleichenden Anthropologie* in *Werke*, Vol. I, pp. 337–75.
9   *'Innere Geistesform'* in *Werke*, Vol. I, p. 347.
10 *'Massstäbe'* in *Werke*, Vol. I, p. 507.
11 Education in the sense of inner development.
12 *'Innere Bildung'* in *Werke*, Vol. I, p. 511.
13 *Ueber die Aufgabe des Geschichtsschreibers.* Published first in *Abhandlungen der historisch-philosophischen Klasse der königlich Preussischen Akademie der Wissenschaften aus den Jahren 1820–1822*, Berlin, pp. 305–322, 1822 (Humboldt 1971, pp. 289–304).
14 *Ueber den Einfluss des Theismus, Atheismus und Skeptizismus auf die Sitten der Menschen* (1788/1789) (Humboldt 1971, pp. 69–92).
15 *'Innere moralische Bildung'* (Humboldt 1971, p. 92).

See also

In this book: Arnold, Kant, Mill, Locke, Rousseau, Plato

Humboldt's major writings

The Spheres and Duties of Government, London, 1854.
Studienausgabe, Vol. 2, *Politik und Geschichte*, ed. K. Müller-Vollmer, Frankfurt am Main, Fischer Taschenbuch Verlag, 1971.
Werke, ed. A. Flitner and K. Giel, Vol. II, *Schriften zur Altertumskunde und Aesthetik. Die Vasken*, 3rd edn, Darmstadt: Wissenschaftliche Buchgesellschaft, 1979.
Werke, ed. by A. Flitner and K. Giel, Vol. I, *Schriften zur Anthropologie und Geschichte*, 3rd edn, Darmstadt: Wissenschaftliche Buchgesellschaft 1980.

Further reading

Baldwin, A. and Hutton, S. (eds), *Platonism and the English Imagination*, Cambridge: Cambridge University Press, 1994.
Hankins, J., *Plato and the Italian Renaissance*, Leiden/New York/Köln, E.J. Brill, 1994 (Columbia Studies in the Classical Tradition, ed. by W.V. Harris, Vol. XVII).
Menze, C., *Die Bildungsreform Wilhelm von Humboldts*, Hannover/Dortmund/Darmstadt/Berlin, Hermann Schroedel Verlag 1975 (*Das Bildungsproblem in der Geschichte des europäischen Bildungsdenkens*, ed. E. Lichtenstein and H.-H. Groothoff, Bd. XIII).
Mill, J.S., *On Liberty.* ed. G. Himmelfarb, Harmondsworth/Middlesex: Penguin Books, 1974 (first edn 1859).
Oelkers. J., 'The Origin of the Concept of "Allgemeinbildung" in Eighteenth-Century Germany', *Studies in Philosophy of Education*, 18 (1–2), pp. 25–41, 1999.
Scurla, H., *Wilhelm von Humboldt. Werden und Wirken*, Düsseldorf: Claassen Verlag, 1976 (first edn 1970).

JÜRGEN OELKERS

GEORG WILHELM FRIEDRICH HEGEL 1770–1831

[O]urs is a birth-time and transition to a new era.[1]

G.W.F. Hegel was born in Stuttgart on 27 August 1770. At the age of 18 he attended the seminary at Tübingen where he befriended the poet Hölderlin and F.W.J. Schelling. Having completed his studies at the seminary, Hegel embarked upon a career as a private tutor, serving families in Berne and Frankfurt. During this period of employment, Hegel wrote several theological and political studies which anticipate many of the themes of his later philosophy. Upon the death of his father in 1799, Hegel received a modest inheritance, which allowed him to concentrate upon his studies and travel to Jena, which – largely due to the influence of Fichte and Goethe – had become the capital of German letters. At Jena, Hegel resumed contact with Schelling, who had earned a reputation as an innovative disciple and expositor of Fichte. In 1801, Hegel wrote a brief essay which was instrumental in Schelling's break with Fichte.[2] In this essay, Hegel outlined the difference between Fichte's merely 'subjective idealism' and Schelling's 'Identity Philosophy' (*Identitätphilosophie*). Yet he also subtly articulated his own conception of philosophy. Hegel soon received a teaching post at Jena University, and began to lay the foundations for his system of Absolute idealism. Shortly thereafter, he decided to write his *Phenomenology of Spirit*, a work intended as the 'introduction' and 'first part' of his philosophical science. In 1806 Napoleon invaded Jena. The first edition of the *Phenomenology of Spirit* was published in 1807.

Hegel moved to Bamberg and, after a brief period as a newspaper editor, he accepted the post of headmaster of Nuremburg Gymnasium. There, he refined and developed his philosophical system, teaching a 'Philosophical Propaedeutic' to his students. In 1812, Hegel published the first part of his monumental *Science of Logic*, a work which sought to articulate the dialectical development of the 'Concept'. Hegel conceived of this inter-related system of categories as constituting the fundamental structure of reality, determining the basic features of thought and being. It was, in other words, a logical ontology – the categories determining reality in all its diversity. In 1816, Hegel was appointed professor at Heidelberg University, where he continued to teach and develop his system, lecturing on the history of philosophy, political philosophy and aesthetics. 1817 saw the publication of his *Encyclopaedia of the Philosophical Sciences*.

From 1818 to 1831 Hegel lectured at the University of Berlin. In 1820, he published his highly influential systematic political philosophy – the *Philosophy of Right*. At Berlin, Hegel reached the zenith of his reputation, becoming Prussia's most celebrated and influential philosopher. In 1830, he became rector of the university of Berlin but, the following year, died of cholera. He was buried, somewhat ironically, next to J.G. Fichte – the very philosopher whose influence he had helped to undermine.

Whilst Hegel's early work is largely concerned with political and theological issues, it anticipates many of the themes of his later philosophy. In his early essays on religion, Hegel inveighs against the transformation of Christianity into a body of 'positive' doctrine – a set of external laws which are simply to be obeyed.[3] Such a body of doctrine, Hegel claims, stifles the living nature of religion, subordinating religious sentiment and feeling to religious authority. In contrast to this conception of religion, Hegel praises the 'folk religion' of Greek society, a political, public religion expressed in festivals, celebrations and the customs of everyday life. Hegel therefore supports the notion – characteristic of writers such as Hölderlin and Schiller – that the age of the Greeks was an age of unity, in which individual and community, state and society, thought and feeling were inseparably united. For these writers, this age of unity is irretrievably lost to us, having given way to the divisive, fragmented nature of modern society. Yet Hegel also held the view that the contradictions of modern society would be resolved in a new age, modernity giving way to a new period of unity. This re-established unity would differ from that of the Greek period, insofar as it retained and incorporated the differences of the modern age. It was to be a higher unity, a unity in which the contradictions of modern society were 'sublated' (*aufgehoben*) – simultaneously transcended, cancelled and preserved.[4]

It was this conception of the divided, fragmented nature of modern society that Hegel brought to his study of the philosophy of his day, a study largely inspired by the young Schelling. For Hegel, modern philosophy was characterized by fundamental oppositions and contradictions. It opposed knowledge to faith, reason to inclination, the infinite to the finite, thought to being, and subject to object. Whilst Kant's critical philosophy had emphasized the spontaneity of thought, it had imposed limits upon this spontaneity, retaining an unknowable realm of things in themselves. And whilst Fichte's idealism had advanced Kant's idealism by establishing the Absolute subject as the source of all reality, it had done this at the expense of objectivity and nature. It was, according to Schelling and Hegel, a merely 'subjective idealism' which failed to grasp the true nature of the Absolute, the true nature of the absolutely unconditioned reality (in theological terms 'God' – not as a transcendent entity, but as the totality of all that is).

Following Schelling, Hegel argued that this merely subjective idealism – in which thought produced being – had to be complemented by an account of the way in which being produced thought. The Absolute had to be grasped as the identity of subject and object, as the identity of thought and being. Yet Hegel considered Schelling's conception of this identity as an undifferentiated conflation of terms to be unsatisfactory.[5] The Absolute must, Hegel maintained, be understood as the 'identity of identity and non-identity' – the separation characteristic of finite experience must be given its due.[6] Far from being an immediate, original unity, the Absolute must be grasped as a cumulative *process* of interrelated moments, the entirety of this process being the Absolute. An adequate system of 'Absolute idealism' must display the Absolute in its entirety, grasping the fundamental structures of the Absolute and its expression as humanity and nature.[7]

This desire to present the Absolute in its entirety provided the inspiration for one of the most ambitious philosophical systems ever constructed. Hegel conceived of this system as the culmination and completion of all philosophy. Yet he also felt that it was of the utmost significance for humanity, allowing it to realize its true potential. It would allow humanity to overcome its divided, fragmented state and ascend to a new age. Philosophy would not create this new age, but merely facilitate the transition. Yet if philosophy was to fulfil this role, it had to be accessible to *all*. It could not, *contra* Schelling, be merely the 'esoteric possession of a few' talented individuals.[8] This desire to make truth accessible to all led Hegel to provide an account of the way in which ordinary consciousness comes to attain knowledge of the Absolute. It is this account which lies at the heart of the *Phenomenology of Spirit*.

Central to Hegel's account of education in the *Phenomenology* – and to his concept of education in general – is the term *Bildung*. This term does not simply mean 'education', but also 'cultivation' and 'formation'. A popular literary genre in late-eighteenth-century Germany was the *Bildungsroman* – a novel in which the protagonist acquired knowledge through a series of experiences. Examples of this genre include Goethe's *Wilhelm Meister's Apprenticeship* (1795–6) and Novalis' *Henri von Ofterding* (1802). The idea of education developed in these works influenced Hegel's *Phenomenology* – a work which he describes as 'the detailed history of the *education* [*Bildung*] of consciousness itself to the standpoint of Science'.[9]

The *Phenomenology* opens with a consideration of how natural consciousness can be compelled to loosen its grip on its knowledge (a knowledge riven with division) and embark on the path to Absolute Knowing. Clearly, some sort of critique is necessary – and therefore a 'criterion'. The problem of the 'criterion' (*Maßtab*) is central to Hegel's strategy, and its solution constitutes one of his most central innovations. The philosopher cannot, Hegel argues, simply judge knowledge against certain preconceived standards and norms. For to assume that a certain conception of knowledge is valid is simply to beg the question, to judge knowledge by a standard that itself requires justification and which ordinary consciousness does not recognize. There is, however, a solution to this problem – a solution that lies *within* ordinary consciousness. This is that we let ordinary consciousness criticize *itself*, judge its *own* knowledge against its *own* conception of truth. We therefore 'do not need to import criteria, or to make use of our own bright ideas and thoughts during the course of the inquiry'. Rather we must engage in the activity of 'pure looking on' (*das reine Zusehen*), simply observing the process that unfolds when ordinary consciousness is left to its own devices.[10] Here the influence of Fichte is clearly evident, the philosopher observing the development of the non-philosophic consciousness.

This process consists of a series of interrelated 'forms of consciousness' – particular relations of consciousness to its reality. These 'forms' consist of natural consciousness' conception of its relation to its object (its conception of knowledge) and its conception of what truth really is. The latter is the 'criterion' against which consciousness tests its knowledge. Now consciousness inevitably finds that the attempted realization of its conception of knowledge conflicts with its conception of truth, destroying both conceptions. It is therefore driven to a new form of consciousness – a new conception of truth and a new conception of knowledge corresponding to this conception.

This repeated destruction of its knowledge is a highly traumatic experience for natural consciousness. The negation of its knowledge seems a merely empty, abstract negation – simple destruction. Furthermore, each form of consciousness is not simply an abstract theoretical conception of knowledge and truth, but a relation of consciousness to its world. Hegel therefore describes the progress of natural consciousness as the 'pathway of *doubt*, or more precisely as the way of despair', consciousness constantly being driven from one unsatisfactory view of its world to another.[11]

Yet what seems, from the 'one-sided' perspective of natural consciousness, to be a 'pathway of despair', has a quite different aspect for the observing philosophical consciousness. What appears to natural consciousness to be a meaningless, destructive process is seen by the 'we' who observe as a gradual progression towards truth occurring 'behind the back' of natural consciousness.[12] From our privileged perspective, 'we' see the necessity whereby each form of consciousness, through internal contradiction, passes into the next. We also see that each form of consciousness is 'preserved' by its successor, each new form of consciousness containing the trace of the preceding forms. What natural consciousness saw as merely empty, abstract negation, we grasp as *'determinate* negation' (*bestimmte* Negation),[13] as negation with *content*.

We see, in other words, the cumulative dialectical process whereby natural consciousness ascends to the position where it can attain to Absolute Knowing. The *Phenomenology* is therefore described by Hegel as the 'science of the experience of consciousness', and the process which consciousness undergoes is its 'education' or 'cultivation' (*Bildung*) to the standpoint of Absolute Knowing.

It should be noted that this formative process is also a social and historical process, consciousness coming to know itself as Spirit (*Geist*) through the realization that it is inseparably related to a community of other selves. The concept of Spirit is first introduced in Hegel's discussion of self-consciousness, Hegel claiming that a relationship of *mutual 'recognition'* (*Anerkennung*) between agents is the condition for the possibility of self-consciousness. For Hegel, the foundation of self-consciousness is a community of selves in which each grants the other the dignity and freedom she herself requires. This '"I" that is "We"', and "We" that is "I"' is precisely the Concept of Spirit.[14] Natural consciousness, however, has yet to attain 'the experience of what Spirit is'.[15] It must first pass through the asymmetrical relation of Lordship and Bondage,[16] and several forms of fractured, divided subjectivity. It must also pass through the forms of Reason, finally coming to question its conception of itself as an independent, individual rational agent. Having reached Spirit, consciousness must now follow its complex historical development. Starting with the collapse of the unified Greek city-state, consciousness passes through the fragmented, alienated world of 'Culture' (*Bildung*) and finally reaches the 'moral world-view' of critical philosophy and the Romantic notion of 'Conscience.' An examination of the conflict between the latter two positions leads consciousness first to Religion (an attempt to grasp the Absolute through images and metaphors) and then to Absolute Knowing. There, consciousness attains the realization that both the social world and the world of nature are expressions of Absolute Spirit, that its experience is both the manifestation of, and means for, the Absolute's self-realization. Its world of experience is no longer riven with contradiction, but fundamentally intelligible as the expression of the Absolute. Having attained this insight, consciousness may now proceed to Hegel's logical ontology – to an exploration of the fundamental structure of the Absolute. Yet it may also, and this is of crucial importance, actively contribute to its age, consciously aiding the development and realization of Absolute Spirit.

Natural consciousness has thereby undergone a formative process in which it passed from sense certainty to Absolute Knowing. It has acquired truth through a painful and difficult process, the true significance of which was not apparent to it. Yet having completed this process it is wiser and more experienced. For Hegel, then, truth is not to be gained through isolated study or rumination, but through the vicissitudes and adversities of experience. Knowledge and truth are cultivated through experience.

Hegel's influence upon educational thought is, like his influence upon philosophy in general, monumental. He exerted a profound influence upon Marx, whose account of history as a progressive, conflict-driven process drew inspiration from Hegel's historical dialectic. Whilst many Marxists rejected Hegel as a source of inspiration, G. Lukács drew upon Hegel's *Phenomenology* to provide an account of the formation of class consciousness. T.W. Adorno – writing from a position fundamentally opposed to that of Lukács – drew upon Hegel's emphasis on negativity to provide an account of experience in capitalist society. Hegel also exerted a significant influence on the pragmatism of J. Dewey. The latter's concept of education owes a considerable debt to Hegel's 'science of the experience of consciousness'.

Notes

1   Hegel, *Phenomenology of Spirit*, trans. A.V. Miller, Oxford: Oxford University Press, p. 6, 1977.
2   Hegel, *The Difference Between Fichte's and Schelling's System of Philosophy*, trans. H.S. Harris and W. Cerf, Albany: SUNY Press, 1977.
3   Hegel, *Early Theological Writings*, trans. T.M. Knox, Chicago: University of Chicago Press, 1948.
4   This conception of *Aufhebung* is first articulated in the 1800 revision of the *Spirit of Christianity and its Fate* in ibid.
5   This is the source of Hegel's oblique criticism (in the *Phenomenology of Spirit*) of Schelling's conception of the Absolute as the 'night in which all cows are black'. Hegel, *Phenomenology of Spirit*, p. 9.
6   This conviction is first expressed in the 1801 essay *The Difference Between Fichte's and Schelling's System of Philosophy*, p. 156.
7   As Hegel writes in the *Phenomenology* – 'The True is the whole. But the whole is nothing other than the essence consummating itself through its development', p. 11.
8   Ibid., p. 7.
9   Ibid., p. 50.
10 Ibid., p. 54. Translation modified.
11 Ibid., pp. 49–50.
12 Ibid., p. 56.
13 Ibid., p. 51.
14 Ibid., p. 110.
15 Ibid., p. 110.
16 This infamous section of the *Phenomenology* clearly has affinities with Marx's account of the class struggle. A highly influential Marxist reading of the *Phenomenology* which regards this section as central is provided in A. Kojève, *Introduction to the Reading of Hegel*, trans. J. H. Nichols, Jr., Ithaca and London: Cornell University Press, 1980.

See also

In this book: Kant, Fichte, Dewey

Hegel's major writings

Werke in zwanzig Bänden, ed. E. Moldenhauer and K. M. Michel, 20 vols, Frankfurt: Suhrkamp Verlag, 1969ff.
Hegel's Phenomenology of Spirit, trans. A.V. Miller, Oxford: Oxford University Press, 1977.
Hegel's Science of Logic, trans. A.V. Miller, Atlantic Highlands, New Jersey: Humanities Press, 1989.
Hegel's Logic, trans. W. Wallace, Oxford: Oxford University Press, 1975.
Hegel's Philosophy of Nature, trans. M.J. Petry, 3 vols, London: Allen & Unwin, 1970.
Hegel's Philosophy of Mind, trans. W. Wallace and A.V. Miller, Oxford: Oxford University Press, 1971.
Hegel's Philosophy of Right, trans. T.M. Knox, Oxford: Oxford University Press, 1967.

Further reading

Beiser, F.C. (ed.), *The Cambridge Companion to Hegel*, Cambridge: Cambridge University Press, 1993.
Inwood, M., *A Hegel Dictionary*, Oxford: Blackwell Publishers Ltd, 1992.
Mure, G.R.G., *The Philosophy of Hegel*, London: Oxford University Press, 1965.
Taylor, C., *Hegel*, Cambridge: Cambridge University Press, 1975.
Westphal, M., *History and Truth in Hegel's Phenomenology*, Bloomington and Indiana: Indiana University Press, 1998.
Wood, A. 'Hegel on Education', in A. Rorty (ed.), *Philosophers on Education – New Historical Perspectives*, London and New York: Routledge, pp. 300–18, 1998.

JAMES A. CLARKE

JOHANN FRIEDRICH HERBART 1776–1841

> Pedagogy, considered as a science ... has to contend with a special difficulty. ... All its major concepts lie within the circle of common talk and likewise in the well-worn rut of what everyone thinks he knows.[1]

It could be argued that the most influential pedagogical theory of the nineteenth century was that of Herbart. At the same time it was the theory most easy to forget. Herbart's pedagogy was the first internationally received system of education, sucessful in almost every civilized country, yet this success happened *after* Herbart's death in 1841. During his lifetime he was a well-known German philosopher who occasionally wrote on educational subjects but was not regarded as the founder of a pedagogical school of thought. His few pupils were theologians and philosophers who had loose contact among each other and were not over-zealous in propagating their teacher's work as the leading theory in philosophy and education. This was done by the pupils more than a decade after Herbart's main work was written.

Johann Friedrich Herbart was born and raised in Oldenburg, a residential town in northern Germany near Bremen. Herbart studied the philosophy of Kant while he was still in school. He quit the *Gymnasium* of Oldenburg in 1794 with a Latin speech that compared the practical philosophy of Cicero and Kant, one of Herbart's lifelong interests. In October of the same year he began his studies at the University of Jena where he became the 'first pupil' of Johann Gottlieb Fichte and was completely overwhelmed by the power of Fichte's philosophy and lectures. Fichte was appointed to the University of Jena only half a year before Herbart arrived. In Jena, Fichte developed his teachings on science and freedom,[2] but his radical views alienated the pupil from his teacher. Herbart broke off his studies and left Jena for a private tutorship in Switzerland.

From 1797 to 1800, Herbart taught the sons of Karl Friedrich Steiger, who represented one of the leading families of the Canton of Berne. During this stay Herbart visited Pestalozzi in Burgdorf several times, and this inspired his critique of the Pestalozzian method. This critique, published in 1802, was Herbart's first publication in the field of education.[3] At that time Herbart lived in Bremen while preparing his return to university. In 1802 he became *Privatdozent* at the University of Göttingen[4] and a member of the Faculty of Philosophy in 1805 after he refused a call to the University of Heidelberg. Herbart was appointed *professor extraordinarius* for philosophy, but went in 1809 to the University of Königsberg to take over the Chair earlier held by Kant. Herbart stayed in Königsberg for more than twenty years, developed his own system of philosophy, and returned to Göttingen in 1833. In 1811 he married Mary Jane Drake (1791–1876), daughter of an English businessman in Memel.

Herbart's life was unspectacular with one exception, the protest of the so-called '*Göttinger Sieben*' – seven professors of the University of Göttingen[5] – against a change of constitution that was proclaimed by the King of Hannover, Ernst August, in 1837. At that time Herbart was Dean of Faculty and became jointly responsible for the removal of the Seven. Because the Seven were liberals, Herbart was accused of being 'reactionary', although in a formal sense their removal was correct. But from then on Herbart's philosophy and his system of education were often considered to be 'conservative', or at least *not liberal*, in a political sense. This ascription is astonishing because Herbart argued strongly against the conservative or collectivistic form of state education that became influential in Prussia and Germany after the famous *Addresses to the German Nation* of his former teacher Fichte.[6] Fichte's *Addresses* were one of the main sources for Germany's nationalistic theory of education in the nineteenth century that was built around the notion of *Gemeinschaft*, originally a term of political Romanticism and then used as the basis of a corporative concept of national political education. Herbart warned *against* 'a pedagogy serving the state'[7] and criticized the politization of education. A 'true education' is one that does not concern itself with the state and political interests, but is education *for its own sake.*

This was the main point in Herbart's later famous, but at time of publication largely unnoticed,[8] *General Education* of 1806.[9] The child's *individuality* is the focus for education. Education must leave individuality as undisturbed as possible, but at the same time it should have results which change children. To solve this paradox, Herbart distinguished between a child's 'very recognizable' individuality and the development of 'character'. Children have to learn the rational use of their will; 'will' meaning the opposite of 'moodiness' or 'longing'. Neither of these, unlike the will, involves *resoluteness*:[10] 'character' is the *manner* of resoluteness. But this is only half of what must constitute education, because individuality needs a second dimension, namely *many-sideness*. Character is one-sided, but individuality is more than character because it has will *and* interests. Interests do not need resoluteness but instruction. So the art of education is to protect individuality and develop its two dimensions.

The most popular part of Herbart's *General Education* is the chapter on instruction, not that on education in the sense of moral training of character. But both, instruction and education, belong together, because both serve the two general purposes of education. Herbart made a strict distinction between *possible* and *necessary* purposes, between those purposes that prepare the pupil for what he might possibly encounter as an adult, and those that are necessary for any future that is to come. The first purpose is associated with many-sidedness and personal interests, the second with morality[11] and character. Morality excludes acting by chance while many-sidedness requires virtuosity. This, Herbart called his 'major consideration' in educational theory.

His complaints about the flatness of education as a science, its proximity to trivial public affairs and its lack of sharp categories were communicated in 1824 as part of Herbart's annual report on the *Pedagogical Seminar* in Königsberg. Herbart was director of this Seminar alongside his duties as Chair of philosophy and education. The Seminar trained teachers and Herbart often complained that the 'rights of theory' were neglected or despised within teacher training. It is ironic that the international success of 'Herbartianism'[12] was mainly caused by the development of teacher training in the second part of the nineteenth century in Europe and the United States. Herbart, who had direct experience of the narrow and vague application of educational terms in teacher training, postulated a theory of education that should be 'profound, precise and complete', and the teaching of which must demand high standards and 'rigorous thinking'.[13]

Herbart's *General Education* of 1806 served as something of a blueprint for work to come, but what came afterwards lost contact with the initial version of his educational theory. Roughly speaking, Herbart developed and refined his metaphysics, mathematical psychology and ethics, but not his theory of education. He tried to bind education to psychology and ethics, claiming in his later work[14] that the aims of education are set by ethics and its means by psychology, yet he never showed in any detail how this would work out. In a sense, Herbart, who is often considered to be the 'founding father' of a scientific approach to education, quite failed to develop a 'science of education', located *between* psychology and ethics.

Herbart's later attempt to found 'pedagogy' upon psychology and ethics changed neither the earlier theory nor its terminology.[15] The main distinction between 'will' and 'character', on one hand, and 'interest' and 'many-sidedness', on the other, remained. What was really influential was the *scheme* of 'means' and 'ends' that seems to be at the heart of methods in education right up to the present. But the later concept was not connected with what was very early[16] called 'educational tact', that is, the delicate balance between theory and praxis in the realm of pedagogy that was considered to require the mediation of educational science. 'Tact' is regarded as a middle way between too much and too little theory and this way has to be sought in every educational situation through personal judgment. Herbart, in a certain way, gave up this aesthetical approach to education in his later work in favour of psychology and ethics. Not only did this shift the problem, but the connections between psychology, ethics and education were left undetermined.

Nor is this an accident, since Herbart's psychological theory says nothing about children, their education and its aims. It is a general psychology based on a mathematical calculus and developed around the concept of the rise and fall of ideas in the mind,[17] the dynamic of which could be described mathematically. This 'physics of mind' influenced many psychological theories in the nineteenth century up to Freud, but was not, or at least not successfully, used in education. Similarly Herbart's realistic – in contrast to idealistic – metaphysics has been influentual, especially in American Pragmatism,[18] as has been his critique of Kant and his alternative to Kant's critique of practical reason. Herbart rejected the idea that the basic problem of morality can be solved through Kant's categorical imperative. Instead he developed a theory of 'practical ideas' that lay behind all moral institutions and all moral reasoning. But he never succeeded in transferring his general theories to education. His *General Practical Philosophy*[19] hardly mentioned education and made no attempt to demonstrate the application of ethics to education. Even though closely coupled by Herbart[20] himself, ethics and education seemed to belong to two different worlds.

The failure is interesting and far-reaching in so far as the theory or science of education cannot simply be regarded as the combination of psychology and ethics. In this connection, the early work of Herbart is of crucial importance. Later he concentrated his philosophy on other disciplines that were heavily influenced by a *non-idealistic* approach that helped to develop post-Kantian psychology, ethics and metaphysics. The first to overcome 'Herbartianism' was psychology. The empirical turn in the mid-nineteenth century made clear that Herbart's psychology is neither observational nor empirical and could not be used for statistical descriptions or laboratory experiments. The last discipline to overcome 'Herbartianism' was educational theory, mainly because Herbartian pedagogy had no real rivals for several decades. This changed at the end of nineteenth century with the rise of child psychology and progressive education.[21] After that Herbart's international influence on theory of education vanished surprisingly quickly.

Notes

1 Herbart, *Sämtliche Werke*, Vol. 14, p. 223 (trans. Dunkel 1970, p. 68).
2 *Wissenschaftslehre, Freiheitslehre*. For the *Jena Wissenschaftslehre* see Perrinjaquet (1994).
3 *Pestalozzis Idee eines ABC der Anschauung untersucht und wissenschaftlich*

ausgeführt (1802). The second edition (1804) is important due to the additions (especially the essay on 'the aesthetical presentation of the world being the main business of education').

4 It was very unsual to present dissertation and habilitation-work in one year.

5 Led by the liberal historian Friedrich Christoph Dahlmann (1785–1860).

6 *Reden an die deutsche Nation* (1808). Fichte's 'Reden' (lectures) were given in Berlin starting on 13 December 1807 while Berlin was still occupied by Napoleon's troops. The core of the argument is a radical theory of national liberation organized by educational institutions that should work on the basis of Pestalozzi's method.

7 'Pädagogik im Dienste des Staates' quoted from: *Ueber Erziehung unter öffentlicher Mitwirkung* (Education under public participation) (1810) (Herbart 1964, pp. 143–51).

8 Herbart was a newcomer to an established scene of writers in education in Germany. Around 1800 the discourse was far-reaching and led by figures such as August Hermann Niemeyer (1754–1828) and Friedrich Heinrich Schwarz (1766–1837) who wrote successful textbooks with profound theories of education.

9 *Allgemeine Pädagogik aus dem Zweck der Erziehung abgeleitet* (Göttingen 1806; English translation, Herbart's *Science of Education*, 1892).

10 *Sittlichkeit.*

12 The story of 'Herbartianism' has newly gained research interest, after having been considered for a long time to be just a story of decay (see Metz 1992, Cruikshank 1993, Coriand and Winkler 1998).

13 *Sämtliche Werke*, Vol. 14, p. 234.

14 *Umrisse pädagogischer Vorlesungen* (second edn 1841) (Herbart 1964-5, pp. 155–283).

15 See Oelkers (2001, chs 2–3).

16 *Erste Vorlesungen über Pädagogik* (1802).

17 *Vorstellungen.*

18 Charles Sanders Peirce used Herbartian concepts for his general philosophy.

19 Written after *General Education* and published in 1808.

20 The aim of moral education is to implant the ideas of the right and the good into the mind of the child so that they can be object if his will in all their sharpness (Herbart 1964-5, p. 43).

21 See Metz (1992).

See also

In this book: Pestalozzi, Kant, Fichte

Herbart's major writings

Sämtliche Werke: In chronologischer Reihenfolge, ed. K. Kehrbach and O. Flügel, vols 1–19, Langensalza: Hermann Beyer & Söhne 1997–1912 (reprinted Aalen: Scientia, 1964).

Pädagogische Schriften, vols 1–3, ed. W. Asmus. Düsseldorf/München: Helmut Küpper, 1964-5.

Allgemeine Praktische Philosophie, new edition, Leipzig: Leopold Voss, 1873.

Zwei Vorlesungen über Pädagogik. Diktate zur Pädagogik, in B. Adl-Amini, J. Oelkers and D. Neumann (eds), *Pädagogische Theorie und erzieherische Praxis. Grundlegung und Auswirkungen von Herbarts Theorie der Pädagogik und Didaktik*, Bern/Stuttgart: Paul Haupt, pp. 106–19, 1979.

Science of Education, trans. H. and E. Felkin, Heath: Boston, 1892.

Outlines of Educational Doctrine, trans. A. Lange, London: Macmillan, 1901.

Further reading

Asmus,W., *Johann Friedrich Herbart. Eine pädagogische Biographie*, vol. I: *Der Denker. 1776–1809*, vol. II: *Der Lehrer. 1809–1841*, Heidelberg: Quelle & Meyer, 1968, 1970.

Coriand, R. and Winkler, M., *Der Herbartianismus – die vergessene Wissenschafts-geschichte*, Weinheim: Deutscher Studien Verlag, 1998.

Cruikshank, K., 'The Rise and Fall of American Herbartianism. Dynamics of an Educational Reform Movement', Ph.D. Diss., University of Wisconsin, 1993.

Dunkel, H.F., *Herbart and Herbartianism: An Educational Ghost Story*, Chicago/London: The University of Chicago Press, 1970.

Metz, P., *Herbartianismus als Paradigma für Professionalisierung und Schulreform. Ein Beitrag zur Bündner Schulgeschichte der Jahre 1880 bis 1930 und zur Wirkungs-geschichte der Pädagogik Herbarts und der Herbartianer Ziller, Stoy und Rein in der Schweiz*, Berne *et al.*, Peter Lang, 1992.

Oelkers, J., *Einführung in die Theorie der Erziehung*, Weinheim/Basel: Beltz, 2001.

Perrinjaquet, A., *Some Remarks Concerning the Circularity of Philosophy and the Evidence of Its First Principle in the Jena Wissenschaftslehre*, in D. Breazeale and T. Rockmore (eds), *Fichte. Historical Contexts, Contemporary Controversies*, New Jersey: Humanities Press, pp. 71–95, 1994.

JÜRGEN OELKERS

FRIEDRICH WILHELM FROEBEL 1782–1852

> By this, in the period of childhood, man (the child) is placed in the center of all things, and all things are seen only in relation to himself, to his life.[1]

Froebel was born in Oberweissbach, Thuringia on 21 April 1782. His mother died when Friedrich was 9 months old. His father, a Lutheran minister, remarried. Friedrich's stepmother left him to the care of servants and his older brothers. For a time he was sent to a school for girls. He gained a reputation as 'stupid, mischievous, and untrustworthy'.[2]

From 11 to 15 he lived with his mother's brother, who sent him to a school for boys. Those were happy years, though due to 'his general backwardness and lack of strength and agility, it was some time before he could take his proper share in the games'.[3] Still he was frustrated that school was unconnected to real life. This early frustration became a central theme in his educational thought – the importance of practical activity as integral to children's education. Judged by his father and stepmother unfit for university, at 15 he was apprenticed to a forester for two years. There he began a lifelong 'religious' relationship with nature, discovering in nature the harmony he found lacking between people.

In 1799, he used a small legacy from his mother to enter the University of Jena to study science and mathematics. There he loaned money to a brother, who did not repay him. Falling into debt, he spent nine weeks in the university jail until his father paid his debt on the condition that he give up his paternal inheritance. For the next three years he worked in various jobs – in a forestry department, as a surveyor, and as an estate manager.

In 1805, with a small inheritance from his uncle, the 23-year-old Froebel went to Frankfurt to study architecture, but instead began his career as an educator. Anton Gruener persuaded him to teach in his Model School and to visit Pestalozzi's Institute at Yverdon. At Gruener's school, he taught a class of between thirty and forty 9- to 11-year-old boys for two years. In 1807, he left the school to tutor three brothers. He took them to Yverdon and stayed there for two years. Froebel deeply admired Pestalozzi and was particularly fascinated by the boys' play and the nature walks that Pestalozzi conducted. In the end, however, he concluded that Pestalozzi's educational system was incomplete, and he determined to develop a complete system.

In 1811, Froebel entered the University of Göttingen to study language and natural science. In 1812 he moved to Berlin to study natural history and mineralogy with Professor Weiss, who convinced Froebel that underlying all life was one law, which was the basis for all development. Froebel would later translate this idea into his 'law of the Divine Unity', writing, 'The most pregnant thought which arose for me ... was this: all is unity, all rests in unity, all springs from unity, strives for and leads up to unity, and returns to unity at last.'[4]

In 1813 Prussia declared war on France. Froebel volunteered. In the military he befriended Heinrich Langenthal and Wilhelm Middendorf, who, with Middendorf's nephew Johannes Barop, became lifelong colleagues (Middendorf would deliver Froebel's eulogy). His regiment was disbanded in 1814, and Froebel worked for Weiss for two years at the Mineralogical Museum in Berlin. In 1815 he turned down a post as a mineralogist in Stockholm. In 1816, he resigned from the museum to devote his life to education.

On 13 November 1816, in a peasant's cottage in Griesheim, Froebel, now 34, opened the 'Universal German Educational Institute'. He had five pupils, all nephews. In 1817 Langenthal and Middendorf arrived, and they moved the school to Keilhau. In 1818 Froebel married Henrietta Wilkelmine Hoffmeister, whom he had met at the Museum in Berlin. The school grew to sixty students, but was financially troubled. Froebel was an impractical man, poor at business, and financial problems plagued him throughout his life. Local opposition led to a government inspection of the Institute. The report was favourable, but the school's reputation had been damaged. By 1829, the Institute had only five students.

In 1826, Froebel published privately *The Education of Man*. In it he discussed his general education principles, child development and school instruction. He focused on the first few years of elementary school, his interest in early schooling was still nascent. The book, as his writing in general, is difficult to understand today and challenged even his contemporaries. His writing is mystical and heavily symbolic, '[p]onderous in style, obscure in philosophy, and frequently repetitious',[5] with 'formidable difficulties of presentation and meaning ... verbose ... convoluted ... [with] long rhetorical passages, peculiar word-plays and eccentric emphases'.[6] His lack of skill at explaining his views to the public no doubt contributed to the opposition he frequently faced.

In 1828, offered by Xavier Schnyder the use of his Castle at Wartensee, Froebel left for Switzerland. He encountered opposition from local Catholic clergy (Froebel and his colleagues were Protestant), and the castle proved ill-suited for a school. Invited by local merchants, they relocated to Willisau. The school opened with thirty-six students. In 1835, Froebel moved to Burgdorf, Switzerland, to oversee an orphanage. There he turned his attention to young children. In 1836, his wife in poor health, they returned to Germany. She died in 1839.

In 1837, at the age of 55, Froebel opened a school for young children in Keilhau, but was troubled that he could not think of a proper name for it. One day in 1840, on a walk in woods with Barop and Middendorf, Froebel suddenly exclaimed, 'Eureka! Kindergarten shall the institute be called!' In 1840 he founded kindergartens in Rudolstadt and Blankenburg for the purpose of providing 'the psychological training of little children by means of play and occupations'.[7] Froebel described the kindergarten as 'an institution for self-instruction, self-education, and self-cultivation of mankind, as well as for all sided and therefore for individual cultivation of the same through play, creative self-activity, and spontaneous self-instruction'.[8]

To facilitate these features he developed play materials that he called *gifts* and *occupations*. The gifts and occupations are of historical interest but have long since disappeared from practice. Froebel developed ten gifts, small manipulative materials such as a series of six coloured yarn balls, wooden balls, cubes, brick-shaped blocks, wooden tablets with different shapes, lines, and others. Gifts were to exercise and develop intellectual powers and knowledge. Froebel saw the gifts as a whole whose parts explain and advance each other. According to his principle of the continuity of development, 'each object given must condition the one which follows; each new gift fulfills and interprets its predecessor, by making explicit what it implied'.[9] Occupations were ways of producing skill in the use of knowledge. They were craft activities – clay, cardboard work, wood-carving, paper-folding, paper-cutting, weaving, drawing, and others. Each gift and occupation had its own purpose in accordance with the progress of the development of children's minds.

In 1843, Froebel published his most popular book, *Mutter und Kose-Lieder*, a collection of songs for mothers of infants of young children. From 1844 to 1847 Froebel lectured extensively in Germany. Frustrated by the negative response of men and professional educators to his ideas, Froebel increasingly turned to women. He began training women as kindergarten teachers, moving in 1849 to Liebenstein for this purpose. That year he also met Baroness Bertha von Marenholtz-Bülow, who was to become his most influential disciple, devoting the rest of her life to travelling and lecturing throughout Europe. In July 1851 he married Luise Levin, one of his students, who would carry on his work. The following month, August 1851, tragedy struck. The Prussian government, confusing Froebel with a socialist nephew Carl Froebel, banned kindergartens. Despite efforts by Froebel and his colleagues, the ban was not rescinded until 1860. Ironically, the ban hastened the spread of kindergartens abroad, particularly to England and the US. Froebel died two months after his seventieth birthday, on 21 June 1852. He was buried in Liebenstein, his grave marked by a column of a cube, cylinder and ball, inscribed with Goethe's words, 'Come let us live for our children.'

Had Froebel not, relatively late in his life, turned his attention to early schooling, he would today be a minor figure in the history of education.

Instead, he is a major figure in the history of early childhood education. The idea that early childhood is different from later childhood and adolescence and, therefore, schooling for young children must be different from schooling for older children did not originate with Froebel, but its strength and persistence owes a great deal to him. Influenced by Comenius, Pestalozzi and Rousseau, seminal thinkers in the field, he transformed their ideas as he forged his own philosophy. For example, for Froebel, children's freedom, independence and individuality were achieved by following the eternal law of development rather than, as Rousseau argued, by protecting them from 'unnatural' society.

Froebel was also strongly influenced by philosophers of his time, particularly Hegel, Schelling, Fichte and Schiller. His writings must be understood within the context of German Idealism, for which, 'The empirical world ... was the appearance of the real world; the real world was not to be reached by plodding empiricism and cold reason but by mystical experience or intuition ... [it] was spiritual in nature.'[10] What to the contemporary reader may appear mystical was in Froebel's Germany a metaphysical explanation of the nature of being, the origin and structure of the world, and the nature of knowledge. Curiously, he rarely mentioned these thinkers, educators and philosophers, in his writing.

Froebel's influence on contemporary early schooling is elusive. Over the years the meanings underlying the terms he used have changed. Not surprisingly, given the difficulty of his writing, he was often interpreted selectively. For example, his pantheistic idealism made him attractive to the American transcendentalists, particularly Elizabeth Peabody, who started the first English language kindergarten in the United States. Froebel's emphasis on society and self-activity appealed to the American Hegelians Susan Blow and William Torrey Harris who, in St Louis, introduced kindergartens into the public schools. Nevertheless, he had a profound impact in a number of areas, discussed below.

One most important contribution he made was simply the name *kindergarten*, literally *child's garden*, which has flourished long after the Froebelian nature of the kindergarten waned. With the name kindergarten, he solidified the metaphor, long dominant in the discourse of early schooling, of the child as a plant to be cultivated in accordance with nature's laws. But he also wanted the kindergarten to be a garden *for* children – in fact, he proposed that each child in the kindergarten have an individual garden, and all share two large gardens, one for flowers and one for vegetables.

Froebel opened up the profession of teaching to women. He devoted his last years to the education of women, calling German women to the holy mission of womanhood. The spread of the kindergarten, primarily in England and the United States, was due to women followers, notably Baroness Bertha von Marenholtz-Bülow, noted earlier, Berthe Ronge in England, and Elizabeth Peabody and Susan Blow in the United States. Since Froebel, many important figures in early childhood education and most teachers have been and continue to be women.

Froebel explicitly linked teaching children to a knowledge of the laws of their development. The essence of teaching, then, was adapting the subject to the present stage of development of the child. Children in kindergarten were not to be schooled but 'freely developed'. To this day knowledge of children's development is considered essential to teaching young children. For Froebel, education must follow the divine laws of development, which he specified as the law of opposites, the law of the part-whole of life, and the law of connection. For example, the law of the part-whole enhanced the awareness of the importance of early childhood in the whole development of the person. Froebel saw early childhood and later childhood as stages that were significant in the whole development of an individual, not simply preparation for adulthood. Froebel introduced the notion of continuity in human development, which originated in his observation of the growth of trees. He saw the stage of a new bud as continuing in the whole development of tree. In the same way, the full development of childhood continued into adulthood. If a prior stage was not fully completed, then the next stage could not be fully developed.

Froebel divided childhood into two main periods, early childhood (from birth to age 8) and later childhood or the 'scholar period'. The idea that early childhood extends from birth to age 8 remains strong today. For Froebel, children's intellectual capacity was limited in early childhood. Learning abstract knowledge at school did not match young children's developmental characteristics. Instead, young children should act on objects in their world in order to gain knowledge of the real world. Froebel considered the instruction in infant schools of his time ill-suited to developing children's thinking ability. 'The principal consideration is the child, his nature, and the strengthening, invigorating, developing, drawing out, and educating of the little one.'[11]

Froebel's emphasis on play has had a profound effect on practice. Froebel argued that in the earliest childhood, young children's play was their primary way of learning about the real world. Young children acquire knowledge of physical nature by acting on it using their senses, an activity he called play. Acting on concrete and external objects in their environment, children gain knowledge of them. Young children learn through their senses rather than through reasoning. The function of play is to represent in children's inner mind objects in the physical world – 'self-active representation'. Play involved *gifts* and *occupations* (described earlier) and games. For Froebel play was not the free play emphasized in the infant schools of his time. Through play children become self-conscious and intellectual. Froebel brought a new meaning to play: an educational medium for understanding the external world.

The term child-centred originated with Froebel, first appearing in *The Education of Man* (quoted at the beginning of the chapter). Child-centredness would become a central theme in early schooling. Froebel's view of child-centredness grew out of his view that early childhood was characterized by limited intellectual ability. Because children's intellectual limitations prevented them from gaining knowledge of the world abstractly, children needed to be placed in the centre of things because 'all things are seen only in relation to himself, to his life'. The children were to be put as it were, in the words of a jazz standard, 'smack dab in the middle'. The critical dimension is that children were not, as they were later to become as the idea of child-centredness evolved, the centre of schooling. Rather they were to be placed *at the centre* of their world, there to act directly on their world.

Kilpatrick wrote of Froebel, 'Perhaps the most valuable of all is the practical demonstration which Froebel through the kindergarten has given the world of how happy a group of children can be when engaged in educative activity. ... Froebel's kindergarten stands as "a city set on hill".'[12] It is an apt tribute.

Notes

1 F.W. Froebel, *The Education of Man*, trans. W. Hailmann, New York: D. Appleton, p. 97, 1889.
2 R.B. Downs, *Friedrich Froebel*, Boston: Twayne, p. 12, 1978.
3 H.C. Bowen, *Froebel and Education by Self-Activity*, London: Heinemann, p. 8, 1893.
4 F.W. Froebel, *Autobiography of Friedrich Froebel*, trans. E. Michaelis and H. K. Moore, Syracuse, NY: C.W. Bardeen, p. 69, 1889.
5 M.S. Shapiro, *Child's Garden: The Kindergarten Movement from Froebel to Dewey*, University Park: Pennsylvania State University Press, p. 20, 1983.
6 I. Lilley, *Friedrich Froebel: A Selection From his Writings*, New York: Cambridge University, p. 3, 1967.
7 J. White, *The Educational Ideas of Froebel*, London: University Tutorial Press, p. 13, 1907.
8 F.W. Froebel, *Pedagogics of the Kindergarten*, trans. J. Jarvis. New York: D. Appleton, p. 6, 1900.
9 Ibid, p. 98.
10 P. Edwards, *The Encyclopedia of Philosophy*, New York: Macmillan, p. 302, 1967.
11 F.W. Froebel, *Education by Development*, trans. J. Jarvis, New York: D. Appleton, p. 278, 1899.
12 W.H. Kilpatrick, *Froebel's Kindergarten Principles*, New York: Macmillan, pp. 205–6, 1916.

See also

In this book: Pestalozzi, Comenius, Rousseau

Froebel's major writings

The Education of Man, trans. J. Jarvis, New York: A. Lovell, 1886.
Autobiography of Friedrich Froebel, trans. E. Michaelis and H.K. Moore, Syracuse, NY: C.W. Bardeen, 1889.
Pedagogics of the Kindergarten, trans. J. Jarvis, New York: D. Appleton, 1900.
Froebel Letters, ed. A.H. Heineman, Lothrop: Lee & Shepard, 1893.
Mother-Play and Nursery Songs, New York: Lee & Shepard, 1879.

Further reading

Downs, R.B., *Friedrich Froebel*, Boston: Twayne Publishers, 1978.
Shapiro, M.S., *Child's Garden: The Kindergarten Movement from Froebel to Dewey*, University Park: Pennsylvania State University Press, 1983.
Von Marenholtz-Bülow, B., *Reminscences of Friedrich Froebel*, trans. H. Mann, Boston: Lee & Shepard, 1877.
Woodham-Smith, P., Slight, J.P., Priestman, O.B., Hamilton, H.A., Issacs, N., *Froebel and English Education*, New York: Schocken Books, 1969.

DANIEL J. WALSH, SHUNAH CHUNG AND AYSEL TUFEKCI

JOHN HENRY NEWMAN 1801–90

> His education is called 'liberal'. A habit of mind is formed which lasts through life, of which the attributes are, freedom, equitableness, calmness, moderation, and wisdom; or what in a former Discourse I have ventured to call a philosophical habit. This then I would assign as the special fruit of the education furnished at a University, as contrasted with other places of teaching or modes of teaching.[1]

John Henry Newman was a Londoner by birth, and attended a school in Ealing before proceeding to Trinity College Oxford, where he began residence in 1817. He was successful in his studies, but not in his degree, for which he over-read and was awarded only a bare pass. But in 1822 he secured a Fellowship at Oriel College, which was then regarded as the greatest achievement possible in the University. He became a tutor there, and in 1828 the Vicar of St Mary's, the University Church. In 1832, disagreements with the Head of his College led him to resign his tutorship, and from then on he dedicated himself at Oxford to the study of ecclesiastical history and religious topics. In 1833 there began what is known as 'the Oxford Movement', a reaction against what was regarded as dangerous liberalism from the Whig ministry at the time. Newman's part in this began when he started the series of *Tracts for the Times*, defending the Catholic inheritance of the Church of England. His sermons at St Mary's proclaimed the same message, and Newman achieved an unrivalled place in notoriety and influence at Oxford. But his reading of Church history led him to doubt whether the Anglican position was tenable; in 1841 his Tract 90, attempting to give a Catholic sense to some of the 39 articles, was repudiated by the University, and the series of the Tracts came to an end. Newman withdrew from public life at Oxford, and in October 1845 was received into the Roman Catholic Church.

After a stay at Rome he returned to England, and founded at Birmingham a religious house, the Oratory, on the model of what had been begun in Italy by Philip Neri, a sixteenth-century saint whom Newman admired; later, an Oratory was founded also in London. In 1854, at the invitation of the Irish bishops, Newman went to Dublin as Rector of a planned Catholic university there. Although the venture was not a success, Newman's *Idea of a University*, with allied works, remains as a memory of the attempt, and as an exposition of his views on higher education.

He founded the Oratory School in Birmingham in 1859, and combined his own pastoral work as Rector with lecturing and writing. In 1864, the controversy with Charles Kingsley over his own honesty led to the *Apologia*, his best-known work, and to the resumption of relations with many of his Oxford friends. From that time onwards, Newman was better known and better understood by his fellow countrymen.

His life in the Church of Rome was in many respects a trial. Plans of his – for an Oratory at Oxford, for a new translation of the Latin Bible – foundered on the indifference or hostility of his superiors. He was out of sympathy with the noisy aggressiveness of other converts to the Church of Rome like Manning and W.G. Ward; he thought the tactics used by the successful party at the First Vatican Council were wrong; he argued, in a controversy with Gladstone in 1874, that the decrees of the Council did not impugn the civil allegiance of Roman Catholics.

His later years saw a brightening of his fortunes. Trinity College elected him an Honorary Fellow in 1877, and he was glad to return to Oxford after so many years. In 1878 the new Pope, Leo XIII, made Newman a Cardinal, and he was able to spend the remaining years of his life at the Birmingham Oratory, while the collected edition of his works was produced, and he himself was regarded, not only as one of the great masters of English style, but as one who had, in a long life, surrendered much and achieved much.

Much of what Newman wrote – discourses, sermons and the rest – embodies or expresses his views on education, but it is his writings to do with the Dublin plan that have a first claim on our attention here. They have been excellently edited by I.T. Ker, with a copious introduction, helpful notes, and a lucid account of the many textual changes subsequently made in them by Newman. To understand them, we need to know their setting; from what Ker writes, I give a brief account of the occasion of their composition.

In 1845, Peel made a gesture of reconciliation towards Catholics in Ireland, who were barred – in theory though not always in practice – from attending the (Anglican) Trinity College Dublin. There were to be non-denominational Queen's Colleges, and these would offer a university education to all. Some Irish Catholic bishops approved but most did not, and decrees from Rome were just as unfavourable. Cardinal Cullen, the Archbishop of Dublin, asked Newman in 1851 for help in founding a Catholic university there. Newman's acceptance of the office of Rector was tempered with apprehension because of the administrative work involved (he had wanted to be Prefect of Studies only). In November 1851 – while his own life was darkened with the prospect of a libel action – he began to write a series of discourses on university education, and the first five were delivered in Dublin in the May and June of 1852. Back in England, Newman wrote seven more discourses, giving all twelve to a Dublin publisher, who brought them out in 1853. The School of Philosophy and Letters was opened in 1854, and in the same year began the *Catholic University Gazette*. Newman contributed to this a series of articles on university topics, and these were collected and published as 'lectures' in 1858. The two parts – the discourses and the articles – make up *The Idea of a University*, of which the full title, as in Ker's edition, is in the bibliography.

It is a tribute to Newman's vigour of mind that he was able to write what he did amid so many distractions; but we need to remember something of what these were, if we are to judge aright the discourses and the articles. Some of the Irish bishops resented the arrival of an Englishman to be the university's Rector, and suspected him of imposing Oxford ideas on them. Some people told Newman that there was no party among Catholics that wanted a university. Bishops – especially Cardinal Cullen – wanted to keep a tight control on it. The whole idea of secular learning was regarded as dangerous by many clerics, whose education had been entirely ecclesiastical. Newman had to challenge, to conciliate, to explore; and he also had to take account of what might be said, in Ireland, England or Rome. What he wrote cannot but bear the marks of these tensions. So what he wrote needs to be read generously, and in generous measure. It will be enough here to indicate some of its recurrent themes. I give reference to the Discourses, with the pagination in Ker's edition.

Newman takes 'university' as suggesting a universality of concern for all branches of knowledge. None is to be excluded from the start, and 'they demand comparison and adjustment' (V; Ker 94). The student may pursue only a few of these, but he profits by the intellectual tradition of the place, and acquires a grasp of principles that gives to him that frame of mind which Newman described in the opening quotation to this section. This enlargement of his mind is more than a passive reception of new ideas. It lies in the mind's 'energetic ... action ... upon these new ideas'; there needs to be a comparison of ideas and a systematizing of them (VI; Ker 120).

This action connoted by a liberal education lies wholly apart from what Newman claims is the danger of his own time: the enfeebling of the mind by an unmeaning profusion of subjects, as if we could be almost unconsciously enlightened by the mere multiplication of volumes. A university is an Alma Mater to its children, not a treadmill. And Newman goes on to say that, faced with a choice between a university that did no more than award degrees after an examination (dispensing with residence and tutorial supervision), and a university that had no examinations at all, but simply brought young men together, he would – if judging simply on academic grounds – choose the latter. Minds would be enlarged there as they would not be in the former (VI, Ker 127–9). Such knowledge is a state or condition of mind, such a condition is worth cultivating for its own sake. This knowledge is itself a treasure, and a sufficient remuneration for years of labour (V; Ker 105).

But if Newman regards a liberal education as the purpose of a university, and judges such knowledge to be its own end, he denies that such an education can be adequate for moral training in a world that is marked by darkness and sin. Divorced from a dependence on religion, a liberal education puts a moral sense in the place of an awareness of sin, and a quest for refinement in the place of a struggle for virtue. And Newman goes on, in a famous passage that needs reading in its context for its drift to be appreciated, to describe 'the gentleman' who is the product of a liberal education (VIII; the passage about the 'gentleman' is there, at Ker 179–81). And so, in the last of the Discourses as printed, he speaks of the need for a direct and active jurisdiction of the Church over the Catholic university (IX; Ker 184).

I said that the pressures under which Newman wrote demand that what he wrote be read in generous measure. I feel a greater need to say the same, after offering this summary. Newman himself, in the course of repeated revisions of the Discourses, inserted qualifications and reservations; these need to be read, if obvious questions we should put are to receive any answers; so should the Lectures, because they take up and adjust the balance of what had been said in the Discourses. Newman's own policies in the setting up of the university should also be borne in mind, if we are to seize the full content of his thought here.

For instance, he says that the university's task lies in the diffusion of knowledge rather than in its advancement, and speaks – in a way that has become remote to us – of academies and private research as more proper for advancing knowledge. But in one of the Lectures he does consider scientific investigation, and does more justice to the theme of 'philosophy and research' (Lecture VIII: Ker 370). In a Lecture on Christianity and Letters, he takes it for granted that training in humane disciplines, with the classics at their centre, will be the main instrument of a liberal education. But the seventh Discourse, on knowledge and professional skill, shows other concerns; and Newman was well aware of the limits of what could be done in Dublin (see Ker's Introduction, xxiv–xxv). And Ker rightly records that Dublin was one of the first universities to possess a Chair of English Literature (lxii, footnote).

Readers today, whatever their beliefs, may find the stress on theology and on Church jurisdiction strange. But although this would have been encouraged by the setting in Dublin, Newman in his Oxford days was just as insistent on the point. It was only later in his life, when he was brought up against the harsh realities of the Roman Curia, that Newman came to see what could be the results of ecclesiastical interference.[2]

Perhaps the greatest question raised for us by what Newman wrote is the matter of *time*. In today's multiplication of syllabuses and faculties, do his ideas retain any sense that is more than just Utopian? I hope it is not fanciful to go for an answer to this to the fourth of the Lectures, 'Elementary Studies'. This is a very perceptive (and very amusing) presentation of two candidates for admission to the university, one of whom lacks accuracy of mind and one who has it; to which Newman adds a correspondence with their respective fathers. The specific character of the conversations and letters brings out vividly what Newman means by accuracy of mind, and how indispensable it is for what he wants a university to provide. Set beside this two other pieces by Newman, both printed in Ker's Introduction. One touches his labours of composing the Discourses: 'For three days I sat at my desk nearly from morning to night, and put aside as worthless at night what I had been doing all day' (Ker xxxii). The other piece Newman wrote in 1869, in a letter to one who had praised his English style: 'I have been obliged to take great pains with everything I have ever written ... my one and single desire and aim has been to do what is so difficult – viz. to express clearly and exactly my meaning; this has been the motive principle in all my corrections and re-writings' (Ker xlii).

And yet Newman's style is regarded as luminous and personal – as unmistakably his. If today's universities insist that their students labour to cultivate accuracy and clarity in writing, they will be doing something, in a very different age, not alien to what Newman did in his own.

Notes

1 *Idea of a University*, Discourse V; Ker 96.
2 I have considered this theme in my contributions to Nicholls and Kerr (1991).

Newman's major writings

An Essay on the Development of Christian Doctrine. The Edition of 1845, edited with an introduction by J.M. Cameron, London: Penguin Books, 1973.
The Idea of a University Defined and Illustrated: I In Nine Discourses Delivered to the

Catholics of Dublin. II In Occasional Lectures and Essays Addressed to Members of the Catholic University, edited with introduction and notes by I.T. Ker, Oxford: Clarendon Press, 1976.
Apologia pro Vita sua, ed. M.J. Svaglic, Oxford: Clarendon Press, 1967.
Ward, W. (ed.), *Newman's Apologia pro Vita sua. The Two Versions of 1864 and 1865. Preceded by Newman's and Kingsley's Pamphlets*, Oxford University Press, 1931. (This older edition of the *Apologia* and connected writings has not lost its usefulness.)
An Essay in Aid of a Grammar of Assent, edited with introduction and notes by I.T. Ker, Oxford: Clarendon Press, 1985.

Further reading

Newman, J.H., *Letters and Diaries*. Begun in 1961, and superlatively edited, these give a day-to-day picture of Newman's activities, with biographical details on persons mentioned.
Nicholls, D. and Kerr, F. (eds), *John Henry Newman: Reason, Rhetoric and Romanticism*, The Bristol Press, 1991.
Tristram, H. (ed.), *The Idea of a Liberal Education: A Selection from the Works of Newman*, Harrap: London, 1952 (a useful collection).
Ward, W., *The Life of John Henry Cardinal Newman*, 2 vols, London: Longmans, Green, 1912.

P.J. FITZPATRICK

JOHN STUART MILL 1806–73

Education and opinion, which have so vast a power over human character, should so use that power as to establish in the mind of every individual an indissoluble association between his own happiness and the good of the whole.[1]

Philosopher, political theorist, economist, Member of Parliament, and champion of women's emancipation, John Stuart Mill was the most celebrated intellectual figure of mid-nineteenth-century England, exerting an influence on public life greater than any other British philosopher has ever done. Mill's godfather was the founder of British utilitarianism, Jeremy Bentham (1748–1832), of whom his father, the political economist and historian of India, James Mill, was a close friend and virtual disciple. Under his father's tutorship, John Stuart received the remarkable education chronicled in his *Autobiography*. By the age of 8, he knew Greek and Latin and was reading Plato and Homer, a taste that he was surprised to discover was 'not universal' among boys of that age. Aristotelian and Scholastic logic, political economy, history, natural science and much else were soon to follow in his father's exacting curriculum.

As a teenager, Mill was already an intimate of liberal radicals, such as David Ricardo, in his father's and godfather's circle, and was contributing to, indeed editing, their mouthpiece, the *Westminster Review*. He was soon, however, to undergo a period of deep depression that he partly attributed to his extraordinary education. It had failed, he judged, sufficiently to 'create those feelings', like loving sympathy, able 'to resist the dissolving influence of analysis', with its tendency to 'wear away the feelings'.[2] Mill's depression – eventually lifted through immersion in the poetry of Wordsworth – was, like the upbringing which partly caused it, profoundly to shape his later views on the methods and goals of education.

Most of Mill's professional life was spent in the London office of the East India Company. The majority of his most famous works, including *On Liberty* and *Utilitarianism*, were written after the dissolution of the Company in 1858 and, in the same year, the death of his wife, Harriet Taylor, a widow and early feminist who had been his 'most valued friend' long before their marriage in 1851. After a brief, but typically energetic spell as Liberal MP for Westminster during the 1860s, Mill retired to Avignon in France, partly in order to be close to his wife's grave. He died there in 1873.

The general tenor of Mill's thinking was that of robust empiricism. Nothing, he held, should be accepted as true that does not pass the stern test of experiential evidence. His lifelong critical target, in consequence, was the view that human beings are possessed of an innate capacity for 'intuitive' knowledge which precedes, and hence does not require confirmation by, experience. In his *System of Logic*, Mill argued that inductive inference from observed data of experience is the only method necessary, or indeed permissible, for arriving at reasonable beliefs about the world. Even the truths of logic and mathematics, he held, are empirical generalizations, confirmed at 'almost every instant of our lives', and not the necessary, *a priori* ones logicians imagine them to be.[3] In both the *Logic* and the massive *An Examination of Sir William Hamilton's Philosophy*, Mill's acknowledged debt is to the 'associationist psychology' of eighteenth-century empiricists like David Hartley, himself a follower of John Locke. According to this, all our concepts are the products of combining the simple, atomic 'sensations' which are all that is truly 'given' to experience. So-called external or material objects, therefore, are intelligible only as 'permanent possibilities of sensation'.[4]

Mill's empiricism was as decisive for his moral philosophy as for his logic and theory of knowledge. Like his father and godfather, he subscribed to 'the principle of utility': to the view that 'the greatest happiness of the greatest number' provides the sole criterion for what is right and properly to be desired. Nothing, he argues, can establish that something is desirable beyond the fact that 'people do actually desire it', and the evidence is overwhelming that the only thing which each human being desires as an end is his own happiness. Hence we have 'all the proof the case admits of' for the principle of utility.[5] In several respects, however, Mill's version of utilitarianism was subtler, though arguably less consistent, than Bentham's. To begin with, the testimony of people who have enjoyed wide and varied experience shows that some kinds of happiness or pleasure are 'higher' than others. Poetry and 'tranquil contemplation' may not yield a greater quantity of pleasure than pushpin but, *pace* Bentham, they are to be preferred. 'It is better to be a human being dissatisfied than a pig satisfied.'[6] Second, Mill was keen to scotch the impression, created by some Benthamites, that a person should pursue the happiness of others only because this is a means towards his or her own happiness. It is essential to recognize, he insists, that the good of others, indeed of mankind at large, is 'the greatest and surest source ... of happiness' for each individual.[7] Finally, Mill places much greater emphasis than Bentham on the cultivation of feelings that, however unobviously, do in fact inspire beneficial behaviour. His experience during his depression had convinced Mill that so remote and abstract a goal as universal well-being may fail to engage a person's emotions and enthusiasm: hence the need to inspire a feeling for, say, natural beauty that, albeit indirectly, helps towards achievement of that goal.

The principle of utility provided Mill with the main stated reason for his famous 'principle of liberty': 'the only purpose for which power can be rightfully exercised over any member of a civilised community, against his will, is to prevent harm to others. His own good ... is not a sufficient warrant.'[8] Since each person is, generally, the best judge of what makes him happy, interference with people's voluntary decisions must, *ceteris paribus*, reduce the sum of happiness. It is apparent, however, that Mill's passionate investment in individual liberty exceeds anything warranted by utilitarian considerations alone. A life of subjection to others, or to public opinion, is, for him, a betrayal of an authentically human existence. As the closing words of *The Subjection of Women* make clear, 'restraint on ... freedom of conduct' not only 'dries up ... the principal fountain of human happiness', it impoverishes 'all that makes life valuable to the individual human being'[9]

Mill wrote no extended work on education but, in addition to smaller pieces on this topic,[10] such major books as *On Liberty* and the *Autobiography* contain many reflections on the methods and goals of education. Mill's educational views may be roughly divided into two groups: proposals for particular educational reforms, and general reflections of a more philosophical character.

Mill's most important and radical proposal was for compulsory universal education. 'Is it not almost a self-evident axiom that the State should require ... education up to a certain standard, of every ... citizen?' It is as great a 'moral crime' to fail to provide for 'the training of the child's mind' as to ignore the child's need for food.[11] But while the state should compel education, it should not 'direct' it. Mill 'deprecates' state-schooling out of the fear that it would make for uniformity and control of opinion. A second radical proposal was a demand for equal access of women to education, including entrance to university. In order to debar women from access, one would have to show, impossibly, that 'no women at all are fit for ... functions of the highest intellectual character'.[12] A third contentious proposal of Mill's was that on 'disputed subjects' – notably religion – children should not be taught or examined on 'the truth or falsehood of opinions', since this cannot be ascertained through any reliable evidence. Hence, for Mill, himself an agnostic in religion, 'all attempts by the State to bias the conclusions of its citizens on disputed subjects are evil'.[13] He would, presumably, have approved of current guidelines on religious education in the UK. If, on most educational issues, Mill's position was radical, on a few he was, however, more traditional. He held, for example, that mastery of Greek and Latin was essential to a disciplined training of the intellect.

Mill's wider philosophical reflections on education flow, predictably, from his empiricism. Leaving us in no doubt where he stands on the 'nature vs nurture' issue, Mill credits education with an immense power to form our beliefs and intellects. 'The only real hindrance' to the attainment of happiness by almost all people, he states, is 'the present wretched education, and wretched social arrangements'.[14] Mill's own education had convinced him that, since he himself had no special, innate intellectual superiority, much more may be 'well taught' to children than is 'commonly supposed'. Only a benighted belief in 'natural' constraints on the abilities of most children, or a misguided urge to teach children only what they enjoy learning, stands in the way of imposing a demanding curriculum from which virtually all children eventually benefit, above all by acquiring 'the power to form opinions of their own'. Mill was no Rousseauian romantic or 'child-centrist', and would have been sickened by the contemporary tendency to require of children nothing that is 'disagreeable' to them. 'A pupil from whom nothing is ever demanded which he cannot do, never does all he can.'[15]

It is in the 'moral influences' of education, at once 'more important than all others' and 'the most complicated', that Mill perceives to be its greatest potential.[16] Without appropriate influences, the young will not develop the 'mental culture' necessary for an independence of thought and autonomy of action which are the proper moral state of human beings. Moreover, children are, in Mill's opinion, inordinately selfish, not in the cold, calculating manner of some adults, but in always acting 'under the impulse of a present desire'.[17] As the opening citation makes clear, it is therefore imperative to exploit the power of education to cultivate those desires whose satisfaction is at least compatible with the good of people as a whole and which, ideally, are desires for the happiness of others.

John Stuart Mill remains one of the most widely read and frequently invoked of English philosophers. While his radically empiricist accounts of logic and knowledge find few subscribers today, they remain ones which supporters of rival positions need to take seriously. It is Mill's, rather than Bentham's, version of utilitarianism that the majority of contemporary utilitarians prefer and attempt to develop. It is, however, his defence of individual liberty that is Mill's most vital legacy. No debate on alleged issues of liberty – from 'gay rights' and censorship to fox-hunting and independent schooling – is conducted without appeals, often from the opposed parties to such debates, to Mill's pronouncements. It is ironic, perhaps, that Mill's greatest impact upon educational policy in the years after his death was in furthering the processes, not of freedom from coercion, but of compulsory education and the compulsory admission of women into higher education.

Notes

1 *Utilitarianism*, in John Stuart Mill, *Utilitarianism, On Liberty, Essay on Bentham*, p. 269.
2 John Stuart Mill, *Autobiography*, pp. 114–15.
3 *A System of Logic*, Bk 2 sect. 5.4.
4 *An Examination of Sir William Hamilton's Philosophy*, Toronto: University of Toronto Press, p. 184, 1979. Mill is often, but perhaps inaccurately, interpreted as a 'phenomenalist', holding that statements about material objects are translatable into ones about actual and possible sense-data. See John Skorupski, *John Stuart Mill*, London: Routledge, 1989.
5 *Utilitarianism*, p. 288.
6 Ibid., p. 260.

7   *Autobiography*, p. 115.
8   *On Liberty* (see n. 1), p. 135.
9   *The Subjection of Women*, Indianapolis: Hackett, p. 109, 1988.
10 A notable example is 'Inaugural address delivered to the University of St Andrews', where he argues for the benefits of university education for both society and the 'mental culture' of the individual.
11 *On Liberty*, pp. 238–9.
12 *The Subjection of Women*, p. 54.
13 *On Liberty*, p. 241.
14 *Utilitarianism*, p. 264.
15 *Autobiography*, pp. 25, 58, 45.
16 Ibid., p. 49.
17 Quoted in Mary Warnock's Introduction to Mill's *Utilitarianism, On Liberty, Essay on Bentham*, p. 29.

See also

In this book: Locke, Rousseau

Mill's major writings

A System of Logic, London: Longmans, Green & Co, 1886.
Utilitarianism, On Liberty, Essay on Bentham, ed. by M. Warnock, London: Collins, 1962.
Autobiography, Harmondsworth: Penguin, 1989.
These and all other writings mentioned in the text and notes are also included in *Collected Works of John Stuart Mill*, 33 vols, Toronto: University of Toronto, 1963–.

Further reading

Anderson, E., 'John Stuart Mill: Democracy as Sentimental Education', in A. Rorty (ed.), *Philosophers on Education: New Historical Perspectives*, London, pp. 333–52, 1998.
Cavenaugh, F. (ed.), *James and John Stuart Mill on Education*, London: Cambridge University Press, 1931.
Robson, J., *The Improvement of Mankind: The Social and Political Thought of John Stuart Mill*, Toronto: University of Toronto Press, 1968.
Ryan, A., *The Philosophy of John Stuart Mill*, London: Macmillan, 1970.
Skorupski, J., *John Stuart Mill*, London: Routledge, 1989.

DAVID E. COOPER

CHARLES DARWIN 1809–82

[Written in 1831] I am often afraid I shall be overwhelmed with the number of subjects which I ought to take into hand. It is difficult to mark out any plan & without method on shipboard I am sure little will be done. The principal objects are 1st, collecting observing, & reading in all branches of Natural history that I possibly can manage. ... If I have not energy to make myself steadily industrious during the voyage, how great & uncommon an opportunity of improving myself shall I threw away. May this never for one moment escape my mind & then perhaps I may have some opportunity of drilling my mind that I threw away whilst at Cambridge.[1]

[Written in 1871] The main conclusion arrived at in this work ... (and now held by many naturalists who are well competent to form sound judgment) is that man is descended from some less highly organized form.[2]

The first quote, dated 13 December 1831, appeared in Charles Darwin's diary as he prepared for his voyage aboard HMS *Beagle*. The second appeared forty years later in 1871 in the concluding chapter of *The Descent of Man*. The quotes epitomize the intellectual growth of a man and the development of a set of ideas that altered the history of the world and man's place in that history.

For an educator audience, it is important to note that Darwin, born in 1809, was the son of a very successful physician and the grandson of a physician and poet. His mother was a Wedgwood and part of that well-to-do, distinguished family of potters. His older brother was trained as a physician at Edinburgh. Charles' education began by being tutored at home by an older sister and later at Rugby, a school he did not like and where he was an undistinguished pupil. Later he tried medicine at Edinburgh which he also found unsatisfying. Finally he went to Cambridge to study for the ministry and a possible post as a rural parson. Here, too, he was an unexceptional student except for his growing interest in natural history and his contacts with the botany professor, John Stevens Henslow. He gained the reputation as 'the man who walks with Henslow'. At the finish of his formal education, Henslow nominated him for the position of naturalist on HMS *Beagle*, the ship that was to spend two years charting the longitude of the coasts of South America. His father thought that such a voyage was foolish and would not give his permission for him to go unless Charles could find some 'sensible person' who would recommend it. Charles' well-respected uncle Josiah Wedgwood answered the negative arguments and commented that for a young man of 'enlarged curiosity' it would be an excellent experience.

The voyage lasted five years. In his autobiography[3] Charles called it the 'most important experience of my life'. He worked assiduously as a natural historian – collecting specimens of plants, animals and fossils of all kinds, kept a lengthy diary which was converted and expanded later into his *Journal of Researches*[4] and wrote long letters home to his sisters and friends. His mentor Henslow briefly presented, edited and published some abstracts of these observations and interpretations while Charles was still at sea, thereby assuring him of a warm and respected reception on his return. He had departed England as a 22-year-old amateur naturalist, he returned five years later as a young but major scientist ready to make important forays into geology, zoology and botany. The voyage served as a major educational experience for what he called his 'self taught' intellectual development. The 'lessons' to be learned from this brief account are vividly controversial for concerned educators living two centuries later.

In the spring of 1837, less than a year after his return from the *Beagle* voyage, Darwin began a series of notebooks containing his preliminary thoughts on evolution. In 1842 and 1844 he wrote two unpublished beginning 'outlines' of what became the *Origin of Species*[5] in 1859, almost twenty years later. The *Journal of Researches* appeared in 1839 and established a new standard for provocative and readable natural history. Five special volumes on the zoology of the *Beagle* were produced collaboratively between 1839 and 1843. He authored three volumes on the geology of the voyage that appeared between 1842 and 1846. One of these, *The Structure and Distribution of Coral Reefs*, offered a new theoretical analysis and synthesis of the formation of coral reefs through subsidence of land masses, a theory that has essentially lasted into the present. That book alone would have assured him a position and status as an outstanding scientist of the nineteenth century. In that decade between his mid twenties and his mid thirties he established himself as a pre-eminent natural historian.

But it was the *Origin of Species* in 1859 that became the defining legacy of Darwin's ideas. Evolution of species rather than 'special creation' as argued in the Book of Genesis of the Bible received its definitive statement at the time. The critical addition to the discussion of evolution was Darwin's hypothesis of natural selection as the major mechanism for evolution. This was the major intellectual stroke that ordered a mélange of ideas and data. Huxley in a review thought it so simple an idea and wondered why he, Huxley, hadn't thought it. The book revolutionized Western views in everyday thought, in philosophy, in science, and perhaps most of all in theology and religious thought. Evolution through natural selection continues to roar through discussions and debates – in churches modern and fundamentalist, liberal and conservative. All schools teach biology and biological science, the core of which is evolutionary theory; in school politics 'creation science' remains among citizens and elected officials one of the most political issues in schooling.

While 1859 remains the critical publication date, the ideas had a long and not easy history in Darwin's thinking. He left Cambridge in 1831, a confirmed 'Bible-as-truth Christian', planning on becoming a minister interested in natural history, a not uncommon hobby for a rural or village parson. During his five-year voyage on HMS *Beagle* only a few references appear in his notebooks and diary that suggest any evolutionary thoughts. While still on board, he published a paper with Captain Fitzroy extolling the virtues of missionaries as they had encountered them in the voyage. From his ornithology notebook Barlow[6] presents a statement of Darwin's that she dates from 1835 that makes an evolutionary claim. More recently, Himmelfarb[7] questions the dating and argues that it came later. No one questions that Darwin opened his 'transmutation notebook' in 1837 less than a year after his return from the *Beagle* voyage. The initial fumblings in his notebook received major clarification when he read Malthus' population essay which stressed the idea of the disastrous consequences of a population that tends to grow exponentially while food supplies grow arithmetically. From this, Darwin moved easily to the beginnings of an explanation of evolution through the struggle for existence and the survival of 'favorable varieties'.

In 1842 Darwin wrote a 35-page 'sketch ' of his developing ideas and in 1844 he wrote a more detailed 'outline' of some 230 pages. At the time he urged his wife Emma to show the manuscript to Hooker or Lyell if something were to happen to him. The earlier sketch was lost until 1896 after Darwin's wife died and the family was cleaning up the house. Both of the essays were published in 1909 by Darwin's son Francis Darwin[8] at the time of the fiftieth anniversary of the publication of *The Origin of Species*. The story of the idea took a dramatic turn in 1858 when Alfred Russel Wallace sent Darwin a letter and essay expressing the same idea of evolution through natural selection which he had arrived at independently. Devastated, Darwin talked to Hooker and Lyell, good friends, colleagues and eminent scientists who knew of his longstanding work. They proposed that two papers be presented together at the summer meeting of the Linnean Society. The papers caused little stir at that meeting. In a year, 1859, Darwin finished writing and published his developing book. That began the larger controversy over the ideas, a controversy that continues to the present.

One of the most memorable controversial episodes occurred at the Oxford Meeting of the British Association in 1860, the year following the publication of *The Origin*. T.H. Huxley debated the scientific merits of the ideas with Bishop Wilberforce early in the meeting and Wilberforce was to speak the next day. Although he had been intending to leave, Huxley decided to stay another day for the lecture and was caught up in another exchange. After a long speech on the inadequacies of Darwin's theory, the bishop concluded with a turn to Huxley and a question as to whether it was through his grandfather or his grandmother that he claimed descent from a monkey. Huxley is alleged to have commented to a nearby colleague, 'The Lord hath delivered him into mine hands.' Huxley again rebutted the scientific arguments and concluded with a devastating comment something like 'If I had to choose between a poor ape as ancestor or a highly gifted and influential individual who uses his gifts to introduce ridicule into a scientific discussion and to humble seekers after truth, he would affirm his preference for the ape.' Considerable commotion followed, one woman allegedly fainted. Bishop Wilberforce, seemingly acknowledging defeat, chose not to reply.

A half century later in America, the state of Tennessee voted to outlaw the teaching of evolution in the public schools.[9] This set the stage for a young science teacher, John T. Scopes to be accused of breaking the law and in 1925, he was tried in court. The trial became known as 'the Scopes Trial', 'the monkey trial', and 'the trial of the century'. It pitted the American Civil Liberties Union (ACLU) against fundamentalist Protestant clergy and world-famous, eloquent lawyers, Clarence Darrow for the defence and William Jennings Bryan for the prosecution. The issues were complicated – Protestant modernism with its 'higher criticism' of Biblical interpretation, freshly stated tenets of fundamentalism from seminaries such as Princeton, variations of the meaning of evolution, constitutional issues ranging from separation of Church and state to rights of free speech, and broader social concerns, as articulated by Bryan, of Darwinian theory representing 'the law of hate – the merciless law by which the strong crowd out and kill the weak'. Scopes was convicted against a background of national publicity and he was eventually freed on a technicality. The law itself was not repealed until 1967. The debates continue.

But to return to *The Origin* itself, the novice reader from any of the many possible different intellectual persuasions will be struck by many aspects of the book. First, it is a big book – over 400 pages. It summarizes a vast amount of a multitude of different kinds of scientific investigations at the time and the conventional common-sense wisdom of animal and plant breeders. Second, no reference appears to human beings except in a sentence in the conclusion that in future scientific work 'Much light will be thrown on man and his history' (p. 449), perhaps the understatement of all time. Third, the organization of the book has a powerful rhetorical quality. The book moves from chapter length, data heavy reports and discussions of variation under domestication and variation in nature, then into the 'struggle for existence' and 'natural selection or the survival of the fittest' and 'laws of variation'. Darwin, in a major disarming rhetorical move, then shifts the presentation with two chapters titled 'Difficulties of the theory' and 'Miscellaneous objections to the theory of natural selection'. He then takes up two special issues – 'instinct' and 'hybridism'. The argument then turns to geology, another domain and kind of evidence, with chapters 'on the imperfection of the geological record' and 'on geological succession of organic beings'. Then once again he shifts the argument to another line of thought and evidence with two chapters on geographical distribution of plants and animals with accounts of 'barriers' and distances in geographical settings as they pertain to evolution through natural selection. Then he veers off into a larger scope account of 'mutual affinities of organic beings: morphology, embryology, and rudimentary organs'. The last chapter, 'recapitulation and conclusion' does just that. All in all it presents a well-written, vivid, detailed and synthetic argument.

Darwin's intellectual life continued until his death at 73 years in 1882. Among his many books three might be mentioned. Darwin extended the ideas in *The Origin* to human beings in a large two-part volume with the title, *The Descent of Man and Selection in Relation to Sex*, each part over 400 pages with a total of some twenty-one chapters. It might be argued that *The Origin* did away with the need for special creation and *The Descent* with its strong materialistic flavour eliminated any need for a deity whatsoever. Further, Darwin took on directly the human issues of intellectual and moral development. In a kind of comparative analysis of physical and behavioural characteristics, Darwin raises the idea of a continuum of differences rather than categorical difference among animals and between man and other animals. A third volume in the sequence, if it be that, was his *The Expression of the Emotions in Man and Animals.*[10] In this book also, Darwin continues his wide-ranging and sharply critical review of what is known about morphology and behaviour of animals and men. He is clear in his evaluations of other scientists: one he compliments '[he] built up a noble structure' (p. 2) but of another he wrote 'He throws, however, very little light on the subject' (p. 3), and about some anatomical drawings he wrote 'the best I believe ever published' (p. 5), and so the discussion moves along. The observation of detail in his comparative analyses of emotional expressions in animals and man is careful, broad ranging, integrated and intellectually powerful.

Finally one needs to read Darwin on Darwin in his Autobiography, a book written late in life for his family. The careful reader needs to know that the original publication in Francis Darwin's *Life and Letters of Charles Darwin*[11] was expurgated of some of his more pithy statements about colleagues and also a considerable amount of his religious comments. Later Nora Barlow published the 'de-edited' version restoring the deleted material. Such is another part of the trail of intellectual history.

Several major concluding ideas follow on the previous discussion. One of the most remarkable aspects of Darwin's intellectual life occurred in the continuity, differentiation and integration of his thought. Hints of evolutionary ideas arose in his diary and journal and became more explicit in his notebooks shortly after his return from the long voyage. These continued through two outlines in the early 1840s and finally were more fully developed in *The Origin* and a decade later in his *The Descent of Man*. One might argue an *idée fixe*.

One of the most controversial aspects of Darwin's legacy resides in the questions – why was it Darwin who created this world-shaking set of ideas? A number of hypotheses are suggested by Darwin himself, his contemporaries and later commentators – family background, great intelligence, luck, hard work, plagiarism and propitious times. One of the most convincing hypotheses raised by Ghiselin is that 'Darwin thought. He reasoned systematically, imaginatively, and rigorously, and he criticized his own ideas'.[12] And he did this in a similar and consistent way across domains of problems, data and ideas. As indicated, the unity of his thinking, the level of synthesis is remarkable and visible mostly by reading his work carefully, following the chronology, and noting the tangents and his veering off the immediate target.

But even in his mode of thinking and methods of inquiry controversy exists. At one extreme is the Baconian view of making many observations and slowly and inductively coming to a theoretical position. At times, Darwin himself indicated this was his approach. At the other extreme is the evidence from his journals and notebooks that what he did was very different. Gruber, a recent analyst, commented about 'The pandemonium of Darwin's notebooks and his actual way of working, in which many different processes tumble over each other in untidy sequence – theorizing, experimenting, casual observing, cagey questioning, reading, etc.'[13] Pat formulas for scientific inquiry fall apart in the Darwin story.

At a substantive level, controversy within and without science exists to a marked degree, no matter how great the ideas and the status of the proponents. In the late nineteenth and early twentieth centuries biologists contested strongly Darwin's thesis of evolution through natural selection, the origin of species in general, and the origin of man in particular. Much of these debates focused on assumptions that were necessary because of the limited knowledge of the times. For instance, the absence of a theory of genetics (Bateson coined the term in 1908) was most crucial. Mendel's early experiments had not filtered out of Germany until their rediscovery at the turn of the century, long after Darwin's death. Similarly fossil records were vague and sketchy with the all-important controversy of the 'missing link' at the forefront of argument. Within biology, evolution remains the great organizing principle. In a simple way, one sees that each new edition of one of his books carries a brief introduction by a noted scientist who attests how this or that particular book opened up lines of inquiry continuing on into the present. His was a remarkable achievement.

As indicated, the controversy spilled over into religion in theology and politics in government and both in the lay public. And these were not minor quarrels. School curricula and teaching, as well, were far from being omitted in the debates. In short, when world views are contested, everyone becomes involved. The controversial Darwin remains with us.

Notes

1   N. Barlow (ed.), *Charles Darwin's Diary of the Voyage of H.M.S. 'Beagle'*, Cambridge: Cambridge University Press, p. 14, 1933.
2   Charles Darwin, *The Descent of Man and Selection in Relation to Sex*, Princeton, NJ: Princeton University Press, p. 385, 1871/1981.
3   N. Barlow, N. (ed.), *The Autobiography of Charles Darwin, 1809–1882*, New York: W.W. Norton, 1958.
4   Charles Darwin, *Journal of Researches*, London: Henry Colburn, 1839.
5   Charles Darwin, *The Origin of Species, by Means of Natural Selection or the Preservation of Favoured Races in the Struggle for Life*, New York: New American Library, 1859/1959.
6   N. Barlow, 'Charles Darwin and the Galapagos Islands', *Nature*, 136, p. 391, 1935.
7   G. Himmelfarb, *Darwin and the Darwinian Revolution*, Chicago: Ivan R. Dee, 1959/1996.
8   F. Darwin (ed.), *The Foundations of the Origin of Species, Two Essays Written in 1842 and 1844 by Charles Darwin*, Cambridge: Cambridge University Press, 1901/1987.
9   S.N. Grebstein (ed.), *Monkey Trial, the State of Tennessee vs. John Thomas Scopes*, Boston: Houghton Mifflin Co., 1960.
10 Charles Darwin, *The Expression of Emotions in Man and Animals*, Chicago: University of Chicago Press, 1872/1965.
11 F. Darwin (ed.), *Life and Letters of Charles Darwin*, 3 vols, London: John Murray, 1887.
12 M.T. Ghiselin, *The Triumph of the Darwinian Method*, Berkeley, CA: University of California Press, 1969.
13 H.E. Gruber, *Darwin on Man, a Psychological Study of Scientific Creativity*, second edition, Chicago: University of Chicago Press, 1981.

Darwin's major writings

Barlow, N. (ed), *Charles Darwin's Diary of the Voyage of H.M.S. 'Beagle'*, Cambridge: Cambridge University Press, 1933.
—— *The Autobiography of Charles Darwin, 1809–1882*, New York: W.W. Norton, 1933.
Darwin, Charles, *Journal of Researches into the Geology and Natural History of the Various Countries Visited by H. M. S. Beagle Under the Command of Captain FitzRoy, R. N. From 1832–1836*, London: Henry Colburn, 1839.
—— *The Origin of Species, by Means of Natural Selection or the Preservation of Favoured Races in the Struggle for Life*, New York: New American Library, 1859.
—— *The Descent of Man, and Selection in Relation to Sex*, Princeton, NJ: Princeton University Press, 1871/1981.

Further reading

Desmond, A. and Moore, J., *Darwin*, London: Michael Joseph, 1992.
Ghiselin, M.T., *The Triumph of the Darwinian Method*, Berkeley, CA: University of California Press, 1969.

Grebstein, S.N. (ed.), *Monkey Trial, the State of Tennessee vs. John Thomas Scopes*, Boston: Houghton Mifflin Co., 1960.

Gruber, H.E., *Darwin on Man, a Psychological Study of Scientific Creativity*, 2nd edition, Chicago: University of Chicago Press, 1981.

Huxley, J. and Kettlewell, H.B.D., *Charles Darwin and his World*, New York: The Viking Press, 1965.

LOUIS M. SMITH

JOHN RUSKIN 1819–1900

No changing of place at a hundred miles an hour, nor making of stuffs a thousand yards a minute, will make us one whit stronger, happier, or wiser. There was always more in the world than men could see, walked they ever so slowly; they will see it no better for going fast. And they will at last, and soon too, find out that their grand inventions for conquering (as they think) space and time, do, in reality, conquer nothing; for space and time are, in their own essence, unconquerable, and besides did not want any sort of conquering; they wanted using. A fool always wants to shorten space and time: a wise man wants to lengthen both. A fool wants to kill space and kill time. A wise man, first to gain them, then to animate them. Your railroad, when you come to understand it, is only a device for making the world smaller: and as for being able to talk from place to place, that is indeed, well and convenient; but suppose you have, originally, nothing to say. We shall be obliged at last to confess, what we should long ago have known, that the really precious things are thought and sight, not pace.[1]

John Ruskin was born in 1819 and died in 1900. The last decade of his life, like that of his contemporary Nietzsche, was passed in a state of mental collapse. Unlike Nietzsche, during his lifetime, every word that Ruskin wrote was attended to. He was one of the great prophets of his time, the Victorian age, influencing thoughts and minds on pretty well every important topic, from art and architecture, to capitalism and the nature of society, through to the nature of science, the impact of technology and the significance of religion. For fifty years, as Kenneth Clark pointed out, to read Ruskin was accepted as proof of the possession of a soul. However, since the early years of the twentieth century, Ruskin's star has been in decline, just as Nietzsche's has been in the ascendant. This may be partly because of embarrassing aspects of Ruskin's biography, now much dwelt on.

Or, more fundamentally, it may be because of the deeply unfashionable nature of Ruskin's thinking. How are we supposed to take seriously someone who declared that the vote of the working man was not 'worth a rat's squeak'? Or who was a fierce opponent of liberalism and a complete unbeliever in equality? Or who insisted that the Gothic style was to be preferred to the classical largely on moral grounds, that in the former but not in the latter, the soul of the individual craftsman was allowed to express itself? Or who fiercely attacked the division of labour on the grounds that it is not just the labour which is divided, but the labourers themselves, 'divided into mere segments of men, broken into small fragments and crumbs of life, so that all the little piece of intelligence which is left in a man is not enough to make a pin, or a nail, but exhausts itself in making the point of a pin or the head of a nail?'[2] Or who based much of his criticism of capitalism on the (surely erroneous) premise that 'whenever material gain follows exchange, for every plus there is a precisely equal minus?'[3]

One of the difficulties of reading Ruskin is the sheer volume of his works. Another is their highly idiosyncratic approach and style. And a third is the wholly unsystematic nature of his mind and thought. Add to these his apparent changes of mind, and it may seem that unearthing Ruskins' views on a topic like education is hardly going to be worth the trouble.

However, beneath all the surface difficulties and even the changes of mind, there are themes of great importance, which also have relevance to education. Of these, two are pre-eminent (and on these Ruskin never really wavered). If only because they are not the sorts of thing 'educators' normally discuss, there is a strong case for taking the trouble.

The first of these points is the distinction Ruskin continually makes between science and what he calls higher contemplation (or *theoria*). Ruskin admits that scientific pursuits are to be praised, in raising us (or some of us) from inactive reverie to useful thought. But they are to be feared or blamed, he says, precisely in their tendency to check impulses towards higher contemplation. They have a tendency to chill and subdue the feelings and to resolve all things into atoms and numbers:

> For most men, an ignorant enjoyment is better than an informed one; it is better to conceive the sky as a blue dome than a dark cavity, and the cloud as a golden throne than a sleety mist. I much question whether any one who knows optics, however religious he may be, can feel in equal degree the pleasure or reverence which an unlettered peasant may feel at the sight of a rainbow. And it is mercifully thus ordained, since the law of life, for a finite being, with respect to the works of an infinite one, must always be an infinite ignorance. We cannot fathom the mystery of a single flower, nor is it intended that we should; but that the pursuit of science should constantly be stayed by the love of beauty, and accuracy of knowledge by tenderness of emotion.[4]

So, in Ruskin's terms, there is a science of the aspects of things, as well as of their nature. During his life he vacillated on whether their nature was to be understood in Christian terms, as to whether the world was to be seen as God's handiwork in the traditional biblical sense, and on whether in appreciating nature we were engaging in a specifically Christian activity. But what he did not vacillate on was in drawing a distinction between what he called *aesthesis* and *theoria*, which is the second Ruskinian theme of educational significance.

Aesthesis is mere pleasure in appearance, whereas *theoria* is what emerges in responding to beauty with one's whole moral being. Throughout his life Ruskin was worried that arts which remained on the level of *aesthesis* would 'sink into a mere amusement', and become 'ministers to morbid sensibilities, ticklers and fanners of the soul's sleep'.[5] (Hence his misguided spat with Whistler, misguided if only because, whatever Whistler said about his art, in practice there is far more in what he does than the 'mere amusement' of art for art's sake.) *Theoria*, on the other hand, could reach into the true nature of the thing represented, which for Ruskin always contained a spiritual-cum-moral element, even though he pretty certainly abandoned orthodox Christianity. But he continued to see beauty in quasi-Platonic terms, as intimating a level of experience beyond the material and beyond what science could reveal.

Obviously for a thinker like Ruskin, education could not be utilitarian. Nor could it focus on science. In fact, it would have to be fundamentally education in morality, taking morality in its widest sense as embracing something like a whole philosophy of life. So in the first lecture in *The Eagle's Nest* (of 1872) we find Ruskin developing a notion of the university not unlike that of Newman's:

> The object of University teaching is to form your conceptions; – not to acquaint you with arts, nor sciences. It is to give you a notion of what is meant by smith's work, for instance; – but not to make you blacksmiths. It is to give you a notion of what is meant by medicine, but not to make you physicians. The proper academy for blacksmiths is a blacksmith's forge; the proper academy for physicians is an hospital. Here you are to be taken away from the forge, out of the hospital, out of all special and limited labour and thought, into the 'Universitas' of labour and thought, that you may in peace, in leisure, in calm of disinterested contemplation, be enabled to conceive rightly the laws of Nature and the destinies of Man.[6]

It is not necessarily an objection to a conception that it does not exist, and maybe never has existed. What is interesting about Ruskin's Universitas is that while many in higher education might be prepared to play lip-service to something of the sort, at the beginning of the third millennium we are further away from it than ever. Academic departments have become ever more specialized and narrow, while governments and administrators become ever more instrumentalist about the point of the university, and ever more all-inclusive and consumerist about its clientele.

For Ruskin the very notion of a 'consumer' of education would have been an oxymoron, for in education the task is to guide and to convert people who do not yet know how to chose wisely. Indeed in his lecture on 'The Future of England' (of 1869), Ruskin addressed the governing classes with the words 'The people are crying to you for command, and you stand there at pause, and silent. ... "Govern us", they cry with one heart, though many minds. ... You alone can feed them, and clothe, and bring into their right minds, for you only can govern – that is to say, you only can educate them. Educate, or govern, they are one and the same word. Education does not mean teaching people to know what they do not know. It means teaching them to behave as they do not behave.'[7]

So the leaders, perhaps the university people as well as the aristocracy, would teach the rest. What they would teach them is laid out, somewhat impressionistically, in *Sesame and Lilies* (of 1865) and also in *The Eagle's Nest* (of 1872). In the former he castigates those who think of education as a matter of social and material advancement. True education is about reading and learning to read, and it is about reading an author who has 'something to say which he perceives to be true and useful, or helpfully beautiful', and which he has said or can say. Such an author will be able to say of his work 'this is the best of me; for the rest, I ate, and drank, and slept, loved and hated, like another; my life was as the vapour, and is not; but this I saw and knew: this, if anything of mine, is worth your memory'.[8] Books of this kind have been written in all ages by their greatest men, Ruskin says. As a nation we should build libraries full of their work 'accessible to all clean and orderly persons at all times of the day and evening', with strict laws being enforced for cleanliness and quietness – all a valid sense of lifelong learning, though without the idolatry of the new, the noisy and the mindlessly busy.

Girls and women must be given this education as much as men, and both sexes should learn science, history and mathematics, and engage in sports. But the point of all of it, as of painting, sculpture and above all architecture, is to instil in ourselves a sense of the 'advancing power of human nature', in the sense that the mortal part of it would one day be swallowed up in immortality, though, of course, Ruskin did not believe in the orthodox doctrine of an after-life. But what he did believe was that life could be ennobled, and that although the vanity of life was given in vain, there was something behind the veil of it, which was not vanity.

He also believed that the first lesson which the arts had to teach us was that nothing can be truly noble which is not imperfect. The great artists always work beyond their powers of execution. Much of what they do is, like nature itself, unfinished and irregular. These irregularities are signs of life. And hence, paradoxically, of beauty too. The search for perfection is, in fact, a readiness to accept the perfection of the dead, of the mediocre. It also usually means that sub-workers in a task have to suppress their own personalities in order to work towards some pattern ordained by another. 'But accurately speaking, no good work whatever can be perfect, and the demand for perfection is always a sign of a misunderstanding of the ends of art.'[9] It is, of course, part of the virtue of the Gothic that it allows imperfection and irregularity to flourish within its overarching and transcendent vision.

What this might actually mean is spelled out in *The Eagle's Nest*. Sight is a spiritual power. It is the source of all necessary knowledge in art. Reading and writing are in no sense education unless they lead us to feeling kindly towards all creatures. And in order that we should understand what natural things and the works of man are, in themselves, drawing is 'vital education of the most precious kind'. All of this takes us back to what in *Modern Painters* he had referred to as the science of aspects – that understanding of things and the world in human terms, in their human relevance and meaning, and in the way that relevance and meaning lead to the transcendence implied by *theoria*, all quite distinct from the abstractions and de-mystifications of science – and which the great painters, Turner above all, had so triumphantly demonstrated.

Ruskin has nothing to say which would be comprehensible to today's political and educational leaders, and very little to our cultural élite either.

That is a comment on our times, rather than on the value of what he had to say.

Notes

1 John Ruskin, *Modern Painters*, vol. III, part IV, ch. 17, 1856; Collected Works (see below), vol. V, p. 381.
2 John Ruskin, *The Stones of Venice*, vol. II, 1853, 'The Nature of the Gothic', as in John Ruskin, *Unto This Last*, ed. Clive Wilmer, Penguin Books, p. 87, 1985.
3 John Ruskin, *Unto This Last*, essay 4, 'Ad Valorem', p. 213, 1860.
4 John Ruskin, *Modern Painters*, vol. III, part IV, ch. 17; Collected Works (see below), vol. V, pp. 386–7.
5 John Ruskin, *Modern Painters*, vol. II, part III, ch. 1; Collected Works (see below), vol. IV, p. 33.
6 John Ruskin, *The Eagle's Nest*, Lecture 1, Section 18, 1872.
7 John Ruskin, 'The Future of England', 1869, Collected Works (see below), vol. XVIII, pp. 500–3.
8 John Ruskin, *Sesame and Lilies*, 1865; Collected Works (see below), vol. XVIII, p. 61.
9 John Ruskin, 'The Nature of the Gothic', p. 91.

See also

In this book: Nietzsche

Ruskin's major writings

The standard edition of the Collected Works is still the 39-volume edition edited by E.T. Cook and Alexander Wedderburn and published by George Allen in London between 1903 and 1912.

Further reading

Anthony, P.D., *John Ruskin's Labour: A Study of Ruskin's Social Theory*, Cambridge: Cambridge University Press, 1983.
Batchelor, John, *John Ruskin, No Wealth But Life*, London: Chatto and Windus, 2000.
Fuller, Peter, *Theoria*, London: Chatto and Windus, 1988.
Hewison, Robert, *Ruskin and Oxford, The Art of Education*, Oxford: Oxford University Press, 1996.
Hilton, Tim, *John Ruskin, The Early Years*, Yale University Press, 1985; and *John Ruskin, The Later Years*, Yale University Press, 2000.

ANTHONY O'HEAR

HERBERT SPENCER 1820–1903

> Children should be led to make their own investigations, and to
> draw their own inferences. They should be told as little as
> possible, and induced to discover as much as possible.[1]

These pregnant words were written by Herbert Spencer in 1861. He had little experience of teaching but he had the most far-reaching influence on teaching and teacher training; he was compared by R.H. Quick in his *Essays on Educational Reformers* (1868) with Mulcaster, Ascham and Locke, and H.E. Armstrong advised all teachers to read Spencer's *Education* to 'have clear ideas on the subject'.[2]

Herbert Spencer was born in Derby on 27 April 1820 to a family of ardent Wesleyans; his paternal grandfather Matthew was a schoolmaster, while his father George was a man of fixed and stubborn social and religious views who had married Harriet Holmes, the daughter of a local plumber, in 1819. Spencer's early education was however neglected and at the age of 13 he was sent to live near Bath with his uncle Thomas, a radical thinker and priest. He learnt a lot from the former don at Cambridge and was offered a place at the university at the age of 16, which he declined. For three months in 1837 he was assistant to a schoolmaster in Derby. He left to be assistant to Charles Fox, the resident engineer of part of the London–Birmingham Railway. He did well and became private secretary to Captain Moorson, the engineer-in-chief.

Upon the completion of the railway in 1841 he was sacked. He became honorary secretary of the Derby Branch of the Complete Suffrage Movement and then sub-editor of the organization's newspaper, *The Pilot*. He was obliged to return to his railway career between 1846 and 1848, but found a secure position as sub-editor of the *Economist* in 1848. In this post he met many of the leading intellectuals of the day and in 1850 published *Social Statics: or the Conditions Essential to Human Happiness* which aimed to show 'every man has freedom to do all that he wills, provided he infringes not the equal freedom of any other man'. His friend G.H. Lewes (1817–78), the partner of George Eliot, the writer, was editor of the *Leader*, a radical paper, and it was in that journal that Spencer in an article on 'Development Hypothesis' in March 1852 defended the theory of organic evolution, some seven years before Charles Darwin published *The Origin of Species*. He was endeavouring to discover scientific laws within his evolutionary framework by which individuals could manage their own lives without interference from government. Where Darwin confined his theory to biology, Herbert Spencer applied evolution to all nature and society. His thinking influenced Alfred Russell Wallace (1823–1913), the naturalist, who also made an important pre-Darwinian contribution to the theory of evolution.

A legacy from his uncle Thomas freed him in 1853 from the need to earn his living for some years. He travelled in England and Scotland and to Switzerland where physical over-exertion caused a cardiac disturbance from which he never recovered. He wrote *The Principles of Psychology* (1855) but mental overwork led to a nervous breakdown from which again he never fully recovered. The book was innovative in its evolutionary psychology and sowed the seeds of his devotion of most of the rest of his life to the development of what he called *Synthetic Philosophy*. The study was not completed until 1896, though he set out the scheme for it in the preface to his *First Principles* in 1862. It was made possible over the years by inheritances from his father and his uncle William and in later years by profits from the sale of his books. He deduced laws of evolution from changes in the solar system, in the structure of the earth, in climate, in flora and fauna, in individuals and in societies. Evolution he held to be a universal process, 'a change from a less coherent form to a more coherent form' (p. 327). Thomas Huxley (1825–95) said of Spencer that he was the most original of thinkers though he never invented a new thought. The originality lay in his applying the laws of evolution to the study of so much of knowledge – psychology, biology, geology and geography, sociology, education and ethics. Indeed he coined the phrase 'the survival of the fittest' and he deemed philosophy to be the science of sciences because of its generalizing qualities. He was much concerned with the process of differentiation, with the change from a homogenous to a heterogenous condition. As he put it in *First Principles*:

> Comparing the rule of a savage chief with that of a civilized government, aided by its subordinate local governments and their officers, down to the police in the streets, we see how as men have advanced from tribes of tens to nations of millions, the regulative process has grown large in amount.[3]

Equally, this differentiation has occurred, he argued, in language, painting and sculpture. His biographer, Hugh S.R. Eliot, in the *Dictionary of National Biography for 1901–11* called *Synthetic Philosophy* 'the best synthesis of the knowledge of his times'.[4]

Though his experience of teaching and of young people was very limited, he pronounced with great authority in his dogmatic way but also with great acclaim on the whole gamut of education – child development, curriculum, teaching methods. In 1861 he brought together in *Education: Intellectual, Moral and Physical* four articles which he had published in the 1850s – 'The Art of Education', *North British Review*, May 1854; 'Moral Discipline for Children', *British Quarterly Review*, April 1858; 'Physical Training', *British Quarterly Review*, April 1859; 'What Knowledge is of Moral Worth?', *Westminster Review*, July 1859. His reputation as an educationalist rests upon this book which urged the claims of science as having paramount value as a discipline and advocated training children not by fear but by freedom, letting them learn from the natural consequences of wrong behaviour without parental involvement. Since the mind moves from homogeneity towards heterogeneity, education, he argued memorably, should proceed from the simple to the complex and lessons from the concrete to the abstract. His contention that 'education should be a repetition of civilization in little'[5] attracted less support. The book went into many editions, selling thousands of copies, and was translated into many languages. It appealed to progressive educationalists and was used extensively in training teachers. Spencer was himself influenced by Johann Pestalozzi (1746–1827) and through the work of John Dewey (1859–1952) his thinking had great influence on British primary education, though his emphasis on science in the curriculum was not adopted widely, except in Russia, and it took some decades before his axiom was to be generally accepted:

> To prepare us for complete living is the function which education has to discharge.[6]

He was appalled that so little was done to prepare for parenthood and for citizenship.

An agnostic, Spencer died at Brighton on 8 December 1903 and was cremated at Golders Green after a secular address by Leonard Courtney.

Notes

1 H. Spencer, *Education: Intellectual, Moral and Physical*, p. 94, 1861.
2 H. E. Armstrong, *The Teaching of Scientific Method*, p. 381, 1903.
3 H. Spencer, *First Principles*, p. 395, 1862.
4 H.S.R. Eliot, *sub* Spencer in the *Dictionary of National Biography for 1901–11*, p. 366, 1920.
5 H. Spencer, *Education*, p. 83, 1861.
6 H. Spencer, *Education*, p. 10, 1861.

See also

In this book: Pestalozzi, Darwin

Spencer's major writings

The place of publication is London unless otherwise stated

Social Statics, Williams and Norgate, 1850.
The Principles of Psychology, Longman, 1855.
Education: Intellectual, Moral and Physical, Williams and Norgate, 1861.
First Principles, Williams and Norgate, 1862.
The Principles of Biology, Williams and Norgate, 1864–7.
The Study of Sociology, The International Scientific Series, volume 5, 1872.
Descriptive Sociology, Williams and Norgate, 1873–81.
The Principles of Sociology, 3 volumes, Williams and Norgate, 1876–96.
The Principles of Ethics, 2 volumes, Williams and Norgate, 1892–3.
Autobiography, 2 volumes, Williams and Norgate, 1904.
Cavanagh, F.A. (ed.), *Herbert Spencer on Education*, Cambridge: Cambridge University Press, 1932.
Duncan, D. (ed.), *The Life and Letters of Herbert Spencer*, Madras, 1908.
Low-Beer, A. (ed.), *Selections, Herbert Spencer*, Educational Thinkers Series, Macmillan, 1969.
Offer, J (ed.), *Political Writings*, Cambridge: Cambridge University Press, 1994.

Further reading

Armstrong, H.E., *The Teaching of Scientific Method*, Macmillan, 1903.

Compayré, G., *Herbert Spencer and Scientific Education*, New York: TY Crowell & Co., 1907.

Eliot, H.S.R., *Herbert Spencer*, Makers of the Nineteenth Century, 1917.

Kennedy, J.G., *Herbert Spencer*, Boston: Twayne Publishers, 1978.

Lauwerys, J.A., 'Herbert Spencer and the Scientific Movement', in A.V. Judges (ed.), *Pioneers of English Education*, Faber & Faber, 1952.

Peel, J.D.Y., *Herbert Spencer: The Evolution of a Sociologist*, Heinemann, 1971.

Quick, R.H. (Revd), *Essays on Educational Reformers*, new edition, Longman, 1902.

Wiltshire, D. *The Social and Political Thought of H. Spencer*, Oxford: Oxford University Press, 1978.

G.R. BATHO

MATTHEW ARNOLD 1822–88

> The idea of perfection as an inward condition of the mind and spirit is at variance with the mechanical and material civilisation in esteem with us, and nowhere, as I have said, so much in esteem as with us. The idea of perfection as a general expansion of the human family is at variance with our strong individualism, our hatred of all limits to the unrestrained swing of the individual's personality, our maxim of 'every man for himself'. Above all, the idea of perfection as a harmonious expansion of human nature is at variance with our want of flexibility, with our inaptitude for seeing more than one side of a thing, with our intense energetic absorption in the particular pursuit we happen to be following. So culture has a rough task to achieve in this country.[1]

Matthew Arnold lived from 1822 until 1888. As well as being a noted poet and literary critic (and Professor of Poetry in Oxford in 1857), Arnold had a considerable personal and professional interest in education. His father was Dr Thomas Arnold, the reforming headmaster of Rugby, while he himself was one of Her Majesty's Inspectors of Schools from 1851 until 1886. Although, in this capacity, Arnold was mainly involved with the state of elementary schools in England, he travelled widely in Europe on educational missions and campaigned vigorously for the establishment of secondary schools in Britain. Aside from his specifically educational writings, his essay *Culture and Anarchy* (of 1869) has obvious educational relevance, and has over the years been taken as a major statement of the virtues of what has come to be known as 'liberal' education. As will become apparent, in this context liberal signifies non-instrumental. It does not mean that a liberal education is not prescriptive – it will be highly prescriptive – nor does it mean that the state has no role to play in its provision; on the matter of state education, Arnold take quite the opposite view to that of his fellow high-minded liberal reformer, John Stuart Mill.

In common with many Victorian thinkers, Arnold is highly critical of the state of his society. The England of his time is brutalized by class division and also by an unthinking pursuit of wealth and power, by which it (erroneously) measures its progress. But what is all this wealth for? It cannot be an end in itself, and making it such blinds us to better, less Philistine ends.

As things stand in the England of 1869, society is divided into three classes. There is no overarching vision of culture to unify and harmonize the different levels of social existence.

As a result, each is cut off from the rest, and lacking any vision other than self-interest, each remains immured in its own characteristic vices. Thus the aristocracy are, in Arnold's terms, Barbarians. They are noble in a sense, but chiefly interested in external display – their great houses, their codes of manners, their high spirits and their field sports. They remain woefully inadequate in intelligence, and can conceive of no form of existence than their own. No more can the middle classes, the Philistines. Again they are not wholly vicious. They display the virtues of hard work and philanthropy, but they have their own narrowness of vision, they are illiberal in spirit, and even in their philanthropy mechanistic and dismal. The lower classes, the 'vast residuum' or Populace as Arnold terms them, are raw and half-developed. They have long remained hidden in poverty and squalor, but they are now emerging from their hiding places 'to assert an Englishman's heaven-born privilege of doing as he likes, and is beginning to perplex us by marching where it likes, meeting where it likes, bawling where it likes, breaking what it likes'.[2] Arnold did not like liberty, which he found hard to distinguish from anarchy. Goodness knows what he would have said of popular taste or of social mores at the start of the third millennium.

For Arnold saw culture as the great unifier of society, releasing the best instincts of each class and harmoniously integrating them, and in our time the provider of the inward goals we all need to produce a drive to personal perfection, and hence our only defence against the anarchy of unrestrained individual choice and selfishness. (Remember that Arnold was the author of 'Dover Beach', and believed that public, dogmatic religion had had its day.) He also saw the state, in a society pervaded with true culture, as that through which each person's best self would be realized in a way impossible when each simply pursued his or her individual goals.

What, though, was culture? It is not, as its critics allege, a smattering of Greek and Latin, nor is it a frivolous or optional addition to the good life. It is, rather, the disinterested study and adumbration of the ideal of human perfection, as it emerges through 'all the voices of human experience which have been heard upon it, of art, science, poetry, philosophy, history, as well of religion'.[3] And the ideal of perfection which is supposed to arise from this study and propagation of the 'best that is thought and known in the world' will counter both our materialism (because of its inwardness) and our individualism and class divisions (because it aims at a general expansion of the whole human family). It is, in Arnold's terms, a pursuit of what he calls total perfection, a matter of continual becoming rather than just a state of being once achieved; and we achieve this state of becoming by continually bringing up ingrained habits of mind by continual reading, observing and thinking in the light of the best that has been thought and known.

To readers who have experienced the culture wars of the late twentieth century, Arnold's view of culture will seem remarkably optimistic in its belief about the civilizing power of culture, and remarkably confident that the best that has been thought and known can be identified. As to the latter, Arnold can be defended by appeal to the test of time, and also by the thought that neither he nor any other defender of traditional culture needs to assert that canons are inflexible. What they do need to assert is that some works have, by all reliable judges over much time and in many places, been regarded as exemplary: *The Iliad, The Oresteia, The Aeneid, The Divine Comedy, Hamlet, Phèdre, Paradise Lost, Faust, Eugene Onegin, La Comedie Humaine, Middlemarch*, etc., etc. In the light of the standards implicit in these judgments, other works can be added or even subtracted. And, as everyone knows, one of the delights of cultural literacy is finding new treasures, and everything Arnold says about flexibility, creativity and joy suggests that he is as aware as anyone of the benefits of new cultural experiences.

But what Arnold does rule out, and correctly rule out is the notion that we should give the masses some inferior intellectual fare. He sees it as the special role of the middle classes to educate their own ranks in culture – first by setting up secondary schools for their children – and then to spread what they have learned through the whole of society:

> Only it must be real thought and real beauty; real sweetness and real light. Plenty of people will try to give the masses, as they call them, an intellectual food prepared and adapted in the way they think proper for the actual condition of the masses. The ordinary popular literature is an example of this way of working on the masses. Plenty of people will try to indoctrinate the masses ... but culture works differently. It does not try to teach down to the level of inferior classes; it does not try to win them for this or that sect of its own, with ready-made judgements and watchwords. It seeks to do away with classes; to make the best that has been thought and known in the world current everywhere; to make all men live in an atmosphere of sweetness and light, where they may use ideas, as it uses them itself, freely – nourished, and not bound by them.[4]

To which, given the number of contemporary sacred cows this proposal will offend, one can only add 'amen'. In an age when so-called higher education, far from tracking down to the lower classes, actually maintains that there are no real distinctions between higher and lower culture, and a man like Mr Greg Dyke becomes the head of the BBC and the driving force of a campaign to educate the masses through soap operas, one can only applaud Arnold's sentiments here while regretting that they will no longer be taken seriously.

But that is not to say that Arnold's own position on culture is without difficulty. In the first place his interpretation of culture in general, and of Greek culture in particular, in terms of sweetness and light looks parochial and narrow. Maybe the words are unfortunate, and Arnold should not be held to them too rigidly, but in *Culture and Anarchy* and the discussion in it of Hellenism he shows little of the toughness and excitement of Nietzsche's *Birth of Tragedy*, a book which transformed our attitude to classical antiquity so that the Arnold-cum-Lord Leighton view of ancient Greece is hardly sustainable.

Arnold's view of classical antiquity and of the purifying, elevating power of culture and indeed of the role of the state in promoting a noble national culture owes not a little to German commentary, to Wincklemann, to

Goethe, to Schiller, to Schelling, to Humboldt. For it was these German romantics above all who saw culture in organic terms, and who thought that the modern state could recreate a kind of new Athenian age through its cultural and educative activities, as did Arnold himself, who thought of the state as the 'nation in its collective and corporate character' and who saw state secondary schools as means par excellence for promoting the best of the culture of the nation.

It is easy to sneer at all this as hopelessly optimistic in the light of the Nazi high command in the Berlin Philharmonie, and to take Auschwitz – an atrocity perpetrated by the most cultured of nations – as a kind of excuse for not even making the effort of educating our young in high culture. So we leave them with horizons bounded by whatever Mr Dyke chooses to give them, and insult upon insult, pretend that key skills and 'media studies' can constitute some sort of education. Against this sort of tracking down – not tolerated for a moment by those parents in this country who can afford to pay for their children's education – Arnold's words in his Rede lecture of 1882 are pertinent:

> If we know the best that has been thought and uttered in the world, we shall find that the art and poetry and eloquence of men who lived, perhaps, long ago, who had the most limited natural knowledge, who had the most erroneous conceptions about many important matters, we shall find that this art, and poetry, and eloquence, have in fact not only the power of refreshing and delighting us, they also have the power, – such is the strength and worth, in essentials, of their authors' criticism of life, – they have a fortifying, and elevating, and quickening, and suggestive power, capable of wonderfully helping us to relate the results of modern science to our need for conduct, our need for beauty.[5]

And in his reports as Inspector of Schools, he constantly affirmed the way in which good poetry both suggests high purposes of action and, in its eloquence, inspires the emotions necessary to put those purposes into practice.

This is surely right. Good poetry – Shakespeare, Milton, Wordsworth, Arnold himself – does expand and liberate the mind. It does raise us above the utilitarian. It does suggest possibilities and aspirations beyond those of the everyday. It does take us out of our narrow self-centredness. It intimates grace, tragedy, nobility, pathos and many other perceptions we might otherwise never come to have, and it can and does inspire. However clumsily, it was this which Arnold was convinced by, and this which he wanted to release in a project of national regeneration. The critics are right to suggest that there is no necessary connection between any of this and good behaviour, and surely also right to demur at Arnold's corporatist hopes for the state, but they are wrong to imply that a life without the inspiration which culture alone can give would be anything but narrow and unfulfilled.

In pre-Arnoldian days religion did much of what he wanted in culture, though, as he himself pointed out, in a 'Hebraic', dogmatic and moralistic way. Even in religious times, the fierce Hebraic conscience needed to be tempered by the Hellenistic intelligence and love of beauty. One of our problems today is that we have forgotten that beauty, grace and the type of light-footed, positive intelligence valued by Arnold could have any role at all, either in education or in culture more widely. We may find Arnold's stress on sweetness and light insipid, and his prose writing lacklustre. But, if this is what we experience on reading Arnold, we should turn the mirror on ourselves and our culture, high and low. Insipidity and lack of lustre are not the worst of faults, if the underlying thinking is valid – or once was. Perhaps the real problem with Arnold is that we have a culture in which the sort of ambitions he has for either the masses or the middle classes have been rendered simply inconceivable by the actions of politicians, educators and, most damning of all, by the very cultural élite whose position in public life, esteem and subsidy the thought of Arnold did so much to establish.

Notes

1 Matthew Arnold, *Culture and Anarchy*, New York: Chelsea House, p 10, 1983 [1869].
2 Ibid., p. 66.
3 Ibid., p. 8.
4 Ibid., p. 31.
5 Matthew Arnold, 'Literature and Science', in *The Oxford Authors: Matthew Arnold*, ed. Miriam Allott and Robert H. Super, Oxford University Press, pp 456–71, at p 468, 1986 [1882].

See also

In this book: Mill, Nietzsche, Humboldt

Arnold's major writings

Arnold. *The Complete Prose Works*, ed. R.H. Super, Michigan: Ann Arbor, 11 vols, 1960–77.
Apart from numerous editions of Arnold's *Culture and Anarchy*, there is a Penguin education special *Arnold and Education*, ed. Gillian Sutherland, Harmondsworth: Penguin Books, 1973.

Further reading

Allott, Kenneth (ed.), *Matthew Arnold*, Writers and their Backgound Series, London, 1975.
Connell, William F., *The Educational Thought and Influence of Matthew Arnold*, London, 1950.

ANTHONY O'HEAR

THOMAS HENRY HUXLEY 1825–95

> Surely it would be the most undesirable thing in the world that
> one half of the population of this country should be accomplished
> men of letters with no tincture of science, and the other half
> should be men of science with no tincture of letters?[1]

Born above a butcher's shop in Ealing, then on the outskirts of London,
Thomas Henry (Hal) was the seventh of eight children of Rachel and George
Huxley, an unsuccessful schoolmaster. Despite having very little formal
schooling, he won in 1842 a scholarship to Charing Cross Medical School,
where he did well but lacked the funds to complete a medical degree. Qualified
at the lower grade of surgeon, he enrolled in the Royal Navy. Sir John
Richardson, explorer and the Navy's senior doctor perceived his talents, and
arranged his posting as Assistant Surgeon on HMS *Rattlesnake* setting out on
a voyage of discovery in 1846 to survey the passage between Australia and
New Guinea. Provided they kept the crew healthy, surgeons on such voyages
were expected (in a tradition going back to the eighteenth century) to
investigate the natural history they encountered. The Captain was the sickly
Owen Stanley, son of an aristocratic parson-naturalist who had become a
Bishop and President of the Linnean Society of London; and he himself
was keen to advance science, in the tradition of James Cook and Matthew
Flinders. Voyages had become a recognized route to scientific eminence.

On the voyage Huxley dredged up previously unknown marine
invertebrates; but he found great frustration in what he perceived as the
Captain's neurotic reluctance to allow prolonged visits ashore. Huxley did in
fact participate in an overland expedition through the jungles of tropical
Australia, which nearly ended badly for him; and was tantalized by Stanley's
refusal to allow more than superficial contacts with the natives of New
Guinea (no doubt because of their fearsome reputation). His relationship
with Stanley, who evidently took a fatherly interest in him, was fraught;
refusing to be patronized, Huxley would not be the Captain's pet. Placing
himself as plebeian, identifying with the crew and the poor patients at
Charing Cross, he was to see himself throughout his life as the scourge of the
establishment – even when he had in later life become part of it. In Australia
the awkward surgeon met Henrietta Heathorn, and they fell in love. The
ship returned to England in 1850, and after an engagement conducted by
letters taking up to six months each way, she joined him and they were
married very happily in 1855 and founded an intellectual dynasty.

Huxley's research was so outstanding that in 1851 he was elected a
Fellow of the Royal Society; but this brought him no income. Given three
years leave to write up his discoveries, when it came to an end he decided to
abandon the Navy and carry on with a career in science. Richard Owen
became his patron, subsequently like Stanley to be despised as patronizing.
After honing his literary skills, supporting himself by journalism and
translation (notably from German), Huxley was appointed in 1854 Lecturer
at the School of Mines in London. This involved shifting his interests to
fossils and teaching students. In the evenings he gave courses to working
men; these were not a new idea of Huxley's, but were something in which he
particularly delighted and where his rhetorical skills were particularly

evident. He also held forth at the fashionable Royal Institution in London's West End, where for half a century mixed intellectual audiences had gathered to be entertained and stimulated by Humphry Davy, Michael Faraday, and now John Tyndall, a physicist, contemporary with Huxley, who shared his rhetorical abilities and his distaste for the prominence of smooth but shallow Oxford and Cambridge men, often clergy, in the educational and learned world – in stark contrast to Germany, with its research universities.

His teaching at the School of Mines, and later at the Normal School at South Kensington (both later became part of Imperial College, London, where Huxley's papers are preserved) can be sampled in his famous textbook, *The Crayfish* (1880). Its bulk is taken up with anatomy, physiology and taxonomy; only within the last 10 per cent do we find a discussion of the evolutionary relationships of crayfishes and other crustaceans. This formal teaching shows a clear separation of fact and theory in the tradition of Francis Bacon; though it would be surprising if students hooked by Huxley's attractive language and masterful sketching on the blackboard could resist his eloquent conclusion. He saw science[2] as 'trained and organised common sense' thus demystifying it. Making it accessible and momentous, he never sought to blind with science. His view of science went with his rejection of organized religion; opposing dogma wherever he found it he coined the word 'agnostic' to describe his own position. The agnostic 'does not know', being content to doubt what nobody is sure about. Atheists were seen as ignoring the Ten Commandments and unperturbed by the prospect of a Last Judgement; Huxley lived a strictly moral life, and made agnosticism respectable.[3] For Huxley, agnosticism was the proper common-sense guide to life in science and beyond it; while training and organizing were the keys to building up a professional scientific community.

He had written a devastating review of a new edition of the anonymous evolutionary book, *Vestiges* (1844), slating it for its inaccuracies; but Charles Darwin perceived that if Huxley could be won around, he would be evolution's apostle. Never fully convinced that natural selection was sufficient to explain development, Huxley did accept that *The Origin of Species* (1859), a lantern in a dark world, made the case for evolution sufficiently strong even for an agnostic. He sharpened his beak and claws in readiness to fight for Darwin. Professing was for him a performance art, and his lectures were compelling, especially when spiced with a little aggression: and in evolution he now had a framework within which to make sense of biology. His predecessors had relied mainly on natural theology, evidence for the wisdom and benevolence of God; Huxley could get by without that. He brought prominently into science the language, astonishingly popular ever since, of warfare against ignorance, bigotry and disease, but urged that, unlike religion and politics, science had never done any harm.

At the Royal Institution in February 1860 he lectured on the origin of species and to Darwin's disappointment presented it agnostically as a hypothesis; then switching into a rant about how England might 'prove to the world, that for one people, at any rate, despotism and demagogy are not the necessary alternatives of government; that freedom and order are not incompatible; that reverence is the handmaid of knowledge; that free discussion is the life of truth, and of true unity in a nation'.[4] He pleaded that science be cherished and preserved from foolish meddlers who thought they did God a service by preventing the study of his works; and ended with a quotation from Tennyson. His hearers were duly excited, affronted and polarized. Such soldiering was not to the taste of Darwin and other gentlemen of science; but in the summer at the British Association for the Advancement of Science Huxley took on Bishop Samuel Wilberforce in a poorly reported debate at Oxford. This inconclusive confrontation ensured that evolution would not be laughed out of court, and Huxley turned into a public figure. His book *Man's Place in Nature* (1863) resulted from these debates.

Students required one kind of rhetoric, and élite audiences at the RI or BAAS another; for working men he adopted a different style. Never patronizing, he made a case like a lawyer before a jury, drawing them in and after presenting the evidence inviting them to come to a conclusion. A particularly memorable talk, delivered in 1868, was 'On a piece of chalk': he used this most basic teaching aid as a way into a truer 'conception of this wonderful universe, and man's relation to it, than the most learned student who is deep-read in the records of humanity and ignorant of those of nature'.[5] Taking his audience through the fossil record, he asked them if they could really believe that all this was the result of endless special creations, ending with a flourish: if the chalk had been placed in a hot flame it would have blazed up like the sun – instead it had been used to illuminate the abyss of the remote past. He knew that working men could never really, like his students, hope to become scientists: he urged upon them the idea that science was not so different from the reasoning they did all the time, and that it was exciting and liberating.

In 1870 Huxley was chosen President of the BAAS; he also in due course became President of the Geological, Ethnological and Palaeontographical Societies, and of the Royal Society. He participated in the opening of Johns Hopkins, the first research university in the USA. His research was particularly important in exploring evolutionary connections between reptiles and birds: study of the hips of dinosaurs convinced him that many had run on their hind legs like ostriches rather than slithered like crocodiles; and he closely studied the fossil bird archaeopteryx. But from the 1860s his role in education was crucial, and his personal research took second place. At South Kensington he inaugurated laboratory teaching and research in zoology; by the time he died most professors of biology in England had been his students, and biology was a secular professional discipline distinct from medicine and from natural history. His campaign to replace clergy in the learned world by meritocrats expert in their field, and aristocratic patrons by powerful professors, had succeeded. His triumphs included getting Charles Darwin buried in Westminster Abbey when he died in 1882. With Tyndall, Herbert Spencer and others he formed the X-club which played a backstage role as a somewhat sinister pressure group within scientific societies. Nevertheless as a sage and admirer of the Old Testament prophets who had fearlessly rebuked tyrants, he came to reject the idea that evolution was the key to ethics: doing right involved putting women and children (the weak) first, rather than letting the fittest survive at their expense. Science alone was not the key to living well.

Extraordinarily active, he collapsed periodically into depression and 'blue devils'. He served on ten royal or other official commissions, was in constant demand as a speaker, and was much involved in publishing projects including scientific journals and the important 'International Scientific Series' of advanced textbooks. In 1870, when universal elementary education was finally introduced in England, he was elected to the London School Board. He was a powerful member, resisting claims by members of the various churches who had hitherto provided all the education there was, and promoting science as an essential part of education at all levels. Refusing to see the cholera as a scourge sent from God to the wicked, he saw it as a punishment for ignorance and sloth. He was very widely read, having a great respect for writers; but believed firmly that a literary education alone was a poor preparation for life. His role on the 'Devonshire' commission of 1872 on scientific instruction was particularly noteworthy. He had little patience with the idea that education was merely the imparting of facts, and was deeply concerned to make it widely available.

At the end of his life he was locked in controversy with the great physicist William Thomson (Lord Kelvin), a pioneer of thermodynamics, over the age of the Earth and hence the speed of evolutionary change. Huxley could not follow Thomson's mathematical inferences, and resented physicists' assumption that their science was fundamental: in the event Huxley was later vindicated because Thomson had known nothing of radioactivity, which transforms the calculations allowing a much longer history for the Earth and the Sun.

Huxley had begun as an explorer; and the wide-eyed curiosity of somebody finding themselves in a brave new world never deserted him. His enthusiasm was communicated to his hearers and readers. The science of the twentieth century was more like Thomson's, defying common sense and relying upon abstruse mathematical models, and less attractive to most people; some of Huxley's excitement is still needed in science education.

Notes

1 *Royal Commission on Scientific Instruction and the Advancement of Science*, London: Eyre and Spottiswoode, para. 3,640, 1872.
2 David Knight, 'Presidential Address: Getting Science Across', *British Journal for the History of Science*, 29 (129–38), p. 132, 1996.
3 Bernard Lightman, *The Origins of Agnosticism*, Baltimore: Johns Hopkins University Press, 1987.
4 T.H. Huxley, 'Species and Races and Their Origin', *Proceedings of the Royal Institution*, 3, p. 200, 1858–62.
5 A.P. Barr (ed.), *The Major Prose of Thomas Henry Huxley*, Athens, GA: University of Georgia Press, p. 156, 1997.

See also

In this book: Darwin

Huxley's major writings

Barr, Alan P. (ed.), *The Major Prose of Thomas Henry Huxley*, Athens, GA: University of Georgia Press, 1997.

Winnick, Charles (ed.), *Science and Education, by Thomas Huxley*, New York: Citadel Press, 1964.

Further reading

Barr, Alan P., *Thomas Henry Huxley's Place in Science and Letters*, Athens, GA: University of Georgia Press, 1997.
Desmond, Adrian, *Huxley*, 2 vols, London: Michael Joseph, 1994, 1997.
Jarrell, Richard A., 'Visionary or Bureaucrat: T.H. Huxley, the Science and Art Department and Science Teaching for the Working Class', *Annals of Science*, vol. 55, pp. 219–40, 1998.

DAVID KNIGHT

LOUISA MAY ALCOTT 1832–88

> I'll tell you that one of my favorite fancies is to look at my family as a small world, to watch the progress of my little men, and, lately, to see how well the influence of my little women works upon them.[1]

Many have called Alcott 'the children's friend'.[2] Ralph Waldo Emerson (1803–1882) called her 'the poet of children',[3] although she is best known as a writer of popular domestic fictions, now childhood classics, most notably *Little Women* (1868–9). That autobiographical novel of moral education and its two sequels about two generations of the March family remain 'beloved'[4] worldwide for the stories they tell and the characters they portray. But these texts at the same time also artfully theorized about child-rearing and schooling, teachers and teaching, most especially about the serious possibilities, purposes, practices and problems of coeducation, a topic that few educational theorists in the US have addressed.[5]

The appearance in this volume of Louisa May Alcott rather than her father, Transcendentalist educational theorist and school reformer Amos Bronson Alcott (1799–1888),[6] may mark a noteworthy development in the historical study of educational thought, registered also in a recent telling report that:

> Before 1982, according to indexes of *Dissertation Abstracts International*, dissertations addressing Bronson outnumber those addressing Louisa by more than 2 to 1. Between 1982 and 1987 the valence shifted, with dissertations attending to Louisa outnumbering those attending to Bronson by about 3 to 1. Since then, Louisa has outstripped Bronson by more than 20 to 1.[7]

Louisa Alcott and her elder sister were Bronson's objects of study as infants in one of the first published American diaries of child development.[8] Yet she charted her own way as a teacher, thinker and writer,[9] and her writing supported both her parents in their impoverished old age. With his friends Elizabeth Palmer Peabody (1804–94) and Margaret Fuller (1810–50),

Bronson Alcott had been a daring coeducational innovator at his own inter-racial Temple School,[10] which later became Louisa Alcott's source for Plumfield, the 'home-like school' in *Little Women* and in its sequel, *Little Men* (1870). Ironically, Alcott's educational narratives have not so much celebrated the educational practice of her well-known father, who took Socrates (469–399 BCE) and Jesus as his own pedagogical models,[11] as they have that of her remarkable mother, Abba May. Alcott was home-schooled in this remarkable New England, Unitarian family who experimented with communal life and often depended upon the charity of their friend Emerson because her father's idealism often left them penniless. But both her parents were conversant with educational theory, especially the Swiss idealism of Johann Heinrich Pestalozzi (1746–1827) and the Irish pragmatism of Maria Edgeworth (1767–1849), both of whose influence on *Little Women* is unmistakable. Her mother wrote that women should assert their right 'to think, feel, and live individually' and to 'be something in yourself'.[12] For a time Alcott herself worked as a nurse, and, as an early suffragist, she signed her letters 'yours for reform of all kinds'.[13] Although never a mother herself, she did, as a domestic servant, care for children and, as a spinster aunt, raise at least one of her sister's children at home. Also a teacher, Alcott ran her own schools for children, collaborated with Peabody in the early kindergarten movement, and participated in the abolitionist movement as a teacher of adult literacy. But her primary contribution to education has been as an artistic writer whose thought imaginatively addressed the most perplexing challenges of child-rearing, schooling and sex equality. Alcott was prolific: one detailed bibliography identifies her as author of 270 works, most published in then prominent domestic periodicals.[14] Although more than a dozen of these were full-length fictions, only *Little Women* and its two sequels constitute her recognized educational *oeuvre*.

Alcott was popular as an artistic writer long before her educational thought achieved recognition. By 1880, the *New York Times* reported that she was 'generally regarded as the most popular and successful literary woman in America'.[15] When she died, her funeral notice appeared on the *Times'* front page. A century later in 1986, she was one of only three authors included in the *Ladies' Home Journal*'s list of the twenty-five most important women in US history. Her *Little Women*, which has never fallen out of print, has inspired cartoons, recipes, postage stamps, films, plays, T-shirts, book bags, samplers, puzzles, magnets, note cards, posters, diaries, jewellery, nightgowns and dolls. The professoriate (showing disinterest toward children and scorn both for sentimentalism and for pop culture generally) had little to do with her. Indeed, much evidence exists to support the critical claim that 'there can be few other books in American literary history which have had so enormous a critical impact on half the reading population, and so miniscule a place in the libraries or criticism of the other'.[16] For educated women – librarians and school-teachers – helped maintain the popularity of Alcott's books, as did both highbrow and middlebrow popular culture. Alcott's writings often appeared on lists of recommended children's books and reached children in the form of special school editions. Girl Scout handbooks cited *Little Women* and recommended Louisa May Alcott as someone who embodied an ideal of the educated woman worthy of girls' emulation.[17] Alcott's popularity with American readers has thus persisted despite highbrow men's indifference. Indeed, perhaps thanks to that persistence, significant women intellectuals such as Simone de Beauvoir, M. Carey Thomas, Jane Addams, Gertrude Stein and Adrienne Rich credited Alcott's work with validating their independent aspirations.

In the 1970s, feminist literary critics intensified scholarly interest in Alcott. In the following decade, feminist educational theorists flagged the neglected importance of educational thought evident in *Little Women* and its sequels. Then the teaching of Alcott's Marmee became one counter-example by means of which Jane Roland Martin demonstrated how deeply flawed was the conceptual meaning of teaching which contemporary analytic philosophers had derived from the paradigm case of Socrates' teaching in the market-place and subsequently declared 'standard'. The gender-blind analytic paradigm had no way to accommodate as 'teaching' any teaching like Marmee's, except to dismiss it along with the teaching of Pestalozzi's Gertrude as 'socialization' or 'acculturation' unworthy even of recognition as 'education'.[18] Thus little more than a century after *Little Women*'s publication, it participated in initiating a feminist paradigm shift within the philosophy of education.

As a domestic curriculum for girls and their mothers, *Little Women* dramatized Marmee's child-rearing practices with teen-aged Meg, Jo, Beth and Amy March. The latter two were school dropouts, and the novel was a study of the March girls' miseducation as much as it was a study of their home education. For it critically contrasted these girls' meagre educational opportunities with the abundant educational privileges of a rich, motherless boy next door who took little advantage of them. Meanwhile the March girls playfully struggled to learn about various subjects despite abusive schools, their educated father's absence, and dull domestic duties. However, Marmee taught them and the boy next door much, albeit neither as Socrates taught young men in the market-place nor as professors teach young men and women in seminars and lecture halls today. Her curriculum was not academic; it consisted of the complex art of learning to love and survive, despite whatever troubles came her daughters' way, especially her own absence. This curriculum in arts of love and survival moreover included far more than cooking and other household chores. It often took the form of deliberate experiments in which the girls were freed to make their own choices, followed by collective evaluation of what they learned from the consequences of their choices. Sometimes it took the form of service-learning projects, to help poor neighbours, or sacrifices with the purpose of learning to distinguish wants from needs. By means of family rituals, Marmee taught her daughters social habits vital to love and survival through difficulties: e.g., sharing experiences with one another, thinking aloud about them in the retelling, risking and taking honest criticism, helping each other along with encouragement and praise, recognizing what each had learned through daily difficulties and triumphs, applying a playful and imaginative spirit to the hardest learning tasks of all. (Such as overcoming boredom, humiliation, disappointment, shyness, vanities, raging tempers, laziness, spitefulness, selfishness.) Most brilliantly exemplified in the spunky tomboy Jo's learning, the achievement for which Marmee's teaching definitively aimed was her daughters' growing capacities and responsibility for learning to love and survive despite their troubles. *Little*

Women artfully contrasted Marmee's mothering with that of several other characters whose child-rearing practices would not qualify as teaching either by analytic philosophers' standards or by Marmee's. Such textual construction was in itself rationally analytic, clarifying distinctive educational values and conceptual meanings not through prosaic abstractions, but through narrative parallelisms, ironies, comparisons, contrasts, the play of presence and absence, and the narrative development of consequences both educative and miseducative.

For example, *Little Women*'s portraits of men teachers all more or less exemplified the liberal ideal of the educated man. Alcott satirically placed these men not within public realms of trade and state, but within homes and schools. In sharp contrast to Marmee, Beth, and Jo, these men teachers were unprepared to address the educational needs of thoroughly lovable children who were nonetheless mischievous, timid, sickly, poor, fat, spoiled, orphaned, boisterous, lazy, vain, mean, slow, bookish, and so on. Thus Alcott's critical character studies of teachers composed a theoretical subtext within her bestseller trilogy, a subtext that demonstrated serious problems with any ideal of the educated teacher derived solely from either the ideal of the liberally educated man or that of the home-educated woman.

Little Men's figures of Professor Bhaer and Mrs Jo, Plumfield's founders, suggested a seldom-made distinction between classroom teachers and school teachers while blurring the distinction customarily drawn between mothers and school teachers. For, in that novel, the 'home-like school' Plumfield's curriculum extended beyond classroom to include each child's school life as a whole. Thus Plumfield restructured the family and its relationship to schooling in a way that liberated mothers from domestic confinement without abandoning their children's needs for nurture. Clearly, Alcott's Plumfield was an early US contributor to the tradition of experimental 'home-like schools', which in the twentieth century included Maria Montessori's *casa dei bambini*[19] and Martin's *schoolhome*.

In addition to making these social innovations, Plumfield (for boys only in *Little Women*) became in *Little Men* a utopian experiment in coeducation, and in its sequel, *Jo's Boys* (1886), expanded to include Laurence College, open to 'all sexes, colors, creeds, and ranks'.[20] Alcott's justification for coeducation was the same as that voiced much later by John Dewey in his generally neglected writing on the subject, that it would enable girls to teach boys manners and boys to strengthen girls intellectually.[21] In these two sequels to *Little Women*, however, Alcott narrated a creative adaptation of Marmee's concept of teaching love and survival in the coeducational context, whose difficulties seem to have eluded Dewey. Alcott's text faced squarely the realities of boys' discrimination and harassment against girls and demonstrated how crucial mutual collaboration between women and men teachers could be to teach girls the necessary collective assertiveness and to teach boys the necessary sensitivity and humility, to eradicate these problems. Thus Alcott is one of the first known American educational theorists to have constructed a feminist pedagogy for coeducational schooling that addressed such problems firmly and strategically, made athletic activity available to both sexes, challenged girls intellectually, and encouraged them to become independent, reform-minded women in the arts and professions. Moreover, a century before the emergence of women's studies in US higher education, Alcott's fictional Laurence College offered women an early version of it while encouraging both sexes to be pro-suffrage. For Jo gave women 'lectures on health, religion, politics, and the various questions in which all should be interested, with copious extracts from ... excellent books wise women write for their sisters, now that they are waking up and asking, "What shall we do?" '[22] Louisa May Alcott was more than 'the children's friend'. As an educational theorist, she was nearly unique insofar as she was also women's friend.

Notes

1 Louisa May Alcott, *Little Men: Life at Plumfield with Jo's Boys*, New York: Grosset & Dunlap, p. 369, 1947.
2 Janice M. Alberghene and Beverly Lyon Clark, introduction to *Little Women and the Feminist Imagination*, ed. Alberghene and Clark, New York: Garland, p. xxi, 1999.
3 Quoted in epigraph to Madeleine B. Stern, *Louisa May Alcott*, Norman: University of Oklahoma Press, p. xv, 1950.
4 Alberghene and Clark (1999, p. xxii.)
5 Susan Laird, 'Learning from Marmee's Teaching: Alcott's Response to Girls' Miseducation', in Alberghene and Clark (1999, pp. 285–321).
6 For a brief introduction to him, see Frederick C. Dahlstrand, 'Alcott, Amos Bronson (1799–1888)', in *Philosophy of Education: An Encyclopedia*, ed. J.J. Chambliss, New York: Garland, pp. 13–14, 1996. This article makes no mention of his more famous daughter Louisa, whom other entries in this encyclopedia do prominently mention, although it contains no entry on Louisa May Alcott.
7 Alberghene and Clark (1999, p. xxvii).
8 Sarah Elbert, *A Hunger for Home: Louisa May Alcott and Little Women*, Philadelphia: Temple University Press, p. 23, 1984; Sarah Elbert, *A Hunger for Home: Louisa May Alcott's Place in American Culture*, New Brunswick: Rutgers University Press, pp. 26–29, 1987; Martha Saxton, *Louisa May: A Modern Biography of Louisa May Alcott*, Boston: Houghton Mifflin, pp. 76ff., 1977.
9 Beverly Lyon Clark, 'Domesticating the School Story, Regendering a Genre: Alcott's *Little Men*', *New Literary History*, 26, p. 332, 1995.
10 Elizabeth Palmer Peabody, *Record of Mr. Alcott's School, Exemplifying the Principles and Methods of Moral Culture*, Boston: Roberts Brothers, 1874.
11 Walter Harding (ed.), *Essays on Education (1830–1862) by Amos Bronson Alcott*, Gainesville, Fla.: Scholars' Facsimiles and Reprints, 1960.
12 Sarah Elbert, *A Hunger for Home: Louisa May Alcott and Little Women*, Philadelphia: Temple University Press, p. 86, 1984.
13 Quoted in Elbert, *A Hunger for Home: Louisa May Alcott's Place in American Culture*, p. xiii.
14 Stern (1950, pp. 342–60). This bibliography does not include some works recently found and posthumously published.
15 Ibid.
16 Elaine Showalter, cited by Jan Susina, 'Men and *Little Women*: Notes of a Resisting (Male) Reader', Alberghene and Clark (1999, p. 161).
17 *Girl Scout Handbook*, New York: Girl Scouts, Inc., p. 17, 1920; *Girl Scout Handbook: Intermediate Program*, New York: Girl Scouts of the U.S.A., p. vi, 1953.
18 Jane Roland Martin, 'Excluding Women from the Educational Realm', in *Changing the Educational Landscape: Philosophy, Women, and Curriculum*, New York: Routledge, chapter 1, 1994.
19 Could Maria Montessori have read these popular children's books? She was

born in the year of *Little Men*'s first publication. *Little Women* was translated into Japanese as early as 1906; unfortunately, American research on other foreign-language translations is still in need of development. Aiko Moro-oka, 'Alcott in Japan: A Selected Bibliography', p. 377, and Beverly Lyon Clark and Linnea Hendrickson, 'Selected Bibliography of Alcott Biography and Criticism', p. 382, both in Alberghene and Clark (1999).

20 Louisa May Alcott, *Jo's Boys: A Sequel to 'Little Men'*, New York: Grosset & Dunlap, p. 260, 1949.
21 Susan Laird, 'The Ideal of the Educated Teacher: *Reclaiming a Conversation* with Louisa May Alcott', *Curriculum Inquiry*, 21(3), p. 276, 1991.
22 Alcott, *Jo's Boys*, p. 262.

See also

In this book: Addams, Dewey, Montessori, Pestalozzi, Socrates, Jesus of Nazareth.
In *Fifty Modern Thinkers on Education*: Jane Roland Martin

Alcott's major writings

Little Women, New York: Penguin, 1989.
Little Men: Life at Plumfield with Jo's Boys, New York: Grosset & Dunlap, 1947.
Jo's Boys: A Sequel to Little Men, New York: Grosset & Dunlap, 1949.
Madeleine B. Stern, 'Bibliography', in *Louisa May Alcott*, Norman: University of Oklahoma, pp. 342–60, 1950.

Further reading

Alberghene, J.M. and B.L. Clark (eds), *Little Women and the Feminist Imagination*, New York: Garland, 1999.
Clark, B.L. and L. Henrickson, 'Selected Bibliography of Alcott Biography and Criticism', in *Little Women and the Feminist Imagination*, eds Alberghene and Clark, New York: Garland, pp. 381–420, 1999.
Clark, B.L., 'Domesticating the School Story, Regendering a Genre: Alcott's *Little Men*', *New Literary History*, 26, pp. 325–44, 1995.
Douglas, A., *The Feminization of American Culture*, New York: Avon, 1977.
Doyle, C., 'Transatlantic Translations: Communities of Education in Alcott and Bronte', in Alberghene and Clark (eds), *Little Women and the Feminist Imagination*, New York: Garland, pp. 261–83, 1999.
Elbert, S., *A Hunger for Home: Louisa May Alcott's Place in American Culture*, New Brunswick: Rutgers University Press, 1987.
—— *A Hunger for Home: Louisa May Alcott and Little Women*, Philadelphia: Temple University Press, 1984.
Laird, S., 'Who Cares About Girls? Rethinking the Meaning of Teaching', *Peabody Journal of Education*, 70 (2), pp. 82–103, winter 1995.
—— 'Teaching in a Different Sense: Alcott's Marmee', in *Philosophy of Education 1993*, ed. A. Thompson, Urbana, IL: Philosophy of Education Society, pp. 164–72, 1994.
—— 'The Ideal of the Educated Teacher: *Reclaiming a Conversation* with Louisa May Alcott', *Curriculum Inquiry 21*, 3 (1991), pp. 271–97.
Langland, E., 'Female Stories of Experience: Alcott's *Little Women* in Light of *Work*', in *The Voyage In: Fictions of Female Development*, ed. Abel, Hirsch, Langland, Hanover, University Press of New England, 1983.
Martin, J.R., *Reclaiming a Conversation: The Ideal of the Educated Woman*, New Haven: Yale, chapter 5, 1985.

—— *The Schoolhome: Rethinking Schools for Changing Families*, Cambridge: Harvard, 1992.

Murphy, A.B., 'The Borders of Ethical, Erotic, and Artistic Possibilities in *Little Women*', *Signs*, 15, pp. 562–85, spring 1990.

Saxton, M., *Louisa May: A Modern Biography of Louisa May Alcott*, Boston: Houghton Mifflin, 1977.

Stern. M.B., *Louisa May Alcott*, Norman: University of Oklahoma Press, 1950.

SUSAN LAIRD

SAMUEL BUTLER 1835–1902

'It is not our business,' he said, 'to help students to think for themselves. Surely this is the very last thing which one who wishes them well should encourage them to do. Our duty is to ensure that they shall think as we do, or at any rate, as we hold it expedient to say we do'.[1]

The opening quotation suggests a reason for including Samuel Butler among the great educators even though he was neither a teacher nor, strictly speaking, a philosopher of education. In his great semi-autobiographical novel, *The Way of All Flesh*, he shows us convincingly and dramatically the tragic effects of cruel and stupid methods of child-rearing. In *Erewhon*, he satirizes the absurdities of academic instruction. Just as important from an educational perspective, in all of his works, he illustrates how difficult (and sometimes undesirable) it is to resolve ambiguities. People educated along Butlerian lines will claim their ideas (almost like material possessions) as their own, but they may find cogent reasons to argue more than one side of an issue.

Butler was the son of a clergyman and grandson of a bishop. His father expected, and very nearly demanded, that Samuel prepare for the ministry, but the boy refused to meet this expectation. He wanted to be an artist and, indeed, his talent was considerable; his work was good enough to be exhibited occasionally in the Royal Academy. He was also talented in music, studied piano, and was a lifelong enthusiast for the music of Handel. He even composed passable pieces in Handel's style. However, no career in the arts was acceptable to his father and, to escape the ministry, Samuel compromised and – with a substantial loan from his father – went to New Zealand to become a successful sheep-rancher.

It is perhaps not surprising, then, that he used a 'lost lamb' metaphor to describe the loneliness of his own childhood:

no sound save a lost lamb bleating upon the mountain side, as though its little heart were breaking. Then there comes some lean and withered old ewe, with deep gruff voice and unlovely aspect, trotting back from the seductive pasture; now she examines this gully, and now that, and now she stands listening with uplifted head, that she may hear the distant wailing and obey it. Aha! they see, and rush towards each other. Alas! they are both mistaken; the ewe is not the lamb's ewe, they are neither kin nor kind to one another, and part in coldness. Each must cry louder, and wander farther yet; may luck be with them both that they find their own at nightfall.[2]

Butler made a success of sheep-ranching, sold out, and returned to London. Here he planned to pursue his painting but, because a stellar reputation in art eluded him, he also wrote. Even while sheep-ranching, he had written essays and opinion pieces, and he was to continue his commentaries on evolution. He accepted the basic idea of evolution and, initially, even received kind messages from Darwin. However, as it became clear that Butler propounded a form of Lamarkianism – insisting that purpose must underlie the changes thought by Darwinians to be random – his views were widely criticized. A comprehensive biography of Butler would, of course, include full discussion of his position on evolution and, also, the very interesting conclusion of his analysis of *The Odyssey*. In *The Authoress of the Odyssey*, Butler suggested and defended the notion that the writer was not an old man (Homer) but a young woman.[3]

I will not comment further on these two great interests of Butler but, from an educational perspective, it is worth noting that he had tremendous intellectual courage and passion. He was not afraid to embrace ideas rejected (or unthought of) by others, and he was not embarrassed to be 'carried away' by enthusiasm. These, clearly, are two intellectual virtues rarely found in even the most successful students. Indeed he anticipated Freud and Jung in his discussion of unconscious memory, and his analysis of machines (in *Erewhon*) reminds today's readers of the lively debates surrounding Turing machines and the 'lives' of computers.

The two works of special interest to educators are *Erewhon* ('nowhere' spelled – almost – backwards) and *The Way of All Flesh*, published posthumously. It has been hard for critics to decide whether *Erewhon* is a utopia, an anti-utopia, or a satire. It has elements of all three, and some critics at the time denounced it as inconsistent and even incoherent.[4] *Erewhon* has not always fared better in more recent reviews.[5]

Readers certainly cannot label *Erewhon* a purely utopian tract, because the Erewhonians exhibit clearly objectionable behaviours and beliefs. Neither is it wholly anti-utopian, for many of their ways suggest improvement on our own. And its satirical elements are not all directed at Butler's own society; many are directed at the ways of fictional Erewhon. The work is shot-through with ambiguities and ambivalence and, in these, Butler shows a depth of mind to be admired. For example, many of us approve of the Erewhonians' treatment of crime as a disease to be treated and cured, but we find their treatment of illness as criminal (something to be punished, not helped) both cruel and ignorant. Butler makes his point by satirizing both societies.

Butler's satire of education encourages a thoughtful reader to apply it over a wide range of practices. In Erewhon's 'Colleges of Unreason', young Erewhonians are taught a 'hypothetical language', one that was 'originally composed at a time when the country was in a very different state of civilization to what it is at present'.[6] Butler's narrator Higgs, the visitor to Erewhon, thinks this is ridiculous, and he questions the coercion used on students who would rather not study this highly honoured (but seemingly useless) language. In addition to the forced study of hypothetics, students are carefully trained in 'unreason':

> The arguments in favour of the deliberate development of the unreasoning faculties were much more cogent. But here they depart from the principles on which they justify their study of hypothetics; for they base the importance which they assign to hypothetics upon the fact of their being a preparation for the extraordinary, while their study of Unreason rests upon its developing those faculties which are required for the daily conduct of affairs. Hence their professorships of Inconsistency and Evasion, in both of which studies the youths are examined before being allowed to proceed to their degree in hypothetics. The more earnest and conscientious students attain to a proficiency in these subjects which is quite surprising; there is hardly any inconsistency so glaring but they soon learn to defend it, or injunction so clear that they cannot find some pretext for disregarding it.[7]

Ah, reader, Butler seems to suggest, choose your favourite university subject and, in your saner and more humorous moments, ask yourself whether the usual instruction is Erewhonian.

Erewhonian education, and by implication traditional Western education, also discourages genius:

> Their view evidently was that genius was like offences – needs must that it come, but woe unto the man through whom it comes. A man's business, they hold, is to think as his neighbors do, for Heaven help him if he thinks good what they count bad. And really it is hard to see how the Erewhonian theory differs from our own, for the word 'idiot' only means a person who forms his opinions for himself.[8]

In this observation, we hear something of a personal lament, for Butler's own genius was often denied, and his popularity was long contested. But his interest in genius went far deeper than egotism. One reason, a powerful one, for rejecting the random variation claimed by Darwinians is, according to Butler, the emergence of genius. On this he followed several earlier writers – Edward Young, Johann Herder, and Immanuel Kant – in making genius the foundation for a belief in progress. More personally, he insisted that the genius of Handel (the composer he virtually worshipped) could not possibly have emerged from random processes. The actuality of genius, he said, demonstrates that *purpose* must somehow be involved in what Darwinians call 'natural selection'. Even today, the question is interesting and challenging.

Through speculation on such issues, Butler came to the conclusion that it was reasonable to believe in God as a 'first cause' – a power interested (perhaps) in the human race in general, and this interest manifests itself in the production of genius. But, said Butler, it is unreasonable to believe in a personal God – one interested in the affairs of individual human beings. For such a belief there is no evidence; similarly, Butler deplored belief in Christian miracles, claiming that anyone who believed in them must have a 'screw loose'.[9]

His criticisms of education are satirical and very funny in *Erewhon*, but they become concrete and practical in *The Way of All Flesh*. Butler's suffering under the educational efforts of his father is dramatically described here (and perhaps exaggerated). Ernest Pontifex, the fictional representation of Butler, was certainly ill-treated: 'When Ernest was in his second year, Theobald [his father] ... began to teach him to read. He began to whip him two days after he had begun to teach him.'[10] Severe punishment was the approved method of instruction:

> Before Ernest could well crawl he was taught to kneel; before he could well speak he was taught to lisp the Lord's prayer, and the general confession. How was it possible that these things could be taught too early? If his attention flagged or his memory failed him, here was an ill weed which would grow apace, unless it were plucked out immediately, and the only way to pluck it out was to whip him, or shut him up in a cupboard, or dock him of some of the small pleasures of childhood. Before he was three years old he could read, and after a fashion, write. Before he was four he was learning Latin, and could do rule of three sums.[11]

To what end? Ernest, although possessed of a loving nature, was a 'lost lamb' in the world – comically and touchingly naïve. Eventually, he separated himself from his parents, after suffering years of what amounted to unrequited love. Ultimately, after a disastrous marriage that turned out to be no marriage at all (his wife was a bigamist), he gave both of his children into the care of loving foster parents, fearing to repeat the horrors of his own upbringing. As a successful writer and investor, he became quite wealthy and supported his children generously; he was a benefactor to his children but not a father. Moreover, he never allowed them to visit their grandfather, Theobald. Butler, of course, saw this as a positive move. The family connection – the 'way of all flesh' – was to be broken.

Critics disagree on whether (or how much) Butler exaggerated his childhood miseries. However, we know from many other accounts of nineteenth- and early-twentieth-century schooling that education both at home and at school caused many bright children great suffering. The schoolboy stories of George Orwell and Winston Churchill, for example, tell of similar cruelties inflicted by schoolmasters. Butler offered a warning to such men:

> Oh schoolmasters – if any of you read this book – bear in mind when any particularly timid, drivelling urchin is brought by his papa into your study, and you treat him with the contempt which he deserves, and afterwards make his life a burden to him for years – bear in mind that it is exactly in the disguise of such a boy as this

that your future chronicler will appear. Never see a wretched little heavy-eyed mite sitting on the edge of a chair against your study wall without saying to yourselves, 'Perhaps this boy is he who, if I am not careful, will one day tell the world what manner of man I was.' If even two or three schoolmasters learn this lesson and remember it, the preceding chapters will not have been written in vain.[12]

Besides his cogent warning to nasty schoolmasters, Butler has powerful messages for all educators. Criticized for inconsistency, he has also been praised for open-mindedness. He rejected the traditional religion in which he was raised as cruel, illogical and pleasure-hating, but he remained open to the possibility of God as purpose in the universe. As he himself wanted to think freely and 'possess' his own thoughts, he advocated that all students should be encouraged (not forced) to think creatively and critically. He revealed his independence of mind in accepting evolution but rejecting random variation and, again, in defending the astonishing claim that *The Odyssey* was written by a woman. (On this last, those he convinced included George Bernard Shaw, Lord Grimthorpe, and Robert Graves.) His passion to investigate and learn is illustrated in this comment:

What can it matter to me where the Odyssey was written, or whether it was written by a man or a woman? From the bottom of my heart I can say truly that I do not care about the way in which these points are decided, but I do care, and very greatly, about knowing which way they are decided by sensible people who have considered what I have urged in this book.[13]

Butler was often wrong, but he did his research with a passion, and he sought evidence on all reasonable sides of the questions that interested him. Not a bad habit to encourage in today's teachers and students.

Notes

1 Samuel Butler, *Erewhon*, London, Penguin Books, p. 189, 1970. The speaker is a Professor of Worldly Wisdom in Erewhon's Colleges of Unreason.
2 Ibid., p. 43.
3 Butler, *The Authoress of the Odyssey*, London: Longmans, 1897.
4 See the discussion in Lee E. Holt, *Samuel Butler*, Boston: G.K. Hall, 1989.
5 See, for example, the acidic comments of Malcolm Muggeridge, *The Earnest Atheist: A Study of Samuel Butler*, London: Eyre and Spottiswoode, 1936.
6 Butler, *Erewhon*, p. 186.
7 Ibid., pp. 186–7.
8 Ibid., p. 189.
9 The comment appears in Holt, *Samuel Butler*, p. 16. Holt cites as the source Henry Festing Jones, *Samuel Butler, Author of Erewhon (1835–1902), A Memoir*, London: Macmillan, 1919.
10 Butler, *The Way of all Flesh*, New York: Library Publications, p. 110, n.d.
11 Ibid., pp. 106–7.
12 Ibid., p. 144.
13 *The Authoress*, p. 281.

See also

In this book: Darwin, Kant

Butler's major writings

Works of Samuel Butler, ed. Henry Festing Jones and A.T. Bartholomew, London: Jonathan Cape, 1923–26.
Erewhon, or Over the Range, London: Trubner, 1872.
Life and Habit, London: Trubner, 1878.
The Authoress of the Odyssey, London: Longmans, 1897.
The Way of all Flesh, London: Grant Richards, 1903.
The Note-books of Samuel Butler, ed. H.F. Jones, London: Fifield, 1912.

Further reading

Furbank, P.N., *Samuel Butler (1835–1902)*, Hamden, CT: Archon Books, 1971.
Holt, L.E., *Samuel Butler*, Boston: G.K. Hall, 1989.
Jones, H.F., *Samuel Butler, Author of Erewhon (1835–1902), A Memoir*, London: Macmillan, 1919.
Muggeridge, M., *A Study of Samuel Butler, the Earnest Atheist*, London: G.P. Putnam, 1936.

NEL NODDINGS

ROBERT MORANT 1863–1920

> In how many towns and villages in England is money ... being unwittingly wasted in giving to a boy either an education which is quite unsuited to his capacities and which will leave him stranded and out of employment at the end of it, or else a base, fraudulent, and spurious imitation of education, which is far worse in its effects upon him than if the lad had gone out immediately to the work of life on leaving the elementary school.

These words from Robert Morant's *Report on the French System of Higher Primary Education*, 1897, p. 335 (PP 1897 XXV, (Cd. 8477)) typify his forthrightness of approach and his opposition to higher grade schools as deleterious to the development of proper secondary education.

Robert Morant was born at Hampstead on 7 April 1863 the only son of Robert Morant, a decorative artist, and Helen Berry, the daughter of the headmaster of Mill Hill School. Educated, despite his mother's poverty after his father's early death, at Winchester and New College, he studied hard and lived abstemiously, excelling at boxing and gaining a First in Theology in 1885. He taught briefly at Temple Grove Preparatory School before going to Siam in November 1886 as tutor to the nephew of King Chulalongkorn and subsequently to the Crown Prince. In the eight years that he spent there he laid the foundations of the system of public education in that country.

Upon his return to England, he went to Toynbee Hall. There, the artist W.B. Richmond used him as a model for Christ on the ceiling above the altar at St Paul's Cathedral; his boss later, Michael Sadler, referred to Morant's 'austere and episcopal appearance'. He met and became the confidant of Sir John Gorst, Vice President of the Council from 1896. Thus Morant secured appointment to the Civil Service as assistant director of special inquiries in the Education Department. His report, *The National Organisation of Education of All Grades as Practised in Switzerland* (PP 1898 XXV Cd. 8988) provided a blueprint for English education for the early part of the twentieth century, for a system in short of national education locally administered. Morant believed that the central authority, the Board of Education, had to be 'an aristocracy of brains' and his work presaged the 1902 Education Act which established local education authorities as junior partners to the Board in the service of education.

As his successor, Sir Lewis Selby-Bigge put it in his entry on Morant in the *Dictionary of National Biography 1912–1921* (1927):

> His achievement, as a relatively junior officer, in mobilizing and marshalling the political, municipal, and educational forces of the country for the not unhazardous enterprise of constructing an early and comprehensive system of public education out of incoherent and antagonistic elements, is one of the romances of the civil service.

His reward was to be made Permanent Secretary to the Board in April 1903. Primary, secondary and higher education made great strides under his leadership.

He reported, 26 February 1902, on the education of pupil teachers and the new regulations of 1903 required them not to be employed normally until they were 16 and to have limited hours of classroom contact together with minimum hours of instruction. As Professor Eaglesham put it in *The Foundations of Twentieth-century Education in England*, 1967, p. 56:

> At the back of Morant's mind was the typical product of a pupil teacher centre: starchly clean, with a provincial accent, a brain crammed with facts, skilled in techniques, but with not a vestige of the culture that Winchester and Oxford can foster.

Morant is credited with responsibility for the introduction to the 1904 *Code of Regulations for Public Elementary Schools* (PP 1904 LXXV Cd. 2074). Though he did not necessarily write it he would have agreed with the main aim (p. vii):

> to form and strengthen the character and to develop the intelligence of children ... and to make the best use of the school years available, in assisting both girls and boys, according to their different needs, to fit themselves, practically as well as intellectually, for the whole of life.

The Regulations for Secondary Schools (PP 1904 LXXV Cd. 2128) followed five weeks later and set the scene for the rise of the county grammar schools which were such a major force for social mobility in the years between the Balfour Act of 1902 and the Butler Act of 1944. The Regulations laid more emphasis on the humanities than had hitherto been the case and the curriculum was not markedly dissimilar to that which was to be laid down in the 1988 National Curriculum.

Regulations for training and technical colleges followed later in 1904 and a handbook on grants to universities appeared in 1911. Perhaps even more significant, however, was the larger part played as a result of his initiatives by the School Medical Service. The integration of the provision of school meals as well as a programme of medical inspection under the Service, a policy not fully implemented until his successor's time, was fundamental to that improvement in the health of children which made possible higher achievements of education among ordinary people between the world wars.

As the HMI, quoted by F. Smith in his *A History of Elementary Education 1760–1902* (1931), p. 340, stated as long before as 1896:

Instead of making education conform to the views of the educator, we are endeavouring to make the educator conform his views to the nature and capabilities of the child.

It was a noble aspiration and a great achievement to have shifted attitudes so far which fully deserved the honours given him (CB 1902, KCB 1907) and it was a strange decision which was taken to transfer him in 1911 to be chairman of the National Health Insurance Commission where he initiated many important innovations including the payment of insurance contributions, the provision of sanatorium benefits, the foundation of a system of national aid for medical research, the institution of a service of general practitioners and indeed, after the Ministry of Health Act of 1919, a redefinition of the functions of both the central and the local authorities concerned with public health.

Morant ate and slept administration and it was not perhaps surprising that he died in his fifties, for he permitted himself no relief from labour. His premature death in London on 13 March 1920 left his colleagues in the civil service bereft of, as Selby Bigge put it in the *DNB*, 'one of the greatest figures it had ever produced – great by both character and achievement'.

Morant married in 1896 Helen Mary, daughter of Edwin Cracknell of Wetheringsett Grange, Suffolk; they had a son and a daughter.

Morant's major writings

The French System of Higher Primary Schools, Special Reports on Educational Subjects, 1896–97, 1, Education Department, PP 1897, XXV, Cd. 8477.

The National Organisation of Education of All Grades as Practised in Switzerland, Special Reports on Educational Subjects, 3, PP 1898, XXV, Cd. 8988.

Code of Regulations for Public Elementary Schools, Board of Education, PP 1904, LXXV, Cd. 2074.

Regulations for Secondary Schools, Board of Education, PP 1904, LXXV, Cd. 2128.

Further reading

The place of publication is London unless otherwise stated.

Aldrich, R. and Gordon, P., *Dictionary of British Educationists*, Woburn Press, 1989.
Andrews, L., 'The School Meals Service', *British Journal of Educational Studies*, 20 (1), pp. 70–5, 1972.
Banks, O., 'Morant and the Secondary School Regulations of 1904'. *British Journal of Educational Studies*, 3, pp. 33–41, 1954.
Chester, D.N., 'Robert Morant and Michael Sadler', *Public Administration*, 29, pp. 109–15, 1950.
—— 'Morant and Sadler – Further Evidence', *Public Administration*, 31, pp. 49–54, 1953.
Daglish, N., 'The Morant – Chulalongkorn Affair of 1893–94', *Journal of Educational Administration and History*, 15, pp. 16–23, 1983.
—— 'Robert Morant's Hidden Agenda? The Origins of the Medical Treatment of School-children', *History of Education*, 19, pp. 139–48, 1990.
—— *Education Policy-Making in England and Wales: The Crucible Years, 1895–1911*, Woburn Press, 1996.
Eaglesham, E.J.R., 'The Centenary of Sir Robert Morant', *British Journal of Educational Studies*, 11, pp. 5–18, 1963.
—— *The Foundations of 20th Century Education in England*, Routledge & Kegan Paul, 1967.
Holmes, E.G.A., *What Is and What Might Be*, Constable, 1911.
Lowe, R., 'Robert Morant and the Secondary School Regulations of 1904', *Journal of Educational Administration and History*, 16, pp. 37–46, 1984.
Markham, V., 'Robert Morant – Some Personal Reminiscences', *Public Administration*, 28, pp. 249–62, 1950.
Selby Bigge, L.A., 'Morant, Robert', in *Dictionary of National Biography, 1912–21*, ed. H.W.C. Davis and J.R.H. Weaver, Oxford University Press, 1927.
—— *The Board of Education*, G.P. Putnam's Sons, 1927.
Smith, F., *A History of English Elementary Education, 1760–1902*, University of London Press, 1931.

G.R. BATHO

EUGENIO MARÍA DE HOSTOS 1839–1903

> In order for humans to be humans, that is, worthy of realizing their life goals, nature bestowed them with awareness of herself, the ability to know their own origins, their own strengths and frailties, their own transcendence and interdependence, their rights and obligations, their own freedom and responsibilities, the capability for self-improvement and for self-ennobling of their ideal existence.[1]

Eugenio Maria de Hostos has been thought of as the John Dewey of the Spanish-speaking world.[2] While there are remarkable similarities between these two educator-philosopher-political scientist-humanists, the fact remains that Hostos preceded Dewey by twenty years and died several years before Dewey published his influential works, *How We Think* (1910) and *Democracy and Education* (1916). Hostos was an educator and writer who wrote more than fifty books (published and unpublished) as well as essays and treatises on social-science topics from moral development to education to the political sciences. Several editions of his works have been published since his death including the recent University of Puerto Rico's 'critical edition' of his *Complete Works*. In addition to being a central figure in education, law, politics, sociology, ethics and other fields in his native Puerto Rico, Hostos travelled extensively making similar contributions in several countries (Argentina, Brazil, Chile, Cuba, Dominican Republic, Peru, Spain, Venezuela), often playing a major part in the reconstruction of their educational systems.

Hostos was an early advocate of the education of women in the sciences and for self-government for Puerto Rico as well as an outstanding writer. His 'Critical Essay on Hamlet', originally published in Germany and translated into several languages, was considered one of the four great works on Shakespeare. Most of his other essays are regarded among the best in Latin American literature. Hostos also composed music and nursery songs for children, wrote poetry, and three one-act plays (comedies). His work and traditions are kept alive by contemporary educators, poets, novelists, short-story writers and essayists.

Hostos was educated in a private school in San Juan, then attended the University of Bilbao and the Central University in Spain. While in Spain he wrote and spoke at the Madrid Athenaeum in favour of autonomic reforms and of the abolition of slavery in Cuba and in Puerto Rico. His first book, *La Peregrinación de Bayoán* (The Pilgrimage of Bayoán) exposed, under the veil of fiction, the restrictions of the Spanish colonial regime. His democratic ideas led him to join the Republican Party in Spain. He later went to Paris and joined the party's Board which Castelar, Salmeron, Prim and other distinguished Spanish republicans had constituted there. This, and his determination not to receive a degree from a monarchical government, made him quit his studies short of graduation.

After Paris Hostos went to New York, where he offered his services to the Cuban Revolutionary Board. For the next two years he argued this cause in public and in the press as a speaker, as director of the Board's newspaper *La Revolución* (The Revolution), and as a writer for the newspaper *Puerto Rico*.

In 1871 Hostos went to South America to expand his political and educational activities. In Peru Hostos conducted a campaign in favour of Chinese workers who were being exploited. In 1873, while working in Chile, his renowned essay 'La educación científica de la mujer' (The Scientific Education of Women), proposed a comprehensive programme for women's education because, as he explained, women provide the foundation for the formation of humanity. Additionally, he became a member of the 'Academia de Bellas Letras' (the Academy of Fine Letters) of Santiago; and published his celebrated essay on Hamlet.

In Argentina he lobbied for building a transandean railroad, and in recognition the first engine to climb the Andes was named 'Hostos'. In Brazil, he wrote a series of articles on the prolific nature of the country, published in *La Nación* (The Nation) of Buenos Aires. In 1877 Hostos moved to Caracas, Venezuela where he taught in a local college, directed a school, and began to implement his educational ideas. Before he could introduce and test his educational theories at a national scale, however,

General Gregorio Luperon, his benefactor and leader of the recently triumphant liberal sector in the Dominican Republic, asked him in 1879 to lead the educational reform in that country.

Hostos undertook the task of rebuilding a devastated public education system in the Dominican Republic. He drafted the bill of law for the establishment of normal schools as well as other legislation required for the reform. In February 1880 the Normal School opened under his direction. In that prestigious institution he set new pedagogical standards lecturing on science and constitutional, international and penal law. Hostos successfully spearheaded the educational reform from his dual position as director and professor at the Normal School for the preparation of future teachers as well as at the 'Instituto Profesional de Enseñanza' (Professional Institute for Teaching), where he also taught political economy. At the time, this latter Institute functioned as the only university in the country. During nine years of intensive work, Hostos fulfilled his mission, establishing the foundation for the Dominican school system that, in turn, transformed the country into one of the world's most progressive in terms of politics, philosophy and educational organization and practices. Simultaneously, he wrote almost all his textbooks during this same period.

Hostos' positivistic and liberal ideas (especially his advocacy of the separation of Church and State and for the development of laic and women's education) positioned him as an adversary in conflict with conservative political groups and Church authorities. In 1888 Hostos, appalled at the political manoeuvrings of President (dictator) Hereux and having received repeated invitations from Chile's President Balmaceda, fled the Dominican Republic and returned to Chile. There, he became involved in a number of cultural struggles. As director (and professor) of the Amunátegui School, he greatly influenced the development of Chilean public education, providing an alternative to more conservative Europeanized trends. His contributions are especially noteworthy in legal education reform and the preparation of barristers, in which he insisted on sociological and ethical preparation along with the technical fundamentals.

When the Cuban Revolution broke out, Hostos left Chile with an eye on Puerto Rico. Reluctantly, the Ministry of Public Education commissioned him to study in the United States at the Institute of Experimental Psychology. Upon his arrival in New York, General Miles' expedition (which later invaded Puerto Rico on 25 July 1898) was already organizing. With the fall of Spanish sovereignty in Puerto Rico, brought on by the invasion of the United States, and fearful that Puerto Rico would become a US colony, Hostos returned to his homeland with the intention of organizing a political-educational movement: the 'Liga de los Patriotas' (League of Patriots). The League sent a commission to Washington to meet with President McKinley in January 1899. Along with other prominent members, Hostos attempted to persuade US authorities to recognize the right of the Puerto Rican people to self-determination through a plebiscite. They submitted an extensive report on issues concerning Puerto Rico, for McKinley's consideration, and requested a suitable resolution of the island's situation.

On the island, the League tried to educate Puerto Ricans about the values and political system of the United States and to initiate an educational reform. Hostos' intention was to situate Puerto Ricans in a position to claim independence from the United States. He established a College of Agriculture and a Municipal College and sought to establish a rational system of public education in Puerto Rico. The town of Juana Diaz was the first to subscribe to his ideas and held the first assembly to inaugurate a campaign. Other assemblies followed throughout the island. US Republicans and local politicians, however, squashed his efforts.

An invitation from his supporters (who led a new triumph of the liberal party) in the Dominican Republic prompted his return to that country in 1900. Back in Santo Domingo, Hostos directed a new educational reform effort against the opposition of traditionalist factions. He took charge of the central college and shortly thereafter was made inspector general of public education. Until his death on 11 August 1903, Hostos devoted his time to establishing schools and progressive institutions as well as curriculum development and the drafting of laws.

Hostos' educational theory draws his philosophical inspiration both from the evolutionary positivism of August Comte (1798–1857) and Herbert Spencer (1820–1903) and from the idealism of Karl Krause (1781–1832). In Hostos' philosophical perspective, physical, social and spiritual (moral and intellectual) reality is the result of a particular set of conditions or relations that evolves, over time, toward the realization of its full potentiality. Hence, it is subject to laws; knowledge about it can be constructed; and it can be learned, grasped and articulated conceptually through a medium that is able to discover and express these laws. This medium is human reason and its most important by-product is science. Knowledge of the conditions or laws of reality grants rational control over it. Only the human species is able to organize its relationship to reality through knowledge of these laws, and the power obtained through this knowledge provides and allows for its reorganization pursuant to the species' interests and values. In terms of knowledge and power over reality, science has become the most important mechanism used by human beings to organize their relationship to the environment. It is the necessary condition for the possibility itself of a new humankind to reach its rational destiny through work and planning. Out of this conception of reality and of knowledge Hostos developed his own sociology (*Tratado de Sociologia*), ethics (*Tratado de Moral*) and psychology of thought (*Tratado de Lógica*). Hostos applied the conceptual frame provided by these disciplines to the particular historical context of Latin America to create the theoretical foundations of his educational theory.

For Hostos, the last quarter of the nineteenth century was the advent of an era of moral reconstruction. The substance of this reconstruction was embedded in the underpinnings of science. In the newly founded American republics, Hostos saw the historical elements for such a reconstruction. For him, America[3] is 'a land unknown to itself, oblivious to its power, and if it were aware of this potential, it would create a wondrous future'.[4] But the lingering conditions of colonialism are an obstacle to this destiny. The republican political revolutions failed to establish the ideal that spawned them. American societies are still ailing. Anarchy, the absence of rational order, is the social trait that best describes them, 'their sociological condition is a state of sickness'. Hostos summarizes this by saying: 'Our [Latin American] peoples are evolved societies whose strong growth is impeded by traditionalism: like the small corpses we know are children whose lives are sacrificed by the misguided brother in his quest for gold. ... All of our people of Latin background who, in the old country identified with diverse nationalities, are immersed in a borrowed ideology that is a poor fit for our young societies'.[5]

Hostos saw education that limits the development of reason due to a one-sided focus as the perfect instrument for domination. The degree of freedom of an individual or a society is directly related to the manner in which one is educated to think. Domination, more than anything, is oppression of the human mind. An oppressed individual's existence resides in underdeveloped thinking. Neocolonial education becomes an instrument of domination in the measure in which it produces a sick mind devoid of conscience, truth, freedom or justice.

This happened through an educational process that denied those conditions needed for developing one's mind. The order and development of intellectual skills was obstructed, thus strengthening those skills that would facilitate the quickest, the blindest and the most servile transmission of ideas, reasoning, judgments and knowledge already shaped by others. Instead of direct contact with reality and the discovery of its laws, a one-sided emphasis on memory and imagination occurred. According to Hostos, 'Adolescence in Latino countries, rather than being based on mental health grounded in the physiology of the human mind, is mentally dominated and enslaved by an intellectual order concerned only with overwhelming and sickening the adolescent mind.'[6]

Colonial education guided by medieval scholasticism or the aestheticism of the renaissance (the classics) had a serious impact on new generations of Americans. It created a false ideal of the human being, uprooted Americans from their land, and neglected development of rationality and scientific thought. Education, Hostos argued, was an instrument of domination because it has lacked:

1   a clear sense of what education is for;
2   scientific knowledge of the nature of the students and of how they may meet educational goals;
3   educational methods based on this knowledge to help educators guide their students toward the attainment of these goals;
4   an objective understanding of educational experiences and of knowledge and its organization that educators can use to stimulate their students.

For Hostos, the ultimate goal in education is developing the mind. Development of the mind implies simultaneous intellectual and moral development because the mind is a composite of organisms, of forces that manifest their activity according to three basic functions: feeling, loving and thinking. Like every other organism, the mind has needs and purposes that must be met through its activity. Specifically, it needs to discover, to know and to own the truth in order to do 'Good'. As Hostos puts it: 'the most infallible way to know if a person has developed fully in his/her capacity for thinking, is the evidence of his or her own life. If he/she causes harm, it [the capacity for thinking] is not rational enough.'[7]

The thinking process consists of a series of interconnected operations in a determined sequence. Hostos identifies four basic functions in the thinking process: intuition, induction, deduction and systematization. Each function may be subdivided into simpler operations. Operations such as memorizing, imagining and paying attention are parts of every function. Each function produces a result or intellectual product upon which the subsequent functions act and upon which it elaborates further. Knowledge results from this thinking process. Therefore 'knowledge' that is not related to intuitions (notions), induction (principles) and deductions (judgments), lacks a real reference and is, hence, considered meaningless. Meaningless knowledge is transmitted by providing students with concepts, formulas, principles and theories, without access to the intuitions, inductions and deductions from which these were generated. The mind is an active organism; knowledge is the result of processes that the learner must carry out. Education is the product of knowledge construction and the development of the mind. This process is the essence of the mind itself. As Hostos states: 'The mind does not receive ideas that are complete but, rather, forms them on its own and depends on the information from its senses.'[8]

Hostos' educational reform clearly defines its liberating purpose. It is founded upon comprehension of the forces and conditions affecting the development of the mind and, in harmony with these conditions, organizes knowledge and educational experiences into a plan of study that follows both a logical and a psychological sequence. Implementation of this educational reform calls for a corps of 're-formed' teachers capable of transforming education. Educators who wish to direct teaching towards development of thinking, and help it to produce knowledge, must contend with its structure and sequence of functions and operations. Teaching must move from intuition to induction, to deduction, and finally towards generalizing or systematizing. Throughout this process, educators must instruct learners in the different functions and operations as they move through an appropriate consecution.

According to Hostos, the mind is a developing organism:

Once the natural order of the mind has been established, one must acknowledge that, like every organism, the mind is born, develops and grows, and is subject in its development to the same laws that affect its functions. In other words, there are times when mind is above all intuition and other times when it leans towards induction based on intuition. At still other times it depends on induction to deduce, from general principles, the concrete truths that it could not previously discover or see. Finally, mind flourishes during systematization when it functions clearly aware of its own process, and of all of the elements of knowledge that are part of it.[9]

Implicitly, educators must ground their teaching not only in the structure and processes of the minds, but also in their particular stage of development. Ultimately, the teacher's task goes beyond connecting the mind and its contextual reality. Rather the task becomes to urge students to develop their minds to the fullest potential allowed by the current developmental stage of the human species (that is, positive scientific systematization). Through an education directed towards development of the mind, in a lifetime, an individual's mind may reach a level of development that formerly encompassed thousands of years for the human species to attain. This is why the educator must understand not only the structure and natural development of the human mind, but also the structure of the knowledge attained by the human species and its objective classification:

> The hierarchy of knowledge does not evolve naturally and spontaneously from any other classification than that derived from the hierarchy of objects of knowledge available to the mind and which evolve naturally from the mind. ... Feeding itself from reality is the way through which collective reason has evolved; the way it has constructed an abundance of positivist truths; and the way it has created a scientific legacy of its thought processes for the thinking and conscientious species. Similarly, it is by nurturing it with natural events and ideas based on observation, and the analysis of these, that the individual mind can appropriate the richness of collective reason and avoid having to replicate the enormous amount of effort human understanding has exerted to dominate reality.[10]

A school curriculum should therefore be the compilation of the developmental paths of the human mind. When following these paths, the learner takes ownership of the highest level of mental development attained by humankind. For Hostos, modern experimental science is the highest achievement of the human mind, and education of the mind is education in scientific methods.

Although Hostos did not conduct rigorous experimental research pertaining to the mind and its development, his encyclopaedic knowledge of philosophy, linguistics, psychology, sociology, history and other disciplines gave him a coherent conceptualization and an operational model of mind. As both theoretician and practitioner, Hostos' work synthesizes the goals, structure and evolving processes of human development that education must encourage toward collective and personal emancipation. Transforming this pedagogical system into practice is where Hostos exhibits the most creativity. He proposes a progressive 'concentric' curriculum similar to what Bruner calls 'spiral'. Likewise, he practised such methods and didactic techniques as deductive lectures; Socratic dialogues; cooperative learning; experimentation; the use of manipulatives, spheres and visual resources; exhibits; field trips; problem-based learning; and many other interactive and meaningful ways of learning. Moreover, Hostos produced texts and didactic manuals for teaching languages, literature, geometry, geography, history, theatre, law and physical education.

In sum, Hostos' work is extraordinarily thorough and vigorous. It is comparable to that of Pestalozzi (1746–1827) in Europe, Giner de los Ríos (1839–1915) in Spain and, more recently, that of Dewey (1859–1952) in the

United States. As such, Hostosian thought is a precursor of many twentieth-century attempts to construct educational theory and pedagogy for fostering human development, such as Jean Piaget's constructivism, Lev S. Vygotsky's socio-cultural perspective, and Paulo Freire's liberatory pedagogy.

Hostos' extraordinary educational frameworks, as well as his struggles for a Latin American educational reform geared at the liberation of its people, establishes him as the most important Latin American educator. If we consider the role of educational philosophy to be that of synthesizing philosophical and scientific knowledge about human nature and drawing implications for its nurturing and advancement, Hostos must also be considered among the world's great philosophers of education.

Notes

Our grateful thanks to Dr Xaé Reyes, University of Connecticut at Storrs, for her generous assistance with much of the translation required for this article.

1 Hostos, *Obras Completas. Edición Crítica, Vol. XII.*
2 This biographical section borrows liberally the entry on Hostos in E.F. Garcia, F.W. Hoadley, and E. Astol (eds), *El Libro de Puerto Rico* (The Book of Puerto Rico), San Juan: El Libro Azul Publishing Co., 1923, and other sources.
3 In this article, the terms 'America' and 'American' refer to the whole of America and to all Americans not just to the United States of America or its citizens.
4 *Obras Completas. Edición Crítica. (Complete Works. Critical Edition), Vol. XIII*, San Juan: Editorial de la Universidad de Puerto Rico, University of Puerto Rico Press, p. 159.
5 Ibid., p. 299.
6 Ibid., p. 204.
7 Ibid., p. 299.
8 Ibid., p. 214.
9 *Obras Completas. Edición Crítica, Vol. XVIII*, San Juan: Editorial de la Universidad de Puerto Rico, p. 29.
10 Manuel Maldonado Denis, *Eugénio María de Hostos: sociólogo y maestro*, Rio Piedras: Editorial Antillana, p. 190, 1981.

See also

In this book: Dewey, Spencer, Socrates, Pestalozzi,
In *Fifty Modern Thinkers on Education*: Piaget, Vygotsky, Freire

Hostos' major writings

'Tratado de Moral', *Obras Completas. Edición Crítica. [Complete Works. Critical Edition], Vol. IX Filosofía, Tomo I*, San Juan, Puerto Rico: Editorial de la Universidad de Puerto Rico, 2000.
'Lecciones de Derecho Constitucional', *Obras Completas, Tomo XV*, San Juan: Editorial Coquí, 1969.
'Tratado de Lógica', *Obras Completas, Tomo XIX*, San Juan: Editorial Coquí, 1969.
'Ciencia de la Pedagogía', *Obras Completas. Edición Crítica, Vol. VI, Educación, Tomo I*, San Juan: Editorial de la Universidad de Puerto Rico, 1991.
'La Peregrinación de Bayoán', *Obras Completas. Edición Crítica, Vol. I, Literatura, Tomo I*, San Juan: Editorial de la Universidad de Puerto Rico, 1988.

'Tratado de Sociología', *Obras Completas. Edición Crítica, Vol. VIII, Sociología, Tomo I*, San Juan: Editorial de la Universidad de Puerto Rico, 1989.
'Diario (1866–1869)', *Obras Completas. Edición Crítica, Vol. II, Diario. Tomo I*, San Juan: Editorial de la Universidad de Puerto Rico, 1988.
'Epistolario (1865–1878)', *Obras Completas. Edición Crítica, Vol. III, Epistolario. Tomo I*, San Juan: Editorial de la Universidad de Puerto Rico, 1988.

Further reading

Bosh, Juan, *Hostos, el sembrador*, La Habana: Editorial Trópico, 1939.
Henriquez Ureña, Camila, *Las ideas Pedagógicas de Hostos*, Santo Domingo: Secretaria de Estado de Educación, 1994.
Hostos, Eugenio Maria de, 'La Educación Cientifica de la Mujer', *Obras Completas*, Vol. XII, San Juan: Editorial de la Universidad de Puerto Rico.
Maldonado-Denis, Manuel, *Eugenio María de Hostos: sociólogo y maestro*, Rio Piedras: Editorial Antillana, 1981.
Pedreira, Antonio S., *Hostos, Ciudadano de América*, San Juan: Editorial Edil, 1976.
Rojas Osorio, Carlos, *Hostos: Apreciación Filosófica*, Humacao: Instituto de Cultural Puertorriqueña, 1988.
Sisler, Robert Frank, *Eugenio Maria de Hostos: A Comparative Study of the Educational and Political Contributions*, New York: New York University Press, 1962.
Villarini Jusino, Angel R., 'La Enseñanza Orientada al Desarrollo del Pensamiento Según Eugenio Maria de Hostos' in *Actas del Primer Encuentro Internacional sobre el Pensamiento de Eugenio María de Hostos*, San Juan: Editorial de la Universidad de Puerto Rico, 1997.

ANGEL VILLARINI JUSINO AND CARLOS ANTONIO TORRE

FRIEDRICH NIETZSCHE 1844–1900

> The hardest task still remains: to say how a new circle of duties may be derived from this ideal and how one can proceed towards so extravagant a goal through a practical activity – in short, to demonstrate that this ideal educates.[1]

Friedrich Wilhelm Nietzsche was born on 14 October 1844 to Franziska and Karl Ludwig who was the pastor of the small village of Röcken, Germany. Nietzsche was descended on both sides from devout Lutheran families and theology had been his intended course of study right up to his inscription in philology at the University of Bonn. His father died when Nietzsche was just 4 years old of what was then called 'softening of the brain'. This diagnosis haunted Nietzsche throughout his life since from an early age he too suffered from debilitating headaches. After the death of his father Nietzsche's mother moved the family to Naumburg where he attended the Dom school. In 1855 Nietzsche was awarded a residential scholarship to attend Schulpforta which was one of the best schools of classical education in the Prussian Gymnasium system. Upon leaving Pforta Nietzsche pursued higher education at the University of Bonn but transferred to the University of Leipzig after just one year following an unfortunate power struggle between his supervisor Otto Jahn and the chairman of the faculty Friedrich Ritschl. Although Nietzsche initially supported Jahn, he followed Ritschl to Leipzig. The debate was significant for Nietzsche because it was his first contact with the political nature of professional scholarship and because his decision to follow Ritschl came back to haunt him in the form of vehement attacks against his first book, *The Birth Of Tragedy*. These attacks came from Nietzsche's younger contemporary, Ullrich von Wilamowitz-Moellendorff. This latter event marked Nietzsche's withdrawal from professional academia and the beginning of his concentration on his philosophical development. In 1867 Nietzsche entered military service as an artillery officer and after his discharge due to injury he was appointed to the chair of classical philology at the University of Basle in 1869. He was just 24 years of age and one of the youngest scholars ever to be appointed to such a position. While there can be little doubt that his success at such an early age was due in part to the support of Ritschl, who once called him the 'idol of the whole young philological world',[2] Nietzsche had long been recognized as a classicist and scholar of the highest rank.

In 1871 Nietzsche's first book, *The Birth of Tragedy*, met with exaggerated indignation from the academic community. The attacks mentioned above confirmed Nietzsche's suspicions that so-called professional scholarship was far too politically motivated to accommodate his interests. He subsequently reduced his active service at the University, and he retired from the chair at Basle. From 1871 onwards Nietzsche gave up the academic world and concentrated on the development of his philosophy, which was committed to the revitalization of culture, education and society through the rejection of the dogmatic reception of tradition. His work in this regard remains a model of philosophical inquiry into the development of modern intellectual opinion to this day. One of the most significant parts of Nietzsche's philosophy is the importance he places on the role of education and teachers in society and their relationship to the development of culture.

Nietzsche collapsed in 1888 and was bedridden from then until his death on 25 August 1900. Between 1871 and 1888 Nietzsche produced eleven major works dealing with many aspects of modern cultural and intellectual life. Many of his works are written as collections of essays and he often preferred the terseness of aphorisms to the exhaustive plodding of the treatise. He wrote with a style and eloquence that has seldom been equalled. His work has had immense influence both within and outside academic circles. Nietzsche's influence on education began to be exerted in the early part of the twentieth century and he has held the attention of educational thinkers ever since.

Nietzsche's importance to pedagogical philosophy can best be understood through an appreciation of his larger philosophical project and the changes that occurred during the first half of the nineteenth century. Throughout his career Nietzsche held a deep concern for what he considered the stagnation of intellectual life and the fragmentation of society through the increased emphasis on material wealth and comfort over cultural and social development. His cultural criticism was motivated by what he saw as the decline in education, the increasing professionalization of scholarship and rising state control over both education and culture. During the first half of the nineteenth century both secondary schools and universities in Germany underwent something of a revolution.[3] The old professional degrees of Law, Medicine and Theology were being challenged for primacy by the Humanities and Natural Sciences. Unfortunately, where once the Humanities, or Liberal Arts, were pursued out of a genuine interest in the development of human understanding, the nature of modern scholarship promoted an attitude of competitive academic work which placed position and reputation in a more central role; one that Nietzsche felt was contrary to the true objectives of education. This had the effect of increasing the fragmentation not only between the various disciplines, but also the various specialities within each discipline. In his inaugural lecture at Basle Nietzsche called his discipline an admixture of blood and bone, or in other words, that which gives life and that which remains after death. He described philology as consisting of the most diverse interests and skills and he urged his colleagues to resist the growing tendency to idealize antiquity, which he felt was the result of over-specialization itself, and to seek the 'real' antiquity which might stand as an exemplar for cultural and societal progress. The overriding tone in Nietzsche's work during the early period, up to 1867, is one of frustration and this drove his desire to develop a pedagogical philosophy which could accommodate his objectives. After this period he became concerned with the repair of the situation which led to the development of his well-known method of criticism, genealogical analysis and reconstruction. Insofar as Nietzsche sought to understand the development and proliferation of these negative forces in society education took a central role in his whole philosophical project.

Underlying Nietzsche's philosophy of education is the notion of 'higher' culture and 'true' education. He described contemporary culture as philistine. This was characterized by what he felt was a tendency towards dilettantism and he attacked this most vehemently in the first of his four published *Untimely Meditations*, 'David Strauss: confessor and writer'. In this essay, he identified philistine culture as the creator of 'whole philosophies: the sole provisio [of which is] that everything must remain as it was before, that nothing should at any price undermine that "rational" and the "real", that is to say, the philistine'.[4] His point was that when academic endeavour is defined by those with little or no vision or initiative education becomes a lifeless process of transferring a body of facts rather than a process of developing human understanding. This situation, Nietzsche argued, was in part the result of the decline of linguistic education. Too much emphasis had been placed on the development of specialized interests within a given field of study at the expense of the scholar's ability to convey his or her conclusions and contribution in an articulate and concise manner. The central role Nietzsche placed on language in education was first presented to his audience in a series of five public lectures titled 'On The Future Of Our Educational Institution', given at Basle in 1872. During the course of these lectures Nietzsche outlined what he felt was wrong with the German educational system. He argued that education had been degraded by its subordination to the state, and had become composed of two detrimental forces which combine to destroy education and thereby culture as well: the greatest possible expansion of education, and the narrowing and weakening of it.[5] He felt that emphasis ought to be placed on strict instruction and guidance. More precisely, the student must be given the tools and guidance to develop his or her own abilities rather than being handed an image to imitate. The ultimate goal of Nietzsche's philosophy of education, as with his whole philosophical system, was the development of true culture through the production of fully authentic individuals or what he called the higher type of humanity, for through the production of such individuals all of society would find its justification and so reap the greatest rewards.

Nietzsche's educational philosophy is concerned, in essence, with the future. He was a harsh critic of the values of modern society and charged these with responsibility for the modern sense of dislocation and isolation. He could make no sense of progress, and here it is cultural and human progress that is meant, unless it was the result of the critical assessment of the past. This is to be done by deciding what ought to be maintained for its useful and beneficial nature with regard to the continued development of the individual and so, through the individual, the whole of society. The goal of education in Nietzsche's opinion was the production of true culture and 'higher types', 'free spirits' and eventually the 'overman'. These are individuals possessed of the ability to decide for themselves what has value and what does not without reliance on the dogmatic reception of tradition. The highest form of life is the fully authentic individual who understands that the illusions and necessary fictions of which he is author are the ones that are right for him and that not everyone is capable of flourishing in the same way under the same conditions. Nietzsche felt that modern society could be characterized by its lack of authenticity. The drive towards ever-greater material wealth and comfort creates a levelling effect which in turn precipitates the stagnation of all culture, education included. This levelling effect results in a desire to have every individual place the same values on the same things and so to eradicate the individual altogether. This is one of the most important attitudes that Nietzsche worked against since its only outcome is nihilism: the feeling that since everything has the same value for everyone, nothing has any appreciable value at all. It is precisely here that Nietzsche's educational philosophy gains its greatest importance, for he held that the purposes of education were the same as those of society, and as such, if society decides that there is no appreciable value to anything, education, in the sense of development and progress, becomes equally meaningless. Against this Nietzsche emphasized the importance of the formation of authentic individuals through, on the one hand, self-reflection and the critical analysis of one's 'true educators', and on the other, through a strong and strict educational system capable of re-establishing the ability of the individual to posit value and thereby re-establishing society's ability to do the same. The attainment of the goals of this form of education are what gives sense to or justifies the society we create.

This 'true' education is, by definition, not within the realm of possibility for everyone; it is for the few. The majority, or herd, require a different type of education, that is, one that provides them with the ability to sustain themselves, but one which ought not be seen as less valuable since it too will allow those individuals to attain their highest possible level of authenticity. Nietzsche's argument is that full authenticity requires sacrifice and commitment on a scale that is exceptionally rare. For Nietzsche there were very few individuals who could be said to have approached the status of the 'higher type' and that only by accident. No overman 'has yet walked the Earth'. This status should not be mistaken for that of the hereditary aristocracy since when he says 'noble' Nietzsche is 'not speaking of the little word "von" '.[6] He is rather speaking of an aristocracy of spirit and intellect, which is to say that anyone who aspires to greater authenticity ought to be able to access the means to that development. It is, therefore, not one's birthright but one's convictions, attitudes and interests that are important. Nietzsche held that a society's interest in such higher types was the same as a concern for all of society. The idea is that we are as great as our greatest examples and in that sense they justify us. For example, Julius Caesar, Pericles or Napoleon, as examples of their society's highest values, are identified with Rome, Athens and France. For Nietzsche, a society is to be judged by the quality of its educational goals and its insistence on the attainment of those goals. On the basis of such educational aims the social, political and economic structure of society will be geared towards its own development in a more authentic manner. When this relationship is reversed, progress becomes synonymous with economic growth and technological advance and this, in turn, perpetuates the levelling effect which is contrary to authentic individuals and lives.

Although during his lifetime Nietzsche occupied the periphery of the intellectual community, his influence has steadily increased since his death. One of the main reasons for this is that his philosophy resists the standard approach of dissection and categorization. Indeed, this approach is responsible for some the greatest abuses and misinterpretations of his philosophy. Perhaps the most significant of these are the Nazi distortions of some of Nietzsche's key concepts for the purpose of justifying their own abominable practices and policies. While Nietzsche did write only three works that deal specifically with education, to take these as his complete pedagogical philosophy would be to fall into the nearsightedness which he devoted himself to correcting. Education is a central theme in Nietzsche's work from the time of his first autobiography at the age of 14 through to his last works. His approach to education came at a time when modern educational systems were first coming into being, and it stood as a warning. Unfortunately ignored during his own time, his work is becoming more and more recognized as important in all of the subjects to which he directed his extraordinary intellect. His thought has had foundational influence on existentialism, critical and literary theory and postmodernism during the twentieth century. Time has done little to reduce the relevance of his approach, his analysis and his conclusions.

Notes

1 *The Will to Power*, translated by W. Kaufmann and R.J. Hollingdale, New York: Vintage Books, section 942, 1967.
2 F. Ritschl quoted in F.A. Lea, *The Tragic Philosopher*, London: Methuen & Co. Ltd, p. 30, 1957.

3 See Wilhelm von Humboldt in this volume. See *also Die deutschen Universitäten und das Universitätstudium*, by Friedrich Paulsen, Berlin pp. 60–77, 1902.
4 'David Strauss: confessor' and writer in *Untimely Meditations*, translated by R.J. Hollingdale, New York: Cambridge University Press, p. 11, 1996.
5 *Werke: Kritische Gesamtausgabe*, G. Colli and M. Montinari (eds), Berlin: Walter de Gruyter, Berlin, III, ii, p. 139, 1967.
6 *The Will to Power*, translated by W. Kaufmann and R.J. Hollingdale, New York: Vintage Books, 942, 1967.

See also

In this book: Humboldt, Hegel

Nietzsche's major writings

The Birth of Tragedy (1872), trans. W. Kaufmann, New York: Random House, 1967.
Untimely Meditations (1873–76), trans. R.J. Hollingdale, Cambridge: Cambridge University Press, 1996.
Human, All Too Human (1878–80), trans. M. Faber and S. Lehmann, London: Penguin, 1984.
The Gay Science (1882), trans. Walter Kaufmann, New York: Vintage Books, 1974.
Thus Spoke Zarathustra (1883–92), trans. R.J. Hollingdale, London: Penguin, 1969.
Beyond Good and Evil (1886), trans. W. Kaufmann, New York: Vintage Books, 1966.
Genealogy of Morals (1887), trans. W. Kaufmann, New York: Vintage Books, 1967.
Twilight of the Idols (1888), trans. D. Large, Oxford: Oxford University Press, 1998.
The Will to Power (1883–1888), trans. W. Kaufmann and R.J. Hollingdale, New York: Vintage Books, 1967.
Werke: Kritische Gesamtausgabe, ed. G. Colli and M. Montinari, Berlin: Walter de Gruyter, 1967ff.

Further reading

Aloni, N., 'The Pedagogical Dimension of Nietzsche's Philosophy.' *Educational Theory*, 39, pp. 301–6, 1989.
Cooper, D.E., *Authenticity and Learning: Nietzsche's Educational Philosophy*, London: Routledge and Keagan Paul, 1983.
Hollingdale, R.J., *Nietzsche*, Cambridge: Cambridge University Press, 1999.
Murphy, T.F., *Nietzsche as Educator*, Maryland: University Press of America Inc., 1984.
Rosenow, E., 'What Is Free Education: The Education and Significance of Nietzsche's Thought', *Education Theory*, 23, 345–70, Fall 1973.

THOMAS E. HART

ALFRED BINET 1857–1911

> The use of tests is today very common, and there are even
> contemporary authors who have made a specialty of organizing
> new tests according to theoretical views, but who have made no
> effort to patiently try them out in the schools. Theirs is an
> amusing occupation, comparable to a person's making a
> colonizing expedition into Algeria, advancing always only upon
> the map, without taking off his dressing gown. We place but slight
> confidence in the tests invented by these authors and we have
> borrowed nothing from them. All the tests which we propose have
> been repeatedly tried, and have been retained from among many,
> which after trial have been discarded. We can certify that those
> which are here presented have proved themselves valuable.[1]

Alfred Binet was born on 8 July 1857 in Nice, France. He was a
contemporary of Sigmund Freud, who was born the year before, Francis
Galton, whose *Inquiries into Human Faculty* was published in 1883, Auguste
Rodin, whose *Gates of Hell* was commissioned in 1880, Victor Hugo, whose
Les Misérables was published in 1862, and Charles Darwin, whose *On the
Origin of Species* was published in 1859. Binet's father was a physician, but
his parents separated and his mother raised him. Little is recorded about
Binet's childhood. His mother took him to Paris at the age of 15 to continue
his education. In Paris, Binet studied both law and medicine, but found
neither satisfactory. He received a law degree in 1878, and then enrolled in
the Sorbonne to study natural sciences. At the same time, in his early 20s,
he began to read psychology at the Bibliothèque Nationale. Eventually, he
became a psychologist without formally enrolling in psychological studies,
and never pursued law. In 1884 Binet married Laure Balbiani, with whom he
had two daughters, Madeleine (b. 1885) and Alice (b. 1887).

Binet was introduced in about 1883 to the Salpêtrière, a Paris hospital
that was originally a gunpowder factory which Louis XIV converted into a
hospital and asylum for the poor. It was at the Salpêtrière that Binet met
Jean-Martin Charcot, a physician and professor who had established there
the greatest neurological clinic of the time. Charcot and the institution were
world-renowned and attracted such people as Binet and Freud. One avenue
of research that Charcot and his colleagues were pursuing was hysterics
under hypnosis, and Binet joined in such studies during the 1880s. He
enthusiastically entered into the publishing fray, which included a
controversy between the researchers of the Salpêtrière and those of the
Nancy school, from the city of Nancy. The Belgian mathematician Joseph-
Remi-Leopold Delboeuf was also critical of the research results coming
from the Salpêtrière, particularly of a series of studies that Binet performed
with Charles Feré.

The debate, described in detail by Wolf[2], centred on whether Binet and
Feré were observing experimentally induced phenomena in hypnotized
patients, as they claimed, or whether they were observing only the results
of suggestibility. The results included transferring hypnotically induced
paralysis on one side of the body to the other, and radically changing
hypnotically induced emotional displays from laughing to crying, all by
merely placing magnets near key areas of the body. Delboeuf agreed with the

Nancy school that the results were due to suggestibility after he observed the researchers discussing their expectations in front of the hypnotized patients. It turned out Delboeuf was correct, and Binet was disgraced. However, Binet was so influenced by his experience at the Salpêtrière that he later published a book titled *La suggestibilité* as well as other articles on the topic. Importantly, he became careful about gathering data to support his views, and became sceptical and critical of armchair theorizing as suggested by the epigraph to this entry.

Since about 1890, Binet had been observing and writing about his two daughters, Madeleine and Alice (whom he called Marguerite and Armande in published work). While baby biographies were not uncommon at the time, his studies do not entirely fit the baby biography mould because they were more experimental. His experiences observing, questioning and analyzing his children's behaviour and responses appear to have influenced his thoughts about individual differences, intelligence and how to measure intelligence. His work foreshadowed some of Swiss psychologist Jean Piaget's ideas, including conservation of number. In fact, in 1920, Piaget worked with Théodore Simon, one of Binet's closest collaborators, and was surely aware of Binet's work.

In 1891, Binet volunteered at the newly established Laboratory of Experimental Psychology at the Sorbonne. He became director in 1894, a post he filled until his death in 1911. In 1894, he established, with Henri Beaunis, *L'Année Psychologique*, which is still a major French psychology journal. Much of his work appeared in *L'Année*, including his writing on intelligence with Simon. A measure of the dedication and fervour that Binet felt for psychology is indicated by the fact that he had an independent income and was not paid for his positions at the Salpêtrière or at the Sorbonne.

Binet was active in studying amazingly diverse areas and in foreshadowing research of many years later. For example, in 1894 he published, with L. Félix Henneguy, a book describing phenomenal mental calculators and chess players. Binet was particularly interested, given controversies regarding thought as image, in the contrast between one calculator's lack of use of visual imagery and another's reliance upon it. The book also described the thought of expert chess players. In addition, Binet published on topics as diverse as prose memory, eye witness testimony, intelligence, fear, fetishes, hypnosis, handwriting analysis, suggestibility, creative writing and conformity to social influence.

Although Binet's work on intelligence was extremely influential across the globe, his other areas of research were much less influential. Why? As Siegler wrote, 'In economics terms, Binet's product was strong, but his marketing was weak.'[3] Binet was uninterested in travel or presenting at conferences; it appears that he did not leave France to attend any conference and may not have attended those in France.[4] His death at age 54 may also have been a factor; he simply did not live long enough to leave the mark of others who lived and published much longer.

While Binet was developing his ideas on intelligence, other scientists such as Francis Galton and James McKeen Cattell were attempting to discover whether that characteristic could be measured through physical and psychophysiological measurement – including measures of head circumference, reaction time, keenness of vision, ability to discriminate colour, and so forth. Binet also engaged in such research, but he believed that the measurement of intelligence required more complex tasks. In an 1896 paper, Binet and Victor Henri expressed astonishment that other researchers were using 'simple processes' to attempt to measure intelligence; they asserted that 'superior processes' would have to be tapped.

In 1899, Binet joined La Societé Libre pour l'Étude Psychologique de l'Enfant (The Free Society for the Psychological Study of the Child). In 1904, the French Ministry of Public Instruction appointed a Commission on the Education of Retarded Children, which included four members of La Societé; Binet was one of the four. The Commission's charge was to generate a method for diagnosing mental deficiency in order to accurately predict who would benefit from normal schooling and who would need an alternative form of education. This fit nicely with Binet's existing interest in understanding individual differences in children's intelligence. Collaborating with Simon, Binet devised the 1905[5, 6] tests which comprised thirty cognitive tasks that became the Binet–Simon scale. Revised versions were published in 1908[7] and 1911.[8] The items included tasks such as distinguishing morning and evening, copying geometric figures, counting money, repeating digits, placing weights in order, comprehending a mixed-up sentence, stating sixty words in three minutes, and stating differences between abstract words (e.g., What is the difference between idleness and laziness?). Binet and Simon graded the tasks according to age. Thus a 7-year-old was administered the 7-year-old tasks. If he or she was successful, the 8-year-old tasks were administered; if unsuccessful, the 6-year-old tasks were administered. The use of mental age as a criterion for selecting and scaling items has been called 'Binet's most original contribution'.[9]

The Binet–Simon scale was individually administered by a trained tester and was designed for children. Recalling Binet's experience with suggestibility, Binet and Simon cautioned that 'An inexperienced examiner has no idea of the influence of words; he talks too much, he aids his subject, he puts him on the track, unconscious of the help he is thus giving. He plays the part of the pedagogue, when he should remain psychologist.'[10] While Binet claimed to be attempting to measure natural intelligence independent of instruction, his writing shows a clear understanding that social conditions would affect such measures.

In the United States, the Binet–Simon scales were introduced and popularized by Henry Goddard. Lewis Terman published the Stanford–Binet scale, after several years of development, in 1916. In an amusing footnote, Binet and Simon noted that when their tests were translated into English, some sentences were criticized as too gruesome and were changed. For example, Binet and Simon wrote, 'We refer particularly to the woman cut into pieces, of an accident on the train which produced 48 deaths, and the man who committed suicide; it appears that these stories seem frightful to the American youth. Our Parisian youths laugh at them.'[11] Of scientific import is the fact that Binet and Simon insisted that revised or translated sentences be tried out experimentally and not be assumed to be valid; this is an area of psychometric research that has become increasingly recognized by current scholars.

In their writing, Binet and Simon provided guidance for scoring the individual test items such that children were scored as being at age, advanced by so many years, or retarded by so many years. The German psychologist William Stern introduced the idea in 1911 of dividing the child's mental age by its chronological age to give a 'mental quotient'. Lewis Terman and his associates multiplied the mental quotient by 100 to eliminate decimals resulting in the familiar 'intelligence quotient' (IQ).

Binet would likely have been disturbed by these manipulations because he was not comfortable with a single number being used to describe a person's intelligence; he believed that intelligence is too multifaceted and complex. He was interested in the specific things that children could do or not do. Binet also rejected the notion that intelligence represented a relatively fixed, hereditary trait. For example, he wrote:

> A few modern philosophers seem to lend their moral support to these deplorable verdicts when they assert that an individual's intelligence is a fixed quantity which cannot be increased. We must protest and react against this brutal pessimism. ... With practice, training, and above all method, we manage to increase our attention, our memory, our judgment, and literally to become more intelligent than we were before.[12]

Binet's legacy lives on in various ways. For example, the Stanford–Binet test, a descendant of the Binet–Simon, was the dominant individually administered intelligence test until the introduction of the Wechsler scales. The fourth revision of the Stanford–Binet was introduced in 1986 and continues to be a major instrument. Binet's conceptualization of an increasing function to represent the relationship between chronological age and cognitive ability foreshadowed the modern mental measurement model, Item Response Theory. Finally, today's special education and gifted education programs are reminiscent of Binet's attempts to examine individual differences in children's abilities, and thus provide them with an appropriate educational experience.

Notes

1   Alfred Binet and Théodore Simon, trans. Elizabeth S. Kite, *The Development of Intelligence in Children*, Baltimore: Williams & Wilkins Company, 1916; reprinted New York, Arno Press, 1973.
2   Theta H. Wolf, 'Alfred Binet: A Time of Crisis', *American Psychologist*, 19, pp. 762–71, 1964.
3   Robert S. Siegler, 'The other Alfred Binet', *Developmental Psychology*, 28, pp. 179–90, 1992.
4   Siegler (1992, p. 181).
5   Alfred Binet and Théodore Simon, 'New Methods for the Diagnosis of the Intellectual Level of Subnormals', *L'Année Psychologique*, 12, pp. 191–244, 1905; reprinted in Binet and Simon, *The Development of Intelligence in Children* (see note 1).
6   Alfred Binet and Théodore Simon, 'Application of the New Methods to the Diagnosis of the Intellectual Level Among Normal and Subnormal Children in

Institutions and in the Primary Schools', *L'Année Psychologique*, 12, pp. 245–336, 1905; reprinted in *The Development of Intelligence in Children* (see note 1).

7   Alfred Binet and Théodore Simon, 'The Development of Intelligence in the Child', *L'Année Psychologique*, 14, pp. 1–94, 1908; reprinted in *The Development of Intelligence in Children* (see note 1).

8   Alfred Binet and Théodore Simon, 'New Investigations Upon the Measure of the Intellectual Level Among School Children', *L'Année Psychologique*, 17, pp. 145–201, 1911; reprinted in *The Development of Intelligence in Children* (see note 1).

9   Arhur R. Jensen, 'Individual Differences in Mental Ability', in John A. Glover and Royce R. Ronning (eds), *Historical Foundations of Educational Psychology*, New York: Plenum Press, pp. 61–88, 1987.

10 Binet and Simon, *The Development of Intelligence in Children*, p. 44 (see note 1).

11 Ibid., p. 274 (see note 1).

12 Binet (1909). Cited in Siegler (1992, p. 183). From *Les idées modernes sur les enfants*.

See also

In this book: Darwin

Binet's major writings

Binet, Alfred, *La suggestibilité*, Paris: Schleicher, 1900.

Binet, Alfred, *Modern Ideas about Children*, trans. S. Heisler (originally published in Paris, 1909 as *Les idées modernes sur les enfants* by Flammarion).

Binet, Alfred, and Henneguy, L. *La psychologie des grands calculateurs et joueurs d'échecs*, Paris: Hachette, 1894.

Binet, Alfred, and Simon, Théodore. *The Development of Intelligence in Children*, see note 5 (includes Binet and Simon's articles from L'Année psychologique in 1905, 1908, and 1911 describing the intelligence scales).

Further reading

Fancher, R.E., *The Intelligence Men: Makers of the IQ Controversy*, New York: Norton, 1985.

Pollack, R.H. and Brenner, M.W. (eds), *The Experimental Psychology of Alfred Binet: Selected Papers*, New York: Springer, 1969.

Reeves, J.W., *Thinking about Thinking*, New York: Dell, 1965.

Siegler, R.S., 'The Other Alfred Binet', *Developmental Psychology*, 28, pp. 179–90, 1992.

Wolf, T., *Alfred Binet*, Chicago: University of Chicago Press, 1973.

DAVID A. BERGIN AND GREGORY J. CIZEK

ÉMILE DURKHEIM 1858–1917

> We must never lose sight of the fact that the class is a small society.[1]

Amongst disciplines such as philosophy and psychology, which have contributed to educational studies, the last on the scene was sociology. In England at least, one of the reasons was the slowness of sociology to be accepted as a creditable university discipline. The pionéer who showed the value of sociology to educational studies was Émile Durkheim, born in Epinal in Lorraine in 1858, who may truly be called the father of the sociology of education. Part of the reason for such a claim was his dedication to establishing sociology as a science, as he defined it, in French academe. Before his time, Auguste Comte (1798–1857) and Frédéric Le Play (1806–82) wrote on sociology, but their work was never accepted in universities, whereas Durkheim's sociology later was. Another factor related to the training of teachers at all levels which, from the time of the French Revolution, was taken more seriously in France than it was, for example, in England, where colleges of education were established only later in the nineteenth century. The French colleges, the Écoles Normales and the Écoles Normales Supérieures were created under Napoleon. From the time when Durkheim went as a lecturer to the University of Bordeaux in 1887 until his death, when he was Professor at the Sorbonne, he lectured in education. This he did despite his considerable output of books and articles on sociology, along with the production of the very influential journal, *L'Année sociologique.*[2] Interestingly enough the journal never included a section on education and nearly all his publications on education appeared posthumously.

Although he felt that so much lecturing on education prevented him from working on sociology itself, he was fully aware of the paramount importance of education for the continuance of any society. Education in the widest sense had existed ever since human societies began. Education is therefore an essential part of society as an ongoing process and is hence an eminently social matter. Sociology was therefore just as important, if not more important, to educational theory as the then more popular approach based on the individual (and therefore on psychology), such as that found in Herbert Spencer (1820–1903).

Basically Durkheim saw education as part of a socializing process which begins when the child is born and prepares him or her for adulthood in society. A person is made human by living in a society. Each society needs a certain degree of homogeneity for it to operate. The task of education is to give what the collective life requires and to make the individual truly human. Some might argue that socialization is a never-ending process. But for Durkheim, and for most practitioners, education meant focusing on the period when the child is educated in school and perhaps in university. He rejected the notion that education had the task of changing society: the young were not to be taught to carry out this task. But neither were they puppets of the ideology of the state. He held that each child was to be envisaged as an individual who, as a result of education, was to achieve his or her autonomy within society. Here stands his basic ideology of liberal humanism. He maintained that the true function of education was first and foremost to bring out and develop such seeds of humanity as we all have. He emphasized the point that education is where the individual and the social meet. Hence the need of sociology for those involved in teaching.

His influence on would-be primary school teachers was enormous and he did not teach students but made disciples of them (Lukes 1973: p. 369). Of all the lectures which have come down to us, none is more provocative and important than those given to would-be primary school teachers. The book of lectures, as its title *L'Éducation morale* (1925) suggests, did not concentrate so much on the techniques of teaching as on wider issues. In short, Durkheim expounded the policies educationalists should adopt. As a man who was convinced that the highest human action was moral action, he felt it necessary to proclaim the imperative of imparting moral education, not based on a traditional religion, but on rational, secular humanism. This was entirely in keeping with the ideology of the Third Republic. In order to displace the Catholic stranglehold on social life, he followed the government line of making the local schoolmaster or schoolmistress in the thousands of villages in France assume the role of the *curé* in instructing the young. Obviously Catholics opposed such a take-over. However, Durkheim agreed with Catholics in one respect. He saw that the problem of teaching secular morality was to find some kind of authority akin to that of traditional religion. He fully realized the close relation of religion and morality, the former giving the latter a sacred base, and thus a transcendental authority. Secular morality has the dual tasks of offering the justification for a moral precept as well as accounting for moral change. In acknowledging these problems Durkheim showed that he was not an old-fashioned, 'anti-religion' rationalist.

For Durkheim the actual content of morality was relative: each society had a system which fitted its own needs. But how does a child see one system as authoritative and demanding respect, obedience and loyalty? Where is the imperative? For Durkheim the answer was in society which he held to be virtually sacred or quasi-divine. Can a child understand such an idea, and will not the idea lead to a near worship of the state, as some critics have asserted? Such worship Durkheim would have strongly repudiated. But as a non-believing Jew who was born into a rabbinic family, he thought that he had a further answer in trying to establish a 'religious/secular' base for the teaching of morality. It could be found in the new humanistic religion which was in fact coming into being and superseding Catholicism and Protestantism. It was the cult of the individual. Here many people would consider him prophetic in the light of what is happening today but some would question whether the cult of the individual was functionally a religion in the generally accepted meaning of the word.

He held that humanism or the cult of the individual was axiomatically connected with science. After the disastrous 1870 war with Germany, it was felt that the French educational system needed to be changed to one more scientifically orientated, such as that of the Germans. For philosophical and practical reasons Durkheim appeared to agree in that he constantly stressed the importance of science in the school curriculum, as being the key to knowledge. Although himself well versed in the classics, he downgraded their importance in schools and universities. He took a negative attitude towards the arts on account of their tendency to detract from reality by allowing too much scope for the imagination.[3] Writing during the First World War, Durkheim was pleased with what the French educational system had achieved in giving to its soldiers a great sense of duty to the country and to humanity.

Durkheim held that the classroom should be looked upon as a micro-society, in which children interact and relate to one another. The school and the classroom are reflections of society. However, in one sense while the classroom has this social quality, it cannot ever be a perfect mirror of adult society, since there exists in the school and classroom the special relation of the teacher to the pupils and a form of authority in that relationship which does not exist in the wider society. For example, in Durkheim's eyes, pupils do not have democratic rights and children are subject to the authority of their parents as well as that of the teacher.

Both society and the school mete out punishments for offenders. Here there is a difference – in society as a rule it takes time for punishment to be handed down. In school it is more immediate, nor of course is punishment there as extreme as it is in the wider society. Discipline is necessary for both school and society. Although Durkheim presented a puritanical and ascetic persona, he was strongly opposed to physical punishment in schools. He held it to be degrading and dehumanizing.[4] Here stands the true humanist. Nevertheless he admitted that corporal punishment was valid for children up to the age of 7, because he believed that it was the only 'language' they could understand. At birth the child is egoistic – a little animal – and cannot respond to rational argument: shades indeed of Freud! There is nothing innate to suggest that the child is moral by nature. In the matter of the education of children, Durkheim was much influenced by Jean-Jacques Rousseau (1712–78). In his deep desire to stress the reality of the environment he found appealing Rousseau's emphasis on things and nature as foci in a child's education. He also admired Rousseau's concept of freedom.

Durkheim stressed the importance of history for an understanding of educational practices, policies and institutions. His lectures, *L'Évolution pédagogique en France* (1938), which he was reluctant to give, were magisterial in their historico-sociological approach. They were compulsory for those planning to teach in a *lycée* or university. In these much neglected lectures, he concentrated on the period from the early Church to recent times in Europe. His aim was to comment on the complicated phases through which educational policies had passed. He demonstrated the importance of the role of the Church in education all down the ages and how its policies varied over the centuries. Much of the controversy turned on the clashes between educational ideals of the ancient world and those of the Church, set within periods of cultural change. Durkheim was particularly critical of the goals of education which encouraged knowledge for its own sake, and ideals based on rhetoric, which the Jesuits supported. Indeed the Jesuits succeeded in stamping a lasting influence on French educational ideals and culture. Education has to be related to reality and to the well-being of society. Hence, while students may come to the university without any immediate vocational concern, it is while they are in a university that specialization begins and they start to prepare themselves to become doctors, teachers, scientists, writers and so on. Knowledge and education are for the benefit of humanity, which means coming face to face with society as it is and that means accepting the achievements of science and the scientific method. Durkheim in his innovative work offered no simple, mono-causal factor to account for changes in the university world, but a combination of factors, operating at different times. These included religion, politics, economics and so on. Such an analysis included the influence of individual thinkers and policy-makers such as Abelard, Comenius and Rabelais.

Durkheim's contributions to educational studies have not received as much recognition as they deserve, although sociology has now an accepted place in such studies. An issue such as the class bias of schools in terms of language used by pupils has been developed by Basil Bernstein in Britain. Kohlberg in the United States, however, has attacked Durkheim's attitude over moral teaching (see Walford and Pickering 1998, chapter 4) and Dewey, with his psychological approach, remains a popular opponent of those leaning towards the sociology of education (ibid., chapter 10). Nevertheless the strengths of Durkheim's distinctive ideas are slowly gaining recognition.

Notes

1 Durkheim (1925, pp. 171–2). In the English translation, 1961, p. 150.
2 The journal was first published in 1898 and finished in 1913 with volume 12. Series 2 and 3 of the journal continued after Durkheim's death.
3 Durkheim emphasized *la vie sérieuse* – the serious side of life. Some relaxation was necessary for the well-being of society, but it must never be dominant. Life is full of difficulties which have to be tackled with an awareness of reality. All knowledge, therefore, was to be cultivated to such an end.
4 Incidentally, in France at the time, sexual education was openly debated. Both in the matter of sexual education for children and need for monogamous marriage, Durkheim's attitude was virtually the same as those of Catholics and Protestants.

See also

In this book: Comenius, Dewey, Rousseau
In *Fifty Modern Thinkers on Education*: Bernstein

Durkheim's major writings

Éducation et sociologie, introduction by Paul Fauconnet, Paris, Alcan, 1922, trans. S.D. Fox, *Education and Sociology*, Chicago: Free Press, 1956.
L'Éducation morale, introduction by Paul Fauconnet, Paris, Alcan, 1925, trans. E.K. Wilson and H. Schurer, *Moral Education: A Study in the Theory and Application of the Sociology of Education*, edited, with an introduction, by E.K. Wilson, New York: Free Press, 1961.
L'Évolution pédagogique en France, 2 vols, Paris: Alcan, 1938.
The Evolution of Educational Thought in France, trans. P. Collins, London and Boston: Routledge and Kegan Paul, 1977.
Lecture, 'L'Enseignement de la morale à l'école primaire', 1991 in Pickering 1995.

Further reading

Cardi, F. and Plantier, J. (eds), *Durkheim, sociologue de l'éducation*, Paris: L'Harmattan, 1993.

Filloux, J.-C., *Durkheim et l'édcuation*, Paris: Presses Universitaires de France, 1994.

Lukes S., *Émile Durkheim. His Life and Work: A Historical and Critical Study*, London, Allen Lane, 1973; new edition, London: Penguin, 1992.

Pickering, W.S.F. (ed.), *Durkheim: Essays on Morals and Education*, London, Boston and Henley: Routledge and Kegan Paul, 1979.

—— 'Durkheim and Moral Education for Children: a Recently Discovered Lecture', *Journal of Moral Education*, 24 (1), pp.19–36, 1995.

Walford, G. and Pickering, W.S.F. (eds), *Durkheim and Modern Education*, London and New York: Routledge, 1998.

WILLIAM PICKERING

ANNA JULIA HAYWOOD COOPER 1858–1964

> We take our stand on the solidarity of humanity, the oneness of life, and the unnaturalness and injustice of all special favoritisms, whether of sex, race, country, or condition ... and that ... not till race, color, sex, and condition are seen as accidents, and not the substance of life; not till the universal title of humanity to life, liberty, and the pursuit of happiness is conceded to be inalienable to all; not till then is woman's lesson taught and woman's cause won – not the white woman's nor the black woman's, not the red woman's but the cause of every man and of every woman who has writhed silently under a mighty wrong.[1]

The life and writings of Anna Julia Haywood Cooper represent her 'voice' as educator, feminist, historian, linguist, scholar, social activist, and writer. She has also been described by the many roles she undertook: human rights advocate, lecturer, principal, professor, scholar, teacher, university president, and writer. Moreover, she is known as the mother of black feminism and her thinking and writing on issues of education, equality, feminism, and race, provide insights into the life of African Americans during the later half of the nineteenth century through the mid twentieth century. As contemporary as the 'voice' of Anna Julia Haywood Cooper appears at the dawn of the twenty-first century, to truly appreciate her life and career it is imperative to understand it within the socio-historical context in which it evolved.

Anna Julia Haywood was born in 1858 in Raleigh, North Carolina. In a brief undated and privately published autobiography, she recalled 'my mother was slave and the finest woman I have ever known. Though untutored she could read her Bible and write a little'. Presumably, her father was George Washington Haywood, her mother's white master. A man whose large family had amassed considerable wealth and land and who had for generations owned and bartered slaves throughout Alabama, North Carolina and Tennessee. Anna Haywood was very aware of her mixed race lineage and did not romanticize about its occurrence, and through correspondence with a Haywood cousin, confirmed his paternity in 1934.

Throughout Anna's early childhood she learned several important lessons from her mother that served as a foundation for her life's work: 'commitment to family and to others in the community; strategies to resist race, class, and gender oppression; and her strong religious belief in God's benevolence'.[2]

A history of segregation and laws barring literacy and education to African Americans preceded Anna Julia Haywood's birth. However, in 1867, at the age of 8 she enrolled in the St Augustine's Normal School and Collegiate Institute, a religious school built on 110 acres of land owned by the Haywood family of Raleigh, according to Cooper biographer Louise Hutchinson. St Augustine's was established by Episcopalians to offer newly freed African Americans teacher training and training for the ministry. Anna Haywood secured a scholarship to attend the school that she fondly referred to as the centre of her life. A precocious child, Anna later in life recalled 'I had devoured what was put before me, and ... was looking for more. I constantly felt (as I suppose many an ambitious girl has felt) a thumping from within unanswered by any beckoning from without'.[3] At the age of 10, Anna began to support herself in part, by tutoring other students. From 1871 to 1887, Anna, along with another early female entrant, Jane Thomas, was employed as a teacher at St Augustine's College.

Anna's experiences as a student at St Augustine's foreshadowed her life's commitment to equality, women's rights, and higher education for African American women, when she fought and won the right to take courses that were designated for males. She enrolled in the classical education programme, designed for males interested in the ministry. However, when the school's curriculum was changed and reorganized to offer classes in the Greek language only for males studying for the ministry, Anna protested to the school's new principal, Reverend Dr Smedes, arguing that the class should be opened to women as well. In fact, she remarked 'the only mission opening before a girl in his (Smedes') school was to marry one of those candidates'.[4] After winning the first of her many battles for women's rights and for the pursuit of higher education for African American women, Anna Haywood was admitted to the class, taught by George A.C. Cooper. Later, on 21 June 1877, Anna married George Cooper, an immigrant from the British West Indies (Nassau) and a tailor by trade. He was preparing to become a Protestant Episcopalian clergyman when they met. The young couple continued their studies while teaching at St Augustine's after George was ordained. However, George Cooper died unexpectedly two years later. Anna never remarried but remained at St Augustine's before furthering her education.

Anna Julia Cooper also learned many life lessons from her experiences at St Augustine's including her commitment to excellence and an uncompromising faith. She remained passionately committed to each of these ideas throughout her long life as evidenced in her writings, community service and personal accomplishments. As a widow, social custom dictated that Anna could pursue her life's dream to become a teacher. Despite her academic prowess and independence, she was strongly discouraged from seeking a higher education as there were few colleges and universities that admitted African Americans, and fewer still that admitted African American women. Undaunted, Cooper wrote an inspiring letter of admission to President Fairchild of Oberlin College. She selected Oberlin College because it admitted African American women, supported Christian religious beliefs, and offered work-study scholarship support. Anna's strong academic background from St Augustine's allowed her to enter Oberlin as a sophomore. There she joined several other African American women, Mary Church (Terrell) and Ida A. Gibbs (Hunt), who also were to become community workers and advocates for higher education of African Americans and human rights. These women enrolled in the 'gentlemen's course' or classical course of study that led to a bachelor's degree at Oberlin. The programme consisted of courses in Latin, Greek, modern European languages, literature, philosophy, science and higher mathematics. The course of study required students to enroll in three classes; Anna, however, often requested permission to enroll in a fourth.

She enrolled at Oberlin College in 1881. She graduated with a Bachelor of Science degree in mathematics in 1884. In addition to her studies, Anna taught classes in advanced algebra at Oberlin's academy to white students. After graduation, she taught French and German literature and science briefly at Wilberforce before returning to St Augustine College, to teach, build community support and to support her aging mother. Three years later, Cooper returned to Oberlin and studied for and received her masters degree. While at Oberlin Anna's life was greatly influenced by her instructors and she later acknowledged their contribution and influence on her thinking. She later wrote that they 'inspired my faith, encouraged my hope, and deepened my love in and privilege of a life of service'.[5] Cooper's worldview was enhanced by her experiences at Oberlin, experiences that helped her form her philosophical stance and fight against race, class and gender oppression in her lifelong battle for 'liberation and empowerment of the African American community.[6] Upon completion of her degree, she was recruited by George F.T. Cook, an Oberlin graduate and principal of M Street School. Anna agreed to teach high school mathematics at the prestigious M Street School (later renamed Dunbar High School) in Washington DC.

M Street School, formerly the Washington Preparatory High School, was a prestigious African American college preparatory school in the segregated school system of the nation's capital, by the time Anna Julia Haywood Cooper was hired as a teacher. The socially stratified African American community of Washington, DC, sought to maintain their school's reputation and excellent record of academic achievement. The school's administration, faculty and student body were disproportionately female. The administration and faculty, however, held college and graduate degrees, in numbers greater than their white counterparts. Moreover, the school's administrators, faculty, staff and the African American community held the students to a high standard of academic performance, encouraged their intellectual abilities, and sought scholarships for higher education. M Street School offered two courses of study: classical and vocational education. The majority of students were enrolled in the classical curriculum.

The M Street School and the African American middle-class community of Washington, DC, were a wonderful fit for Cooper who had experienced success under the classical curriculum. She was involved in the school's academic programme, extra-curricular programmes, and within the community. At school she was known to challenge African American students toward academic excellence by setting high standards, desiring to shape a generation of African American leaders. Cooper wanted to cultivate and equip African

American leaders who were not merely interested in self-gain, but leaders who would lead their community, their nation and the world toward social justice. Several scholars have likened Cooper's stance to that of W.E.B. Du Bois, calling her 'the female Du Bois'. Both Du Bois and Cooper believed that it was important to ensure that the most talented African American students were afforded the opportunity to excel academically and to become leaders of the nation, state and local African American community.

Cooper, a talented teacher who quickly earned a reputation for her ability to nurture, became the principal of M Street High School and successfully revised and strengthened the school's academic curriculum. She strongly believed in and encouraged students to participate in the classical curriculum, although she was not an ardent opponent of vocational education. Like many of her contemporaries, she understood the need for both types of curricula. However, she preferred to have students work within the classical curriculum, in stark contrast to the prevailing ideology which saw vocational and industrial education as 'the model for black education'.[7]

Among the many visitors to M Street School during Cooper's tenure were Abbé Klein, a professor at the Institut Catholique de Paris, in 1904; and Booker T. Washington, founder and principal of Tuskegee Institute, in 1905. The Abbé Klein vividly described his impression of Cooper, the school, and the student body as inspiring and scholarly. Cooper's relationship with the Abbé would serve her well later in life.

Under Cooper's tutelage, several students from M Street School were awarded scholarships to prestigious post-secondary institutions including Brown, Harvard, Oberlin and Yale. Students from M Street School received scholarships at a greater rate than white students in the area. According to biographer Leona C. Gabel, part of Cooper's success at M Street School was due to her ability to select her staff, hold special tutorials for students, and the encouragement she gave her staff to seek scholarship aid for students.[8]

Cooper's success came at a time in history when the intellectual capacities of African Americans were part of the public debate and when strong lines were drawn between supporters of W.E.B. Du Bois' and Booker T. Washington's philosophies and theories of education for African Americans. When local and school politics sought to discourage the continuation of the classical curriculum at M Street School, preferring a less classical and less strident curriculum, Cooper was an outspoken opponent to the change. She resigned her position as principal in 1906, rather than change her standards, and upon resignation, promptly left Washington for a position as chair of the modern language department at Lincoln University in Jefferson City, Missouri, where she remained until 1910. Following her work at Lincoln, Cooper returned to the M Street School as a Latin teacher.

In 1914 Cooper began her doctoral studies in Romance Languages at Columbia. However, due to her teaching and familial responsibilities, she could not meet the residency requirement. In partial fulfillment of her studies, however, Cooper translated the eleventh-century French epic, Le Pèlerinage de Charlemagne (1917) complete with a glossary and notes.[9] In the interim, the Abbé Klein encouraged Cooper to complete her doctoral studies at the University of Paris (Sorbonne). While continuing to teach at M Street School and under threat of dismissal, Cooper completed her studies and graduated at the age of 65. Her dissertation, written and defended in French, was titled *Slavery and the French Revolutionists, 1788–1805*. Following this, Cooper returned to her teaching position at M Street School where she remained until 1930. Never one to take life lightly, Cooper published several articles in the 1930s in *The Crisis* that called for the training of African American teachers.

Cooper became the second president of Frelinghuysen University (1930–1940), an institution established in 1906, to offer the working African American adult an opportunity to gain high school, undergraduate and graduate credit in night classes. The students paid tuition and could enroll in several courses of study: academic, religious and vocational. As the president, Cooper established the Hannah Stanley Haywood Opportunity School in honour of her mother. When funding for the school was scarce, Cooper opened up her own home and held classes for the students, before the school closed in 1961.

At the age of 105, Anna Julia Cooper died peacefully at her home on 27 February 1964. Her obituary recalled her 'life of service' as an educator, writer and principal of M. Street School. Services were held at St Augustine's College Chapel and she was buried in North Carolina. A street has been named after her in Washington, DC, the *Anna J. Cooper Memorial Circle* at 3rd and T Streets, NW.

Anna Julia Haywood Cooper's accomplishments were extraordinary for an African American woman of the nineteenth century, a woman whose life began in slavery, and a woman who dedicated her life to the education of others. Early in her life, Cooper became an outspoken proponent of the importance of higher education, especially for African American women, as a means of social and political equality. Like many other African American female educators of her day, Cooper firmly believed that education, especially higher education, could help to 'uplift the race'. She held that African American women were uniquely qualified to deliver such an education to African American youth; an education that could potentially change the life of the student, the community, the nation and the world. Cooper's lifelong commitment to education, her fervent desire to uplift the race, and her high academic standards, paved the way for many African students to pursue post secondary education in prestigious colleges and universities. Moreover, she understood education's potential to create opportunities for all students and sought to transform their lives by setting high academic standards, offering support for those who were struggling, and always encouraging each student to make the most of life. Throughout her life she remained fiercely loyal to improving the educational opportunities of African Americans, especially for African American women.

Cooper steadfastly believed in education's ability to empower and uplift the African American race. Her thoughts on education were often shared in her essays and as early as 1892, she had observed that 'Education, then, is the safest and richest investment possible to man. It pays the largest dividends and gives the grandest possible product to the world – a man. The demand is always greater than the supply – and the world pays well for what it prizes.'[10] Cooper, who was first and foremost a teacher, wrote later in 1930, 'The humor of teaching', published in *The Crisis*. Perceptively she details some of the frustrations of teachers and their need to be more reflective in their practice. In an undated essay, 'On Education', she writes, 'the only sane education, therefore, is that which conserves the very lowest stratum, the best and most economical is that which gives to each individual, according to his capacity, the training of "head, hand, and heart," or, more literally, of mind, body and sprit which convert him into a beneficent force in the service of the world.'[11]

Cooper's 'unbridled passion for learning and sincere convictions that women were equipped to follow intellectual pursuits',[12] led her to use her accomplished skill as an orator to speak at churches, to women's groups and at Pan-Africanist gatherings. In her first public speech, an address to African American clergymen in 1886, Cooper 'held their feet to the fire', asserting that 'We need men and women who do not exhaust their genius splitting aristocratic distinctions and thanking God they are not as others; but earnest, unselfish souls, who can go into the highways and byways, lifting up and leading, advising and encouraging with the truly catholic benevolence of the Gospel of Christ'.[13] Throughout her speeches and writings, Cooper makes clear her devotion to her Christian religious beliefs and values with her constant use of Biblical allusions and references. Although often referred to as the 'mother of black feminism', Cooper's writings mirror current theorizing of black womanist writers as she declared in 1886, ' "I am my Sister's keeper" should be the hearty response of every man and woman of the race, his conviction should purify and exalt the narrow, selfish and petty personal aims of life into a noble and sacred purpose'.[14] Not only was she aware of the discrimination, marginalization and silencing of the voice of African American women within the white women's movement, she attacked the hypocrisy of the white women's movement and African American males. Moreover, she did not hesitate to invoke her Christian beliefs as she challenged both groups to address racial, gender and class injustices.

Cooper believed that as an African American woman and intellectual she had a voice that needed to be heard in the cacophony of voices on both issues, and she captured the uniqueness of her position by stating that African American women are 'confronted by both a woman question and a race question'.[15] A fearless fighter for the voice of African American womanhood, Cooper wrote, 'that this little Voice has been added to the already full chorus. The "other side" has not been represented by one who "lives there". And not many can more sensibly realize and more accurately tell the weight and the fret of the "long dull pain" than the open-eyed but hitherto voiceless black Woman of America'.[16] She understood the importance of stressing the significance and the complexity of the African American woman's position in a racialized society.

Cooper's most notable publication, *A Voice from the South: by A Black Woman of the South* is a collection of essays and speeches (two) written between 1886 and 1892. Her understanding of American social thought and her actions to change the course of events through education are most poignantly stated in this book. Cooper's style, clear and direct, portrays the interconnectedness and complexity of religion, race, gender and class concerns of African Americans in American society. Her address entitled 'The Intellectual Progress of the Colored Women in the United States since the Emancipation Proclamation: A Response to Fannie Barrier Williams', delivered at the 1892 Congress of representative women at the Chicago

World's Fair, established her position as one of the most outspoken and forthright feminists of her era. She artfully wove her vast knowledge and understanding of world history, literature, philosophy, sociology and personal experience together to lay out a scathing rebuke of the hypocrisy of the white women's movement.

Writing years before W.E.B. Du Bois' famous references to second sight and moving beyond the veil, Cooper believed that African American women were a unique and special class of humans who, by experience and faith, were wise discerners of the past, counsellors of the present, and visionaries of the future. To Cooper, the African American experience in America was in its infancy. She described world history and acknowledged the plight of African Americans in America as a challenge to the popular rhetoric of scientific notions of racial superiority espoused by whites. Quickly and decisively she dismisses all theories of white racial superiority with a proverb claiming that 'The devil is always painted *black* – by white painters'.[17] She dismissed theories of the physical, mental and moral superiority of whites and challenged the very 'science' on which they were based. Cooper found particularly abhorrent the use of scientific generalizations and the acceptance of opinions as facts, as used by scientists, white feminists, academics and politicians to continue the oppression of African Americans. She argued 'Whence the self-congratulation of "dominant" races, as if "dominant" meant "righteous" and carried with it a title to inherit the earth. Whence the scorn of so-called weak and unwarlike races and individuals, and the very comfortable assurance that it is their manifest destiny to be wiped out as vermin before this advancing civilization.'[18] It was difficult for Cooper to reconcile the anti-racist teachings of Christianity with the racist propaganda of science.

Cooper was both intimately bound to her philosophical positions and unrelentingly bound to her Christian religious beliefs as she countered the agnosticism and secularism around her. Boldly, she disputed the prevailing ideologies with wit and cunning in her writing:

> In the old days, I am told that two or three Negroes gathered together in supplication and prayer, were not allowed to present their petition at the throne of Grace without having it looked over and revised by a white man for fear probably that white supremacy and its 'peculiar' system might be endangered at the Court of the Almighty by these faltering lips and uncultured tongues![19]

During her long life, Cooper often participated in panel discussions along with W.E.B. Du Bois and Booker T. Washington. She was one of two women invited to speak at the first Pan African Conference in Westminster Hall in London, England, in 1900. Though she understood the pervasiveness of racial, class and gender discrimination, she was not unaware of how many people were unconscious participants.

Cooper's work as an educator and social activist resulted in an extension of her personal philosophies of education into the nation and her community. Using today's language, Anna Julia Haywood Cooper was an African American female educator who used a transformative pedagogy to fight for feminist issues, social justice, class and racial equality and higher educational opportunities. Of her own life's calling, Cooper observed

> I may say honestly and truthfully that my one aim is and has always been, so far as I may, to hold a torch for the children of a group too long exploited and too frequently disparaged in its struggling for the light.
>
> 29 December 1925[20]

Notes

1 Cooper (1893), quoted in Loewenberg and Bogin (1976, pp. 330–1).
2 Karen A. Johnson, *Uplifting the Women and the Race: The Educational Philosophies and Social Activism of Anna Julia Cooper and Nannie Helen Burroughts*, New York: Garland Publishing Inc., p. 36, 2000.
3 Anna Julia Cooper, privately printed and undated autobiography.
4 Ibid.
5 Cooper, quoted in Jackson (2000, p. 46).
6 Jackson (2000, p. xii).
7 Louise D. Hutchinson, *Anna J. Cooper, A Voice from the South*, Washington, DC: Smithsonian Institution Press, p. 45, 1981.
8 Gabel (1982).
9 Ibid.
10 Cooper (1892, pp. 244–5).
11 Ibid., p. 250.
12 Hutchinson (1981).
13 Cooper (1892, p. 64).
14 Ibid., p. 32.
15 Ibid., p. 134.
16 Ibid., p. ii.
17 Ibid., p. 51.
18 Ibid., p. 59.
19 Cooper (1902), reprinted in Lemert and Bhan (1998, p. 214).
20 Cooper (1925), reprinted in Hutchinson (1981, p. 131).

See also

In this book: Du Bois

Cooper's major writings

A Voice from the South, by a Black Woman from the South, New York: Negro Universities Press (original privately printed 1892, Xenia, OH, Aldine Publishing House), 1892.
L'Attitude de la France a l'égard de l'esclavage pendant la Revolution, Paris, trans. F. Keller, 1988, Lewiston, New York: Edwin Mellen Press, 1925.
The Life and Writings of the Grimke Family, privately printed, 1951.
'The Third Step: Autobiographical', in M. Mason and C. Green (eds), *Journeys: Autobiographical Writings by Women*, Boston, MA: G. K. Hall & Co. pp. 138–45) (original privately printed, 1925), 1979.

Further reading

Baker-Fletcher, K., *A Singing Something: Womanist Reflections on Anna Julia Cooper*, New York: Crossroads, 1994.

Collins, P., *Black Feminist Thought: Knowledge, Consciousness, and the Politics of Empowerment*, second edition, New York: Routledge, 2000.

Crenshaw, K., 'Demarginalizing the Intersection of Race and Sex: A Black Feminist Critique of Antidiscrimination Doctrine, Feminist Theory, and Antiracist Politics', in J. James and T. Sharpley-Whiting (eds), *The Black Feminist Reader*, Oxford: Blackwell Publishers Ltd, pp. 208–38, 2000.

Gabel, L., *From Slavery to the Sorbonne and Beyond: The Life and Writings of Anna J. Cooper*, Northampton, MA: Department of History of Smith College, 1982.

Hutchinson, L., *Anna J. Cooper, A Voice from the South*, Washington, DC: Smithsonian Institution Press, 1981.

Johnson, K., *Uplifting the Women and the Race: The Educational Philosophies and Social Activism of Anna Julia Cooper and Nannie Helen Burroughs*, New York: Garland Publishing Inc., 2000.

Lemert, C. and Bhan, E. (eds), *The Voice of Anna Julia Cooper: Including A Voice from the South and Other Important Essays, Papers, and Letters*, Lanham, MD: Rowman & Littlefield Publishers, Inc., 1998.

Loewenberg, B. and Bogin, R. (eds), *Anna Julia Cooper. Black Women in Nineteenth-Century America Life: Their Words, Their Thoughts, Their Feelings*, University Park: The Pennsylvania State University Press, pp. 317–31, 1976.

Pellow, D., 'Anna "Annie" J. Cooper (1858/9–1964)', in J. Smith (ed.), *Notable Black American Women*, Detroit, MI: Gale Research Inc., pp. 218–24, 1992.

Hundley, M., *The Dunbar Story, 1870–1955*, New York: Vantage Press, 1965.

Terrell, M., *Colored Woman in a White World*, Washington, DC: Ransdell, 1940.

ARLETTE INGRAM WILLIS AND VIOLET HARRIS

JOHN DEWEY 1859–1952

> [We must] make each one of our schools an embryonic community life, active with types of occupations that reflect the life of the larger society, and throughout permeated with the spirit of art, history, and science. When the school introduces and trains each child of society into membership within such a little community, saturating him with the spirit of service, and providing him with the instruments of effective self-direction, we shall have the deepest and best guarantor of a larger society which is worthy, lovely, and harmonious.[1]

John Dewey is generally recognized as the most renowned American educator of the twentieth century. In a prolific career that spanned seven decades (his collected works comprise thirty-seven volumes), Dewey focused on a wide range of concerns, most notably within the fields of philosophy, education and politics. As much after his life as during it, Dewey's writings have been the subject of interpretation and reinterpretation by countless scholars. A voluminous literature exists as much about him as by him, with vastly different assessments made of the nature and impact of his work. Ironically and contrary to the assumptions made by some commentators on his books, Dewey's own ideas never really permeated the classroom realities of the American education system, despite his central place in academic discourse throughout this century. Thus his legacy is contradictory, but it is still extremely important as a foundation for a vision of education that is connected to the expansion of democracy to all spheres of social life.

Dewey was born in 1859 in Burlington, Vermont. The United States generally during the late nineteenth and early twentieth centuries was rapidly evolving from a relatively simple frontier-agricultural society to a much more complex urban-industrial nation. The ways in which a genuine and cohesive democratic community could be maintained amidst the wrenching economic and cultural changes of the new industrial order were Dewey's paramount concern throughout his life.

After graduating from the University of Vermont in 1879, he taught Latin, algebra and science for two years at a high school in Oil City, Pennsylvania, and then for a short time was the sole teacher in a rural school near Burlington. During these years, with the encouragement of one of his Vermont professors, he also wrote three philosophical essays which were accepted for publication in the *Journal of Speculative Philosophy*. His success in this area whetted his interest to continue his studies and he subsequently enrolled in the graduate programme in philosophy at Johns Hopkins University. Among the faculty with whom he worked closely were George Sylvester Morris, known for his embrace of German idealism and antipathy toward British empiricism; Charles Sanders Peirce who, with William James of Harvard, laid the basis for pragmatic philosophy; and G. Stanley Hall, a psychologist who advocated intensive study of children and adolescents to determine teaching methods that were developmentally appropriate.

After completing his doctoral dissertation in 1884 on the psychology of Immanuel Kant, Dewey secured a position as instructor in philosophy and psychology at the University of Michigan. In 1888 he left for the position of chair in philosophy at the University of Minnesota, but he returned to Michigan after only one year to take a similar position. In 1894, the University of Chicago offered Dewey the chairmanship of the combined department of philosophy, psychology and pedagogy.

Upon his arrival in Chicago, Dewey witnessed for himself the turbulence of life in a large city at the turn of the century, and in particular the Pullman Strike and the results of President Grover Cleveland's decision to send in federal troops to support corporate interests. The events of the strike, as well as his association with social activists like Jane Addams and educators like Ella Flagg Young, served to enhance his commitment to wide-ranging progressive reforms.

While at the University of Chicago, Dewey established an elementary level Laboratory School to help assess, modify and develop his educational and psychological ideas. However, a dispute with the president of the university resulted in Dewey's resignation from Chicago in 1904. Columbia University immediately offered him a position as professor of philosophy, with arrangements made to also occasionally offer lectures at the university's well-known Teachers College. In 1930, he was appointed professor emeritus of philosophy in residence at Columbia, a position he held until his eightieth birthday in 1939.

Dewey was actively involved in a diverse array of educational, social and political causes throughout his life. For example, he was a fellow of the

National Academy of Sciences; helped to found the American Association of University Professors, the New School for Social Research, and the American Civil Liberties Union; was a charter member of the first teachers' union in New York City; was a regular contributor to a number of influential liberal journals; and during the early 1930s served as president of two groups that attempted to organize a radical third party based on a coalition of labour, farmers and the middle class. In addition, as a further indication of his lifelong commitment to progressive causes, in 1937 (at the age of 78) he travelled to Mexico to head a commission that investigated the charges of treason and murder levelled against the exiled Leon Trotsky during the infamous Moscow purge trials.

Perhaps Dewey's greatest legacy, however, is the many articles and books that he authored, including *The School and Society* (1899), *The Child and the Curriculum* (1902), *How We Think* (1910), *Democracy and Education* (1916), *The Public and Its Problems* (1927), and *Experience and Education* (1938). Dewey conceived of the philosopher's role as engaging intimately with social criticism, rather than participating in abstract exercises of contemplation that remained aloof from practical morality. He was particularly concerned with the enhancement of democratic community in a nation that seemed to be in danger of losing its moral and spiritual compass. For Dewey, genuine democracy did not refer simply to governmental agencies and rituals, but rather to a dynamic process of daily active and equitable participation that included not simply the formal political apparatus but culture and economics, indeed *all* spheres of life.

Intertwined with Dewey's concern for democratic community was the pragmatism that undergirded all of his work. Dewey believed that every idea, value and social institution originated in the practical circumstances of human life. They were neither divine creations nor did they reflect some type of ideal. Truth did not represent an idea waiting to be discovered; it could only be realized in practice. Every institution and every belief, viewed within its specific context, should be subject to the test of establishing its contribution in the broadest sense to the public and personal good.

Dewey viewed change and growth as in fact the nature of things. Thus, social experimentation, rather than absolute principles, was needed to assess the worth of an idea or practice. This experimentation was to be guided not by random trial and error, however, but rather by scientific habits of mind. For Dewey, 'an articulate public' that had developed methods of intelligence, not narrowly defined but broadly with regard to the capacity for rigorous reflective (scientific) inquiry, was the foundation of democratic community. He attacked absolute principles and imposition strategies because, while some good may be accomplished from them, they would not help to establish a genuine form of democracy in a constantly evolving society. Only rational criticism and experimentation, linked to concern for the creation of a humane and just society, could do so.

For Dewey, the key to intellectual development, and consequently to social progress, was schooling, especially at a time when the educational influences of other institutions (the home, the church, etc.) had decreased so drastically. Dewey stressed the social and moral nature of the school and believed that it should serve as a 'miniature community, an embryonic society', especially one that actively fostered the growth of democracy which was being undermined by urban industrial society. This view was in stark contrast to 'the factory system' model being adopted by school planners and 'efficiency experts' across the country, which emphasized students as relatively passive raw materials to be moulded by teachers, repetitious methods of teaching, and subject matter divorced from social content. Not only, then, was universal schooling crucial in a rapidly changing society, but a 'new education' was vital as well, one that was guided by the perspective that school is life, rather than a preparation for it. Thus, the best preparation for democracy was to provide opportunities for students (and teachers) to be actively engaged in democratic life.

The most effective curriculum for such a school would attend seriously to the present interests of children, not as a motivational strategy but as a way to teach the essential relationship between human knowledge and social experience. Dewey severely criticized public schools for silencing or ignoring student interests and experiences, using artificial language (perhaps about some vague future) that only served to alienate students, over-relying on testing to assess student learning, differentiating students according to their presumed ability to partake in mental or manual learning instead of offering both to all, and isolating subjects from one another instead of uniting them around students' lived experience with knowledge. Rather than blaming students for their passivity, Dewey focused attention directly on the pedagogy of schools.

However, it is important to emphasize as well that Dewey strongly disagreed with the more extreme proponents of child-centred progressivism. He made it clear that a crucial role was to be played by teachers in helping to link children's interests to sustained intellectual development and to educative experiences. Thus, for him, education was the construction and reorganization of experiences that add meaning and that increase one's ability to direct the course of subsequence experiences. Freedom for the child in the classroom, for example, was not to be an end in itself.

This dispute with some child-centred educators in part illustrates Dewey's long-held antipathy toward dichotomous thinking and absolute principles. He attacked such common dualisms as theory and practice, individual and group, public and private, method and subject matter, mind and behavior, means and ends, and culture and vocation. His attempt was not to find a compromise but rather to reconstruct the debate so that they were no longer viewed as opposites. Thus, for example, it was not a question of a choice between validating the interests of the child or the subject matter in constructing the curriculum, but rather of understanding and developing the continuum of experiences that links them.

Dewey remained steadfastly in support of an 'intentionally progressive' society throughout his lifetime. He condemned the traditional view of culture as blatantly aristocratic in its inequity and chose instead to ground culture and aesthetics in common experience. Similarly, rather than the school remaining isolated from social life, he advocated it taking on the role of helping in the transformation to a better social order. He recognized the nature of class barriers and distinctions, and argued that schools should help in their elimination. However, it did not follow, according to Dewey, that the school's role in the amelioration of social life in general and the evils of capitalism in particular should include the teaching of any kind of economic or social 'ism'. Instead, through the study of and active engagement in basic social activities (what he referred to as 'occupations'), such as growing food, cooking, building a shelter, making clothing, creating stories and artwork, children could be best initiated into moral social membership. They would be provided with opportunities to learn 'the instruments of effective self-direction', as well as a sensitivity toward social issues and the ability (including reading, writing and problem-solving skills) to act on them. In effect, the classroom was to embrace the kind of democratic community life, concern for human dignity, and scientific intelligence that was sought outside the school. The 'means' were in fact the 'ends'.

Dewey's place in American radical movements has always been somewhat problematic. For example, he wavered in his identification with socialism (e.g. he supported the entrance of the United States into the First World War) and referred to Marxism as 'unscientific utopianism'. Moreover, in his efforts to retain flexibility and oppose dogmatism, and in particular his disavowal of explicit ends decided ahead of time, he appeared too 'neutral' to some of those actively engaged in the struggle for radical social change. His antipathy toward the teaching of fixed social beliefs was in contrast to the approach of many social-reconstructionist educators who believed that such political advocacy was an unavoidable aspect of education. The application of creative and scientific inquiry to social problems was as far as Dewey would go. Indeed, his present-oriented and experimentalist perspective tended to result in rather vague depictions of alternatives to strive for, as he sought to avoid all 'blueprints', class-based or otherwise.

Furthermore, it is questionable whether the kind of common social purpose and active citizenry that Dewey advocated is possible in a capitalist society of such striking inequities of power and wealth and the dominance of consumerism. Some have also argued that Dewey's faith in science was misplaced, since scientific intelligence could be used just as easily to serve bureaucratic purposes or to foster domination.

Despite these criticisms, Dewey still looms as one of the major figures of American education, philosophy and politics, a towering presence whose work deserves to be read closely for its intensive examination of many of the pressing social issues that continue to be of such vital concern today. His articulation of and commitment to participatory democracy, in our schools and elsewhere, represents a major contribution. Indeed, although his optimism about progress, freedom, community, science, and so forth may seem at times to have been out of proportion to the realities of hegemonic culture, it serves to remind us of many of the paths to progressive social change. We may argue with some of the answers that he provided, but John Dewey exemplified attempts to get at the very root of the social world, to not only understand it but also to change it.

Note

1 John Dewey, *The School and Society*, Chicago: University of Chicago Press, pp. 39–40, 1899.

See also

In this book: Addams, Kant

Dewey's major writings

The School and Society, Chicago: University of Chicago Press, 1899.
The Child and the Curriculum, Chicago: University of Chicago Press, 1902.
How We Think, Chicago: University of Chicago Press, 1910.
Democracy and Education, New York: Macmillan,1916.
The Public and Its Problems, New York: Henry Holt, 1927.
Experience and Education, New York: Macmillan, 1938.

Further reading

Archambault, R.D, *John Dewey on Education: Selected Writings*, Chicago: University of Chicago Press, 1964.
Bernstein, R.J., *John Dewey*, New York: Washington Square Press, 1966.
Kliebard, H.M., *The Struggle for the American Curriculum*, New York: Routledge and Kegan Paul, 1986.
Mayhew, K.C. and Edwards, A.C., *The Dewey School: The Laboratory School of the University of Chicago, 1896–1903*, New York: D. Appleton-Century, 1936.
Westbrook, R.B., *John Dewey and American Democracy*, Ithaca, New York: Cornell University Press, 1991.

MICHAEL W. APPLE AND KENNETH TEITELBAUM

JANE ADDAMS 1860–1935

> And yet in spite of the fact that the public school is the great savior of the immigrant district, and the one agency which inducts the children into the changed conditions of American life, there is a certain indictment which may justly be brought, in that the public school too often separates the child from his parents and widens the gulf between fathers and sons which is never so cruel and so wide as it is between the immigrants who come to this country and their children who have gone to the public school and feel that they have there learned it all.[1]

This sentence, the essay from which it is taken, and many other statements by Addams should refute the claim sometimes heard today that she was an 'assimilationist'. Addams wanted to welcome immigrants and help them adjust to American life, but she also wanted to preserve 'old world' cultures and educate the young to appreciate their parents' heritage. The desire to help children understand and appreciate their parents' non-American culture motivated the establishment of the Hull House Labor Museum. Both implements (such as spinning wheels and looms) and products were displayed in the museum, and museum programmes were integrated with other educational activities at Hull House. 'Yet', Addams remarked, 'far beyond its direct educational value, we prize it [the museum] because it so often puts the immigrants into the position of teachers, and we imagine that it affords them a pleasant change from the tutelage in which all Americans, including their own children, are so apt to hold them.'[2] Today, when we struggle to provide immigrants and their second and third generation offspring with the education they need to succeed in their new countries and at the same time commit ourselves to respect their original cultures, we can learn a great deal from Jane Addams.

Addams was born into a well-to-do family in Illinois. Her mother died as a result of premature labour with her ninth child, and Addams – only two at the time – never really knew her. However, she knew her mother's reputation as a woman 'with a heart ever alive to the wants of the poor', one who would be 'missed everywhere, at home, in society, in the church, in all places *where good is to be done and suffering relieved*'.[3] Even as a young girl, Addams was deeply moved by the sights of obvious poverty in the city, and she was well aware of the privilege in which she lived.

Her father, John Addams, was a major influence in his daughter's life. He encouraged her continued education, and she was a good student. When her father remarried, Anna Haldeman Addams became another strong influence in Jane's life. It was she who ensured that Addams would be thoroughly at home with gentle society, music and art, and a step-brother, George, introduced her to nature studies and a love of science. From an early age, Addams was determined to make her life count – to be both independent and committed to service.

Addams, like many other young women, went through a period of indecision and nervous anxiety over exactly what form her life of independence and service would take.[4] It would be too facile to argue that she entered a life of service because there was nothing else available to young women at the time. The exclusion of women from most professions and public positions was, of course, a fact. But Addams could well have become a society matron, living well and giving occasional attention to good works. That she did not reflects a courageous and generous spirit.

In 1889, with Ellen Gates Starr, Addams opened Hull House, a 'settlement house' designed to educate the poor and meet their needs. At first, in addition to starting a kindergarten and classes in cooking, they concentrated on cultural events, but it soon became clear that the neighbourhood had greater needs. Addams and her companions responded to those needs, even helping to deliver babies when the appeal came. Although Addams admitted having reservations about some of these activities, her friends Julia Lathrop and Florence Kelley assured her that it was appropriate, even essential, for Hull House to respond with kindness and help to all genuine needs.[5] Sensitive to the lessons of experience, Addams said, 'I learned that life cannot be administered by definite rules and regulations; that wisdom to deal with a man's difficulties comes only through some knowledge of his life and habits as a whole; and that to treat an isolated episode is almost sure to invite blundering.'[6] The attitude expressed here is very like the one promoted today by an ethic of care.

Another lesson Addams learned – mainly in her European travels – was that social problems do not always yield to intellectual solutions. Indeed, intellectualizing the horrors of poverty could get in the way of responding with tangible help. In an essay of great poignancy, 'The Snare of

Preparation', Addams described her disgust upon realizing that she and so many of her class were 'lumbering our minds with literature that only served to cloud the really vital situation spread before our eyes'.[7] Addams continued to involve herself in both reading and writing, but she did not allow her prolific writing to displace the direct caring she saw as necessary.

Addams also believed that 'the dependence of classes on each other is reciprocal'.[8] Not only do people depend on one another for all sorts of work and services, but the sort of work done by Settlements was seen as a 'subjective necessity' for 'young people ... seeking an outlet for that sentiment of universal brotherhood'.[9] Addams did not comment on how this need to serve would be filled if poverty were actually overcome (there was little likelihood of this happening), and today we worry whether our charities and our need to be charitable might, perversely, help to maintain the very evils we try to relieve. The responsiveness of Addams, combined with a determination to educate, seems adequate insurance against such an unfortunate outcome.

The flexibility and responsiveness characteristic of Addams and her companions in the general conduct of Hull House extended to their educational programmes. Addams directed some criticism at professor-lecturers who could not adjust to their initially eager audiences at Hull House. Enthusiasm sometimes turned to boredom and absence. Of such professors, she remarked: 'The habit of research and the desire to say the latest word upon any subject often overcomes the sympathetic understanding of his audience which the lecturer might otherwise develop, and he insensibly drops into the dull terminology of the classroom.'[10]

The preferred pattern at Hull House was 'socialized education', and teachers were pressed to provide quickly the knowledge needed by new immigrants. However, education at Hull House was not limited to this crucial and instrumental knowledge. Poetry and the arts flourished; Lathrop sponsored a Plato club, and Starr held successful classes on Dante and Browning. Further, teachers at Hull House provided both domestic and vocational training. In designing their programmes with the needs and interests of their students in mind, Addams and her teachers were living examples of John Dewey's progressive education.

Dewey was, in fact, a frequent visitor at Hull House, and he and Addams became close friends. Dewey's daughter Jane was named for Jane Addams, and Addams delivered the eulogy for Dewey's son Gordon who died at the age of 8. It is clear also that Dewey and Addams learned from one another; their practical and theoretical talents were complementary. Moreover, Dewey and Addams worked together on social causes, and both were strong supporters of workers and unions.

In addition to her continuous work at Hull House, Addams wrote extensively and was regularly involved in political issues. Ellen Lagemann presents a succinct summary of this involvement:

> Addams served on the Chicago School Board. She seconded Theodore Roosevelt's nomination as the presidential candidate of the Progressive Party in 1912. She was a member of the first executive committee of the National Association for the Advancement of Colored People, a vice-president of the National American

Woman Suffrage Association, and a founder of the American Union Against Militarism, from which emerged both the Foreign Policy Association and the American Civil Liberties Union. She was elected chairman of the Woman's Peace Party in 1915, and in 1919 she became the first president of the Women's International League for Peace and Freedom, having presided over the 1915 International Congress of Women at The Hague from which the League originated.[11]

The First World War tested Addams' courage and commitment to non-violence. Although her good friend Dewey, after early opposition to US entry into the war, finally endorsed it, Addams remained firmly and outspokenly against US participation. Strongly criticized in newspapers and even in Congress, Addams lost the support of many who had formerly loved and admired her. Having suffered personal losses and agonies over the war, she was at last recognized for her efforts toward international peace with the Nobel Peace Prize in 1931. She was the first American woman to receive the Prize.

Addams' commitment to non-resistance supported a ban on military-like drills in the gymnasium of Hull House but, even on a matter so crucial to her principles, she gave way when it became clear that many neighbourhood boys wanted to engage in such activities. She retells with some humour and some dismay the story of her attempt to get the boys to drill with sewer spades instead of mock guns and bayonets. The request for military drill, she says, 'shocked my nonresistant principles', but – ever responsive – she urged the boys to use the sewer spades to attack (at least in imagination) the filth of Chicago streets. This experiment did not work. Years later, the sight of a sewer spade reminded her of this educational failure. 'I can only look at it', she writes, 'in the forlorn hope that it may foreshadow that piping time when the weapons of warfare shall be turned into the implements of civic salvation.'[12]

In an age when – in the US at least – policy-makers are trying to force all children into a standard academic mould, we might take a lesson from Jane Addams. Although she clearly wanted to make cultural riches available to all who were interested, she refused to force her interests on others. She respected all honest forms of work, and welcomed the participation of all regardless of their educational status. Education at Hull House was truly socialized. When serious requests were made by people who wanted to learn something, someone in the community was found to teach them or to lead them in cooperative learning. Similarly, when someone wanted to teach a beloved subject, to lecture, or to demonstrate some skill, there was usually an eager audience. When there was not, the activity just faded away.

The residents of Hull House were so diverse in their religious beliefs that a brief attempt at Sunday evening services was abandoned. Life at Hull House was proof that people could cooperate, actually live together, despite differences of religion, nationality and economic status. There were no ideological tests at Hull House beyond the common commitment to improve the neighbourhood, Chicago and, more generally, the lives of working people.

A sample of the weekly offerings in Hull House's educational programme includes athletics, drawing, sewing, English composition, lectures on social issues, biology, cooking, Latin grammar, history, singing, needlework, reading groups, arithmetic, French, Shakespeare, algebra, German, clay modeling, English class for Italians, fairy stories ... The list is quite incredible. There were, in addition, scheduled meetings of the Shirt-Makers Protective Union and gymnastic classes especially for members of the Bookbinders' and Shirtmakers' Unions.[13] Reading about the riches provided by Hull House and the eagerness of even the very poor to participate in what was offered, one wonders why schooling has long been so coercive.

Addams believed strongly in using current events to educate. However, she did not mean to 'teach current events' as teachers in our public schools so often do. Rather, she meant to take an event or issue of great current importance and encourage open inquiry and discussion. She used the Scopes trial as a marvellous example. Instead of merely asserting the intellectual superiority of those who defended evolution, Addams pointed out that 'the group of so-called narrow-minded men had made their own contribution to our national education. In the first place, they had asserted the actuality of religion'.[14] Addams went on to show how this event could be used not only for scientific education but, perhaps more importantly, to reopen discussions between young people and elders on religion. Her discussion is a model of even-handed generosity and creative thinking.

She captures the value she sought to promote in using current events this way: 'It seems at moments as if we were about to extend indefinitely what we call our public, and that unless it were stretched to world dimensions, the most significant messages of our times might easily escape us.'[15]

Notes

1 Jane Addams, 'The Public School and the Immigrant Child', in *Jane Addams on Education*, ed. Ellen Condliffe Lagemann, New York: Teachers College Press, pp. 136–7, 1985.
2 Ibid., p. 139.
3 Lagemann's introduction, *Jane Addams on Education*, p. 7.
4 See ibid. Also see the introduction by Victoria Bissell Brown (ed.), Jane Addams, *Twenty Years at Hull-House*, Boston: Bedford/St Martin's, 1999.
5 See Addams, *My Friend, Julia Lathrop*, New York: Macmillan, 1935.
6 Addams, 'Problems of Poverty' in *Twenty Years at Hull-House*, p. 109.
7 Addams, 'The Snare of Preparation', ibid., p. 71.
8 Addams, 'First Days at Hull-House', ibid., p. 80.
9 Addams, 'The Subjective Necessity for Social Settlements', ibid., p. 90.
10 Addams, 'Socialized Education', ibid., p. 198.
11 Lagemann, 'Introduction', *Jane Addams on Education*, p. 30.
12 Addams, 'Socialized Education', p. 203.
13 See the Hull-House Weekly Program in *Twenty years at Hull-House*, pp. 207–18.
14 Addams, 'Education by the Current Event' in *Jane Addams on Education*, p. 214.
15 Ibid., p. 224.

See also

In this book: Dewey

Addams' major writings

Democracy and Social Ethics, New York: Macmillan, 1902.
The Spirit of Youth and the City Streets, New York: Macmillan, 1909.
Twenty Years at Hull-House, New York: Macmillan, 1910.
Peace and Bread in Time of War, New York: Macmillan, 1922.
The Second Twenty Years at Hull-House, New York: Macmillan, 1930.
The Excellent Becomes the Permanent, New York: Macmillan, 1932.
See, also, the Bibliographic Essay in Ellen Lagemann (ed.), *Jane Addams on Education*, New York: Teachers College Press, 1985.

Further reading

Davis, A.F., *American Heroine: The Life and Legend of Jane Addams*, New York: Oxford University Press, 1973.
Diliberto, G., *A Useful Woman: The Early Life of Jane Addams*, New York: Scribner, 2000.
Farrell, J.C., *Beloved Lady: A History of Jane Addams's Ideas on Reform and Peace*, Baltimore: Johns Hopkins University Press, 1967.
Lasch, C. (ed.), *The Social Thought of Jane Addams*, Indianapolis: Bobbs-Merrill, 1965.
Linn, J. W., *Jane Addams: A Biography*, New York: D. Appleton-Century, 1935.
Ryan, A., *John Dewey and the High Tide of American Liberalism*, New York: W.W. Norton, 1995.

NEL NODDINGS

RUDOLF STEINER 1861–1925

> The prophet perceives revelation, that is, the sign of the world of feelings.[1]

Rudolf Steiner was the founder of and inspiration behind today's largest empire of private, non-profit education-providers apart from church-oriented schooling. The Rudolf Steiner Schools are the fastest growing enterprise in schooling in the Western world.[2] This enterprise was founded in 1919, after the First World War, and quickly became one of the most attractive alternatives to compulsory state-schooling. In post-war Germany, the *Waldorf-Schulen*, as they were known, were an integral part of the educational reform-movements where they were accepted as an important contribution to 'new education' irrespective of their specific *Weltanschauung* (Hilker 1924; Oelkers 2001). Throughout the twenties and thirties Steiner Schools were founded all over Europe, and these foundations laid the basis for today's empire. The enterprise is led from Dornach in Switzerland, the centre of power of the 'Anthroposophical Society' which operates world-wide.

The *Weltanschauung* of the schools is called 'anthroposophy' (wisdom of men) and consists of a system of doctrines for which Rudolf Steiner was the *spiritus rector*. Steiner was born and raised in Hungary.[3] He studied mathematics and science at the Technical University of Vienna from 1879 to 1883. At the age of 21 he was apppointed to edit Goethe's scientific writings.[4] From 1884 to 1890 he worked as private tutor in a wealthy Viennese family and in 1886 he published his first book, with the subject, not by chance, being Goethe's philosophy. Steiner completed his doctorate in philosophy at the University of Rostock in 1891. During this period of study he worked at the Goethe-Schiller-Archives in Weimar where he met the insane Friedrich Nietzsche in 1894. In 1895 Steiner published a book on Nietzsche, and in 1897 the conclusions of his studies on Goethe were published. Both Goethe and Nietzsche influenced Steiner's anti-empirical philosophy of spiritual wholeness that was developed against the positivistic reductionism of his time.

The biggest influence on his thinking, however, was Marie von Sievers, who met Steiner for the first time in 1900. He then worked in Berlin as a teacher at the private Worker's High School in Berlin.[5] From 1902 Steiner taught for three years at Berlin's Free College,[6] after he had become General Secretary of the German Section of the Theosophical Society.[7] Here he met Marie von Sievers,[8] later his wife and then his personal manager who organized the development of the German Section and thus the career of Steiner. His switch to mysticism and occult philosophy was made public on 8 October 1902, when Steiner gave his famous lecture on 'Monism and Theosophy' in the town hall of Berlin.

Theosophy is the key to his later work, including his theory of education. The original Theosophical Society, founded by Helena Blavatsky and Henry Steel Olcott, was intended to reactivate Eastern spiritual philosophy against decadence in Western culture. Steiner developed his own 'anthroposophy' of Western spirituality, incorporating medieval mysticism, Paracelsus' occult philosophy of nature, Giordano Bruno's neo-platonic universalism and Jakob Böhme's renewal of esoteric Christianity. In 1912 Steiner broke with the Theosophical Society and developed his own empire, starting with the founding of the Goethanium in Dornach in 1913. From then on Steiner lectured restlessly throughout the German-speaking world and in Europe, creating a large group followers, many of them middle- and upper-class people. The founding of the first Steiner School was sponsored by Emil Molt, owner of the Waldorf-Astoria cigarette factory in Stuttgart. The Waldorf Schools soon became attractive to middle-class parents in search of alternatives to conventional, subject-oriented schooling.[9]

Steiner's philosophical teachings had one central premise, namely the existence and personal reality of what is called the 'spiritual world'. In his autobiography,[10] Steiner (1982, p. 429) spoke of the 'modern form of spiritual knowledge' to be distinguished from older forms of spirituality that had been like dreams rather than knowledge. For Steiner, spirituality is knowledge and not just intuition. Education is thus regarded as that which develops spiritual knowledge of the world and allows the pupil to become a vital part of spirituality. The medium for this is inner experience (ibid., p. 435)[11] and neither observation nor description. The social organization for the dissemination of this inner experience is called the 'secret society'[12] (ibid, p. 447) to indicate the exclusiveness of the kind of knowledge involved. So it is not surprising that Steiner is called the 'leading esoteric researcher of the twentieth century'.[13]

Steiner's anthroposophy stresses the unity of body, mind and soul, not in the sense of a personal but of a cosmic unity. There are three worlds, the

physical, the soulish and the spiritual. Man is part of all three worlds
through the seven forms of his whole existence on earth. He is 'rooted' in the
physical world with his physical, ethereal and soulish body[14] and
'blossomed' into the spiritual world with his spiritual self, his spirit of life
and his spiritual existence. The soul is man's trunk, rooted at one end and
blossoming at the other (Steiner 1994, p. 58). 'Anthroposophy' is nothing
else than the spiritual science[15] for the ripening of the soul that required
research into the spiritual world. Research into the inner world is similar to
research into the external world, Steiner said in his autobiography; with
slightly different methods, but the same approach to truth (1982, p. 458).

Anthroposophy, of course, is a counter project to Western scientific
culture, a project that includes doctrines of cosmic fate and reincarnation
(Steiner 1994, pp. 68 ff.). The soul has 'inner' and 'upper' regions (ibid, pp.
104–5). After carnal death the soul is introduced to the 'world of souls',
upon which it follows the pure laws of spirituality (ibid, p. 110). In this world
the *Urbilder*[16] of all things and beings are to be seen (ibid., p. 121). Between
two incarnations, the spirit of man 'wanders' through the world of souls, and
so on. This purely occult philosophy is applied to education. The child is
considered to be the 'human in being' whose 'substance' is known only when
the 'hidden' or 'secret' nature of man is revealed (Steiner 1948, p. 9).
Education then is part of the *Geheimwissenschaft* that is not publicly known
but revealed only to its believers. This view is in opposition to all that
constitutes modern education since the Enlightenment.

For Steiner and his followers, the basis of education is neither teaching
nor learning, but development. 'Development' refers not to nature, as
Rousseau had stated, nor to mind, as Piaget proposed. Steiner spoke of the
'three births of men' that succeeded one after the other in a sequence of
seven years (ibid., pp. 22 ff.). Up to the age of 7 the child is woven within the
ethereal and astral cover. After the child's second dentition, the ethereal
body is born, at the age of 14 the astral body or the body of sensation is
revealed, and at the age of 21 the 'body of I'[17] is set into spiritual life.
The means of education during the first period are imitation and modelling,
during the second period succession and authority (ibid., p. 34), while in
the third period the road to the 'higher soul of men' is opened (ibid., p. 16).

Teaching in the first periods should not take place in an 'abstract'
manner, but in a concrete way, with 'lively, vivid pictures' representing true
spirituality for the understanding of the child (ibid. p. 36). The educator will
be 'sensitive, warm and imbued with empathy' (ibid., p. 39) as a result of his
studies of the sources of spiritual science. In the end the educator will
represent the 'true knowing of spritual science' and this will be at the heart
of all true education (ibid., pp. 39–40). Up to sexual maturity the teaching
relates to the memory of the child, after that to reason. Working with
concepts is necessary only after sexual maturity. Teaching has one central
principle, namely that memory comes first and only then comprehension.
The better the memory, the better the understanding will be (ibid., pp. 44–5),
so all first schooling should be based upon memorizing.

Steiner's doctrines are absolute. He claims to have solved the secrets of
man and thus the secrets of education. So his 'spiritual science' is the true,
vital and unrivalled basis for the art of education (ibid., p. 40). This strong
dogmatism was the core of anthroposophical reform movements inside and

outside education, such as architecture, agriculture, medicine, all kind of arts and social reconstruction. Steiner's teachings influenced artists such as Wassily Kandinsky and Joseph Beuys, writers such as Christian Morgenstern, and entrepreneurs such as Emil Molt. The influence on education, however, is restricted to his followers. Steiner is not regarded as a 'classic' in educational philosophy,[18] and even his linkage to the international movement of 'new education' is doubtful.

Steiner himself did not discuss the eminent authors of reform pedagogy, such as Maria Montessori, John Dewey and Georg Kerschensteiner, authors of a new generation that did not interest him. When lecturing for the first time in Oxford in the Summer of 1922, Steiner met Margaret Macmillan. After that he read and reviewed her book on education through imagination in quite a typical way, namely as confirmation of his own teachings (Lindenberg 1997, Vol. II, pp. 689 ff.). Apart from this there are no real contributions to what was called 'new education' at the beginning of the twentieth century. Steiner clearly was not child-oriented, he did not call for freedom in education and was no follower of the new pychology of the child. So he and his followers were at the margin of reform pedagogy, preoccupied with their own activities within a closed community.

The core of success was and is the Waldorf/Steiner Schools. In Febuary 1919, Steiner delivered four public lectures in Zürich. These lectures were published soon after as 'the key points of the social question' (Steiner 1919). Steiner developed his later famous principles of the 'trinominal organisation of society', namely economy, law and spiritual life (ibid., pp. 31–2). Education and schooling are part of the spiritual life or the 'geistige Kultur' that can only work when it is compeletely free. Thus schooling should be completely free, too. The Waldorf Schools, following this principle, are non-state enterprises and are in this sense free. They call themselves 'Free Schools' because they operate independent of the curricula of the state.

The building principle of the schools is 'rhythm' not lecturing. There is the rhythm of the day, of the week and of the year. The curriculum is constructed around a seven-year cycle with special forms of teaching such as the epoch-instruction or the learning of eurythmics. The schools are non-selective and know neither marks nor rankings. There is no grading of the pupils, who remain together as a group with one teacher as long as one cycle lasts. The schools are co-educative, have an independent administration and a close connection between teachers and parents. The attempt is made to avoid pressures on children and allow them to work according to their own personal potentials.

Parents interested in Waldorf Schools wish to avoid the stress of normal schooling and especially the stress of too early selection. The actual effectiveness of the Waldorf Schools is unclear because there is virtually no empirical research on their success or failure. Public debate on them tends to be purely ideological, focused on the pros and cons of Steiner's anthroposophy, but without data to judge the praxis of schooling in a fair way. Most of Steiner's occult philosophy is hard to believe. His educational principles are far removed from twentieth-century's 'new education', but that does not necessarily mean that the alternatives he offers do not work in practice. It is somewhat ironic both that Steiner's authorities in education, such as Wilhelm Rein or Theodor Vogt, were Herbartians and not representatives of 'new education', and that most histories of education include the Waldorf Schools as part of the educational reform movement.

Notes

1 *Theosophie*, 1906 (Steiner 1994, p. 41). All translations are my own.
2 More than 600 schools worldwide in 1996.
3 Biographical data from Lindenberg, 1996.
4 The edition was prepared for Kürschner's *Deutsche National-Literatur*, a then famous series of German classical authors.
5 The *Arbeiterbildungsschule* was founded by Wilhelm Liebknecht, a leading German social-democrat.
6 The private *Freie Hochschule* in Berlin was founded in 1902 by Bruno Wille and Wilhelm Bölsche, both authors and activists in modernist Berlin circles.
7 The Theosophical Society was founded in 1875 in New York as a spiritual counterforce to materialistic Darwinism. The Society was one of the main forces behind international reform pedagogy at the end of the nineteenth century.
8 Marie von Sievers (1867–1948) was the daughter of a Russian general. She grew up in St Petersburg and was highly educated. She spoke several languages and practised as an actor.
9 See Steiner (1997).
10 Written immediately before his death, Steiner's autobiography is the last and most personal summary of his work.
11 *Inneres Erleben*.
12 *Geheimgesellschaft*.
13 Rudolf Steiner, Website Gotheaneum (http://www.goetheaneum.ch/leute/esteiner.htm)
14 In later publications the concept of 'astralbody' is added.
15 *Geisteswissenschaft* (but not in Dilthey's sense of a human science).
16 Originals – *Urbild* is a concept in Goethe's morphology of plants.
17 *Ich-Leib*.
18 See, for example, Oksenberg Rorty (1998).

See also

In this book: Nietzsche, Rousseau, Montessori, Dewey
In *Fifty Modern Thinkers on Education*: Piaget

Steiner's major writings

Die Kernpunkte der Sozialen Frage in den Lebensnotwendigkeiten der Gegenwart und Zukunft, Stuttgart: Greiffer & Pfeiffer, 1919.
Die Erziehung des Kindes vom Gesichtspunkte der Geisteswissenschaft, Stuttgart: Verlag Freies Geistesleben, 1907/1948.
Mein Lebensgang. Eine nicht vollendete Autobiographie, edited and with an afterword by M. von Sievers, Dornach, Schweiz: Rudolf Steiner Verlag, 1925/1982.
Theosophie. Einführung in übersinnliche Welterkenntnis und Menschenbestimmung, Dornach, Schweiz, Rudolf Steiner Verlag, 1904/1994. Translated as *Theosophy: An Introduction to the Supersensible Knowledge of the World and the Destination of Man*, London: Rudolf Steiner Press, 1973.
'A Lecture for Prospective Parents of the Waldorf School', 31 August 1919. Translated by R.F. Lathe and N. Parsons Whittaker, wysiwyg://contents.52/http://www.bobnancy.com/lectures/s3829a.html, 1997.

Rudolf Steiner on Education: A Compendium, ed. Roy Wilkinson, Stroud: Hawthorn, 1993.

Further reading

Lindenberg, C., *Rudolf Steiner. Eine Biographie*, Vol. I: 1861–1914. Vol. II: 1915–1925, Stuttgart: Verlag Freies Geistesleben, 1997.
Oksenberg Rorty, A. (ed.), *Philosophers on Education: Historical Perspectives*, London and New York: Routledge, 1998.

JÜRGEN OELKERS

RABINDRANATH TAGORE 1861–1941

> That education is a living, not a mechanical process, is a truth as freely admitted as it is persistently ignored.[1]

When Oxford University conferred an honorary doctorate on the Nobel prize-winning poet, writer, composer, painter and philosopher Rabindranath Tagore in 1940 for the entire range of his achievements, including those as an educationist, there was a unique irony in the award. Not only had Tagore had a loathing for all his Calcutta-based school education as a boy and adolescent and failed to complete a university degree, he had devoted much of his adult life to founding and running both a school (1901) and a university (1921), at Shantiniketan in a poor region of rural Bengal, that together were the most unorthodox educational institutions in twentieth-century India. The paradox is typical of this complex man.

Tagore wrote copiously on education for some fifty years. Perhaps his most famous essay is 'A Poet's School', published in 1926, which was intended to explain his essential approach to sceptical critics, both Indian and foreign. The enchanting, elusive opening is worth quoting in full:

> From questions that have often been put to me, I have come to feel that the public claims an apology from the poet for having founded a school, as I in my rashness have done. One must admit that the silkworm which spins and the butterfly that floats on the air represent two different stages of existence, contrary to each other. The silkworm seems to have a cash value credited to its favour somewhere in Nature's accounting department, according to the amount of work it performs. But the butterfly is irresponsible. The significance which it may possess has neither weight nor use and is lightly carried on its pair of dancing wings. Perhaps it pleases someone in the heart of the sunlight, the Lord of colours, who has nothing to do with account books and has a perfect mastery in the great art of wastefulness.
>
> The poet may be compared to that foolish butterfly. He also tries to translate in verse the festive colours of creation. Then why should he imprison himself in duty? Why should he make himself

accountable to those who would assess his produce by the amount of profit it would earn?

I suppose this poet's answer would be that, when he brought together a few boys, one sunny day in winter, among the warm shadows of the tall straight *sal* trees with their branches of quiet dignity, he started to write a poem in a medium not of words.[2]

Tagore's family was richly endowed, both financially and artistically. His ancestors were among the first Indians to profit by trade with the British. His grandfather Dwarkanath Tagore, a landowner and business entrepreneur, was one of the wealthiest men in Calcutta, famous for the extravagance of his pleasures, his rejection of religious orthodoxy, and his philanthropy, which included the funding of science-based higher education for Bengalis in Calcutta and Britain. He was among the first Hindus of note to visit Europe, where he entertained Queen Victoria and writers such as Dickens and Thackeray and was known as 'Prince' Dwarkanath. He died in London in 1846 at the age of 52.

His son, Tagore's father Debendranath, was sharply different. Until his late teens he led the self-indulgent life expected of him as the spoilt son of a rich man. It took the lingering death of his grandmother on the banks of the Ganges at Benares, attended by the young man, to alter his whole outlook. He renounced worldliness and began a search for enlightenment in the sacred literatures of both East and West, reviving a religious movement of reformed Hinduism known as the Brahmo Samaj and helping to make it highly influential in Indian education until his death in 1905 at the age of 88. He became known as an austere, saintly figure – the Maharshi, or 'Great Sage'.

Rabindranath, the fourteenth of his children, born in 1861, followed a different path from his grandfather and father from the start. In a sense, he took after both of them simultaneously. As he wrote in *Gitanjali*, the verse collection translated from Bengali that won Tagore the Nobel prize in 1913, 'Deliverance is not for me in renunciation. . . . I feel the embrace of freedom in a thousand bonds of delight.'

His early upbringing contributed to this feeling; he was confined entirely to school and to the Tagore mansion in north Calcutta under the control of generally harsh servants and a punishing schedule of private lessons. He seldom saw his parents. In the space of seven years he attended four schools with complete lack of academic distinction and retained memories of them which were 'not the least sweet in any particular'.[3] Both freedom and delight were in short supply and he longed for them.

Commenting on this early experience and the rote-learning he witnessed in the rural schools on the family estates in the 1890s before he decided to start his own school, Tagore remarked:

the men who teach the lower forms of our schools are not adequately trained for their work. Some of them have only passed the Matriculation examination, some have not even done that, and all are lacking in adequate knowledge of English language and literature, English life and thought. Yet these are the teachers to whom we owe our introduction to English learning. They know neither good English nor good Bengali, and the only work they can do is misteaching.[4]

Ignoring school, he read widely from his very early years on, stimulated by the diversely talented members of the family, especially an elder brother, who created an atmosphere of constant artistic and intellectual innovation around him. (The Tagore family is unquestionably the most influential Indian family in the arts.) His first worthwhile poetry appeared in Bengali – like almost all his subsequent fictional creations. He was 16, and he wrote under a pseudonym in a deliberate imitation of the eighteenth-century boy-poet Thomas Chatterton. But his writing and song composing really began to flower in the 1880s after a year-long stay in Britain, where he briefly attended classes at University College London. By now, he had become convinced of the need for Indians to be educated in both the best of their own traditions and the best of the Western (and Far Eastern) traditions – a cosmopolitan attitude which would be the driving spirit behind his university, Visva Bharati, and especially its most productive department, the art school, known as Kala Bhavan. 'Let me state clearly that I have no distrust of any culture because of its foreign character. On the contrary, I believe that the shock of outside forces is necessary for maintaining the vitality of our intellect', Tagore wrote.

> What I object to is the artificial arrangement by which this foreign education tends to occupy all the space of our national mind and hus kills, or hampers, the great opportunity for the creation of new thought by a new combination of truths. It is this which makes me urge that all the elements in our own culture have to be strengthened; not to resist the culture of the West, but to accept and assimilate it. It must become for us nourishment and not a burden. We must gain mastery over it and not live on sufferance as hewers of texts and drawers of book-learning.[5]

This vision exerted an immediate appeal on the British-educated Jawaharlal Nehru, India's first prime minister, who sent his daughter Indira (later also prime minister) to study at Shantiniketan in the 1930s and who himself became chancellor of Visva Bharati, when it was incorporated as a national university in 1951. Tagore's vision also appealed to the Indian-educated Mahatma Gandhi, who sent a group of boys from his South African Phoenix school to Shantiniketan prior to his own return to India in 1915 and who later helped to raise money for Visva Bharati (which was always chronically short of funds). But Gandhi differed from Tagore – and Nehru – in rejecting any educational emphasis on the arts and science, and in believing that Indian rural education should be primarily vocational. 'Education specially labelled as rural education is not my ideal – education should be more or less of the same quality for all humanity needful for its evolution of perfection', Tagore told his English friend, the agricultural economist Leonard K. Elmhirst.[6]

Elmhirst was one of many talented people among non-Indians, including some distinguished scholars (mainly Orientalists), who worked with Tagore at Shantiniketan in the 1920s and 30s. He is unique, however, in having founded his own educational institution in the West, a school and college at Dartington in the Devon countryside of south-west England, directly inspired by his work with Tagore. Dartington, like Shantiniketan, would attempt to educate children and college students by giving each of them as much freedom as possible, by exposing them to nature at every opportunity, and by accenting the arts (especially music) – in direct contrast to the scholastic and games-playing priorities of British urban and public schools of the time; it would also aim to inculcate respect for other cultures, far from the imperial ethos of the official British system and the imitative ethos of its Indian equivalent. In Elmhirst's words about Tagore:

> there was no aspect of human existence which did not exercise some fascination for him and around which he did not allow his mind and fertile imagination to play. Where, as a young man, I had been brought up in a world in which the religious and the secular were separate, he insisted that in poetry, music, art and life they were one, that there should be no dividing line.[7]

For certain gifted individuals, there is no doubt that both Shantiniketan and Dartington were enriching experiences, whatever the undoubted drawbacks of both places for the less receptive. The economist and philosopher (and Nobel laureate) Amartya Sen, who was a schoolboy at Shantiniketan in the 1940s (and whose grandfather was one of Tagore's earliest recruits as a teacher), notes that Shantiniketan was 'rather important' in making him aware at an early age that a worthwhile life requires variety and that narrowness of view is deadening. Sen particularly recalls starting a night school with other teenage students to teach local villagers the three Rs, which was perhaps the beginning of his lifelong adult concern with literacy programmes.[8] A second alumnus, the film director Satyajit Ray, who was a student of painting at Visva Bharati in the 1940s, and is the other towering twentieth-century Indian artist besides Tagore, admitted much later in his life that it was Shantiniketan where he first came to appreciate that there was more to art and culture than the art and culture of the West he had imbibed as a college student in Calcutta. Shantiniketan 'opened windows for me. More than anything else, it … brought me an awareness of our tradition, which I knew would serve as a foundation for any branch of art that I wished to pursue.'[9]

These are significant accolades for the work of any educational pioneer, with a resonance wider than their Indian time and context. But the difficulty is, as always with Tagore, that his ideas cannot be formulated and applied by others; for despite his many heartfelt and eminently rational essays on education – and the textbooks he wrote for children – he developed no concrete theory of education, indeed he said that 'I merely started with this one simple idea that education should never be dissociated from life'.[10]

The advantages and disadvantages of this are clear from Tagore's relationship with Maria Montessori. Before visiting India, Montessori wrote to Tagore: 'I feel that your people have achieved a higher degree of capability for feeling and sentiment than the Europeans, and I am certain that my ideas which are founded only on love for the children would find a good welcome in the hearts of the Indian people' – which was certainly true of Tagore and his school while he lived. Tagore replied: 'the Montessori method is widely read and studied not only in some of the big cities of India but also in out of the way places; the method is, however, not so extensively followed in practice largely owing to the handicap imposed by the officialised system of education prevalent in the country.' When Montessori finally visited Shantiniketan in 1939, she found herself in immediate sympathy with Tagore and his school and he with her, but she realised, one senses, that the success of everything depended on the unique aura of the founder. As she told Tagore's son when she heard of his father's death in August 1941:

> There are two kinds of tears, one from the common side of life, and those tears everybody can master. But there are other tears which come from God. Such tears are the expression of one's very heart, one's very soul. These are the tears which come with something that uplifts humanity, and these tears are permitted. Such tears I have at this moment.[11]

Notes

1 Lecture in Calcutta in 1936, quoted in Dutta and Robinson (1995, p. 323).
2 Tagore (1961b, pp. 285–6).
3 Tagore (1991, p. 37).
4 'The Vicissitudes of Education' in Tagore (1961b, p. 41).
5 'The Centre of Indian culture', ibid., pp. 222–3.
6 Letter to Elmhirst, 19 December 1937, in Dutta and Robinson (1997b, p. 491).
7 Quoted in Introduction to Rabindranath Tagore, *The Religion of Man*, London: Unwin Paperbacks, p. 4, 1988.
8 'Amartya Sen' in Sian Griffiths (ed.), *Predictions: 30 Great Minds on the Future*, Oxford: Oxford University Press, p. 214, 1999.
9 Quoted in Andrew Robinson, *Satyajit Ray: The Inner Eye*, London: Andre Deutsch, p. 55, 1989.
10 Letter to Patrick Geddes, 9 May 1922, Dutta and Robinson (1997b, p. 291).
11 See letter 207 and notes in ibid., pp. 326–7.

See also

In this book: Gandhi, Montessori

Tagore's major writings

Tagore wrote essays on education in both Bengali and English; only those written in English or translated into English are included here. There are also many fictional writings which shed light on his educational ideas; these have been omitted (references will be found in the biography mentioned in Further reading).

The English Writings of Rabindranath Tagore, Volume 3: A Miscellany, ed. Sisir Kumar Das, New Delhi: Sahitya Akademi, 1996.
My Reminiscences, 2nd edn, London: Macmillan, 1991.
Rabindranath Tagore: Pioneer in Education: Essays and Exchanges between Rabindranath Tagore and L. K. Elmhirst, London: John Murray, 1961a.
Towards Universal Man, London: Asia Publishing House, 1961b.

Further reading

Dutta, Krishna and Andrew Robinson, *Rabindranath Tagore: The Myriad-Minded Man*, London: Bloomsbury, 1995.
—— (eds), *Rabindranath Tagore: An Anthology*, London: Picador, 1997a.
—— (eds), *Selected Letters of Rabindranath Tagore*, Cambridge: Cambridge University Press, 1997b.
Elmhirst, Leonard K., *Poet and Plowman*, Calcutta: Visva Bharati, 1975.
Thompson, Edward P., *Alien Homage: Edward Thompson and Rabindranath Tagore*, New Delhi: Oxford University Press, 1993.

KRISHNA DUTTA AND ANDREW ROBINSON

ALFRED NORTH WHITEHEAD 1861–1947

> The solution which I am urging, is to eradicate the fatal disconnection of subjects which kills the vitality of our modern curriculum. There is only one subject-matter for education, and that is Life in all its manifestations.[1]

Alfred North Whitehead, known mainly as a mathematician and philosopher, was one of the most widely read, most quoted, and least understood philosophers of the twentieth century.[2] He is best remembered for his collaboration with Bertrand Russell, from 1910 to 1913, on *Principia Mathematica*, a three-volume treatise on mathematics and logic. Whitehead's views on education can be found scattered in his essays and books, but he did not write a coherent exposition of his philosophy of education in one book where it could be easily read and understood. His best-known educational writings are in *The Aims of Education*, a collection of lectures delivered between 1912 and 1928. The focus of Whitehead's later work, after 1925, is on metaphysics and the development of a cosmological doctrine wherein reality is a process in time.

His English ancestors were yeomen, fishermen and farmers. Those of his forefathers who did not inherit land had become local schoolteachers, clergymen and doctors. At that time no higher education was required for these professions. Alfred North's grandfather, Thomas, was a remarkably enterprising man who was widely read in both history and mathematics. He became a schoolmaster and Church of England clergyman and founded Chatham House Academy in Ramsgate, on the Isle of Thanet, Kent, England. He was the first in the family to give his sons a university education. Thomas' son, Alfred, became an Anglican clergyman as well and took over from his father as headmaster of Chatham House Academy when Thomas accepted the post as Deputy Mayor of Ramsgate at 63.

Alfred North was born on 15 February 1861, at Ramsgate. He was the youngest of Alfred Whitehead and Sarah Buckmaster's four children. He was considered to be a child in delicate health, though he was his father's favourite and was genuinely adored by his siblings. His early years were spent at Ramsgate in his father's tutorage where tangible links with visible historical artifacts pervaded Alfred North's early experience and thought. It is said that St Augustine converted the Saxon King Ethelbert to Christianity near

Ramsgate in 597 under an oak tree that survived until the early nineteenth century. Only sixteen miles away from Ramsgate is Canterbury Cathedral, where English bishops have been consecrated since the thirteenth century.

In September 1875, when Alfred North was 14, he left home to attend Sherborne School, where he stayed for five years. Both of his brothers had preceded him. At Sherborne he received an excellent classical education in Latin and Greek and some mathematics. He read poetry, especially the work of Wordsworth and Shelley.

Cambridge (1884–1910) – mathematics as a discipline

In 1880 Alfred North received a scholarship to attend Trinity College at Cambridge University. There he concentrated on mathematical studies. In 1884 he was elected to join the 'Apostles', an élite discussion club with lifetime membership, founded by Tennyson in the 1820s. Intellectual originality, honesty and having an open mind were the traits most praised by the club. The kinds of questions discussed most often were philosophical rather than political ones. Alfred North began lecturing in mathematics at Trinity College, Cambridge, in 1884. He was much admired by his students as an engaging and forceful lecturer and a pleasant and caring person. He was intrigued by the intellectual discipline of mathematics. One of his first scholarly interests was stimulated by Hermann Gunther Grassmann's work. (Victor Lowe, Whitehead's biographer,[3] claims there is no more striking case of genius-neglect in the history of mathematics than the case of Grassmann's obscurity.) Grassmann proposed a consistent formal mathematical theory of *n*-dimensional space that has uses beyond those of three-dimensional geometry. With his study of Grassmann's theory, Whitehead began his lifelong interest in the exploration of the fundamental nature of mathematics. He was not content with formulae and their applications or the science of mere number and quantity. During the late 1880s he was preoccupied with the extension of Grassmann's and others' novel ideas in logic, mathematics and the philosophy of science. In 1989 he published his first book, *A Treatise on Universal Algebra*, an investigation of systems of abstract mathematical ideas applied to physics.

On 16 December 1890, when he was 29, Alfred North Whitehead married Evelyn Wade. She was almost 25. They had four children, all born in Cambridge: North, 1891; Jessie, 1893; an unnamed son who died at birth; and Eric,1898. Eric, the youngest, was shot down in March 1918, during World War I.

Whitehead is most widely known for his collaboration with Bertrand Russell on the three large volumes of *Principia Mathematica* published in 1910, 1912 and 1913. Russell had been Whitehead's pupil at Cambridge and was 13 years his junior. Russell and Whitehead began their collaboration shortly after 1900. In this work they held that mathematics is less a science of quantity than a deduction from formal logic. Their ideas were much discussed and assessed, but the most common conclusion is that the effort was a failure. Victor Lowe (1985) assesses the voluminous work as follows:

'One of the great intellectual monuments of all time' is the stock assessment of *Principia Mathematica*. Monuments aren't alive, and the book had little influence on living mathematics. Its presence did have the beneficial effect of putting an end to mysticism about mathematics. New developments, which began shortly after its publication, had much to do with its lack of influence. The distinction between mathematics and metamathematics became important; but *Principia* contained no metamathematical theory of its system.[4]

Bertrand Russell (1956) recalled his years of studying under Whitehead and then his collaboration with Whitehead on *Principia Mathematica*:

Throughout the gradual transition from a student to an independent writer, I profited by Whitehead's guidance. ... When, in 1900, I began to have ideas of my own, I had the good fortune to persuade him that they were not without value. This was the basis of our ten years' collaboration on a big book no part of which is wholly due to either. ... In England, Whitehead was regarded only as a mathematician, and it was left to America to discover him as a philosopher. He and I disagreed in philosophy, so that collaboration was no longer possible.[5]

London, 1911–23 – nature and human nature: how do we learn?

In 1911 Alfred North moved from Cambridge to University College, London, to teach mathematics. His reason for moving was that he was 'in a groove' at Cambridge and he wanted fresh challenges. In 1914 he became a professor at the Imperial College of Science and Technology in Kensington. During his years in London, he turned his attention to problems of education and applied mathematics. He questioned how people think, and eventually this led to questions of human nature. He began to ask how and why it happens that people learn and how learning can be improved. He wrote several lectures on education between 1912 and 1928 and published them in 1929 in *The Aims of Education*. Although his main personal concern was mathematics education, he applied his ideas about education to other disciplines such as technical education, science, art, literature and the classics.

His continuing interest in nature and science at this time was mainly concerned with physics; the meaning of relativity; and mathematical concepts such as space, time and motion. Whitehead criticized the mechanistic view of reality and Newtonian physics that portrayed atoms that were moved locally by other particles but that were otherwise unmoved. He thought that Einstein's formulations relied on too narrow an empirical base. During this period he wrote *An Enquiry Concerning the Principles of Natural Knowledge* (1919), *The Concept of Nature* (1920), and *The Principle of Relativity* (1922). Alfred North's own theories about relativity were not accepted by physicists of his time, partially because of his refusal to take into consideration the means by which we measure spatio-temporal relations.[6]

Harvard University, 1924–47 – mathematics, science and religion: what does it all mean?

In 1924, when Alfred North was 63 years old, he accepted an offer from Harvard for a five-year appointment to teach philosophy. He retired from Harvard in 1937 and remained in Cambridge, MA, until his death on 30 December 1947, at 86. His wife, Evelyn, lived until 1961.

At Harvard Whitehead's work attained lasting success. He moved away from strictly formal logic and explored more general questions in *Science and the Modern World* (1926) and *Adventures of Ideas* (1933). He became preoccupied with religion in this final phase, an interest well expressed in two books, *Religion in the Making* (1926) and *Process and Reality* (1929). In all, he wrote seven books during the Harvard years. His ideas about the nature of reality are presented more technically in *Process and Reality* (1929) and are more easily accessible in *Symbolism* (1927), *Adventures of Ideas* (1933), and *Modes of Thought* (1938). After his retirement, his home in Cambridge became a meeting place for visitors who enjoyed his originality of mind and the constant warmth of his personality.

Overview of Whitehead's views on education

Whitehead was influenced by his early study of the classics. He was especially interested in Plato's philosophy. In 'Nature Lifeless', an essay in *Modes of Thought* (1938), he wrote, 'Plato's ultimate forms, which are for him the basis of all reality, can be construed as referring to the metaphysical necessity which underlies historic accident.' Whitehead attempted to reconcile the differences between science and human experience. He proposed a metaphysical system in semi-mathematical form. His objective was to create a pattern of ideas in which everything we can know can be interpreted as a particular instance of a general scheme. His vision was of a universe always in process and subject to a universal force that underlies every event and every sequence of events. He called his philosophy the philosophy of organism.

His writings highlight important themes in education: 'There is only one subject-matter for education, and that is Life in all its manifestations.'[7]

> Education is the guidance of the individual towards a comprehension of the art of life; and by the art of life I mean the most complete achievement of varied activity expressing the potentialities of that living creature in the fact of its actual environment. This completeness of achievement involves an artistic sense, subordinating the lower to the higher possibilities of the indivisible personality. Science, art, religion, morality, take their rise from this sense of values within the structure of being. Each individual embodies an adventure of existence. The art of life is the guidance of this adventure.[8]

He advocated guarding against inert ideas – 'that is to say, ideas that are merely received into the mind without being utilized, or tested, or thrown into fresh combinations'. How must we guard against this 'mental dry rot?'

Whitehead urged, 'We enunciate two educational commandments, "Do not teach too many subjects" and again, "What you teach, teach thoroughly".'[9]
Concerning mathematics, he advises:

> Unless quadratic equations fit into a connected curriculum, of course there is no reason to teach anything about them. ... First, you must make up your mind as to those quantitative aspects of the world which are simple enough to be introduced into general education, then a schedule of algebra should be framed which will about find its exemplification in these applications. We need not fear for our pet graphs, they will be there in plenty when we once begin to treat algebra as a serious means of studying the world.[10]

On science education, he recommends:

> the first thing to do with an idea is to prove it. But allow me for one moment to extend the meaning of 'prove'; I mean – to prove its worth ... either by experiment or by logic, of the truth of the propositions. ... But in so far as either process must have the priority, it should be that of appreciation by use.[11]

About knowledge of history, he maintains:

> The only use of a knowledge of the past is to equip us for the present. No more deadly harm can be done to young minds than by depreciation of the present. The present contains all that there is. It is holy ground; for it is the past, and it is the future.[12]

With regard to teaching itself, he says:

> It should be the chief aim of a university professor to exhibit himself in his own true character – that is, as an ignorant man thinking, actively utilizing his small share of knowledge. In a sense, knowledge shrinks as wisdom grows: for details are swallowed up in principles.[13]

Whitehead claims that there is a threefold rhythm of education in the development of the learner and in shorter cycles of the presentations of lessons. 'Till the age of thirteen or fourteen there is the romantic stage, from fourteen to eighteen the stage of precision, and from eighteen to two and twenty the stage of generalization.'[14] He compares this rhythm to Hegel's thesis, antithesis and synthesis. Romance is at first apprehension of vivid novelty with half-disclosed, half-hidden possibilities. In the stage of precision, exactness of formulation becomes important, where we acquire facts in a systematic order. The final stage of generalization is synthesis or fruition of classified ideas. He says that each lesson should form a repetition of the cycle. Pupils should be encouraged to repeat the stages again and again.

What did Whitehead mean?

Whitehead was a teacher of mathematics. It follows that he was concerned with educational questions. He aspired to make mathematics meaningful, interesting and challenging to his students. He was convinced that learning happens in the interaction when the student applies or tests knowledge. Learning does not happen when the teacher hands over to the student a piece of information (an inert idea). For Whitehead, reality was in the present moment, not the past or future. I am struck by Whitehead's development of an organic theory based on process, his willingness to see reality in terms of interactions in time, his ambitious quest for a cosmic order in nature that encompasses everything knowable, the humility of his own claims to attain mere partial understanding, and his undisputed moral earnestness and generosity. I am disappointed by his refusal (or neglect) to systematize the application of his philosophy to education. Harold Dunkel (1965) wrote an analysis of Whitehead's ideas and terms, as applied to education, in *Whitehead on Education*. The book is a genuinely interpretive attempt to apply Whitehead's ideas, but it is not a compelling synthesis or a rousing call to action as Whitehead might have written.

What is the influence of Whitehead on others?

Whitehead's notions about education seem uncannily up to date today, but he is not well known by many educators. During his lifetime he served on many educational boards, councils and committees; but he was never a professional administrator or student of the educational system. He never set himself up as a philosopher of education. His educational writings are scattered essays. He never attempted to publish a specific philosophy of education or to train teachers in it. Though Whitehead's educational works are widely read, he has left little in the form of specific educational theories or programmes.[15]

Those who have attempted to write biographies of Whitehead have been hindered by a paucity of materials and the lack of written records. Whitehead was not a prolific letter-writer. The few letters that exist are mostly those he wrote to Bertrand Russell during their ten-year collaboration on *Principia Mathematica*, as Whitehead in his will directed that all his letters to his wife be destroyed.[16]

Like-minded thinkers, contemporary with Whitehead, were on fire with novel theories that soared in opposition to entrenched mechanistic views of the time. John Dewey reviewed Whitehead's *Science and the Modern World* (1926), praising Whitehead's encouragement of intellectual change and new ideas. He quoted Whitehead's words in his review:

> [but when] Darwin or Einstein proclaims theories which modify our ideas, it is a triumph for science. We do not go about saying there is another defeat for science, because its old ideas have been abandoned. We know that another step of scientific insight has been gained.[17]

Then Dewey goes on to say:

> Mr. Whitehead, although he does not succeed in making the new ideas intuitive, that is, appreciated in terms of naive, everyday experience, does succeed in a wonderful way in giving readers a sense for the nature of the change and what it imports.[18]

John Dewey wrote the following words in a review of Whitehead's book, *Process and Reality* (1929):

> It is no piece of news that the work of Professor Whitehead has been for the last ten years one of the most stirring influences in serious philosophic thought. ... I close the book also with a sense of the great debt that everyone who is trying to think his way through the muddled modern world owes to the luminous and precise mind of Mr. Whitehead.[19]

In similar fashion, Whitehead wrote of Dewey's influence on contemporary thought:

> Dewey has never been appalled by the novelty of an idea ... we are living in the midst of the period subject to Dewey's influence. ... John Dewey is the typical effective American thinker; and he is the chief intellectual force providing that environment with coherent purpose.[20]

Whitehead guided and influenced many of his contemporaries profoundly. For example, Charles Hartshorne was a young instructor at Harvard when Whitehead arrived to teach. Hartshorne attended many of Whitehead's lectures after 1925. Hartshorne, now well known as a process philosopher, turned his attention to metaphysics and applied Whitehead's approach to a reformulation of the traditional argument for God's existence. Through Hartshorne's work and that of other process philosophers, Whitehead's influence was stronger in the field of metaphysics than in science, mathematics or education theory.

Notes

1 A.N. Whitehead, *The Aims of Education*, New York: Mentor Books, pp. 18–19, 1929.
2 Victor Lowe, *Alfred North Whitehead: The Man and His Work, Volume I: 1861–1910*, Baltimore: The Johns Hopkins University Press, p. 4, 1985.
3 Ibid., p. 153.
4 Ibid., p. 290.
5 Bertrand Russell, *Portraits from Memory and Other Essays*, pp. 99–100, 1956.
6 In an anthology edited by B. MacKinnon, *American Philosophy: A Historical Anthology*, Albany: State University of New York Press, pp. 389–427, 1985, Alfred North Whitehead and Bertrand Russell are discussed together and compared as the two major American process philosophers in the twentieth century.

7 Whitehead, *Aims of Education*, p. 7.
8 Ibid., p. 39.
9 Ibid., p. 1.
10 Ibid., pp. 7–8.
11 Ibid., p. 3.
12 Ibid.
13 Ibid., p. 37.
14 Ibid., p. 38.
15 H.B. Dunkel, *Whitehead on Education*, Ohio State University Press, p. 7, 1965.
16 Lowe, *Alfred North Whitehead*, p. 7.
17 J. Dewey, 'The Changing Intellectual Climate', *New Republic*, 45, pp. 360–1, 17 February 1926, in J. Boydston (ed.), *John Dewey: The Later Works, Volume 2, 1925–1927*, Carbondale and Edwardsville: Southern Illinois University Press, p. 222, 1984.
18 Ibid., p. 223.
19 J. Dewey, 'An Organic Universe: The Philosophy of Alfred N. Whitehead', *New York Sun*, 26 October 26, 1929, in J. Boydston (ed.), *John Dewey: The Later Works, Volume 5, 1925–1953*, Carbondale and Edwardsville: Southern Illinois University Press, pp. 375–81, 1984.
20 A.N. Whitehead, 'John Dewey and His Influence', in P.A. Schilpp and L.E. Hahn (eds), *The Philosophy of John Dewey*, La Salle, IL, Open Court, pp. 475–8, 1939.

See also

In this book: Dewey, Russell

Whitehead's major writings

Cambridge (1882 or earlier until 1910)

A Treatise on Universal Algebra, with Applications, Vol. I (no others published), Cambridge: Cambridge University Press, 1898.
The Axioms of Descriptive Geometry, Cambridge Tracts in Mathematics and Mathematical Physics, No. 5, Cambridge: Cambridge University Press, 1907.
An Introduction to Mathematics, New York: Henry Holt, 1911.
The Organization of Thought, Educational and Scientific, London: Williams & Norgate; Philadelphia, J.B. Lippincott Co., 1917.

London (1910–24)

Principia Mathematica, with Bertrand Russell, vols I–III, Cambridge: Cambridge University Press, 1910–13, 2nd edition, 1925–7.
The Aims of Education and Other Essays, New York: Macmillan Co.; London: Williams & Norgate, 1929 (originally delivered and published between 1912 and 1928, the majority of them antedating 1920).
The Concept of Nature, Cambridge: Cambridge University Press, Tarner Lectures, Trinity College, Cambridge, 1920.
The Principle of Relativity, with Applications to Physical Science, Cambridge: Cambridge University Press, 1922.
An Enqury Concerning the Principles of Natural Knowledge, Cambridge: Cambridge University Press, 1919; 2nd edition, 1925.

Harvard (1924–39)

Science and the Modern World, New York: Macmillan Co., 1925; Cambridge: Cambridge University Press,1926.

Religion in the Making, New York: Macmillan Co., 1925; Cambridge: Cambridge University Press, 1926.

Symbolism: Its Meaning and Effect, New York: Macmillan Co., 1927; London: Cambridge University Press, 1928 (Barbour-Page Lectures, University of Virginia, 1927).

Process and Reality: An Essay in Cosmology, New York: Macmillan Co.; Cambridge: Cambridge University Press, 1929 (corrected ed., edited by David Ray Griffin and Donald W. Sherburne, New York: Free Press, 1978. Gifford Lectures, University of Edinburgh, 1927–8).

Adventures of Ideas, New York: Macmillan Co.; Cambridge: Cambridge University Press, 1933.

Nature and Life, Chicago: University of Chicago Press; Cambridge: Cambridge University Press, 1934 (reprinted as chapters 7 and 8 of *Modes of Thought*, 1938).

Retired in Cambridge, MA (1939–47)

Modes of Thought, New York: Macmillan Co.; Cambridge, Cambridge University Press, 1938 (six lectures delivered at Wellesley College, MA, and two lectures given at the University of Chicago).

Essays in Science and Philosophy, New York: Philosophical Library, 1947; London: Rider & Co., 1948.

Further reading

Dunkel, H.B., *Whitehead on Education*, Ohio State University Press, 1965.

Hartshorne, Charles, *Whitehead's Philosophy: Selected Essays, 1935–1970*, Lincoln, Nebraska: University of Nebraska Press, 1972.

Hendley, B.P., *Dewey, Russell, Whitehead: Philosophers as Educators*, Carbondale and Edwardsville: Southern Illinois University Press, 1986.

Jordan, M., *New Shapes of Reality: Aspects of A.N. Whitehead's Philosophy*, London: George Allen & Unwin, 1968.

Kline, G.L. (ed.), *Alfred North Whitehead: Essays on his Philosophy*, Englewood Cliffs, NJ: Prentice-Hall, Inc., 1963.

Lawrence, Nathaniel, *Alfred North Whitehead: A Primer of His Philosophy*, New York: Twayne Publishers, Inc., 1974.

—— *Whitehead's Philosophical Development: A Critical History of the Background of Process and Reality*, Berkeley: University of California Press, 1956.

Lowe, Victor, *Alfred North Whitehead: The Man and His Work, Volume I: 1861–1910*, Baltimore: The Johns Hopkins University Press, 1990.

—— *Understanding Whitehead*, Baltimore: The Johns Hopkins Press, 1962.

—— with J.B. Schneewind (ed.), *Alfred North Whitehead: The Man and His Work, Volume II: 1910–1947*, Baltimore: The Johns Hopkins University Press, 1990.

Morris, Randall C., *Process Philosophy and Political Ideology: The Social and Political Thought of Alfred North Whitehead and Charles Hartshorne*, Albany, NY: State University of New York Press, 1991.

Russell, Bertrand, *The Autobiography of Bertrand Russell*, London: George Allen & Unwin, 1968.

—— *Portraits from Memory and Other Essays*, New York: Simon and Schuster, 1956.

NANCY C. ELLIS

ÉMILE JAQUES-DALCROZE 1865–1950

> I am beginning to think of a musical education in which the body would play the role of intermediary between sound and thought, so becoming an expressive instrument. Bodily movement is an experience felt by a sixth sense, the muscular sense. This consists of the relationship between the dynamics of movement and the position of the body in space, between the duration of movement and its extent, between the preparation of a movement and its performance. This muscular sense must be capable of being grasped by the intellect, and since it demands the collaboration of all the muscles, voluntary and involuntary, its rhythmic education needs movement of the whole body.[1]

Émile Jaques-Dalcroze was born to Swiss parents in Vienna in 1865.[2] The family later moved to Geneva, which became the base for Dalcroze's life's work. His parents recognized his unusual musical abilities and started his piano lessons at a young age. His education was characterized by richness and diversity, including gymnastics, conducting, composition (with prominent composers such as Bruckner, Delibes and Fauré), and drama at the Comédie Française.[3] In Algiers, where he conducted an orchestra, he discovered the relationship of music and gesture and became intrigued with the intricate, irregular rhythms of Arab music. First as a student, and later as a teacher at the University of Geneva, he came into contact with Europeans who were well known in the fields of music, theatre, pedagogy and psychology, and he maintained these influential links throughout his long life. His close friends included innovative stage designer Adolph Appia, composer Gabriel Fauré and psychologist Adolphe Claparède. These close personal relationships gave him insights into the workings of a range of educational fields and artistic disciplines.

When in 1894 he made his début in pedagogy as professor of harmony at the Conservatoire of Geneva, he became concerned with the technically accurate but lifeless performances of his piano students.[4] He was appalled at their poor sense of rhythm, their lack of feeling for the flow of the music, and their inability to hear what they were writing. He attributed these weaknesses to their conventional training, which taught them to manipulate their fingers, and to complete various theoretical tasks without reference to feeling or to sound. Their musical progress, he claimed was 'retarded by an incapacity to estimate with any exactitude variations of time and rhythmic grouping'. (*Rhythm, Music and Education* (*RME*), pp. vii–viii). He argued that 'The music teacher should make it his first business to create a feeling for beauty in the souls of his pupils' (*RME*, p. 22). Individuals, he asserted, should learn to feel the music before embarking on the study of an instrument.

From his observations of the natural rhythms in human movements he concluded that the brain and the body develop along parallel lines, the one communicating its impressions and sensations to the other, and that therefore physiological training would develop his students' abilities to understand and respond to music. He argued that rhythm, not sound, was the primary form of movement. To support this theory he proposed eight principles.[5]

Dalcroze thus began to develop his method of education, which was based on what he called eurhythmics – literally, good flow, or good rhythm. He refined and expanded his methods, and trained eurhythmics teachers. He developed eurhythmics into a pedagogical tool, a holistic approach involving body, mind and soul, emphasizing the development of a feeling for rhythm moving through time and space. He insisted that understanding and feeling the relationship between time, space and energy were the key to understanding all physical activity. His methods brought innovation to the fields of music education, dance, drama, opera, physical education and therapy.[6]

From 1910 until 1914 Dalcroze was director of the Bildungsanstalt Jaques-Dalcroze, the training college built for him in 1910 by industrialists Wolf and Harald Dohrn at Hellerau, near Dresden, Germany. Hundreds of students of many nationalities came to live and study an extensive curriculum that included solfège, rhythmic gymnastics, keyboard improvisation and advanced music-movement study (referred to also as arts plastique, or plastic arts), music theory and practice, Swedish gymnastics, dance and anatomy. In 1913 at a festival at Hellerau, Gluck's opera *Orpheus* was performed. The choreography was by one of Dalcroze's students and the opera's chorus and soloists received eurhythmics training. The overarching goal was to harmonize movement, music, light and space. More than five thousand people from the worlds of theatre, dance, and literature, came to see the performance.[7] Hellerau became a world centre for education in and through the arts and was the cradle of the modern theatre movement. Dalcroze eurhythmics was introduced into theatres, dance schools and educational centres, and Dalcroze training schools began to be opened in Europe and elsewhere.

In spite of the setbacks of two world wars, Dalcroze continued his work, determined to enrich the lives of individuals through eurhythmic experience. Today, nearly 100 years later, Dalcroze programmes of study flourish in many educational centres in the world, including several European countries, Canada, the United States, Venezuela, Taiwan, Japan and Australia. Individuals wishing to become qualified as Dalcroze instructors, follow a rigorous programme of study whose quality is controlled by the Dalcroze Institute in Geneva. To obtain the Diploma, which is the highest level, requires excellent musicianship and as many as ten years of specialized training.[8]

Overview of his work and influence in the field of education

A Dalcroze education is an education *in* and *through* music – an education not only in music, but an education for life. It accommodates students of all ages, abilities and socioeconomic classes. It is neither exclusive nor élitist.[9] These were novel educational concepts at the beginning of the twentieth century, and it put Dalcroze in the company of other progressive educational thinkers, such as Froebel and Pestalozzi, and his contemporary, Maria Montessori. Dalcroze's methods were unorthodox. A visitor to a typical Dalcroze music class would see teachers and students in bare feet, bloomers and loose clothing moving their whole bodies through space. Traditionalists were scandalized,[10] but progressives welcomed this new approach which reflected the growing discontent with the constraints of European autocracies and socio-political movements towards ideals of freedom[11] and democratic practice.

In a Dalcrozian music education, musicianship begins with the enactment of musical realities in physical space, using the body as the medium of musical expression. The three main components of a Dalcroze education are: eurhythmic games[12] – to comprehend and express the music heard; ear training (solfège) – to sing what the eye sees, to write what the ear hears, and to invent music with the voice; and improvisation – to use the imagination and the skill of inner hearing to invent musical ideas spontaneously. Bodily movement is the physical manifestation of rhythm. In a sense, one can read the music by watching the body.

A fundamental notion in eurhythmics is that music moves through space in time. For example, a basic eurhythmic game is that of walking the beat. Walking the beat is progression in space. As the phrase moves from one note to another, so the walker moves forward in space, in a particular time-frame, using the energy that is appropriate to the tempo and movements that are appropriate to the musical style. As the students walk, they might be asked to clap the downbeat and show the remaining beats by expressing a large circle with the arms. As the arms move in a continuous circle through space, the time that elapses between downbeats is expressed in space. The student must calculate the size of the gesture, and the energy with which to express it, in order that the hands arrive at the appropriate point on the circle to give the next downbeat at the appropriate time.[13]

Eurhythmics and dance have much in common, but are distinct in important ways: in dance, the visual component is primary, while in eurhythmics it is secondary. Dance is an art; eurhythmics is a course of study.[14] Nijinsky and Diaghilev were among the audience at Hellerau, and were therefore familiar with Dalcroze's eurhythmics. Mary Wigman, a prominent German dancer and dance teacher was strongly influenced by Dalcroze. She, in turn, influenced the next generation of dancers. Eurhythmic training gave dancers a better understanding of the music they danced to. Dalcroze wrote that:

> A dancer must be trained to understand the intimate connection between musical and bodily movement, between the developments of a theme, the successive sequence and transformation of attitudes, between sound-intensity and muscular dynamics, between rests and pauses, counterpoint and counter-gesture, melodic phrasing and breathing, between space and time.
>
> (*RME*, p. 125)

Dalcroze was critical of singers, especially those on the opera stage. He observed:

> [they] impose their gestures and attitudes utterly regardless of music, which either they do not understand or understand imperfectly. Their feet are set in motion when they should remain stationary, their arms are raised when they should remain motionless, their bodies no more harmonize with the music than

would their throats if they sang out of tune or suddenly began an air from another opera, while the orchestra continued to play from the original score.

At Hellerau, with the production of Gluck's *Orpheus*, under the direction of Dalcroze and his trained teachers, singers studied eurhythmics to learn how to achieve harmony between their voices and their bodies.[15]

Just as he maintained that children should not begin to learn an instrument without prior training in eurhythmics,[16] so Dalcroze was convinced that those who were involved in physical activities should be similarly trained in eurhythmics prior to embarking on rigorous physical training. 'To the rhythmician', he stated, 'has fallen the difficult task to create a psychophysical technique for the education through rhythm, a specific technique which has no immediate resemblance to the current physical-culture exercises. Our special training would precede the technique of the sportsman, the acrobat or the dancer' (Rosenstrauch – *RME* 1921/ 1967) Eurhythmic training for these individuals would lead to the achievement of balance, grace and self-knowledge.

The broad aim of eurhythmics – to achieve interior harmony through a balance of mind, body and soul, and achieving harmony with others through collaborative and other social interactions – are consistent with the aims of therapy. Therapists use eurhythmic games to help their patients become aware of their bodies and of their emotional selves. Therapists use these games to help patients achieve consciousness of their personal physical space and of the space they share with others.[17]

Dalcroze's experience with the Comédie Française, where he studied breathing, the use of the voice, and the correlation of emotions with posture, attitude and gesture, contributed to the development of his method. His eurhythmics techniques, with their emphasis on the relations of space, time and energy, and feeling and gesture, have been adapted for use in the training of actors in the theatre.[18]

During his lifetime Émile Jaques-Dalcroze received awards and honours for his contributions to education and to the arts. He became a member of the Royal Academy in Sweden, an Officer of the Légion d'Honneur in France, and he received honorary doctorates from the universities of Geneva and Lausanne (Switzerland), Clermont-Ferrand (France) and Chicago. He lived long enough to see Dalcroze training centres open in many parts of the world, and his method applied in state schools, conservatories, colleges, schools of drama and opera, in therapeutic work with the blind, deaf, and mentally and physically handicapped children and adults. It is a measure of his students' gratitude, and the breadth of his influence, that on his seventieth birthday he was presented with a book signed by 10,500 former students, representing forty-six nationalities.

Notes

1   Émile Jaques Dalcroze, in Dutoit (1971, p. 10).
2   He was born Émile-Henri Jaques. In his twenties, when he began to compose, a publisher suggested that he change his name to avoid confusion with another French composer by the same name. He invented the surname Dalcroze, added it

to Jaques, and thereafter was known as Émile Jaques-Dalcroze. He is usually referred to in articles and books simply as Dalcroze or Jaques-Dalcroze. Dalcroze is also often used as a shorthand, to indicate an education based on his philosophy and techniques, as in a Dalcrozian education, or Dalcrozian techniques. I will refer to him here as Dalcroze.

3 His composed works include operas, violin concertos, string quartets, piano pieces and songs.

4 He was also aghast at the way that singing was taught, describing it as 'parrot training' (*RME*, p. 19), the implication being that the students were taught to mimic but not to understand.

5 The eight principles are: 1. Rhythm is movement. 2. Rhythm is essentially physical. 3. Every movement involves time and space. 4. Musical consciousness is the result of physical experience. 5. The perfecting of physical resources results in clarity of perception. 6. The perfecting of movements in time assures consciousness of musical rhythm. 7. The perfecting of movements in space assures consciousness of plastic rhythm. 8. The perfecting of movements in time and space can only be accomplished by exercises in rhythmic movement.

6 While the *The Oxford International Encyclopedia of Dance*, 1998 gives Émile Jaques-Dalcroze six columns, his name does not appear in the *Harvard Dictionary of Music*, either as a composer, or as an educator.

7 Selma Odom (1998) reports in the *Oxford International Encyclopedia of Dance* that among the visitors to Hellerau were Serge Diaghilev, Vaslav Nijinsky, Anna Pavlova, George Bernard Shaw, Darius Milhaud, Paul Claudel and Upton Sinclair.

8 The three levels of teaching expertise are the Certificate, the Licence, and the Diploma, the latter being available only from the Dalcroze Institute in Geneva or its representatives.

9 Dalcroze argued that music education should be for all children, that it should take place during school time, that it should be a compulsory component of the school curriculum, that it should be taught by qualified teachers. He contended that all children could improve their musical skills and understanding with training.

10 Some traditionalists referred to Dalcroze's women teachers as 'lost girls'. This was related to me at a Dalcroze workshop at Carnegie Mellon University by Malou Hatt-Arnold a Swiss teacher of eurhythmics who was instructed by Dalcroze.

11 'Freedom' is a word that comes up frequently in connection with Dalcrozian eurhythmics due, no doubt, to the freedom from constraint, the freedom to create, and the freedom to express oneself. Dalcroze claimed that eurhythmics training would free individuals from intellectual and nervous inhibitions.

12 Dalcroze called eurhythmic activities games, and preached a philosophy of joy – the joy of self-knowledge and the joy that comes from achieving control over one's movements. The notion of 'play' in education is consistent with Piagetian and Vygotskyian notions of the role of play in child development.

13 This is not as easy as it sounds. The only way to truly understand what is required of the student is to do the actions oneself.

14 See Farber and Parker, 'Discovering Music Through Dalcroze Eurhythmics', in *Music Educators Journal*, November 1987, for a more a detailed discussion of the differences and similarities between dance and eurhythmics.

15 See J.T. Caldwell, *Expressive Singing: Dalcroze Eurhythmics for Voice*, 1995 and also A. Davidson, 'Dalcroze Eurhythmics and Contemporary Opera: Applications in the Production of John Adams' *The Death of Klinghoffer*', 1995.

16 What Dalcroze said was, 'It is nothing less than lunacy to set a child to study an instrument before he has been trained to appreciate rhythm and distinguish sounds.' *RME*, p. 53–4.

17 See Dutoit (1971) for details about the therapeutic uses of Dalcroze eurhythmics.

18 See Rogers (1966).

See also

In this book: Froebel, Pestalozzi, Montessori

Dalcroze's major writings

Eurhythmics, Art and Education, trans. Frederick Rothwell, New York: Ayer Company, 1976.

Rhythm, Music and Education, trans. Harold Rubinstein, London, The Dalcroze Society, 1921/1967. A collection of thirteen articles, originally published in French. The titles indicate the era in which he was proposing his method of music education, and show the range of his interests:

'The Place of Ear-Training in Musical Education', 1898.
'An Essay in the Reform of Music Teaching in Schools', 1905.
'The Initiation into the Rhythm', 1907.
'Music and the Child', 1912.
'Rhythmic Movement, Solfège and Improvisation', 1914.
'Eurhythmics and Musical Composition', 1915.
'Music, Joy and the School', 1915.
'Rhythm and Creative Imagination', 1916.
'Rhythm and Gesture in Music Drama and Criticism', 1910–16.
'How to Revive Dancing', 1912.
'Eurhythmics and Moving Plastic', 1919.
'Music and the Dancer', 1918.
'Rhythm, Time and Temperament', 1919.

Further reading

Abramson, R.M., 'The Approach of Emile Jaques-Dalcroze', in L. Choksy (ed.), *Teaching Music in the Twentieth Century*, Englewood Cliffs, NJ: Prentice-Hall, 1986.

Abramson, R.M. and Reiser J., *Music as a Second Language: An Integrated Approach to Ear-Training, Sight Singing, Dictation, and Musical Performance*, New York: Music and Movement Press, 1996.

Andrews, G., *Creative Rhythmic Movement for Children*, Englewood Cliffs, NJ: Prentice Hall, 1954.

Aronoff, F.W., *Move with the Music*, New York: Turning Wheel Press, 1982.

Bachmann, M-L., *Dalcroze Today: An Education Through and into Music*, trans. David Parlett, Oxford: Clarendon Press, 1991.

—— *Theoretical Foundations of Dalcroze Eurhythmics*, London, 1986.

Becknell, A.F., 'A History of the Development of Dalcroze Eurhythmics in the United States and its Influence on the Public School Music Program', doctoral dissertation, University of Michigan, 1970.

Caldwell, J.T., *Expressive Singing: Dalcroze Eurhythmics for Voice*, Englewood Cliffs, NJ: Prentice Hall, 1995.

Davidson, A., 'Dalcroze Eurhythmics and Contemporary Opera: Applications in the Production of John Adams' *The Death of Klinghoffer*, honours thesis, University of New South Wales, 1995.

Dutoit, C-L., *Music, Movement Therapy*, Surrey: The Dalcroze Society, 1971.

Farber, A., and Parker, L., 'Discovering Music Through Dalcroze Eurhythmics', *Music Educators Journal*, November 1987.

Findlay, E., *Rhythm and Movement: Applications of Dalcroze Eurhythmics*, Evanston, IL: Summy Birchard, 1971.

Gell, H., *Music, Movement and the Young Child*, Sydney: Australasian, 1949.

Odom, S.L., *Oxford International Encyclopedia of Dance*, 1998.

—— 'Choreographing *Orpheus*: Hellerau 1913 and Warwick 1991', in *Dance Reconstructed*, ed. Barbara Palfy, New Brunswick, NJ, 1993.

Revkin, L.K., 'An Historical and Philosophical Inquiry into the Development of Dalcroze Eurhythmics and its Influence on Music Education in the French Cantons of Switzerland', doctoral dissertation, 1984.

Ring, R. (ed.), *Hellerau Symposium*, Geneva: Fédération Internationale des Enseignants de Rythmique, 1993.

Rogers, C.M., 'The Influence of Dalcroze Eurhythmics in the Contemporary Theatre', doctoral dissertation, Louisiana State University, 1966.

Rosenstrauch, H., *Essays on Rhythm Music Movement*, Pittsburgh, PA: Volkwein Bros Inc., 1973.

Schnebly-Black, J. and Moore, St., *The Rhythm Inside*, Portland, OR: Rudra Press, 1997.

Spector, I., *Rhythm and Life: The Work of Emile Jaques-Dalcroze*, Stuyvesant, NY, Pendragon Press: 1990.

Steinitz, T., *Teaching Music: Theory and Practice of the Dalcroze Method*, Tel-Aviv: OR-TAV Music Publications, 1988.

JOAN RUSSELL

WILLIAM EDWARD BURGHARDT DU BOIS 1868–1963

> Herein lie buried many things which if read with patience may show the strange meaning of being black here in the dawning of the Twentieth Century. This meaning is not without interest to you, Gentle Reader; for the problem of the Twentieth Century is the problem of the color-line.[1]

Introduction

W.E.B. Du Bois, scholar, historian, sociologist, novelist, editor, political activist, radical democrat, socialist, pacifist, Pan-Africanist, and communist wrote these prophetic words nearly a century ago and they continue to resonate today. He represented the modern intellectual, one shaped by disparate philosophies such as Calvinist Christianity, pragmatism, and political ideologies such as socialism. Du Bois began his emergence as one of America's and the world's public intellectuals with the publication of *The Souls of Black Folk*, a collection of essays about the complexities of race in America. This exquisite collection of essays provided Du Bois with a broader, perhaps more popular, audience than his groundbreaking earlier works, *The Suppression of the African Slave Trade* (1896) and *The Philadelphia Negro* (1899). The former evolved from his prize-winning Harvard University dissertation, a systematic examination of the economic and historic dimensions and effects of the slave trade. The latter, regarded by some as the advent of urban, black sociology, detailed the 'social conditions of the colored population' of Philadelphia's seventh ward. Each of these book's creation, publication and dissemination reflected then ideological stances and realities and the contradictions therein, faced by members of the African diaspora.

What enabled Du Bois to achieve and influence multiple cultural spheres in a time when most men of African descent were uneducated, disenfranchised, oppressed and regarded as intellectual inferiors? Some of the answers are found in his beginnings in Great Barrington, Massachusetts a town and region notable for the assimilation of its small black population and limited racism. Here, Du Bois acquired the persona of the stereotypic reserved, socially conservative and religious New Englander.[2]

Du Bois' roots – West Africa, Europe, the Bahamas, Santo Domingo, Haiti, New England – reflected the patterns of slavery, miscegenation, manumission and the struggles for citizenship found among many in the African diaspora. Du Bois was born on 23 February 1868 in Great Barrington, Massachusetts to Alfred Du Bois and Mary Burghardt Du Bois. Du Bois did not experience the overt racism and acts of violence experienced by his brethren in the Deep South. Instead, he was reared in a relatively benevolent racial environment. By all accounts, Du Bois displayed exceptional intellectual abilities early on and moved ahead quickly in school. The realities of race in America intruded upon his life in subtle ways as he entered high school. Later, he would explore issues of race and gender in several histories, sociological studies, journal articles, and novels, for instance, *The Negro* (1915), a children's magazine, *The Brownies' Book* (1920–1), and a novel, *The Quest of the Silver Fleece* (1911).

Du Bois graduated from high school with high honours, the first black graduate of the school. Du Bois' mother Mary died soon after. Her death affected his educational aspirations in that she could not afford to bequeath him money for his future educational endeavours. Some members of the community provided financial support for his college education. Du Bois preferred Harvard University but some of his white benefactors, who had agreed to donate one hundred dollars annually to his educational costs, rejected that choice. Instead, they selected Fisk University in Nashville, Tennessee as the most appropriate college for a black male. Paternalism of this type was not unusual and these actions foreshadowed one of the great political debates of the century, the future of blacks and the best methods for assuring racial justice and equality. Du Bois would challenge ideological views that would place limits on the intellectual aspirations of blacks and the supremacy of industrial education. His opponents in these ideological skirmishes would be Booker T. Washington, founder of Tuskegee Institute and the most powerful black man in America.

At the age of 17 as a first-year student at Fisk, Du Bois literally stepped within the 'Veil' he so aptly described in *The Souls of Black Folk*. Fisk University was quite the opposite of his predominately white/European American cultural milieu. Fisk represented a total immersion in black cultures, both highbrow and folk, for Du Bois. One of his remembrances centres on his initial impressions of Fisk students and the response to a largely black cultural milieu. 'I was thrilled to be for the first time among so many people of my own color or rather of such various and such extraordinary colors, which I had only glimpsed before, but who it seemed were bound to me by new and exciting and eternal ties.'[3]

Fisk's curriculum featured the traditional classical education: Latin,

Greek, physics, literature, European languages, mathematics, rhetoric, sciences and the arts. Du Bois would excel at Fisk but he noted the lack of preparation among some of the black students and understood this as a direct result of their caste status and lack of educational opportunities. Liberatory education would appear as a major tenet of his work throughout his career, for example the essays contained in the volume, *The Education of Black People, Ten Critiques, 1906–1960*. He would 'live' the idea first as a teacher during the summer vacation periods at Fisk.

The hills of Tennessee presented Du Bois with another introduction to his lifelong, political work – the education of black folk and their caste status. Du Bois wanted to experience first-hand the life of the black in the South.

> I determined to know something of the Negro in the country districts; to go out and teach during the summer vacation. I was not compelled to do this, for my scholarship was sufficient to support me, but that was not the point. I had heard about the country in the South as the real seat of slavery. I wanted to know it.[4]

For two summers, Du Bois taught in schools created shortly after the end of slavery and encountered 'the commonest of mankind'.[5] The irony of sharing the works of Cicero 'in plainest English' to children, teens and adults who did not possess the rudiments of literacy was not lost on Du Bois. Nonetheless, he maintained his desire to impart some knowledge and extract valued cultural knowledge about blacks recently liberated from slavery. One example was Du Bois' appreciation of the 'sorrow songs' or Negro spirituals which was enhanced during this period. The vibrant, participatory, and vocal religious rituals in these hill churches and the music contrasted with the solemnity of Du Bois' Episcopalian and Congregational religious experiences in the Berkshires. Nevertheless, they afforded him the chance to share a sense of community among the poor blacks.

The remainder of Du Bois' time at Fisk proceeded at the expected pace with growing participation in extracurricular activities such as choral groups and the stints as the literary and editor-in-chief of the *Herald*, the school's newspaper. Du Bois' attitudes about religion and race were in flux, too. Prior to graduation in 1888, Du Bois decided to attend Harvard University and pursue doctoral studies. Du Bois was admitted to Harvard as a junior and received a grant from the Price Greenleaf Fund to cover his expenses.

Du Bois was admitted to the 'commonwealth of culture' evident at Harvard.[6] His academic life veered in a different direction under the tutelage of historian Albert Bushnell Hart.[7] Hart introduced Du Bois to the rigorous methods of scholarship and research characteristic of German universities. Du Bois' professors moved him from the provincial thoughts of his upbringing and the racial assumptions underlying his existence and that of other blacks to a more cosmopolitan, liberal stance. Du Bois completed his bachelor's degree in 1890, his master's in 1891, and his doctorate in 1895. His dissertation, *The Suppression of the African Slave Trade*, was selected as the first volume published in the Harvard Historical Series. It remains a model of methodological rigour and a touchstone volume for the study of the African slave trade. The broadening of his intellectual horizons at

Harvard opened the world to him as he embarked on further study in Germany. Throughout his career and life, Du Bois would seek ideological and intellectual connections with people of colour throughout the world and with Europeans and European-Americans who were progressive. This pattern began with the period of study in Europe and would find expression in many of his works and activities.

Du Bois attended Friederich Wilhelm University in Berlin for two years beginning in 1892. German scholars, such as Gustav von Schmoller, Adolf Wagner, Heinrich Rudolf von Gneist and Max Weber, intrigued Du Bois and affected his intellectual development in fundamental ways, primarily to shift it left of centre while providing an understanding of new economic theories and socialism.[8] In contrast, Heinrich von Treitschke reinforced what Rampersad regarded as Du Bois' attraction to élitism and authority despite his disparagement of mulattos and his nationalism. He returned to the United States feeling somewhat prepared to 'teach in a Negro university, to build up a department of history and social science, to collect capable young Negro students and to study scientifically the Negro question past and present with a view to its best solution'. [9] Du Bois sought teaching positions at Howard University, Hampton Institute and Fisk University. Europe left an indelible imprint on Du Bois that would shape his changing philosophical and ideological stances.

Laws and customs circumscribed literacy among blacks, during and after slavery. Among the most notorious laws were the Black Codes of the South and court decisions that mandated 'separate but equal facilities'. In reality, most schools were under-funded or not funded, teachers were inadequately prepared, and facilities and materials were woeful. Some individuals and philanthropic organizations, for instance, free blacks, abolitionists and missionaries sought to provide some schooling during the ante- and post-bellum periods. One of the compromises developed for black education during the post-bellum period was the decision to offer a type of education, manual or industrial, that would maintain the caste status of blacks.[10]

Fatefully, Du Bois did not accept a position teaching mathematics at Tuskegee Institute headed by Booker T. Washington, a school noted for its emphasis on industrial education. Instead, Du Bois accepted a job as chair of the classics department at Wilberforce University. Wilberforce was notable as one of the pre-Civil War institutions of higher education for blacks and a place for the offspring of Southern plantation owners who wished to educate and liberate their slave progeny. Du Bois taught Latin and Greek, mathematics and other courses but was not allowed to teach a course in sociology. He clashed with university officials over traditional matters such as curriculum and appropriate behaviour of faculty members. Du Bois married a Wilberforce student, Nina Gomer, a few months before leaving Wilberforce for a position as a researcher at the University of Pennsylvania.

American racial strictures forced Du Bois and Nina to live among the poor blacks whom he studied. Du Bois' research focused on the documentation of black life in Philadelphia. He spent a year compiling empirical and statistical data. The result was *The Philadelphia Negro* (1899), a classic sociological study. Du Bois' study posited environment, oppression and personal attributes as central causes of the status of Philadelphia's blacks. Rampersad detected a neo-Calvinist tone that permeated Du Bois' descriptions of criminality among some of his study's participants.[11] Rather than blame blacks solely for their condition, Du Bois argued for behaviours that would lead to uplift – moral, educational, economic, cultural and political. Du Bois completed his work in Philadelphia and accepted a teaching position at Atlanta University in Atlanta, Georgia as a professor of economics, history and sociology. Here, Du Bois would unleash the intellectual and artistic leadership that would result in his historic status as a leader. He would affirm his identity as a black, create a programme of research on the Negro question, organize conferences, found journals such as *The Moon* and *Horizon*, experience the death of his beloved son, and write one of the enduring classics of American intellectual history, *The Souls of Black Folk*.

Atlanta University offered an alternative to the philosophy and reality of industrial or manual education as defined by Booker T. Washington at Tuskegee Institute. Progressive educators at Atlanta University such as Asa Ware nurtured an intellectual openness, within restrictions, not available at Wilberforce University. As Du Bois produced more research, organized conferences, and garnered support for his ideas, it became increasingly difficult for him and others to accept the dominance of B.T. Washington in all aspects of black life.

Lauded by black intellectuals such as James Weldon Johnson, Benjamin Brawley, Jessie Redmon Fauset and Ida Wells-Barnett, and former professor William James, *The Souls of Black Folk* succeeded in allowing freer discourse about the status of blacks in opposition to the ideology and power of the 'Tuskegee machine'. According to Rampersad, Du Bois 'sought to convert and to seduce the American people, white and black, into sharing Du Bois' optimistic view of black culture in the United States. It was apparent neither to all black people nor to all whites that the dark people living in America had a fund of spirituality which ennobled their life'.[12] *The Souls of Black Folk* contains fourteen essays, eight of which were previously published and revised for the book. The essays represent a range of genres and are modelled along the lines of Whitman's *Leaves of Grass*. Together, they form a comprehensive view of Du Bois' evolving philosophies and ideological beliefs unfettered by the methodological rigour and dispassionate tone of *The Suppression of the African Slave Trade* and *The Philadelphia Negro*.

Five of the most oft-quoted essays include 'Of our Spiritual Strivings' in which he sets forth ideas about 'living within the Veil' of racial strictures and the 'warring of two souls or double-consciousness' felt by those of African descent. 'Of the Dawn of Freedom', 'Of the Passing of the First-Born' and 'The Sorrow Songs' are cited extensively, too. If Du Bois had only written one paper in his entire life, 'Of Mr. Booker T. Washington and Others', he would have been assured a prominent place in American intellectual life. This collection of essays probably more than anything else among the hundreds of articles, score or more of books, research studies and numerous speeches, is the touchstone work identified with Du Bois. Du Bois boldly challenged the leadership of Washington with these words.

> Easily the most striking thing in the history of the American Negro since 1876 is the ascendancy of Mr. Booker T. Washington. It began at a time when war memories and ideals were rapidly

passing; a day of astonishing commercial development was dawning; a sense of doubt and hesitation overtook the freedmen's son's, – then it was that his leading began. Mr. Washington came, with a simple definite program, at the psychological moment when the nation was a little ashamed of having bestowed so much sentiment on Negroes, and was concentrating its energies on dollars. His program of industrial education, conciliation of the South, and submission and silence as to civil and political rights, was not wholly original. ... But Mr. Washington first indissolubly linked these things; he put enthusiasm, unlimited energy, and perfect faith into this program, and changed it from a by-path into a veritable Way of Life. And the tale of the methods by which he did this is a fascinating study of human life.[13]

Du Bois dissected Washington's ability to curry favour with those supporting a variety of ideas about blacks ranging from paternalism to white supremacy. He also delineated the ways in which Washington acquired political power and the mantle of sole black leader, at least among many whites and blacks that remained unchallenged for years. Equally important, he noted the harm wrought by the silencing of opposition voices and the elevation of one man's aspirations, tenets and beliefs for an entire people. Washington's seeming disdain for the type of education attained by the rest of blacks, fuelled Du Bois' ire and concern. Further, Du Bois viewed the quest for reconciliation and appeasement exhibited by Washington as a capitulation and repudiation of the legitimate demands of an oppressed people. Du Bois reserved particular criticism for Washington's commitment to industrial education. Du Bois recognized the need for such education but always in tandem with university education. The term 'talented tenth' is associated with Du Bois and is often linked with his opposition to industrial education. Some regarded the idea of an élite group of students trained for leadership roles as evidence of Du Bois detachment from the realities of American life. Many, however, viewed it as a sensible solution to the leadership crisis or void embodied in Washington and his policies. The views expressed in this essay and in the idea of the talented tenth were and are polarizing. Nevertheless, Du Bois's essays spurred on opposition to Washington and helped prevent the complete subjugation of black educational aspirations

Additionally, Du Bois helped to mobilize an interracial group of individuals committed to racial justice and equality who participated in what is known as the Niagara Movement, precursor to the National Association for the Advancement of Colored People (NAACP) and the nascent Pan-African movements. The NAACP, with Du Bois in the role of director of research, would undertake actions in the streets, courts and in the offices of influential individuals that would gradually result in some achievement of racial justice and equality. For instance, the *Crisis* magazine, the official publication of the NAACP, would chronicle the lynching of black men, women and children as its editors agitated for a national law against such heinous acts. In this case, Du Bois and others would expand the pioneering efforts of Ida B. Wells-Barnett. The *Crisis* magazine published the fiction of black writers who would emerge as major participants during the Harlem Renaissance. Du Bois continued in these efforts on behalf of the NAACP until his resignation in 1934.

Before and after his resignation from the NAACP and for the next twenty-nine years, Du Bois assisted in the process of internationalizing the struggle of blacks in the United States. He participated in a number of international meetings that sought to link liberation struggles throughout the world. For example, he attended several of the Pan African Congresses held in Europe in which he met many men and women – C.L.R. James, Edward Blyden and others, who would challenge his ideas about imperialism and colonialism.

For more than sixty years, Du Bois would engage in struggle on many fronts and move from a liberal stance to membership in the Communist party and permanent residency in Ghana, West Africa. His contributions are numerous and no other black intellectual has since attained the status he has in academic and political circles. Evidence of his influence is found in the numerous books, essays and journal articles written about his roles in education, sociology, politics and liberation struggles. He remains a figure embodying intellectual ideals and an unwavering desire for freedom. Yet, he also attracted a great deal of criticism; Broderick's 'denunciatory biography' comes to mind.[14] Several examinations of his work authored by Herbert Aptheker, August Meier, Arnold Rampersad, Marable Manning and David Levering, among others, provide balanced analyses of his contributions.

Notes

1   Du Bois (1903/1989, p. 1).
2   D. Levering, *W. E. B. Du Bois: Biography of a Race, 1868–1919*, 1995; A. Rampersad, *The Art and Imagination of W. E. B. Du Bois*, Cambridge, MA: Harvard University Press, 1976.
3   S.G. Du Bois, *His Day is Marching on*, Philadelphia, PA: J.J. Lippincott, 1971.
4   Ibid, p. 114
5   Ibid. p. 114
6   Rampersad (1976).
7   M. Manning, *W. E. B. Du Bois, Black Radical Democrat*, Boston, MA: Twayne Publishers, 1986.
8   Rampersad (1976)
9   J.B. Moore, *W. E. B. Du Bois*, Boston, MA: Twayne Publisher, 1981
10 J. Anderson, *The Education of Blacks in the South, 1865–1930*, Bloomington, IN: University of Indiana Press, 1988.
11 Rampersad (1976).
12 Du Bois (1903; 1989).
13 Ibid., pp. 36–7.
14 Manning (1986).

Du Bois' major writings

The Suppression of the African Slave Trade, New York, NY: Longmans, Green, 1896.
Atlanta University Publications on the Study of Negro Problems, 1898–1913.
The Philadelphia Negro, Boston, MA: Ginn & Co., 1899.
The Souls of Black Folk, New York, NY: Penguin Classics, 1903; 1989.
John Brown, Philadelphia, PA: George W. Jacobs, 1909.

The Quest of the Silver Fleece: A Novel, Chicago, IL: A.C. McClurg, 1911.
The Negro, New York, NY: Henry Holt, 1915.
Darkwater: Voices from Within the Veil, New York: Harcourt, Brace & Howe, 1920.
Black Reconstruction, New York, NY: Harcourt, Brace, 1935.
Black Folk Then and Now: An Essay in the History and Sociology of the Negro Race, New York, NY: Henry Holt, 1939.
Dusk of Dawn: An Essay Toward an Autobiography of a Race Concept, New York, NY: Harcourt, Brace, 1940.
Color and Democracy: Colonies and Peace, New York, NY: Harcourt, Brace & Howe, 1945.

Further reading

Aptheker, H. (ed.), *The Autobiography of W. E. B. Du Bois: A Soliloquy on Viewing my Life from the Last Decade of its First Century*, New York, NY, International Publishers, 1968.
—— (ed.), *The Correspondence of W. E. B. Du Bois*, Amherst, MA, University of Massachusetts Press, 19–

VIOLET HARRIS AND ARLETTE INGRAM WILLIS

M.K. GANDHI 1869–1948

> Had I been without a sense of self-respect and satisfied myself with having for my children the education that other children could not get, I should have deprived them of the object lesson in liberty and self-respect that I gave them at the cost of the literary training. And where a choice had to be made between liberty and learning, who will not say that the former has to be preferred a thousand times to the latter.[1]

Mohandas Karamchand Gandhi, the architect of India's freedom through non-violent struggle, was born in 1869 in Porbander, a princely state in Kathiawar, now in Gujrat. His father and grandfather were chief ministers in Kathiawar. After completing school education, he went to London to study law. After returning home he practised as a lawyer in Bombay and Rajkot, but without success. However, on receiving an unexpected offer he went to South Africa, where two experiences transformed his life. The first occurred when he went to the court in Durban and the judge asked him to take off his turban, which hurt his national pride. The second really opened his eyes to racism. Despite having a first class railway ticket he was literally pushed out of the compartment with his luggage. This prompted him to reflect:

> Should I fight for my right or go back to India, or should I go on to Pretoria without minding the insults, and go back to India? ... It will be cowardice to run back to India without fulfilling my obligation. ... I should try, if possible, to root out the disease and suffer hardships in the process. Redress for wrongs I should seek only to the extent that would be necessary for the removal of the colour prejudice.[2]

An incident during his school days had also had a deep impact on him. A school inspector

had set five words to write as a spelling exercise. One of the words was *kettle*. I had misspelt it. The teacher tried to prompt me with the point of his boot; I would not be prompted. It was beyond me to see that he wanted me to copy the spelling from my neighbour's slate, for I had thought that the teacher was there to supervise us against copying. The result was that all the boys, except myself, were found to have spelt every word correctly. Only I had been stupid. The teacher tried later to bring this stupidity home to me, but without effect. I never could learn the art of 'copying'.[3]

Gandhi's experiments in education started when he returned to South Africa in 1897 with three children, his two sons and a nephew. He could have sent them to the school for European children, but

I was not prepared to send my children there, as I did not like the education imparted in those schools. For one thing, the medium of instruction there would be only English, or perhaps incorrect Tamil or Hindi. I could not possibly put up with this and other disadvantages. I was making my own attempt to teach them but that was at best irregular and I could not get hold of a suitable Gujrati teacher.[4]

He engaged an English governess, but that too was unsatisfactory. He did not have any clear idea as to how to set about the task. The educational needs grew with the growth of the 'Tolstoy farm' that Gandhi was running. It could not afford to pay high wages to qualified teachers, who were scarce and would not be prepared to travel 21 miles from Johannesburg. Gandhi decided to live among the children for twenty-four hours of the day as their father, in the belief that if the foundations of education were firmly laid on the ideals of character-building, the children would learn all the other things themselves or with the assistance of friends.

Daily physical training of the children was deemed important. There were no servants; all the work, from cooking down to scavenging, was done by the inmates. There were some fruit trees, which were also looked after by the children under the guidance of an inmate. Vocational training also became an essential part of the programme. One of Gandhi's colleagues went to a Trappist monastery and learnt shoemaking. Another knew carpentry. Cooking, of course, every youngster learnt. An important rule was that the youngsters should not be asked to do what the teachers did not do. Therefore there was always a teacher co-operating and actually working with them. Classes in the mother tongues of the children were conducted with whatever resources and skills were available among the inmates.

The question of spiritual training was a much more difficult matter. Gandhi did not rely on religious books. Nevertheless, he believed that every student should be acquainted with the elements of his or her religion and have general knowledge of its scriptures. As he came into closer contact with children he saw that it was not through books that one could impart training of the spirit. Just as physical training was to be imparted through physical exercise, so the training of the spirit was possible only through the exercise of the spirit. And the exercise of the spirit entirely depended on the life and character of the teacher.

Gandhi returned to India in 1914 and to the new challenge of the educational reconstruction of the whole nation, which had been deprived of its own traditions built over centuries. Before India was colonized, education was widespread. As one historian observed:

In every Hindu village which has retained its old form, I am assured that the children generally were able to read, write and cipher, but where we have swept away the Village System, as in Bengal, there the village school has also disappeared.

One education officer, writing in 1835, noted that in Bengal and Bihar 'there was a school for every thirty-two boys and that these schools were provided in most of the 150,00 villages'. Max Müller later observed that 'there is such a thing as social education and education outside books; and this education is distinctly higher than in any part of Christendom. It is an education not in the so-called three R's, but in humanity.'[5]

Colonial rule destroyed the earlier Indian system of education. The East India Company created a distinct class among Indians, which was to be educated in the Western mode. The purpose of this class was to fill the minor positions in the administration, which were considered neither sufficiently dignified nor sufficiently lucrative for Englishmen. As Sir Claude Hill put it, 'We must at present do our best to form a class who may be interpreters between us and the millions we govern; a class of persons Indian in blood and colour, but English in taste, in opinions, in morals and intellect.'[6] The other side of the story was that Raja Ram Mohan Roy started the Hindu College in Calcutta, which aimed to combine the best in Indian and English cultures. Social reformers such as Swami Dyananda and Swami Vivekananda stressed the need for a renaissance in education. They opened institutions on classical traditions. But it was only a part of national awakening and was also limited in scope.

On his arrival back in India, Gandhi found that the problem was very complex. The first task was to get rid of the colonial educational system, which was totally unrelated to the life of the people and tended to wean the educated away from their own culture. The second task was to construct a system, which would give the people a sense of self-respect and the skills to be able to educate themselves in a way that would make them responsible for their own lives, individually as well as collectively.

Ravindranath Tagore had founded Santiniketan, in 1901. His philosophy was that real knowledge could be gained only in an atmosphere of freedom. He was firm in his convictions that (a) the medium of instruction at all levels should be the mother tongue, (b) nature was the richest source of knowledge, and (c) creative activities must play a central role in education. When Gandhi's family returned to India, Tagore invited them to consider Santiniketan as their home. A month's stay in Santiniketan helped Gandhi's thinking about the future of education in India. Eventually he set up his *ashram* in Sabarmati, where he also started a school for the *ashram* children.

The First World War ended in great disappointment for Indian aspirations of self-rule. Congress called for a total boycott of legislative bodies, government schools and law courts. This had great impact on the educational scene of the country, leading to the establishment of Vidyapeeths, National University of Gujrat and, in Delhi, Jamia Millia Islamia. These institutions drew the attention of the students to their cultural heritage. According to Gandhi it was imperative that for rejuvenating India education and national freedom were seen as two sides of the same coin.

After the 1935 elections for Legislative Assemblies, Congress ministries were formed in nine provinces, and Gandhi proposed to them a new educational system. In October 1937 he called a conference of education ministers and eminent education experts, where a resolution was passed agreeing on free and compulsory education for every child of 7 to 14. The medium of instruction was to be the mother tongue and education should centre around some handicraft suited to the environment of the child, and the abilities to be developed should be integrally related to it. Hindustani Talimi Sangh was formed to develop the programme and run experimental schools. The first school was set up in Sevagram, Gandhi's *ashram*, and the second in Jamia Millia Islamia, founded by Zakir Hussain.

A wave of educational reconstruction passed over the country. Some provinces appointed education reorganization committees. Teacher training centres and primary schools were opened in various parts of the country. A seven-year syllabus was prepared. 'Basic education' was carried out as an experiment in the states with Congress governments and in some non-governmental institutions. Fourteen training schools and colleges, seven Refreshers Training Centres and over five thousand schools were opened for the experiment.

Towards the end of 1939 Congress ministries resigned, resulting in the closure of government schools. Those run by voluntary bodies continued, which implied that the system had attracted the interest of the people. At a conference in 1941, a report was given on the working of basic schools run by governments and private bodies. It said that the general standard of health, behaviour and intellectual attainment was very encouraging. Children were more active, cheerful and self-reliant. Their power of self-expression was well developed, they were developing habits of cooperative work, and social prejudices were breaking down.

In 1942, Gandhi's call for the 'Quit India' movement resulted in mass arrests. He and thousands of freedom fighters were put in prison. After his release in 1944, Gandhi said:

> I have been thinking hard during the detention over the possibilities of [basic education] ... We must not rest content with our present achievements. We must penetrate the homes of the children ... educate their parents. Basic education must become literally the education for life. ... It had become clear to me that the scope of basic education has to be extended. ... A basic school teacher

must consider himself a universal teacher. ... His village is his universe.[7]

Gandhi called an all-India conference in December 1944 in Sevagram to launch his new scheme. He said:

> Our sphere of work now is not confined to children from seven to fourteen years; it is to cover the whole of life from the moment of conception to the moment of death. ... Our reward, if any, has to come from within and not from without. It should not make any difference to us whether in our quest for Truth we have any company or not. ... I know that true education must be self-supporting.[8]

In November 1944, I myself joined the teacher training institute as an art instructor, working under Gandhi's guidance.

The scheme of education proposed by Gandhi was, schematically, the following: (a) adult education of the whole community, including the parents of the newborn babies; (b) pre-basic schooling from 2 to 7 years; (c) Basic schooling from 7 to 14 years; (d) Post-basic education from 14 to 18 years; and (e) university and teacher training institute education.

The daily schedule in Sevagram was as follows: after the morning prayers we all divided ourselves into groups to do the cleaning of the campus, including the lavatories, an activity which was considering a science as well as an art. After 45 minutes of community cleaning we went to our workshops – some to the farm which produced the food the community needed, some to the spinning and weaving workshops, and some to the kitchen. We all took turns preparing meals every day. Gradually the number of workshops increased according to the needs of the community and the educational programme, for example one for mechanical engineering. I developed the art department with a ceramics section. After a two-hour lunch-break students and teachers went to their studies, which related to the day's work and its various aspects, scientific, mathematical and so on. The principle was to teach academic subjects in a manner related to the work in the workshops or agriculture. It included management and usage of equipment. One principle that greatly mattered was 'Think before doing and think after doing.'

There were music and art classes for all students. Some of the time was devoted to the practice and rehearsals for the celebration of festivals and special occasions related to *all* the religions. Whenever there were performances or festivals, students and teachers did all the decorations. Stagecraft and management were an important part of education. In the afternoon, before dinner, there were games. The evening prayer was ecumenical.

It is necessary to point out that in Nayee Talim there was no place for textbooks as such, but students were constantly encouraged to use the library. Gradually Nayee Talim schools were set up all over the country, drawing inspiration and guidance from Sevagram. Jamia Millia Islamia was another central institute that worked in close co-operation with Sevagram. After the early sixties the quality of Nayee Talim fell rather low. The main reason behind that 'failure' was that the political élite did not care for an educational system that they thought was for villagers only. Ironically, they remained attached to the so-called 'modern educational system' which India had inherited from its colonial past.

Notes

1 Gandhi (1963, p. 123).
2 Ibid., pp. 67–8.
3 Ibid., p. 3.
4 Ibid., p. 122.
5 Reginald Reynolds, *White Sahibs in India*, London: Martin Secker & Warburt, pp. 149–50, 1937.
6 Ibid., p. 278.
7 From Gandhi's inaugural talk at the 1944 Conference in Sevagram, in Gandhi (1962).
8 Ibid.

See also

In this book: Tagore

Gandhi's major writings

An Autobiography or The Story of my Experiments with Truth, translation from Gujrati by Mahadev Desai, Ahmedabad, Navajivan Publishing House, 1963 (first published in 1927).
The Problems of Education: A Compilation of Gandhi's Writings and Speeches on Education, Ahmedabad: Navajivan Publishing House, 1962.
Towards New Education, ed. Bharatan Kumarappa, Ahmedabad: Navajivan Publishing House, 1980.

Further reading

Basic National Education, Report of Zakir Husain Committee and the Detailed Syllabus, Wardha: Hundstani Talimi Sangh, 1939.
Kumarappa, J.P., *Education for Life*, Rajamundry: Hindustan Publishing Co., 1937.
Parekh, Bikhu, *Gandhi's Political Philosophy*, London: Macmillan, 1989.
Two Years Work, Report of the Second Basic Education Conference Jamianagar 1941 Delhi, Wardha: Hundstani Talimi Sangh, 1942.

DEVI PRASAD

MARIA MONTESSORI 1870–1952

> The voice of Séguin seemed to be like the voice of the forerunner crying in the wilderness, and my thoughts were filled with the immensity and importance of a work which should be able to reform the school and education.[1]

Over the protests of her shocked parents, Maria Montessori decided at age

13 to become an engineer. Once enrolled in a technical school, however, she switched her allegiance to medicine. And so it was that in 1896, to everyone's surprise but her own, Montessori became the first woman in Italy to graduate from medical school. Not long after, Montessori also became an educator. The observations she made of young 'idiot children' in asylums and her growing conviction that mental deficiency was at root a pedagogical problem led her directly to the writings of Jean-Marc-Gaspard Itard and Edouard Séguin. From these it was but a short step to the study of pedagogy and the philosophies of Rousseau, Pestalozzi and Froebel. In quick succession thereafter Montessori gave a series of lectures on special methods of education at a teacher training institute in Rome, was appointed director of a medical-pedagogical institute, and taught in the Pedagogic School at the University of Rome. Then in 1980 she opened the first Casa dei Bambini – a school for 'normal' children who were running wild in Rome's tenements while their parents were at work.

In *The Montessori Method*, first published in 1909, Montessori set forth the theory and practice of the Casa dei Bambini. This book was so widely translated and well received that people across the world began flocking to Rome to observe her ideas in action. Montessori, in turn, made several triumphant speaking tours abroad. On the eve of her first visit to the United States in 1913, a news article referred to Montessori's educational ideas as having already taken their place in history next to those of Rousseau, Pestalozzi, and Froebel. Although five years later she was all but forgotten in that country, Montessori continued to lecture to huge audiences and to give training courses throughout Europe. When on a single day in 1935 Mussolini closed down all her schools, she moved to Holland to continue her work and to deliver the addresses that would later be collected in *Education and Peace*. In 1939 she left her new home for India where, during World War II, she trained over one thousand teachers while giving the lectures that formed the basis for *The Absorbent Mind* and *The Discovery of the Child*. Returning to Europe after the war, Montessori spoke, wrote, travelled to conferences, and gave training teacher courses until the very end. At the time of her death she had thrice been nominated for the Nobel Peace Prize.

Responsibility for the decline of Montessori's popularity and reputation in the US lies largely with William Heard Kilpatrick, a member of the faculty of Teachers College, Columbia University and a disciple of John Dewey. In a speech to the International Kindergarten Association and then in a devastating monograph addressed to teachers and school superintendents, Kilpatrick asked where among other systems of education Montessori's belonged. After faulting Montessori for admiring Séguin's work with retarded children, calling her 'illogical', and consistently comparing her unfavorably to Dewey, he answered: 'they are ill advised who put Madam Montessori among the significant contributors to educational theory. Stimulating she is; a contributor to our theory, hardly if at all.'[2]

In 1918, Robert R. Rusk of the University of Glasgow reached an opposite conclusion. Along with many others, Rusk criticized Montessori for overrating the importance of the special devices for sensory training she had introduced into early education. However, his final verdict on Montessori's contribution to educational theory was reflected in his decision to include a chapter on her system in a text entitled *The Doctrines of the Great Educators*.

Over the years, Montessori's ideas about the importance of the child's environment, her system of individualized instruction, the exercises for sensory training and practical living she designed, and her emphasis on auto-education have been admired by many educational thinkers besides Rusk. They have also had – and continue to have – a worldwide influence on educational practice. In 1997 the 22nd International Montessori Congress was held at Uppsala University. As the centennial of the opening of the first Casa dei Bambini approaches, Montessori schools proliferate and Montessori organizations and training courses thrive in North America, Asia, Europe and Australia. And in the US where Montessori was once forgotten, there are now Montessori public schools and independent schools, pre-schools and middle schools, magnet schools and day care homes for migrant children.

Both friends and foes of Montessori have, however, misread a central element of her theory. Speaking at the opening of the second Casa dei Bambini in Rome, Montessori said: 'We Italians have elevated our word "casa" to the almost sacred significance of the English word "home," the enclosed temple of domestic affection, accessible only to dear ones.'[3] Nevertheless, Montessori's term for school has from the beginning been rendered in English 'The House of Childhood' or 'The Children's House'. Indeed, in 1912 the speech containing her cautionary note was published as Chapter III of the first English-language edition of *The Montessori Method* under the title 'Inaugural Address Delivered on the Occasion of the Opening of One of the "Children's Houses"'.

Read 'casa' as house and one's attention is drawn to the child-sized furniture in the schools Montessori established, the exercises in dressing and washing, the self-education, and perhaps the extended day. Read 'casa' as home and one discovers a moral and social dimension that transforms one's understanding of Montessori's theory. A common criticism of her educational thought has been that it ignores interpersonal or social education. When her system is reinterpreted, however, its elements take on a different configuration: where small individuals were seen busily manipulating materials designed especially for learning, there emerges a domestic scene with its own special form of social life and education.

If Montessori's Inaugural Lecture is not in itself convincing evidence that she conceptualized school as home, her use in *Education and Peace* of the image of a womb – a child's very first home – should be decisive. Considering the child a spiritual embryo, Montessori told European audiences that the child 'must no longer be considered as the son of man, but rather as the creator and the father of man'.[4] The spiritual embryo's promise will only be fulfilled if the child is allowed to develop normally, Montessori insisted. Since its psychic life begins at birth, the problem of peace becomes, then, one of educating young children. Just as the physical embryo derives its nutriments from the womb, the spiritual embryo absorbs them from its surroundings. Put children in the wrong environment and their development will be abnormal; they will become the deviated adults we now know. Create the right environment for them and their characters will develop normally. The 'second womb' is what she called the young child's proper environment. From at least age 3 the Casa dei Bambini was to be that second womb.

What is the character of the institution she called home? One dwells in a house. One feels safe, secure, loved, at ease – that is, at home – in a home, at least in the kind of home envisioned by Montessori. Montessori was well aware that not all homes are safe and loving. In addition, this delegate to the 1896 international women's congress in Berlin knew that the sex equality she was building into her idea of school was not an attribute of the ordinary Italian home. However, she did not dream of modelling her school on just any home. Maintaining in her Inaugural Address that the Casa dei Bambini 'is not simply a place where the children are kept, not just an *asylum*, but a true school for their education',[5] she indicated that even in its homelikeness it was to be educative.

One clear implication of Montessori's concept of school as home is that the inhabitants of school constitute a family. Just as the model for school in Montessori's theory is an idealized version of home, an exemplary family serves as the model for the relationship in which those attending school stand to one another. When it does, the social nature of Montessori's system becomes apparent. Instruction in a Casa dei Bambini is definitely individualized. However, like the individual members of the family of Montessori's imagination, even as the children are treated as individuals and their individuality is allowed to flourish, they feel connected to one another and concerned about each other's welfare.

Although Montessori's name is usually associated with the education of young children, in *From Childhood to Adolescence* she applied her idea of school as home to the case of teenagers. In that work she proposed that adolescents live together in the country away from their private homes, and that they run a modern farm, a country store, and 'The Rural Children's Hotel'. Directed by a married couple who would exercise a moral and protective influence on the youths, this home away from home would be an ongoing commercial enterprise. Conserving a tradition by which personal talent was expressed in the fabrication of objects, the store would sell the produce not only of the young people, but also of poor neighbours. Mixing business with friendship, it would also serve as a kind of social centre.

Ignoring the context in which Montessori developed her ideas, most interpreters of Montessori's thought have not realized that the Casa dei Bambini was meant to compensate for the domestic vacuum in the lives of children whose mothers were required to work each day outside their own homes. Even those who were aware of its origins apparently did not realize that the Casa dei Bambini was intended as a surrogate home for children. In consequence, the uncanny relevance for future generations of Montessori's idea of school has never fully been appreciated. To borrow a phrase that William James introduced in a very different context just three years after she delivered her Inaugural Lecture, the Casa dei Bambini was Montessori's 'moral equivalent' of home. Because fathers have left home each day to go to work ever since the Industrial Revolution and many families are headed by single mothers, the exodus of women to the workplace greatly expands this concept of school's range of application.

One reason why Montessori's domestic imagery has been neglected is that it violates basic cultural expectations about the role of school in society.

Implicitly dividing social reality into two parts – private home and public world – members of Western industrial and post-industrial societies take the function of school to be that of transforming children who have heretofore lived their lives in one part into members of the other. Assuming that the private home is a natural institution and that, accordingly, membership in it is a given rather than something one must achieve, they see no reason to prepare people to carry out the tasks and activities associated with it. Perceiving the public world as a human creation and membership in it as something at which one can succeed or fail and therefore as problematic, they make preparation for carrying out the tasks and activities associated with it the main business of education.

Montessori wanted the Casa dei Bambini to form children for life in the public world. But she knew that a public world hospitable to peace would have to be very different from the one of her acquaintance and that those living in it would have to have been formed by a very different kind of school. Envisioning school as an extension of the private home and the world as continuous with school and home, she left no room in her system for the radical dichotomies so often drawn between school and home, home and world, world and school.

Montessori may not have been the only or even the first person in the history of Western educational thought to reject a radical separation between school and home. Since, however, she is the one who built domestic imagery into her theory even as her educational practice acknowledged the importance of the atmosphere, affections, and curriculum associated with home and domesticity, the system that Kilpatrick claimed had nothing new in it of importance is nothing short of revolutionary.

Notes

1 Maria Montessori, *The Montessori Method*, Chicago: Regnery, p. 42, 1972.
2 William Heard Kilpatrick, *The Montessori System Examined*, Boston: Houghton Mifflin, p. 30, 1914
3 Montessori, *The Montessori Method*, Chicago: Regnery, p. 52, 1972.
4 Ibid., p. 104.
5 Ibid., p. 62.

See also

In this book: Dewey, Pestalozzi, Rousseau

Montessori's major writings

Education and Peace, Chicago: Regnery, 1972.
From Childhood to Adolescence, New York: Schocken, 1973.
The Absorbent Mind, New York: Dell, 1984.
The Montessori Method, New York: Schocken, 1964.
The Secret of Childhood, New York: Ballantine, 1972.

Further reading

Kilpatrick, William Heard, *The Montessori System Examined*, Boston: Houghton Mifflin, 1914.

Kramer, Rita, *Maria Montessori: A Biography*, Chicago: University of Chicago Press, 1976.

Martin, Jane Roland. 'Romanticism Domesticated: Maria Montessori and the Casa dei Bambini', in *The Educational Legacy of Romanticism*, ed. John Willinsky, Waterloo, Ontario: Wilfrid Laurier University Press, pp. 159–174, 1990.

—— *The Schoolhome: Rethinking Schools for Changing Families*, Cambridge: Harvard University Press, 1992.

Rusk, Robert R. *The Doctrines of the Great Educators*, 3rd edn, New York: St Martin's, 1965.

JANE ROLAND MARTIN

BERTRAND RUSSELL 1872–1970

The good life is one inspired by love and guided by knowledge.[1]

Bertrand Arthur William Russell has been described as the greatest logician since Aristotle, but during his lifetime he was known equally well for his writings on social, political and educational themes. He was born in Trelleck, Monmouthshire on 18 May 1872, and, after the early deaths of his parents, was brought up in Pembroke Lodge, the home of his paternal grandmother, Countess Russell, the widow of the first Earl Russell. Until the age of 16, he was educated privately at home by a series of, mostly very able, tutors. Then, to prepare him for Cambridge, he was sent to crammer school in London, attended mainly by boys destined to become officers of the British Army. He later remembered his childhood years as solitary, lonely and shrouded in mystery, and he did not discover the joys of companionship until, in October 1890, he went up to Trinity College, Cambridge to study mathematics.

At Cambridge, Russell was elected a member of the famous conversation society, the Apostles, the other members of which included some of the most influential philosophers of the day, most notably, the neo-Hegelian J.E. McTaggart. Stimulated by his discussions with the Apostles and disappointed by his mathematical studies, Russell, after taking Part I of the Mathematics Tripos, switched to philosophy, and in 1894 secured a first class with distinction in moral sciences. The following year, after a brief spell at the British embassy in Paris, he was elected to a fellowship at Trinity on the basis of a dissertation on the philosophical problems created by the construction of non-Euclidean geometries (in 1897 this was published as his first philosophical book, *An Essay on the Foundations of Geometry*).

On 13 December 1894, a few months before his election to a fellowship, Russell, in the face of vigorous opposition from his grandmother, married Alys Pearsall Smith, the daughter of a rich Philadephia Quaker who had settled in England. On his honeymoon, Russell went to Berlin, where he studied the theory and practice of Marxism, and formulated an ambitious plan of writing two series of books, one on the philosophy of the sciences from mathematics to physiology, and the other on social and political questions, the two series constituting one large unified system of philosophy analogous to Hegel's. The plan, in its original form, was never executed, but his very first book, *German Social Democracy*, published in 1896, might be seen as the first step towards its realisation.

Within a few years, Russell abandoned the neo-Hegelian metaphysics that he had derived from McTaggart and that had been the inspiration for his proposed grand synthesis of politics and science. Russell's rejection of idealism is customarily attributed to the influence upon him of G.E. Moore, whose seminal defence of realism, 'The Nature of Judgment', was published in 1899 and had a powerful impact on Russell. An even greater influence, however, was exerted by a group of pure mathematicians, including Weierstrass, Cantor and Dedekind, whose work Russell began to study in 1898. What these mathematicians showed Russell was that the traditional paradoxes of mathematics – those of continuity, infinity and the infinitesimal – were capable of a purely mathematical resolution. Excited by this discovery, and stimulated also by G.E. Moore's attack on idealist philosophical logic, Russell conceived the ambition of providing a realist foundation for mathematics that would demonstrate its essentially logical nature.

The result, published in 1903, is what is generally regarded as Russell's greatest philosophical work, *The Principles of Mathematics*, in which he argues that mathematics in its entirety is nothing but logic and can be shown to be such by the definition of all its fundamental notions (including number and series) and the derivation of all its theorems from within a purely logical theory of classes. By the time he published this book, however, Russell had already discovered the famous paradox of classes which bears his name and which shows that there is something fundamentally amiss with the notion of class that he and, before him, Frege, had intended to use as a foundation for arithmetic. Russell's solution to this paradox, presented in the massive work, *Principia Mathematica*, that he co-authored with Alfred North Whithead and which was published in three volumes between 1911 and 1913, centred on a bewilderingly complicated system of logic called the Ramified Theory of Types which, though technically it solved the problem, raised difficult questions about the nature of logic and doubts about the philosophical purpose of reducing mathematics to it.

These questions were taken up by Ludwig Wittgenstein, who in 1911 arrived in Cambridge to study with Russell who, meanwhile, had largely lost interest in them. To some extent, this was due to the considerable strain on his intellect of finishing *Principia Mathematica*, but it was also due, in no small measure, to the impact upon him of Lady Ottoline Morrell, with whom Russell began a tempestuous affair in 1911 that was to have a tremendous influence on the course of his life. Inspired by Ottoline, Russell began to write in a new, less technical way, aiming to reach an audience far greater than the tiny few capable of understanding *Principia Mathematica*. He began in 1912 with the *The Problems of Philosophy*, a small book that became a surprising bestseller and revealed to the public for the first time Russell's gift for writing, in supremely elegant prose, expositions of difficult ideas accessible to a general readership.

During the period 1911–1914, Russell's philosophical interests shifted from logic to epistemology. A large ambitious book called *The Theory of Knowledge* was abandoned in 1913 due to the severe criticisms it received from Wittgenstein, but the following year Russell published *Our Knowledge of the External World*, which presented a novel form of empiricism according to which the world is regarded as a 'construction' out of sense-data. This view, much debated in the succeeding decades, has now generally fallen out of favour among professional philosophers.

At the outbreak of war in 1914, Russell more or less abandoned philosophy in favour of political campaigning. He considered it disastrous for civilization that Britain and Germany should find themselves at war with one another and wrote several vitriolic attacks on the foreign policy that had led to such a monstrous outcome. When conscription was introduced in 1916, his attacks on the government grew more strident and he became a leading member of the No-Conscription Fellowship (NCF). A leaflet he wrote in support of the NCF brought him into conflict with the authorities and he was fined £100 and, more seriously, was sacked from his lectureship at Trinity College. Undaunted, he continued to pour out, in articles, public lectures and books, unceasing denunciations of the war and the government. In 1918, this led to a six-month prison sentence for publishing an article suggesting that American troops might be employed in Britain in a strike-breaking role.

By this time, Russell's interests had swung back to philosophy. Shortly before serving his prison sentence, he delivered the series of public lectures published as *The Philosophy of Logical Atomism*, and while in prison he wrote *Introduction to Mathematical Philosophy*, intended as a popularization of *Principia Mathematica*. Immediately after the war, he delivered another series of public lectures on philosophy, published in 1921 as *The Analysis of Mind* and, after receiving an invitation to return to Trinity College, it seemed that he might, after all, resume his academic career.

However, having discovered that he rather enjoyed being a freelance writer and a public lecturer, Russell was in no hurry to return to academic life. In 1920, he visited the Soviet Union and was appalled at the cruelty and tyranny of the Leninist regime, a reaction he expressed with great force in *The Practice and Theory of Bolshevism*, written soon after his return. Then, with his lover, Dora Black, he spent the year 1920–21 in China, from where he wrote to Trinity rejecting the offer of a renewed lectureship. In China, to Russell's great delight, Dora became pregnant and, within months of their return to England, she and Russell married so as to legitimize the baby.

The birth of his first son, John, in November 1921 (a daughter, Kate, was added in 1923), was an important turning point in Russell's life, inspiring in him, not only a deep interest in the proper methods of parenting and education, but also, more generally, a fervent concern with political and social reform with an eye to ensuring that the world inherited by his son's generation would be saner, more peaceful and more reasonable than the world that had descended into war in 1914. With this in mind, Russell devoted most of his vast output of journalistic articles and popular books during the interwar years to a fervent espousal of a set of ideas that established him as a leader of a progressive movement that was radically socialist, stridently anti-clerical, openly defiant of conventional sexual morality and committed to 'the scientific outlook'. Many of the books published in defence of these ideas – *On Education* (1926), *Marriage and Morals* (1929) and *The Conquest of Happiness* (1930) – enjoyed large sales and helped to establish Russell in the public eye as a philosopher with important things to say about the moral, political and social issues of the day.

During these years, however, Russell's second marriage came under increasing strain, partly because of overwork, but chiefly because Dora chose to have two children with another man. In 1932, Russell left her for Patricia ('Peter') Spence, a 21-year-old Oxford undergraduate, whom he married in 1936 and with whom he had a son, Conrad, the following year. Worn out by years of frenetic public activity and desiring, at this comparatively late stage in his life (he was then 66), to return to academic life, Russell gained a position at the University of Chicago in 1938. For the next six years, he lived in the United States, where he taught at Chicago and UCLA but was prevented from taking up a post at the City College of New York because of a much-publicized court case brought against his appointment by a woman who claimed that his presence at the college would corrupt the morals of its students. Russell was then saved from financial ruin by Dr Albert C. Barnes, who offered him a job teaching the history of philosophy to the art students at the Barnes Foundation in Philadelphia. These lectures became the basis of Russell's *History of Western Philosophy* which, despite the scorn heaped upon it by professional philosophers, proved to be immensely popular with the general public and was for years Russell's chief source of income.

In 1944, Russell was again invited to return to Trinity College, and this time was only too happy to accept. He was disappointed, however, with the lukewarm reception given by the younger generation of philosophers (among whom Wittgenstein was now the dominant influence) to his last major work on philosophy, *Human Knowledge: Its Scope and Limits*, published in 1948. In the 1950s he launched a series of attacks on the so-called 'Ordinary Language Philosophy' prevalent at Oxford, but this served only to alienate him further from professional philosophers.

In 1952, Russell married his fourth wife, Edith Finch, and at last, at the age of 80, found marital happiness. His last years were devoted to political campaigning, first against nuclear weapons and then against the Vietnam War. In 1961 he received a second prison sentence, serving a week in Brixton gaol, which did nothing to temper his increasingly shrill denunciations of the British and American governments. When he died in 1970, he was better known as an anti-war campaigner than as a philosopher, but there seems little doubt that it is for his great contributions to logic and the philosophy of mathematics that he will be remembered by future generations.

Note

1   'What I Believe' (1925), reprinted in *The Basic Writings of Bertrand Russell*, London: Routledge, pp. 367–90 (quotation p. 372), 1961.

Russell's major writings

The Collected Papers of Bertrand Russell, 15 volumes published so far, London: Routledge, 1983–.
The Principles of Mathematics, Cambridge: Cambridge University Press, 1903.

(with A.N. Whitehead) *Principia Mathematica*, 3 volumes, Cambridge: Cambridge University Press, 1910–13.
Our Knowledge of the External World, London: Open Court, London, 1914.
History of Western Philosophy, London: George Allen & Unwin, 1946.
Logic and Knowledge, London: George Allen & Unwin, 1956.
My Philosophical Development, London: George Allen & Unwin, 1959.
The Basic Writings of Bertrand Russell, London: George Allen & Unwin, 1961.
The Autobiography of Bertrand Russell, 3 volumes, London: George Allen & Unwin, 1967–9.

Further reading

Clark, Ronald W., *The Life of Bertrand Russell*, London: Penguin, 1978.
Grayling, A.C., *Russell*, Oxford: Oxford University Press, 1996.
Monk, Ray, *Bertrand Russell: The Spirit of Solitude*, London: Jonathan Cape, 1996.
—— *Bertrand Russell: The Ghost of Madness*, London: Jonathan Cape, 2000.
Ryan, Alan, *Bertrand Russell: A Political Life*, London: Allen Lane, 1988.
Schilpp, Paul Arthur (ed.), *The Philosophy of Bertrand Russell*, La Salle: Open Court, 1944.
Slater, John G., *Bertrand Russell*, Bristol: Thoemmes Press, 1994.

RAY MONK

E.L. THORNDIKE 1874–1949

> Education is concerned with changes in human beings; a change
> is a difference between two conditions; each of these conditions is
> known to us only by the products produced by it – things made,
> words spoken, acts performed, and the like. To measure any of
> these products means to define its amount in some way so that
> competent persons will know how large it is, better than they
> would without measurement.[1]

Edward Lee Thorndike is perhaps the most influential of all American psychologists. His early work in animal learning helped establish comparative psychology as an experimental science and created the field of psychology that became known as the experimental analysis of behaviour. He introduced important methodological innovations to behavioural science. He laid the methodological and philosophical foundation of the behavioural psychology of John B. Watson and B.F. Skinner. He applied principles of learning developed in the laboratory and quantitative measurement of individual differences to create educational psychology. He produced 507 publications, over 50 of which are books.[2] As a measure of his influence, Tolman observed in 1938 that the psychology of learning, both animal learning and human learning, was largely a matter of agreeing or disagreeing with Thorndike.[3] Psychology has moved on, but Thorndike's influence is still felt today, the result of his impact on the historical development of both psychology and education.

Thorndike was born in Williamsburg, Massachusetts on 31 August 1874. He was the second of four children, all of whom had academic careers and three, including Edward Lee, becoming professors at Columbia University.[4] His father, Edward Roberts Thorndike, was trained in the law and later became a clergyman; his mother, Abigail Brewster Ladd, was a home-maker.[5] He received a BA degree from Wesleyan University in 1895, where he studied literature. He attended Harvard University from 1895 to 1897, receiving a second BA in 1896 and an MA in 1897.

At Harvard, Thorndike became interested in psychology through William James, who had published *Principles of Psychology* in 1890. During his first year in graduate school at Harvard, he began 'mind reading' studies of the ability of young children to read unintended cues from facial expressions or movements while attempting to guess the letter, number or object Thorndike had in mind. When Harvard did not permit continuation of these studies, Thorndike changed his research programme to the study of the behaviour of chickens. This substitution of animals for children was thought odd by others at Harvard, including – in a strange historical connection – Gertrude Stein, who was with Thorndike in a William James' seminar at the time, but it reveals Thorndike's interest in both animals and children from the beginning of his work in psychology.[6] James supported Thorndike's research, even to the point of allowing him to keep his chickens in the basement of the James home, but when he received a fellowship Thorndike and his chickens moved to Columbia University where Thorndike completed graduate work under James McKeen Catell. He received a Ph.D. from Columbia in 1898. His dissertation, which was first published as the *Psychological Review* monograph 'Animal Intelligence',[7] proved to be a major event in the history of psychology.

Following his graduate work, Thorndike spent a year at Western Reserve University as professor of pedagogy and director of the practice school. In 1899 he returned to the Teacher's College at Columbia University as an instructor in psychology, then adjunct professor of psychology from 1901 to 1904 and professor of psychology from 1904 until his retirement in 1940. He died in Montrose, New York on 9 August 1949. His obituary in the *Psychological Review* described him as friendly, generous and kind, with a good sense of humour, qualities which made him a good friend and teacher.[8]

Carrying on the tradition of producing academic children begun by his parents, four of Thorndike's children earned doctorates, two in physics, one in mathematics, and one, Robert L. Thorndike, who became a professor of psychology and education at the Teacher's College, Columbia University, in psychology. Robert L.'s son, Robert M. Thorndike, also became an educational psychologist, working like his father and grandfather in educational measurement and intelligence testing.[9]

Thorndike's dissertation, 'Animal Intelligence', was a landmark in the history of psychology. In addition to being the first psychology dissertation to use animals as subjects,[10] it introduced an experimental methodology that today seems so obvious that it is difficult to appreciate the magnitude of his contribution. Work in the field of animal behaviour at the end of the nineteenth century was anecdotal, anthropomorphic and introspective, attributing complex intellectual and emotional lives to animals based on selected anecdotes and anthropomorphic interpretation of the evidence. Such research was motivated by a debate between deists and evolutionists on the origins of human intellect. Demonstrations of rich intellectual and emotional lives in animals were thought to show a link between animals and humans many believed required by Darwin's theory of evolution. Thorndike's dissertation provided a vigorous critique of anecdote, introspection and anthropomorphism, and employed a set of new methods for studying behaviour systematically and quantitatively under controlled conditions. These methods are familiar to any Introductory Psychology student today: a representative sample of subjects, a carefully described and reproducible experimental situation, quantitative measures of performance, comparisons of groups receiving different treatments, and interpretation of outcomes before the experiment is conducted.[11]

Thorndike's work on animal intelligence over the ten years following his dissertation was published in book form in 1911.[12] This work included his first statement of two general laws of learning derived from his experimental work: the Law of Effect and the Law of Exercise.[13] Thorndike's conception of learning was that it was a matter of forming stimulus-response (S-R) associations. The Law of Effect states that practice alone will not generate an association: the pairing of stimulus with response must be followed by a consequence, or effect. A positive consequence or reward will strengthen the association; a negative consequence or punishment will weaken the association. According to the Law of Exercise, associations are strengthened with practice and weakened without practice. Thorndike believed that these two general laws, with instinct providing basic raw materials of behaviour on which the Laws of Effect and Exercise operated, were sufficient to explain all learned behaviour of all species, including humans. As Thorndike put it, 'the higher animals, including man, manifest no behaviour beyond expectations from the laws of instinct, exercise, and effect',[14] implying that analyses of the effects of reward, punishment and practice performed with animals could produce general laws of learning applicable to humans. This view would later be embraced by the behaviourists John B. Watson and B. F. Skinner and have a monumental impact on the development of psychology through the rest of the twentieth century. It also formed the basis of Thorndike's educational psychology and had an impact of similar magnitude on education.

Thorndike applied the same experimental methodology he used with animals to his research in human learning. One of his earliest and best-known studies of human learning, conducted with Robert S. Woodworth and published in 1901, dealt with transfer of training, showing that the degree of positive or negative transfer between one learning and another is based on the similarity of the two situations.[15] This refuted the long-held belief that there is positive transfer from prior training of any kind, even training in a dissimilar area, a belief that had been used to justify the learning of Latin or Greek as a kind of mental exercise that would benefit later learning of any subject.

During the first fifteen years of the twentieth century, Thorndike moved from animal psychology to education, in part because of his interest in applying his general laws of learning to school learning and in part because more jobs were available in teacher education programmes.[16] Through his research, writing and teaching, Thorndike developed an educational psychology based on S-R associationism, an experimental methodology, and measurement of individual differences. He was teaching undergraduate and graduate education courses at Columbia with titles like 'Application of Psychological and Statistical Methods to Education', a title he soon changed to the newly coined term 'Educational Psychology'. His first book, *The Human Nature Club*,[17] was intended for teachers and adults interested in education. His second book, *Notes on Child Study*, published in 1901, critiqued the naturalistic and unscientific methodology of G. Stanley Hall's child study movement.[18] *The Principles of Teaching*, published in 1906, applied the laws of learning to classroom teaching and emphasized the importance of the scientific approach to education based on 'direct observations of and experiments on the influence of educational institutions and methods made and reported with quantitative precision'.[19] He founded *The Journal of Educational Psychology* in 1910, published *Education* in 1912, a book on educational philosophy, and produced the three-volume *Educational Psychology* in 1913–14, which dealt with his laws of learning, inherited mental abilities and individual differences.

Along with Pearson, Binet and Spearman, Thorndike was part of the early mental testing movement. He believed in the specificity of abilities rather than a single factor and based his scales on a variety of tasks.[20] He helped develop and analyze intelligence tests used by the army in World War I, and following the war began producing rating scales and tests for subjects including writing, spelling, geography and drawing. He developed the Thorndike–Lorge word frequency book for teachers,[21] also well known to verbal learning researchers, and dictionaries[22] and mathematics textbooks[23] written to be understandable by children. Thorndike's success with his tests and curriculum materials led him to develop commercial ventures. He formed the Psychological Corporation in 1921 with Cattell and Woodworth to publish very successful standardized educational and psychological tests.

Late in his career, Thorndike attempted to apply his research methodology to new areas, including the rating of the value of cities as places to live[24] and working toward a science of values that could support social decision making.[25] A progressive, he believed strongly in science's ability to solve all social problems, but moral and social values did not prove to be as tractable as learning.

Most of Thorndike's academic career was dominated by educational psychology and psychometrics.[26] He was a positivist and a progressive, believing in the betterment of mankind and that scientific laws developed through observation and testing would provide the path to social improvement. This belief led him from research on animal and human learning to an applied psychology that included mental testing, educational psychology, and developing mathematics textbooks and children's dictionaries.

Looking back on the twentieth century, it is clear that much of educational practice can be construed as an extension of Thorndike's work or as a repudiation of it. Consider the recurrent swings between viewing education as a science or as an art, between focuses on processes or outcomes, or as based on principles or on interpretative knowledge. Even more important than the contributions made substantively, Thorndike was instrumental in the development of a persistent American interest in pursuing high quality methods in conducting educational and psychological research. When one examines the contribution of the strains of psychology and education developed in the US, the focus on analysis of effects can be traced to Thorndike's influence.

As important a contribution as the substance of his research is in fact the model Thorndike set of great interest, range and intellectual power across the entire field of education. His attention considered domains of basic and applied research, as well as practice and policy. Tom Glennan (196?) calls this unusual facility parallel flexibility. Only a few researchers ever show the ability to traverse the full spectrum of contributions in a field, illustrating the capacity for painstaking, theoretically relevant work and deep understanding of the complexities of affecting the messier worlds of practice and policy.

Notes

1 Thorndike (1918) cited in Berliner (1993).
2 W.W. Cumming, 'A Review of Geraldine Jonchich's The Sane Positivist: A Biography of Edward L. Thorndike', *Journal of the Experimental Analysis of Behavior*, 72, pp. 441–6, 1999.
3 E.C. Tolman, 'The Determiners of Behavior at a Choice Point', *Psychological Review*, 45, pp. 1–41, 1938. Cited in Cumming (1999).
4 Berliner (1993).
5 Woodworth (1952).
6 Jonçich (1968). Cited in H.J. Stam and T. Kalmanovitch, 'E. L. Thorndike and the Origins of Animal Psychology', *American Psychologist*, 53, pp. 1,135–44, 1998.
7 Thorndike (1898).
8 A.I. Gates, 'Edward L. Thorndike: 1874–1949', *Psychological Review, 56*, pp. 241–3, 1949. Cited in Dewsbury (1998).
9 Berliner (1993).
10 Galef, Bennett G. Jr., 'Edward Thorndike: Revolutionary Psychologist, Ambiguous Biologist', *American Psychologist*, 53, pp. 1,128–34.
11 Ibid., p. 1,130.
12 Thorndike (1911).
13 Galef, op cit., p. 1,131.
14 Thorndike (1911, p. 274).
15 Thorndike and Woodworth (1901).
16 D.A. Dewsbury, 'Triumph and Tribulation in the History of American Comparative Psychology', *Journal of Comparative Psychology*, 106, pp. 3–19, 1992.
17 Thorndike (1901a).
18 Thorndike (1901b).
19 Thorndike (1906).
20 Thorndike, Cobb and Woodyard (1926).
21 E.L. Thorndike and I. Lorge, *Teacher's Wordbook of 30,000 Words*, New York: Columbia University Press, 1944.
22 E.L. Thorndike, *Thorndike-Century Junior Dictionary*, Chicago: Scott Foresman, 1935.
23 E.L. Thorndike, *The Thorndike Arithmetics. Books 1–3*, Chicago, Rand-McNally, 1917.
24 E.L. Thorndike, *Your City*, New York: Harcourt, Brace, 1939.
25 Thorndike (1940).
26 Dewsbury (1998).

See also

In this book: Darwin, Binet
In *Fifty Modern Thinkers on Education*: Skinner

Thorndike's major writings

'Animal Intelligence', *Psychological Review*, Monograph Supplement 11, No. 2, Whole No. 8, 1898.

The Human Nature Club: An Introduction to the Study of Mental Life, New York: Longmans, Green, 1901a.

Notes on Child Study (monograph), Columbia University Contributions to Philosophy, Psychology, and Education, 8 (3–4), New York: Macmillan, 1901b.

The Principles of Teaching: Based on Psychology, New York: A.G. Seller, 1906.

Animal Intelligence: Experimental Studies, New York: Macmillan, 1911.

'The Nature, Purposes, and General Methods of Measurements of Educational Products', in *The Measurement of Educational Products* (Seventeenth Yearbook of the Nationan Society for the Study of Education, Part 2, p. 16), Bloomington, IL: Public School Publishing Company, 1918.

Human Nature and the Social Order, New York, Macmillan, 1940.

Thorndike, E.L., Cobb, M.V., and Woodyard, E., *The Measurement of Intelligence*, New York: Teachers College, Columbia University Press, 1926.

Thorndike, E.L., and Woodworth, R.S., 'The Influence of One Mental Function Upon the Efficiency of Other Functions', *Psychological Review*, 8, pp. 247–61, 384–95, 553–64, 1901. Cited in Dewsbury (1998).

Further reading

Berliner, D., 'The 100-year Journey of Educational Psychology. From Interest, to Disdain, to Respect for Practice', in T.K. Fagan and G.R. VandenBos (eds), *Exploring Applied Psychology: Origins and Critical Analyses*, Washington, DC: American Psychological Association, pp. 41–78, 1993.

Dewsbury, D.A., 'Celebrating E. L. Thorndike A Century After *Animal Intelligence*', *American Psychologist*, 53, 1,121–4, 1998.

Galef, Bennett G. Jr., 'Edward Thorndike: Revolutionary Psychologist, Ambiguous Biologist', *American Psychologist*, 53, pp. 1,128–34.

Glennan, T.K., 'Issues in the Choice of Development Policies', in T. Manschak, T.K. Glennan, Jr and R. Summers (eds), *Strategies for Research and Development*, New York: Springer Verlag, pp. 13–48, 1967.

Jonçich, G., *The Sane Positivist: A Biography of Edward L. Thorndike*, Middletown, CT: Wesleyan University Press, 1968.

Woodworth, R.S., 'E. L. Thorndike', in *National Academy of Sciences biographical memoirs*, Washington, DC: National Academy of Sciences, 27, pp. 209–37, 1952.

WILLIAM L. BEWLEY AND EVA L. BAKER

MARTIN BUBER 1878–1965

> This fragile life between birth and death can nevertheless be a
> fulfillment – if it is a dialogue. In our life and experience, we are
> addressed; by thought and speech and action, by producing and
> influencing, we are able to answer. ... The relation in education
> is one of pure dialogue. ... [T]he educator is only one element
> among innumerable others, but distinct from them all by his will
> to take part in the stamping of character and by his consciousness
> that he represents in the eyes of the growing person a certain
> selection of what is, the selection of what is 'right,' of what should
> be. It is in this will and this consciousness that his vocation as an
> educator finds its fundamental expression[1]

Mordecai Martin Buber was born in Vienna on 8 February 1878, the son of
Jewish parents who lived in a house straddling the Danube River. Buber's
mother disappeared when Martin was 3, and young Martin went to live with
his paternal grandparents in Lvov where he stayed until he rejoined his
father, a farmer, at the age of 14. Until the age of 10, Buber was educated
most profoundly by his grandparents – Solomon Buber, a renowned
Talmudic scholar, and Adele, an educated woman who introduced Martin
to languages and literature and inspired the enduring fascination with
linguistic precision and poetic expression which distinguishes his mature
writings. The life of the mind he lived in the home of his grandparents was
balanced by his appreciation of the 'genuine human contact'[2] he observed in
his father's way of being in the world.

Equally as decisive was Buber's longing for the mother who disappeared
without explanation. Buber recalled with great clarity the moment when an
older child to whom his grandmother had temporarily entrusted his care
informed him that his mother would never return: He later coined the term,
'Vergegnung', or 'mismeeting', to 'designate the failure of a real meeting
between men'.[3] Deeply affected by this experience, and surrounded
throughout his lifetime by evidence of the results of missed connections
between individuals and groups, Buber dedicated his life to defining the
ever-present possibility of achieving true meeting through direct response to
the situations that present themselves to us.

Buber attended universities in Vienna, Leipzig, Berlin and Zurich,
studying literature, philosophy, art history, German studies and philology.
He became formally associated with the Zionist movement in 1898, and
through his involvement with the cultural and political activities associated
with Zionism, met Paula Winkler who later became his wife. Buber's
children, Raphael and Eva, were born in 1900 and 1901. In 1901 Buber
became editor of *Die Welt*, the primary publication of the Zionist
organization. In 1904, he completed a Ph.D. at the University of Berlin.
Soon after he began to publish, prolifically, on many subjects related to his
growing interest in Hasidic Judaism. Throughout his career, Buber was both
an original and highly generative thinker, and an interpreter of the works of
others.[4] From 1916 through 1938 Buber lived in the small German town
of Heppenheim near the University of Frankfurt, where he lectured in the
Study of Jewish Religion and Ethics from 1924 to 1933. During this time he
worked closely with Franz Rosenzweig (1886–1929) at the Freies Jüdisches

Lehrhaus (Free Jewish School); together they translated the Old Testament into German. Buber resigned his professorship in Frankfurt immediately after Hitler seized power in Germany, and was soon forbidden to lecture in public. In 1938 he emigrated to Jerusalem where he taught anthropology and sociology at the Hebrew University and participated in discussions of troubled relationships between Arabs and Jews.

In the late forties and early fifties, Buber lectured throughout Europe and the United States. He was nominated twice for the Nobel Prize for Literature (first by Herman Hesse, who described Buber as 'one of the few wise men living in the world today'[5] and again in 1961 by a group which included T.S. Eliot, W.H. Auden, Hesse, Gabriel Marcel and Herbert Read). Though neither nomination was successful, Buber described himself as 'surfeited with honors'[6] in the final years of his life.

More than 30 volumes of Buber's writings have been translated into English, many in multiple editions and variant translations. His works encompass an unusually broad spectrum of topics, reflecting his belief in the integral unity of theological and anthropological concerns, and his commitment to 'the hallowing of the everyday ... which stands in uncompromising opposition to every tendency to make of religion a separate upper story with no binding force in our lives'.[7] All of Buber's writings instantiate the philosophy of dialogue central to his thinking. In keeping with his philosophical commitments, Buber frequently wrote in response to specific occasions, circumstances and concerns of the day.

In 1925, Buber presented a keynote address at the Third International Pedagogical Conference of the International Work Circle for the Renewal of Education, held in Heidelberg. In response to the theme of the conference, 'The Unfolding of Creative Forces in the Child', an ideal cherished by the progressive educators who organized the event and invited Buber's contribution, Buber suggested that, as valuable as the experience of 'origination' certainly was to the growing person, something beyond freedom and the exercise of the creative instinct was needed to establish a genuine education. In the speech later published as the essay, 'Education',[8] Buber reminded his audience that the artist, working in isolation, could not provide an adequate model of human potential; it is only when the artist reaches out and enters into dialogue with another person that solitude is transcended and communion established. In his effort to temper uncritical acceptance of a particular, highly individualized vision of art education as the panacea for the world's ills, Buber reminded us that, whatever the content of a teaching–learning event may be, it is the relation between teacher and student, the interhuman dimension of education, which is most decisive and least expendable.

Perhaps Buber's best-known formulation was the distinction drawn between the relationship he characterized as I–Thou and the way of being he described as I–It. Buber emphasized that these two possibilities, available at every moment in any life, represented choices made moment to moment, alternative responses to particular situations in which we find ourselves. The I–Thou relationship, Buber stressed, is one characterized by full participation in the situation in which one finds oneself, unguarded presence and unmediated openness to the other in his or her particularity. He maintained that it is possible to enter into an I–Thou relationship with nature, with plants or animals, with works of art, with texts. The difference is in the relationship itself rather than in the identity of its participants. Buber clearly understood the I–It relationship as a relaxed, even distracted or automatic, form of attention, but he recognized its ubiquity and its pragmatic value, the necessity of returning continually to the I–It in order to negotiate daily existence. The I–It is our everyday or 'natural attitude'[9] toward the world. The I–Thou is marked off as an achievement, a moment of full participation in communion with another human being; Buber insisted that the Eternal Thou is met in full response to our earthly existence. The I–Thou is achieved in relatively rare moments which cannot be unilaterally willed into being, for they are, by definition, mutually constituted. The individual person can nevertheless be prepared to receive by cultivating true presence, a full immersion in life and its requirements. To live exclusively in the I–Thou is an impossibility; to persist in the I–It, to fail to enter into dialogue with those persons and things who exist over against us as others in their uniqueness, is to live an irresponsible and monological existence, self-absorbed, instrumental and oblivious to the other, refusing to answer when we are addressed. Thus Buber saw the other as essential to the individual's becoming, and the I–Thou relationship as the medium through which the self comes into being.

Buber emphasized the special nature of the dialogue in education. Admitting that the child is constantly educated by everything she encounters in the world, Buber recognized the educator as unique in her[10] conscious will to influence the learner. This decision to become influential in the lives of children, Buber contended, demands abdication of some of the freedom of choice, the personal preference, the Eros, that we are free to exercise when we enter into other relationships, such as friendship, love or collegiality. The teacher meets the random assortment of students who present themselves to her as her responsibility and her destiny; she is not able to choose who it is that she will educate. Unlike the dialogue that may occur between friends, lovers or colleagues, the relation in education is never completely reciprocal: In order to fulfil her responsibility as teacher, the teacher must 'experience the other side'[11] of her encounters with students; she must realize the situation both as it occurs to her and to the particular student standing over against her. The student, however, is unable to experience the teacher's side in the same way, simply by virtue of her situation as student; the teacher's vantage point is unavailable to her. Buber spoke of this 'one-sided experience of inclusion'[12] as an essential characteristic of teaching, healing and forgiving relationships, in which one partner consciously guides another through a landscape upon which the guide enjoys a privileged perspective.

Another consequence of the teacher's willingness to influence students is her tacit agreement to represent to students what Buber termed 'a selection of the effective world', to present to them, both through curricular content deliberately chosen and through the interests and convictions she embodies, a certain perspective on the world, a selection of what is, a curriculum which derives coherence because it is filtered through the life of a single person.

Buber expected much of teachers. He stressed the teacher's personal choice, integrity, authenticity, presence and willingness to respond to all students, regardless of the affection or revulsion they might evoke in the teacher herself, as fundamental to establishment of the trust in the world that the student first experiences as trust in the teacher who brings the world to her.

Buber addressed issues of religious and moral education, aesthetic education, and adult or community education in detail, reflecting his own involvements and interests. His writings on education – primarily found in *I and Thou* (first published in 1958), *Between Man and Man* (1947), and *The Knowledge of Man* (1965) – are invoked frequently by those whose interests in education focus on the dialogical and the relationship between teachers and students. Descriptions of the I–Thou and I–It relationships in teaching, once standard fare in philosophy of education courses for prospective teachers, are less frequently cited today, although critical elaborations of these concepts as they were developed by Buber continue to appear.[13] Yet Buber's influence persists in the published and practical works of Paolo Freire, Maxine Greene, Madeline Grumet, Nel Noddings, and others. Concerns Buber introduced, including the question of 'how to turn toward, address, and respect otherness', figure prominently in postmodern discourses. An example of Buber's enduring relevance is found in the work of Alexander Sidorkin, whose recent publications critique certain aspects of Buber's philosophy of dialogue – suggesting, for example, that Buber's insistence on dialogue as a one-to-one relationship limits its applicability in classroom settings where educative encounters tend to occur.

Notes

1   Martin Buber, *Between Man and Man*, New York: Macmillan, pp. 92, 98 and 106, 1065.
2   Martin Buber, *Meetings*, ed. M. Friedman, La Salle, IL: Open Court Publishing, p. 22, 1973.
3   Ibid.
4   Maurice Friedman, *Martin Buber: The Life of Dialogue*, Chicago: University of Chicago Press, 1976.
5   Maurice Friedman, *Encounter on the Narrow Ridge: A Life of Martin Buber*, New York: Paragon Books, (p. xi), 1991.
6   Ibid., p. 186.
7   Friedman 1976, (p. xi).
8   Buber (1965).
9   Alfred Schutz, *On Phenomenology and Social Relations*, ed. H. Wagner, Chicago: University of Chicago Press, 1970.
10 Throughout his writings Buber used the male pronoun in generic reference to people. In an effort to suit more contemporary sensibilities, I have elected to use the female pronoun in all cases where direct quotation is not involved.
11 Buber (1965).
12 Ibid.
13 See, for example, David Hawkins, *The Informed Vision: Essays on Learning and Human Nature*, New York: Agathon Press, 1974; J.R. Scudder and A. Mikunas, *Meaning, Dialogue and Enculturation: Phenomonological Philosophy of Education*, Center for Advanced Research in Phenomenology and University Press of America, 1985; A. Sidorkin, 'The Pedagogy of the Interhuman', in *Philosophy of Education, 1995*, Urbana, IL: Philosophy of Education Society, pp. 412–19, 1995.

See also

In *Fifty Modern Thinkers on Education*: Freire, Greene, Noddings

Buber's major writings

Between Man and Man, introduction and afterword by M. Friedman, trans. R.G. Smith, New York: Macmillan, 1965.
I and Thou, trans. W. Kaufman, New York: Charles Scribner's Sons, 1970.
The Knowledge of Man, ed. M. Friedman, trans. M. Friedman and R.G. Smith, New York: Harper and Row, 1988.
Meetings, ed. and trans. M. Friedman, LaSalle, IL: Open Court, 1973.

Further reading

Cohen, A., *The Educational Philosophy of Martin Buber*, Rutherford, NJ: Farleigh Dickinson University, 1983.
Friedman, M.S. (ed.), *Martin Buber and the Human Sciences*, Albany, NY: SUNY Press, 1996.
Murphy, D., *Martin Buber's Philosophy of Education*, Dublin: Irish Academic Press, 1988.
Schilpp, P.A. and Friedman, M. (eds), *The Philosophy of Martin Buber*, LaSalle, IL: Open Court Press, 1967.
Sidorkin, A.M., *Beyond Discourse: Education, the Self, and Dialogue*, Albany, NY: SUNY Press, 1999.

CHRISTINE THOMPSON

JOSÉ ORTEGA Y GASSET 1883–1955

> Plato's pedagogy is based on the idea that one must educate the city in order to educate the individual. ... If education is the transformation of a reality according to some better idea that we have and education cannot be other than social, it obtains that pedagogy is the science of transforming societies. We used to call this politics, and so, we now have that politics has become social pedagogy for us and the Spanish problem is a pedagogical problem.[1]

Ortega is one of the most important and attractive Spanish thinkers. An exiled Spanish philosopher said of him that he was 'the pre-Socratic of our tongue, the source to which one must return as or more often than to the Greek pre-Socratics'.[2] The interest and delight of his texts are a result of the profoundly, radically human manner in which he examines the manifestations of culture; the acute penetration of his mind revealing the intimate depths of individual and social human situations; and also his suggestive and exquisite literary style.

Ortega was born and died in Madrid. His family belonged to the enlightened Madrid upper class. He studied with the Jesuits and at the Central University of Madrid. In 1908 he was appointed to the Chair of Psychology, Logic and Ethics in the Escuela Superior de Magisterio in Madrid and in 1910 to the Chair of Metaphysics in the Central University of Madrid.

Ortega's three stays in Germany were decisive in his academic formation as he met Georg Simmel, Hermann Cohen and Paul Natorp, and studied neo-Kantianism and Edmund Husserl's phenomenology. He was impressed by the efficiency and organization of the German people and by the strength of their thought and culture, but he was wary of the excessive importance of collective and military influences on German society of the time.

He soon freed himself of the idealistic effects of neo-Kantianism. One might say that Ortega had sought in Kant an analytical scheme by which to objectify the characteristics of the Spanish problem and take restorative action. Human reality, in its specific historical flow, in its 'radical historicisation', occupied the centre of his attention and, in this sense, he was in agreement with Kierkegaard, Nietzsche and Bergson. Ortega also clearly coincided with Heidegger regarding the individual and personal freedom, to such an extent that at times he made an emphatic point of just how he had given expression to certain ideas before the German philosopher had done so. There is, moreover, an obvious relation between Ortega's perspectivism and Dilthey's radically historical view of life and human existence.

The vision of the subject as a concrete reality that lives 'here and now' and selects impressions or what is given is apparent in Ortega's earliest publications. 1923 marks the beginning of his formulation of the 'ratiovitalist' concept. In a balanced manner, he rejects at one and the same time the abstraction of rationalism and pragmatic, biological and exclusively intuitive interpretations. For Ortega, reason and life must be taken together. Knowledge is certainly rational, but it is rooted in life and all reason is 'vital reason'. In this sense, the person is not a being provided with reason, but a reality that must use reason to live, and living is 'dealing with the world', 'accounting for the world' not in an intellectual or abstract fashion, but concretely and fully.

With this method, Ortega considered some of the most important questions of the twentieth century, aware that this was his vocation and his task. For him, life is a continuous process of self-realization; it is a problem, something to be solved, a task, a programme for life. One can, indeed, shy away from life, but then the person falls into insincerity.

Ortega's pedagogical ideas mainly appear as suggestions when dealing with other questions, although there are works that centre specifically on educational questions, such as *Social Pedagogy as a Political Programme* (*La pedagogía social como programa político*, 1912), *Biology and Pedagogy* (*Biología y pedagogía*, 1921) or *The Purpose of the University* (*Misión de la Universidad*, 1930). Obviously, one should not expect to find technical questions of pedagogy in Ortega. He considers pedagogy to be no other than the application of a manner of thinking and feeling about the world – a philosophy, we might say – to educational problems. His concern is therefore to connect the school with his society and his culture, to overcome individualism, as he understands that if one does not educate for the city, a person cannot be brought to plenitude and that the school tends to operate on preterit principles, when it should educate from the present for the future.

'I am myself and my circumstances, and if I do not save them, I cannot save myself.'[3] This is one of Ortega's definitions that best helps us understand his life and work. He believed that, in order to give to the best of their ability, a person should become fully aware of their circumstances. That is why Ortega is to be understood on the plane of his own life, since for him life is a *unity of dramatic dynamism* between the world and the person that the latter is required to fulfil.[4] Ortega himself attempted to do so by assuming the circumstances of his time and of his country (Spain – a European nation linked to the other European nations), and he constantly exhorted his contemporaries and disciples to undertake the same task.

Part of Ortega's circumstances was the Europe in which World War I broke out and pulverized modernity. Indeed, as Graham has pointed out, Ortega was one of the first thinkers to conceive how the modern era was coming to an end to be replaced by the postmodern era. The Europe that was unable in the interwar period to impose its values on fascism and Nazism, on the one hand, and on Soviet communism, on the other. The Europe that was to return to warfare until its exhaustion in World War II.

However, Spain was even more part of his circumstances. The defeat by the United States of America and subsequent loss of its last colonies in 1898 became for the most lucid Spaniards a clamorous demonstration of a vicious circle closed by society's lack of energy and vitality, a society incapable of rejuvenating a falsified parliamentary monarchy and a political class incapable of confronting the needs of the country's modernization. The monarchy disappeared with the dictatorship of General Primo de Rivera (1923–9) and led to the Second Republic (1931–6), which faced up to the task of overcoming political, social and cultural backwardness with firm decision. However, both internal and international difficulties fomented extremist stances and the military uprising brought about a cruel civil war (1936–9), followed by a period of repression and a long military dictatorship (1939–75).

From the start of his activity, Ortega had felt the urge to commit himself to Spanish society, and he did so, in order of precedence, through his university Chair, through journalism and through politics. He felt the need to connect everything, understand everything, explain everything, to seek new ways to see things and transmit them to his fellow citizens. With all his learning and profound understanding of European culture, Ortega, who was also an independent thinker with marked personal traits and an enormous capacity for seductive and persuasive expression, made an indelible imprint on his pupils. But, not just a teacher, he also had the ability and the desire to be a writer, as shown by the more than six thousand pages of his *Complete Works*. Apart from setting up a means of spreading the best of Spanish and European culture (*Revista de Occidente*), up until his retirement from public life he constantly wrote in the press, in an attempt to connect with the average reader, since he was doubtful of the number of 'expert' readers in Spain and their ability to understand 'profound theories'.

From 1908 to 1933, Ortega's opinion and, at times, his action, was felt in national politics. This was mainly through articles in the press and lectures with broad repercussion. His wish was to contribute to the formation of a new liberal conscience in Spain; his proposals were directed at setting up a national organization led by a minority of intellectuals; his conception was élitist, of clearly Nietzschean inspiration; his programme had as its basis liberty, social justice, competition and Europeanization; his legacy in politics is a questionably open system, with a well-defined direction in intellectual renewal of the country through work and scientific rigour.[5] All of this was set out on the basis of Spain's incorporation into the concert of European nations. This was not a question of assimilation, but rather of growing closer to a broader, more modern cultural context. The solution for the problems of Spain lay in its cultural, social and political articulation in a higher, European sphere, in which Ortega always believed.

> It was historical realism that taught me to see that the unity of Europe as a society is not an ideal, but a very ancient daily fact. Now, once one has perceived this, the probability of a general European state becomes a necessity. The occasion that will suddenly bring this process about could be anything at all, for example, a Chinaman's pigtail showing over the Urals or a quake of the great Islamic magma.[6]

Although Ortega began by preaching a form of liberal socialism – inspired in Saint-Simon and Ferdinand Lasalle but certainly not in Marx – his opposition to chaos, disorder, revolutionary violence and his faith in *natural aristocracy* to lead, inform and save the *masses* were to lead him to conservative, even authoritarian postulates, but never to renounce essential freedom and democracy. The successive failures of his political initiatives, such as the Spanish League for Political Education (1913) in the years of his closest leanings to socialist ideas, and conceived as an instrument to carry out the new politics that was to cause the organic renovation of national life in view of the obvious decadence of the existing model of state, culminated in the Second Republic with the failure of his political activity as Member of Parliament. Because of his opposition to the socialists and his drift away from the radical republicans; because of his aspiration to create a broad national party in which professional people such as doctors, businessmen, engineers, teachers, men of letters and industrialists would exercise their social leadership; because of his defence of interventionism and economic control by the state, with protagonism of the bourgeoisie; and because of his unshakeable fidelity to himself, his active participation in politics came to an end in 1933, never to be renewed. His attitude as an intellectual prevented him from manoeuvring among the political groups and, in his desire to solve the problems of Spain, he underestimated the strength of the conservative oligarchy and other elements, as Robert Wohl points out:

> He also neglected or underestimated other areas of Spanish vitality – the army, anarcho-syndicalism, socialism, the separatist movements – that were going to play decisive roles in Spanish politics during the next twenty-five years. But the shortcomings of the political analysis do not detract from the grandeur of the vision. And the heart of more than one young man of the Spanish 'generation of 1914' was moved by Ortega's message, as a glance at the list of members of the Spanish League for Political Education shows.[7]

Ortega's vision of the Spanish situation was particularly dramatic partly because he compared it with the situations of Germany, Britain and France – he was not to discover North American society until 1949, which filled him with 'hope'. If he had compared Spain with other countries in southern or eastern Europe, he might have understood that modernization was a much more complex phenomenon. In the case of Spain, it was to be achieved on the basis of economic, social, cultural and, finally, political transformation that was late to take place and would be most clearly visible after Ortega's death. This occurred a few years after his return to Spain, when General Franco's dictatorship had become established. Not long after his death this dictatorship undertook strategically important structural changes of an economic nature that led, with notorious political resistance and repression, to the modernization of Spanish society and, after the restoration of democracy, to its complete integration into the Europe that Ortega had once imagined.

Notes

1 J. Ortega, *La pedagogía social como programa político*, en *Obras completas*, Madrid: Revista de Occidente, 11 vols, 1946–69, T. I, 506, 1912.
2 J.D. García Bacca, Suplemento literario de *La República*, citado en Morán, G. (1998) *El maestro en el erial. Ortega y Gasset y la cultura del franquismo*, Barcelona: Tusquets Editores, p. 517, 1955.
3 J. Ortega, *Meditaciones del Quijote*, en *Obras Completas,* T. I, 322, 1914.
4 J. Ortega, *Goethe desde dentro*, en *Obras Completas*, T. IV, 400, 1930.
5 A. Elorza, *La razón y la sombra. Una lectura política de Ortega y Gasset*, Barcelona: Editorial Anagrama, pp. 10–12, 1984.
6 J. Ortega, 'Prólogo para Franceses', en *La rebelión de las masas*, en *Obras Completas*, T. IV, p. 119, 1937.
7 R. Wohl, *The Generation of 1914*, Cambridge, MA: Harvard University Press, p. 134, 1979.

See also

In this book: Plato, Kant, Nietzsche
In *Fifty Modern Thinkers on Education*: Heidegger

Ortega's major writings

Ortega's works in Spanish are to be found in the 11-volume edition of his *Obras completas* published by *Revista de Occidente* between 1946 and 1969 (reissued in 12 volumes by *Alianza Editorial* in 1983).

Meditaciones del Quijote, Madrid, 1914 (*Meditations on Quixote*, New York, 1961).
El tema de nuestro tiempo, Madrid, 1923 (*The Modern Theme*, New York, 1933, repr. 1961).
La deshumanización del arte e ideas sobre la novela, Madrid, 1925 (*The Dehumanization of Art. Ideas on the Novel*, Princeton, NJ, 1948).
¿Qué es filosofía?, Madrid, 1929–30 (*What Is Philosophy?*, New York, 1960).
La rebelión de las masas, Madrid, 1930 (*The Revolt of the Masses*, Notre Dame, IN, 1986).
Misión de la Universidad, Madrid, 1930 (*Mission of the University*, New Brunswick: Transaction Publishers, 1991).

Historia como sistema y Concordia y Libertad, Madrid, 1935 (*History as System and Other Essays toward a Philosophy of History*, Greenwood, CN, 1961).
La idea del principio en Leibniz y la evolución de la teoría deductiva, Madrid, 1947 (*The Idea of Principle in Leibniz and the Evolution of Deductive Theory*, New York, 1971).

Further reading

The *Fundación Ortega y Gasset* provides information relevant to his work on http://www.fog.es and at *fogescom@accessnet.es*

Dobson, A., *An Introduction to the Politics and Philosophy of José Ortega y Gasset*, Cambridge: Cambridge University Press, 1989.
Donoso, A. and Raley, H.C., *José Ortega y Gasset: A Bibliography of Secundary Sources*, Bowling Green, OH: Philosophy Documentation Center, 1986.
Dust, P.H. (ed.), *Ortega y Gasset and the Question of Modernity*, Minneapolis: The Prisma Institute, 1989.
Graham, J.T., *A Pragmatist Philosophy of Life in Ortega y Gasset,* Columbia: University of Missouri Press, 1994.
—— *Theory of History in Ortega y Gasset: the Dawn on Historical Reason*, Columbia: University of Missouri Press, 1997.
Ouimette, V., *José Ortega y Gasset*, Boston, MA: Twayne, 1982.
Rodríguez Huescar, A., *José Ortega y Gasset's Metaphysical Innovation: a Critique an Overcoming of Idealism*, New York: SUNY Press, 1995.
Torras, J. and Trigo, J., *Liberal Thought in Spain in the First Half of the Twentieth Century: José Ortega y Gasset*, Barcelona: Mont Pelerin Society, 1997.
Tuttle, H., *The Crowd is Untruth: The Existential Critique of Mass Society in the Thought of Kierkegaard, Nietzsche, Heidegger, and Ortega y Gasset*, New York: Peter Lang Verlag, 1996.

DIEGO SEVILLA

CYRIL LODOVIC BURT 1883–1971

[I]t is essential to study every aspect of the child's development, physical as well as mental, emotional as well as intellectual ... the child's environment ... both at home and at school, in the past as well as in the present. ... What breaks the camel's back is not the last straw, but the accumulation of straws; and the only sure remedy is to remove each one.
... it would seem that the frequency of the various causes [of subnormality] is approximately as follows ... about two-thirds of the backward suffer from unfavourable *environmental* conditions, often grave enough to require a complete change to something better ... three quarters suffer from unfavourable *physical* conditions – body weakness or ill-health ... more than three quarters are handicapped by defective *intellectual* abilities: here the commonest ... condition is ... sheer lack of intelligence ... about one-third have ... *temperamental* difficulties ... not much more than one-sixth ... [suffer] unfavourable conditions within the *school*.[1]

Cyril Burt was the son of a doctor. The family lived for the first nine years of Burt's life in one of the poorest areas of London, and he attended a London Board School. Burt gained first-hand experience of the problems of living and being educated in a slum area. The family moved to Warwickshire, where Burt went to public school, then to Oxford. In Warwickshire, the Burts lived just three miles from the Galtons, who were patients of his father. Burt was strongly influenced by Galton's thoughts and works. At Oxford, as a student of McDougall, he worked on the standardization of psychological tests. Here he met Pearson, and was introduced to correlation. After spending some time in Würzburg, he was a lecturer in experimental psychology in Sherrington's department in Liverpool for five years (1907 to 1912). He became the first professional psychologist in England when he worked for the London County Council. In 1926 he was appointed to a chair of what is now the Institute of Education (then the London Day Training College), and in 1932, he took over Spearman's founding chair at University College, London. Burt retired in 1951, but wrote at least another 200 articles and reviews, and continued to act as editor of the *British Journal of Statistical Psychology*. Sir Cyril Burt was the first foreigner to be awarded the Thorndike Award by the American Psychological Association.

Burt was an applied psychologist who spent about half of his working life on practical issues. He had considerable skill in handling both practical and political realities, and was able to push psychology to the forefront of decision-making in important fields – education, vocational guidance and criminology. Much of his writing was addressed to working professionals rather than academics. The quotation at the start of the chapter is from a book written primarily for teachers, and collates the major findings from extensive studies of individual children. A strong argument is made for multiple causality and multiple approaches to treatment. In a similar vein, Burt was the first person in Britain to collect data systematically via interviews and assessment in order to study delinquency. In *The Young Delinquent* (1925) he showed that delinquency was associated with a number of factors, notably abnormal family situations, but was not an inevitable consequence of these factors; it also occurred in the apparent absence of all associated causes. His conclusion that good conduct and misconduct are always products of mental life, not life situations, contrasted directly with rival genetic and psychoanalytic theories. Burt set out the principles for, and was instrumental in the establishment of Child Guidance Clinics in the UK in 1927; he also established a special school for the handicapped.

Burt is best known for his work on mental testing. Galton's pioneering work on individual differences had focused on relatively simple cognitive processes such as sensory discrimination and reaction times, and required individual testing. Burt (and others) showed that higher mental functions were better predictors of educational attainment. Burt made significant contributions to psychometrics – which sets out to determine the 'mental characters of individuals' experimentally. To do this, one needs an account of the structure of human abilities. The data are the scores from a large sample of students who have taken a number of cognitive tests (reasoning, sentence completion, maze tests, picture completion etc.); commonly, positive relationships are found between performances on different tests. Some tests are more strongly related than others, and patterns can be seen in the array of correlations – for example, performance on tests which assess some aspect of language usually show strong positive relationships. Psychometricians set out to describe these patterns in terms of a number of 'factors' or dimensions of 'mental space'.

Burt made contributions to the techniques of factor analysis, and invented a practical method of analysis which has a remarkable family resemblance to Thurstone's centroid method, for which Thurstone became famous twenty years later. Burt formulated a 'four-factor' model of intelligence. The factors were general, group, test specific and error. Other accounts (such as Spearman's two-factor theory) he regarded as a simplification of this four-factor model. Burt had a modern view of the relationship between data and theory. He argued that many of the apparent differences between theorists could be explained in terms of the choice of matrix algebra used to analyze their data sets; different analytical methods giving rise to different factor structures. Burt argued that decisions about the underlying factorial structure of intellect should be a matter of theoretical aesthetics; unfortunately, it was often based on a belief (often implicit, and borne of ignorance) in one algebraic approach over another.

Burt developed tests which could be administered by teachers in ordinary classroom settings, based on reasoning, analogies, syllogisms and the like, many of which can be recognized as the basis of current intelligence tests. It was Burt who produced the first written group test of intelligence (rather than American army psychologists working in the First World War, as is often claimed). Tests and psychometrics were a means to an end, not an end in themselves. In work for London County Council, Burt set out to discover ways to maximize the benefits of schooling to children. One aspect was the identification of pupils unlikely to benefit from ordinary schooling, as Binet had done (see *The Backward Child*, 1937), and to estimate the number of such pupils in ordinary schools. He was also concerned with ways to identify highly able students for whom special educational provision might be made (see *The Gifted Child*, 1975).

Burt's concept of intelligence is that of an 'innate, general cognitive efficiency'. This concept of an innate ability is apparent in his earliest works – a paper in *Eugenics Review* (1912) presents evidence on the superior test performance of children of people in higher professional groups, for example. His work on identical twins set out to determine the relative contribution of genetics and environmental factors in determining intellectual functioning. The idea is to look for similarities in the test scores of pairs of individuals ranged on dimensions of genetic similarity and environmental similarity. The genetic dimension is: unrelated children, siblings,and identical twins. The environmental dimension is: reared apart, reared together, reared as twins. How strongly related are the scores on intelligence tests of different pairs of children? If the scores of unrelated children reared together (such as adopted children in the same household) are strongly related, and the scores of identical twins reared apart are weakly related, there is evidence for a strong environmental effect on intelligence. If the opposite is the case, it provides evidence of a strong genetic component. Intermediate pairs on the two dimensions allow one to check the validity of the results from the extreme cases. Burt reported a number of studies on identical twins reared apart which provided evidence of a strong genetic component in intelligence – he estimated that approximately 80 per cent of IQ was determined by genetic factors. Burt reported data on the largest sample of identical twins reared apart at the time, and claimed that his identical twins had all been separated by 6 months of age; he also claimed that there was no correlation between the socio-economic background of the fostering families. The circumstances under which identical twins are reared apart will be extraordinary. In studies by other researchers, a number of twins were reared one by a relative, and one by natural parent(s); twins were reunited for part of the time; attended the same school, and so the claims that they experienced a different environment are harder to sustain. The exemplary nature of Burt's data reported lead to widespread citation.

The evidence that intelligence test scores are a relatively stable attribute of each person is impressive, and widely replicated. One can sample an hour of behaviour (via a paper and pencil test) and can predict a person's likely success in the education system, and even about their likely life successes with modest accuracy (the further apart the test and the predicted behaviour, the weaker the predictive power; specific attempts to improve test scores or educational experiences also reduce predictive power). For a Victorian, raised in the intellectual maelstrom of Darwin's theory of evolution, and exposed at an early age to the person and ideas of Galton (a cousin of Darwin, a pioneer of ability testing, an advocate of the notion of both heritability of human aptitudes, and of eugenics), the ideas of 'intelligence' and of heritability of intelligence paved the way both for a science of human behaviour, and a technology of effective social policy. If individual differences have a strong genetic component, and superior performance is associated with higher social groups, the argument can be made that current social divisions are natural, and a result of evolutionary pressure over a long period. Education can be improved by tailoring educational provision to the needs of individual students – highly able students can be identified by intelligence testing, and can be offered appropriate educational experiences, no matter what their home background or past educational experiences. Students unable to benefit from conventional education can be identified and special provisions can be made for their needs. General social improvement can be attained in the short term by appropriate allocation of students to educational treatments, and in the longer term by accelerating Darwinian selection processes. The theme of scientific beliefs and politics will be explored later.

Burt was appointed senior investigator in charge of vocational guidance at the National Institute of Occupational Psychology. In the interwar years, a large team (around forty people) of psychologists was built up with expertise in staff selection, training, fatigue at work, working practices, ergonomics, personnel management and marketing. This team formed the nucleus for extensive work by psychologists as part of the British war effort in all these areas. The work on vocational guidance, initiated by Burt, led to the development of new tests, and demonstrated the superiority of psychological approaches over conventional approaches (such as interviews or teacher recommendations). Procedures were applied successfully by the armed services during the Second World War, and subsequently by major employers.

A series of government reports to which Burt contributed a good deal of evidence paved the way for the 1944 Butler Education Act which set out to provide an education for each child best suited to the aptitude of that individual. The Act made provision for an IQ test to be given at age 11, which was used as the basis for allocating pupils to one of three educational streams: grammar, technical or modern. The intellectual underpinnings combine four strands: the effectiveness of tests to allocate people to different tracks best suited to their abilities; the idea that IQ tests measured a stable characteristic of a child, and had a large genetic component; evidence that IQ tests are better predictors of educational attainment than any other available measure; and evidence on the unreliability of other forms of assessment (notably teacher reports and school tests).

Burt was keen to promote the study of psychology, and the use of a variety of evidence to inform educational practice. He worked closely with children, and wrote for practitioners and politicians as well as for academics (UK developments taking an evidence-based approach to education were modest in comparison with USA work, associated with Stanley Hall and Thorndike, however).

Burt was arguably the most influential educational psychologist of his generation in the UK, whose works on testing, delinquency and high and low attaining children were viewed as landmark studies. His work on the measurement of intelligence, and on psychometrics were impressive, and had an impact in the UK, though rather little impact abroad (unless one claims that Thurstone used Burt's methods, without attribution). Amongst his influential students, H.J. Eysenck and R.B. Cattell both extended the work on factorial analyses. Burt was a major figure in establishing the centrality of the notion of educational 'aptitude', and in promoting the idea that intelligence has a major genetic component. His twin studies are very widely known – indeed, notorious.

Within five years of his death, Sir Cyril Burt had been accused of fraud, and pilloried in national newspapers. An official biography by a noted historian of British psychology, Leslie Hearnshaw, based on Burt's diaries and personal correspondence, as well as on his published work, confirmed and added to the accusations of fraud. The British Psychological Society accepted Hearnshaw's conclusions. Two later biographies (by Joynson 1989; and Fletcher 1991) cast doubt on many of Hearnshaw's conclusions. A collection of articles edited by Mackintosh (1995) casts further doubt on the status of many of the accusations, but concludes that Burt did, indeed, invent both data and co-workers. Sir Cyril Burt is remembered as a scientific cheat.

One might ask why the fraudulent behaviour was not noticed earlier. One reason is the thoroughness of Burt's early work; another is that much of the fraudulent data presented evidence consistent with evidence elsewhere. Large differences in the IQ of adults in different social classes are widely documented; those children that migrate up social classes have higher IQs, those that move down have lower IQs. IQ does predict educational attainment; a number of studies have shown that people who are close genetically are close intellectually. Other accounts can be offered about why IQ measures are predictive such as their relation with educational advancement, or their cultural loading, however the raw data about the association between IQ and other factors is not in dispute although the heritability data are. Burt's fraud shows something of the constructivist nature of knowledge; evidence shapes world views, and once a world view is established, data that fits is accepted less critically than data which does not.

Any scientist can falsify data for a short while; the power of science resides both in the work of individuals, and in the process of accepting knowledge into the community. The Burt affair provided a stark reminder of the need for effective validation procedures. Burt published extensively in the journal he edited; he was allowed to publish articles with serious methodological flaws in leading journals as late as 1966. Few editors publish their own work; halo effects have been well documented, and modern practice is to review papers anonymously.

The Burt affair also gives us insights into the sociology of science – the alignment of scientists into camps, the conflicting world views, and shifts in scientific paradigm over time. Science can be used (legitimately or illegitimately) as a justification for political action. If IQ is causally related to educational and social success, and IQ has a large genetic component, then there is little point devoting much money to the education of low IQ citizens – little will come of it. Society is the way it is for good Darwinian reasons, and will be improved by accelerating the processes (e.g. the practice of sterilizing 'subnormals' in several States in the USA at one time, according to Gould, 1981), rather than reversing them. However, if IQ is a proxy measure for other causal factors (such as social class, or membership of a particular language community), and it has no genetic basis, then spending money on education is likely to have positive effects for all children, and on society. The debate on heritability, therefore, can be recast as a debate about right-wing and left-wing politics, or even about evil and good. This agenda has been the focus of debate triggered by *The Bell Curve* (1994). The fact that the best evidence for the heritability of IQ was fraudulent provided ammunition relevant to science, politics and morality.

Sir Cyril Burt will be remembered for the failings of his old age, which overshadow the whole corpus of his work. His primary legacy is a reminder that the practice of science is not set in a political or social vacuum; evidence-based policy can be a sharp sword, which should be used with great care.

Note

1   Cyril L. Burt, *The Causes and Treatment of Backwardness*, 1964.

See also

In this book: Binet, Tyler, Piaget, Vygotsky, Darwin

Burt's major writings

The Distribution and Relation of Educational Abilities, London: King and Son, 1917.
Mental and Scholastic Tests, second edition, London: Staples Press, 1947.
The Young Delinquent, fourth edition, London: University of London Press, 1944.

The Causes and Treatment of Backwardness, fourth edition, London: University of London Press, 1964.
The Backward Child, fifth edition, London: University of London Press, 1965.

Further reading

Devlin, B., Fienberg, S., Resnick, D. and Roeder, K. (eds), *Intelligence, Genes and Success: Scientists Respond to The Bell Curve*, New York: Springer-Verlag, 1997.
Fletcher, R., *Science, Ideology and the Media: The Cyril Burt Scandal*, New Brunswick, NJ: Transaction Publishers, 1991.
Gould, S., *The Mismeasure of Man*, New York: W.W. Norton, 1981.
Hearnshaw, L., *Cyril Burt Psychologist*, London: Hodder and Stoughton, 1979.
Herrnstein, R., and Murray, C., *The Bell Curve: Intelligence and Class Structure in American Life*, New York: Free Press, 1994.
Joynson, R., *The Burt Affair*, London: Routledge, 1989.
Mackintosh, N. (ed.), *Cyril Burt: Fraud or Framed?*, Oxford: Oxford University Press, 1995.

JIM RIDGWAY